# Phoenix Wright Ace Attorney™

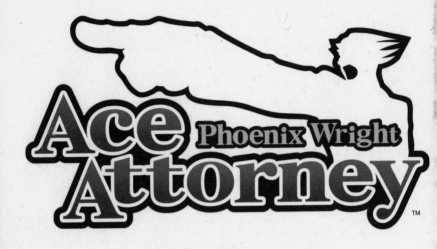

## VOLUME ONE

Story by Kenji Kuroda
Art by Kazuo Maekawa
Supervised by CAPCOM

Translated and adapted by Alethea Nibley and Athena Nibley
Lettered by North Market Street Graphics

KC KODANSHA COMICS

This book is a faithful translation of the book released in Japan on April 6, 2007.

*Phoenix Wright: Ace Attorney* Volume 1 is a work of fiction. Names, characters, places, and incidents are the products of the author's imagination or are used fictitiously. Any resemblance to actual events, locales, or persons, living or dead, is entirely coincidental.

A Kodansha Comics Trade Paperback Original.

Published in the United States by Kodansha Comics, an imprint of Kodansha USA Publishing, LLC., New York.

Publication rights for this English edition arranged through Kodansha Ltd., Tokyo.

First published in Japan in 2007 by Kodansha Ltd., Tokyo.

ISBN 978-1-935-42969-2

Printed in the United States of America.

www.kodanshacomics.com

3 4 5 6 7 8 9

Translators: Alethea Nibley and Athena Nibley
Lettering: North Market Street Graphics

# CONTENTS

# HONORIFICS EXPLAINED

Throughout the Kodansha Comics books, you will find Japanese honorifics left intact in the translations. For those not familiar with how the Japanese use honorifics and, more important, how they differ from American honorifics, we present this brief overview.

Politeness has always been a critical facet of Japanese culture. Ever since the feudal era, when Japan was a highly stratified society, use of honorifics—which can be defined as polite speech that indicates relationship or status—has played an essential role in the Japanese language. When addressing someone in Japanese, an honorific usually takes the form of a suffix attached to one's name (example: "Asuna-san"), is used as a title at the end of one's name, or appears in place of the name itself (example: "Negi-sensei," or simply "Sensei!").

Honorifics can be expressions of respect or endearment. In the context of manga and anime, honorifics give insight into the nature of the relationship between characters. Many English translations leave out these important honorifics and therefore distort the feel of the original Japanese. Because Japanese honorifics contain nuances that English honorifics lack, it is our policy at Kodansha Comics not to translate them. Here, instead, is a guide to some of the honorifics you may encounter in Kodansha Comics books.

*-san:*    This is the most common honorific and is equivalent to Mr., Miss, Ms., or Mrs. It is the all-purpose honorific and can be used in any situation where politeness is required.

*-sama:*    This is one level higher than "-san" and is used to confer great respect.

*-dono:*    This comes from the word "tono," which means "lord." It is an even higher level than "-sama" and confers utmost respect.

*-kun:*    This suffix is used at the end of boys' names to express familiarity or endearment. It is also sometimes used by men among friends, or when addressing someone younger or of a lower station.

*-chan:* This is used to express endearment, mostly toward girls. It is also used for little boys, pets, and even among lovers. It gives a sense of childish cuteness.

*Bozu:* This is an informal way to refer to a boy, similar to the English terms "kid" and "squirt."

*Sempai/*
*Senpai:* This title suggests that the addressee is one's senior in a group or organization. It is most often used in a school setting, where underclassmen refer to their upperclassmen as "sempai." It can also be used in the workplace, such as when a newer employee addresses an employee who has seniority in the company.

*Kohai:* This is the opposite of "sempai" and is used toward underclassmen in school or newcomers in the workplace. It connotes that the addressee is of a lower station.

*Sensei:* Literally meaning "one who has come before," this title is used for teachers, doctors, or masters of any profession or art.

*-[blank]:* This is usually forgotten in these lists, but it is perhaps the most significant difference between Japanese and English. The lack of honorific means that the speaker has permission to address the person in a very intimate way. Usually, only family, spouses, or very close friends have this kind of permission. Known as *yobisute*, it can be gratifying when someone who has earned the intimacy starts to call one by one's name without an honorific. But when that intimacy hasn't been earned, it can be very insulting.

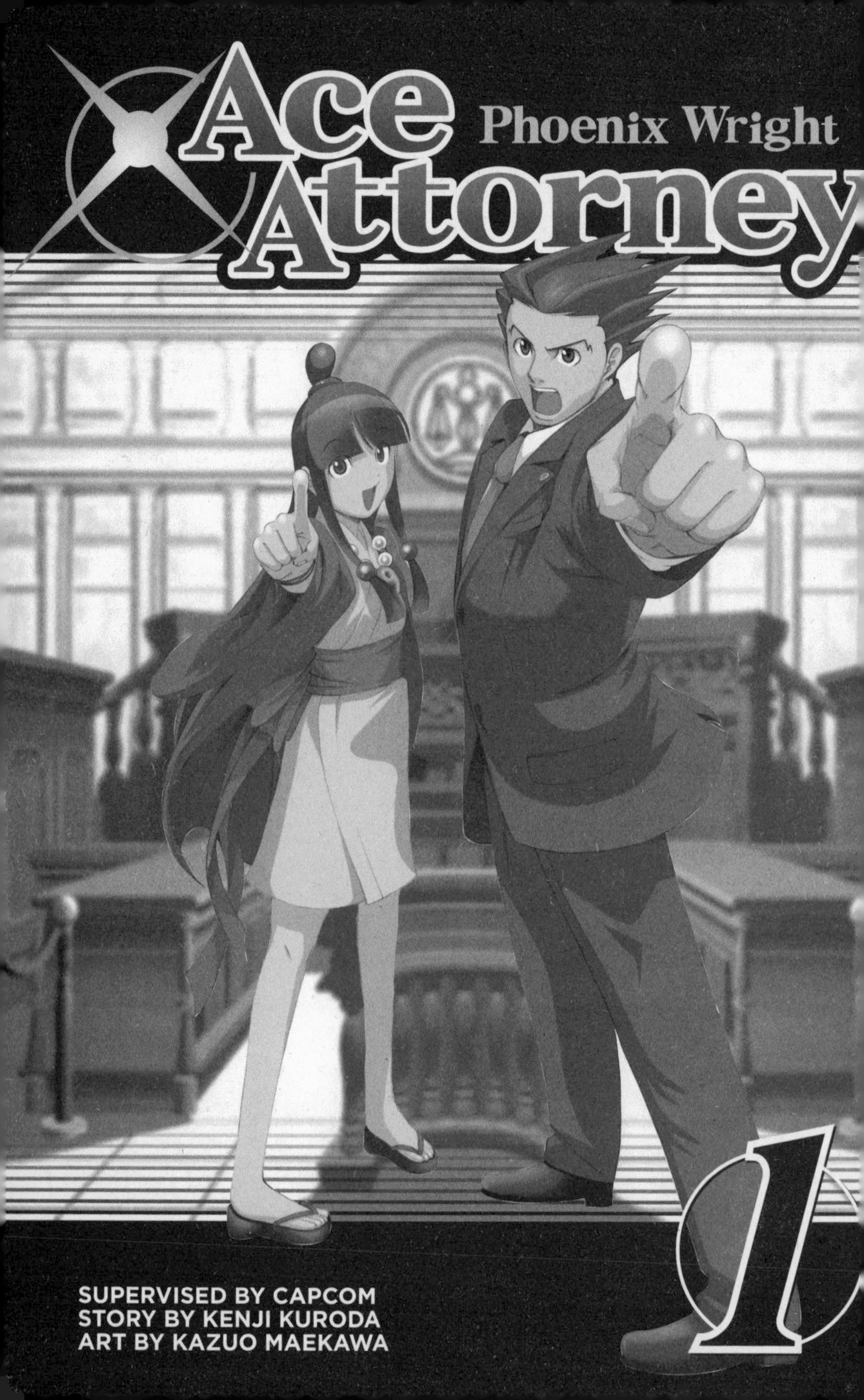
Phoenix Wright
Ace Attorney
1
SUPERVISED BY CAPCOM
STORY BY KENJI KURODA
ART BY KAZUO MAEKAWA

# CHARACTER INTRODUCTIONS

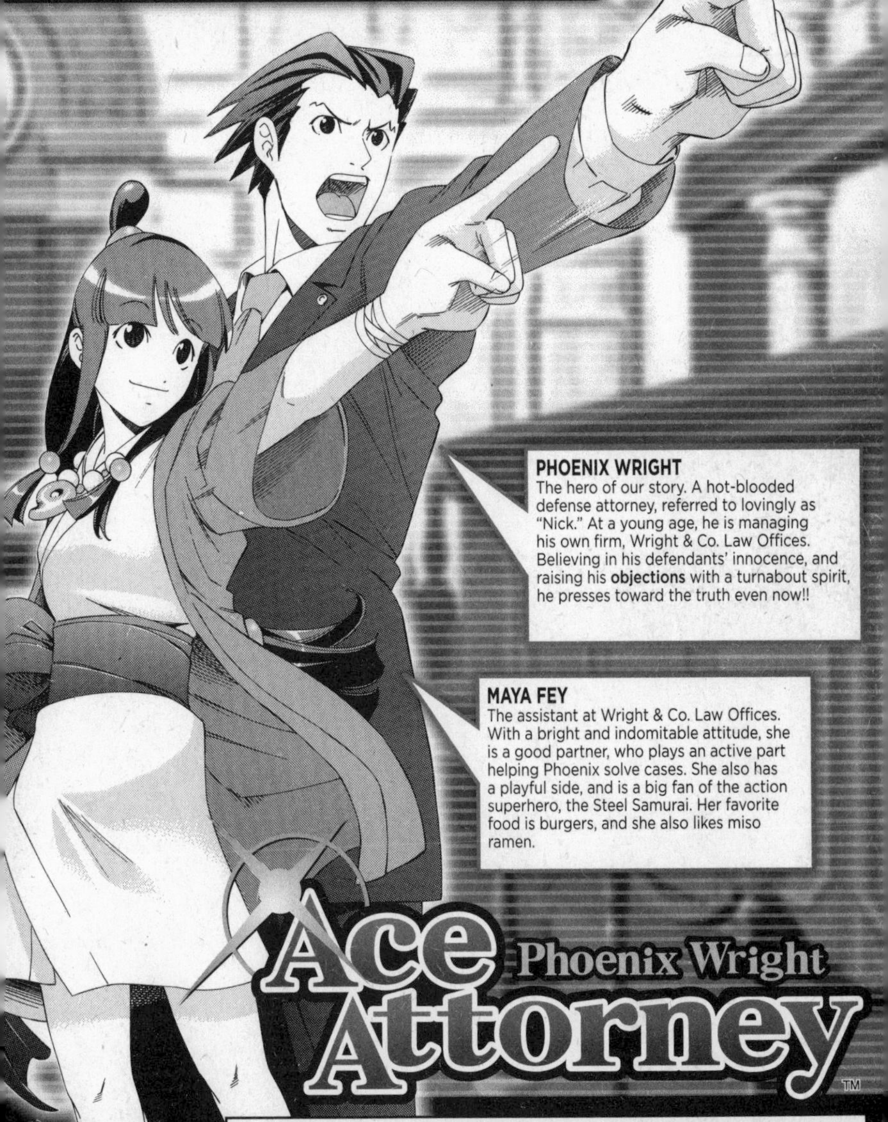
Phoenix Wright
Ace Attorney™

**PHOENIX WRIGHT**
The hero of our story. A hot-blooded defense attorney, referred to lovingly as "Nick." At a young age, he is managing his own firm, Wright & Co. Law Offices. Believing in his defendants' innocence, and raising his **objections** with a turnabout spirit, he presses toward the truth even now!!

**MAYA FEY**
The assistant at Wright & Co. Law Offices. With a bright and indomitable attitude, she is a good partner, who plays an active part helping Phoenix solve cases. She also has a playful side, and is a big fan of the action superhero, the Steel Samurai. Her favorite food is burgers, and she also likes miso ramen.

The characters, laws, and court procedures in this work are all fiction. Accordingly, the court system of this story is set in the near future, where the demand for expedited trials creates a different system than that of present-day.

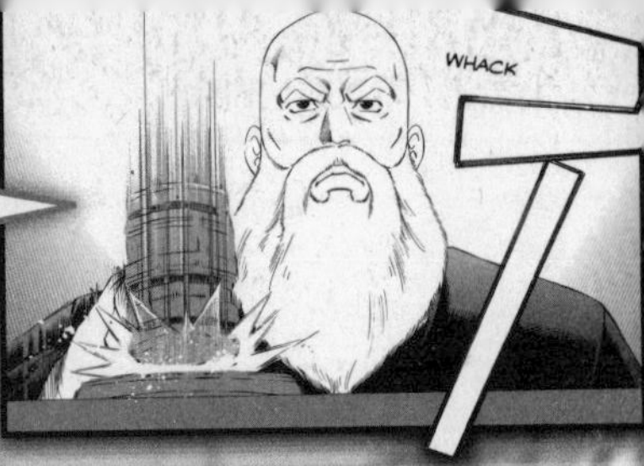
WHACK

**THE JUDGE**
The court judge, who looks dignified but actually is not. He has a habit of gullibly swallowing every scenario fed him by Phoenix or Edgeworth. His name is unknown.

**MILES EDGEWORTH**
Phoenix's greatest rival. He has been known as a genius prosecutor ever since he started out in the profession. In fact, he and Phoenix knew each other as children, and were the best of friends, bound together by trust.

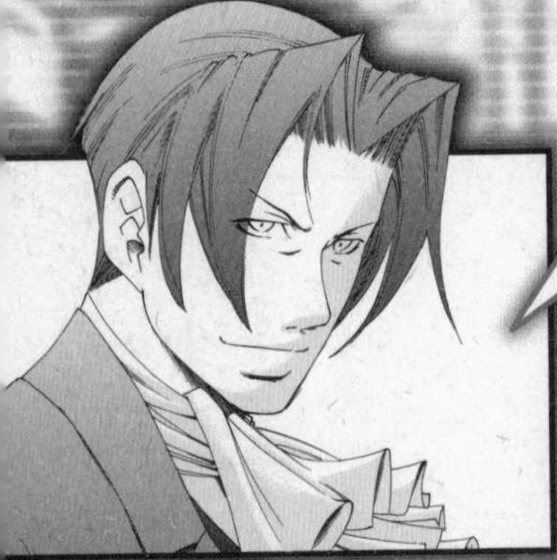

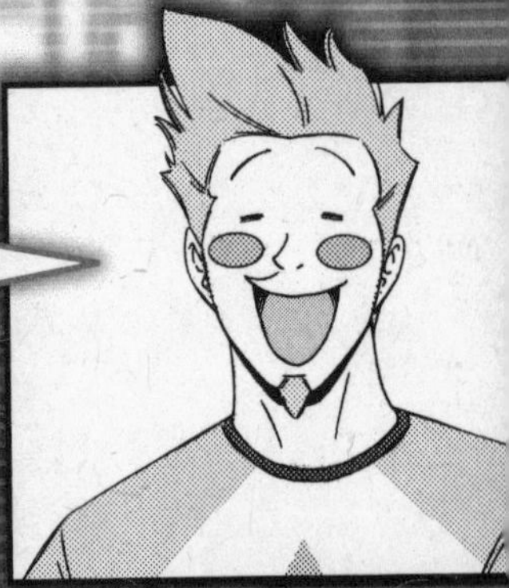

**LARRY BUTZ**
A friend of Phoenix's since grade school. He has a knack for getting into trouble, due to his inherent bad luck. Unfortunately, he also has bad luck in the dating department....

**DICK GUMSHOE**
A detective in charge of murder investigations. He's a few cards shy of a deck, and sometimes misses important clues. Every time he does, he gets a paycut, so his salary is very low.

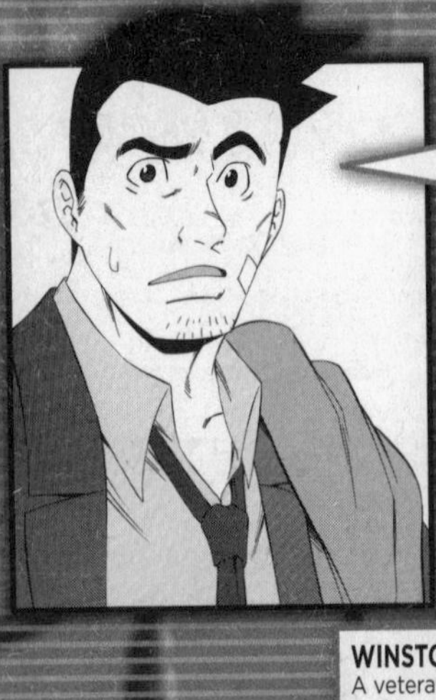

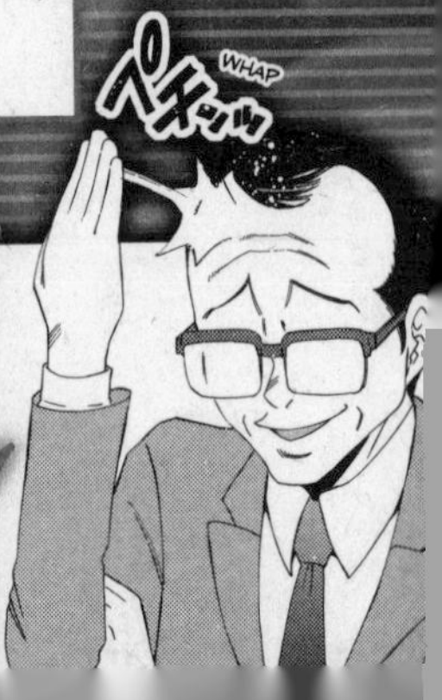
WHAP

**WINSTON PAYNE**
A veteran prosecutor, but he lacks presence, and is completely unreliable. Stress has caused his hairline to recede. In a word, he's dull.

# Chapter 1
# TURNABOUT WITH THE WIND

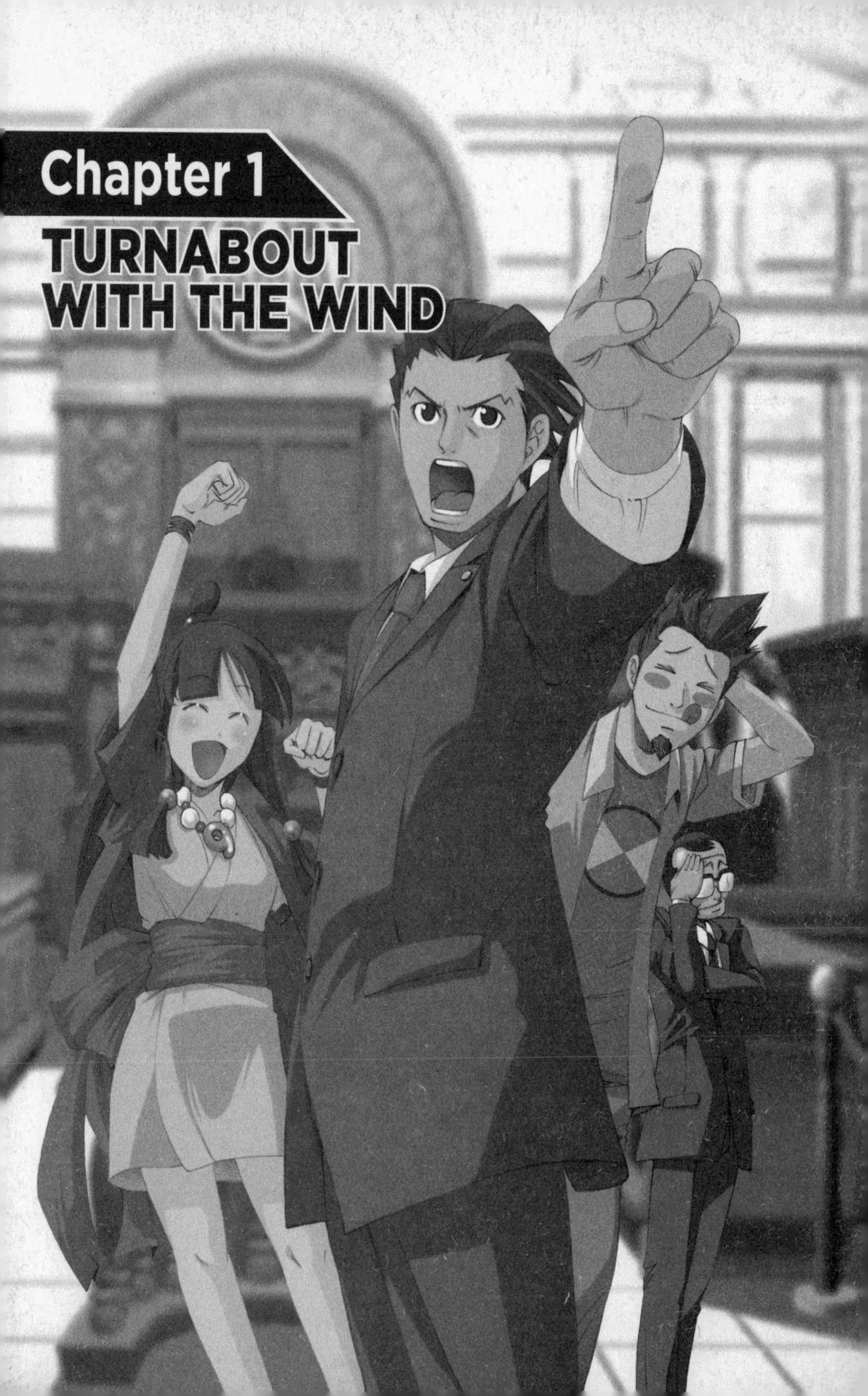

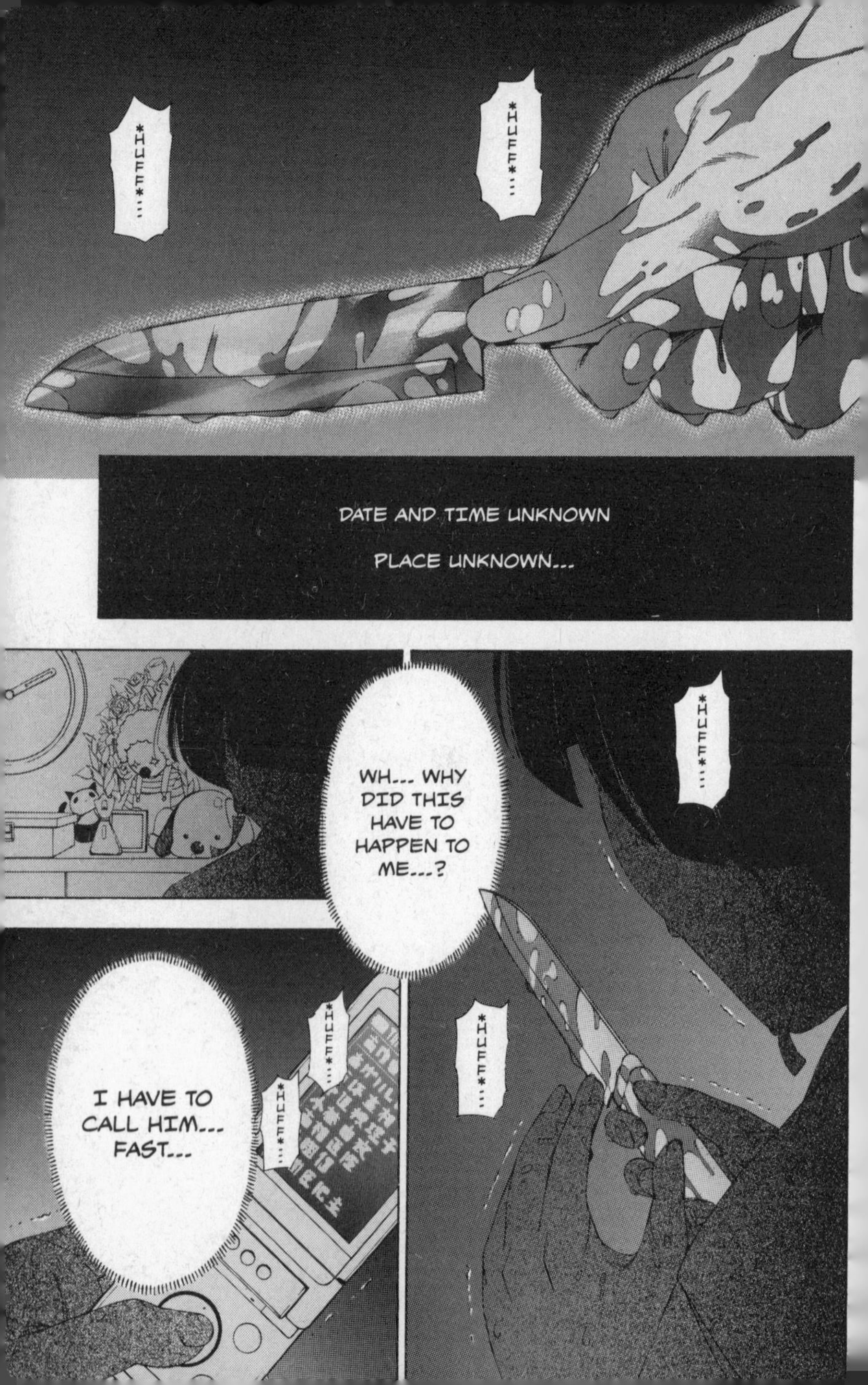
*HUFF*...
*HUFF*...
DATE AND TIME UNKNOWN
PLACE UNKNOWN...
*HUFF*...
WH... WHY DID THIS HAVE TO HAPPEN TO ME...?
*HUFF*...
*HUFF*...
*HUFF*...
I HAVE TO CALL HIM... FAST...

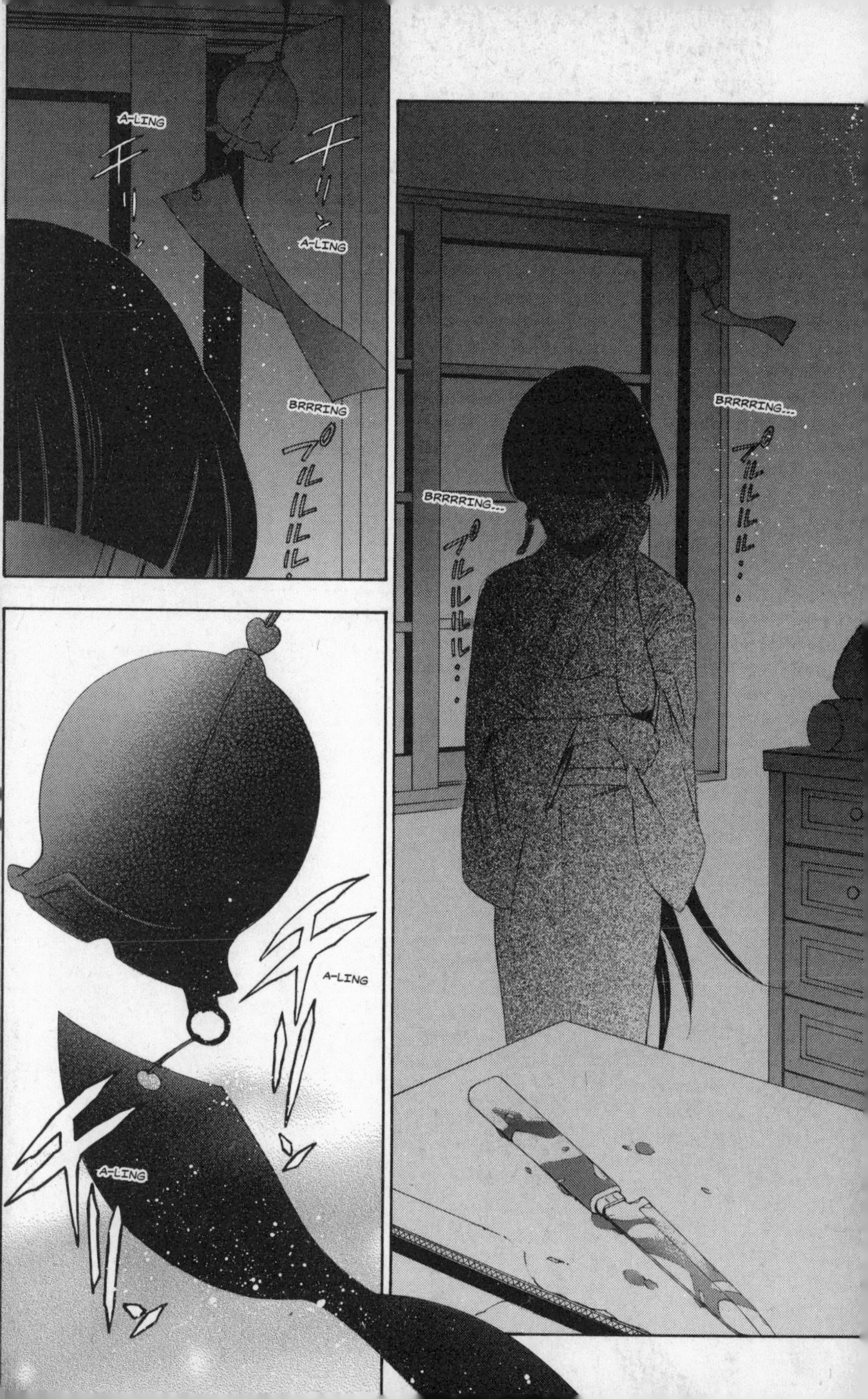
BRRRRING...
BRRRRING...
A-LING
A-LING
BRRRING
A-LING
A-LING

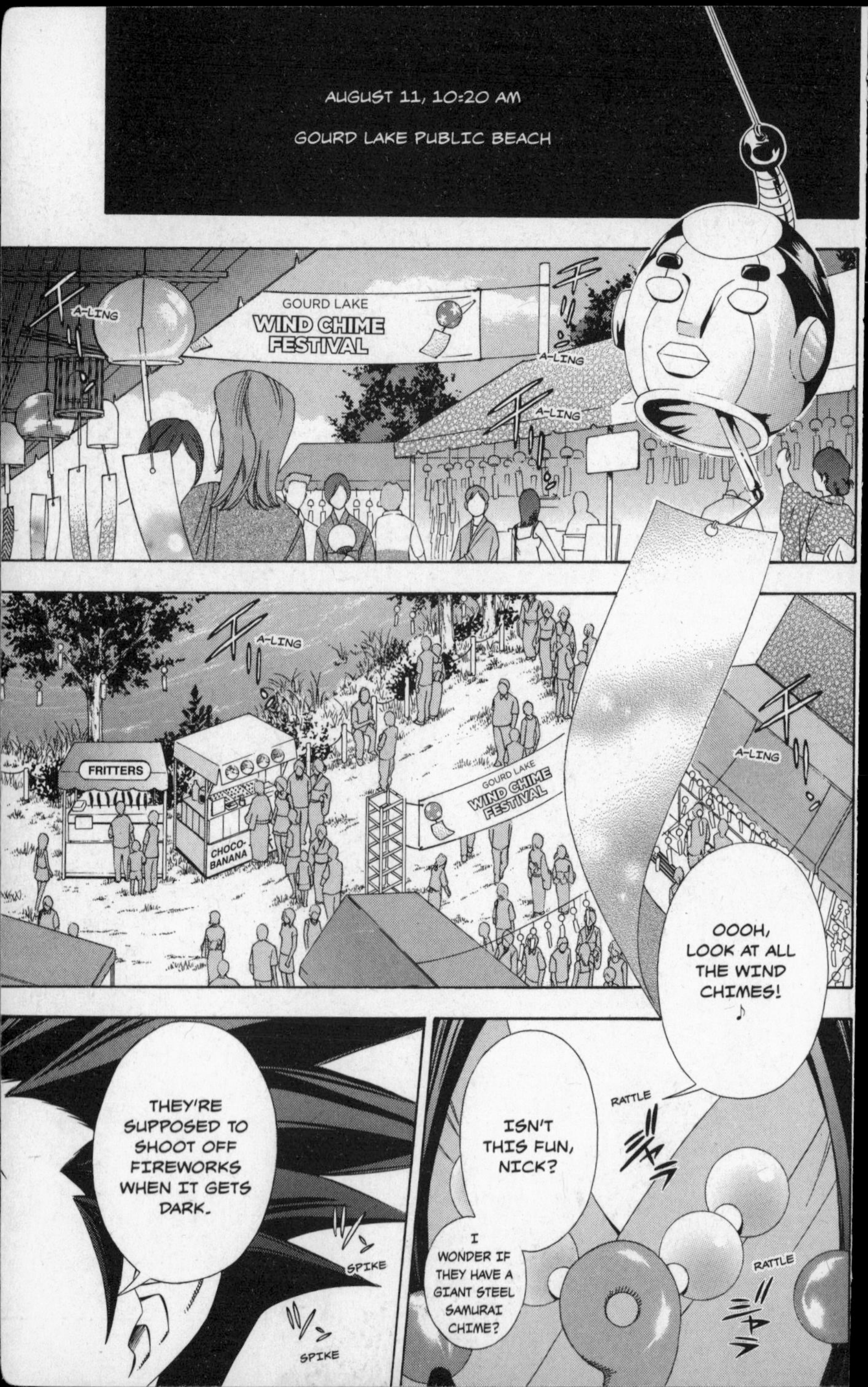
AUGUST 11, 10:20 AM
GOURD LAKE PUBLIC BEACH
A-LING
A-LING
GOURD LAKE WIND CHIME FESTIVAL
A-LING
A-LING
A-LING
GOURD LAKE WIND CHIME FESTIVAL
A-LING
CHOCO-BANANA
FRITTERS
OOOH, LOOK AT ALL THE WIND CHIMES! ♪
RATTLE
ISN'T THIS FUN, NICK?
RATTLE
I WONDER IF THEY HAVE A GIANT STEEL SAMURAI CHIME?
THEY'RE SUPPOSED TO SHOOT OFF FIREWORKS WHEN IT GETS DARK.
SPIKE
SPIKE

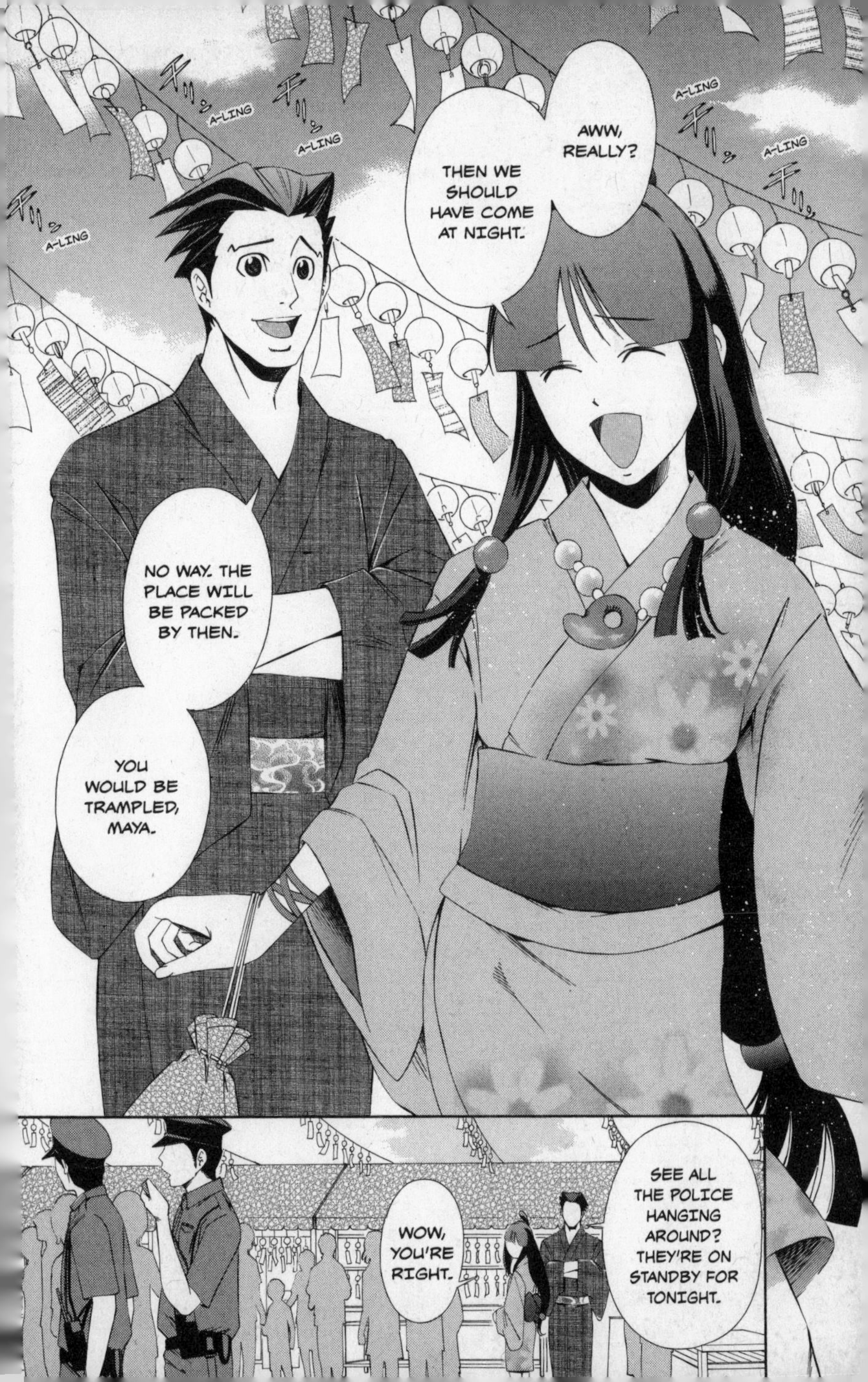
A-LING
A-LING
AWW, REALLY?
THEN WE SHOULD HAVE COME AT NIGHT.
A-LING
A-LING
A-LING
NO WAY. THE PLACE WILL BE PACKED BY THEN.
YOU WOULD BE TRAMPLED, MAYA.
SEE ALL THE POLICE HANGING AROUND? THEY'RE ON STANDBY FOR TONIGHT.
WOW, YOU'RE RIGHT.

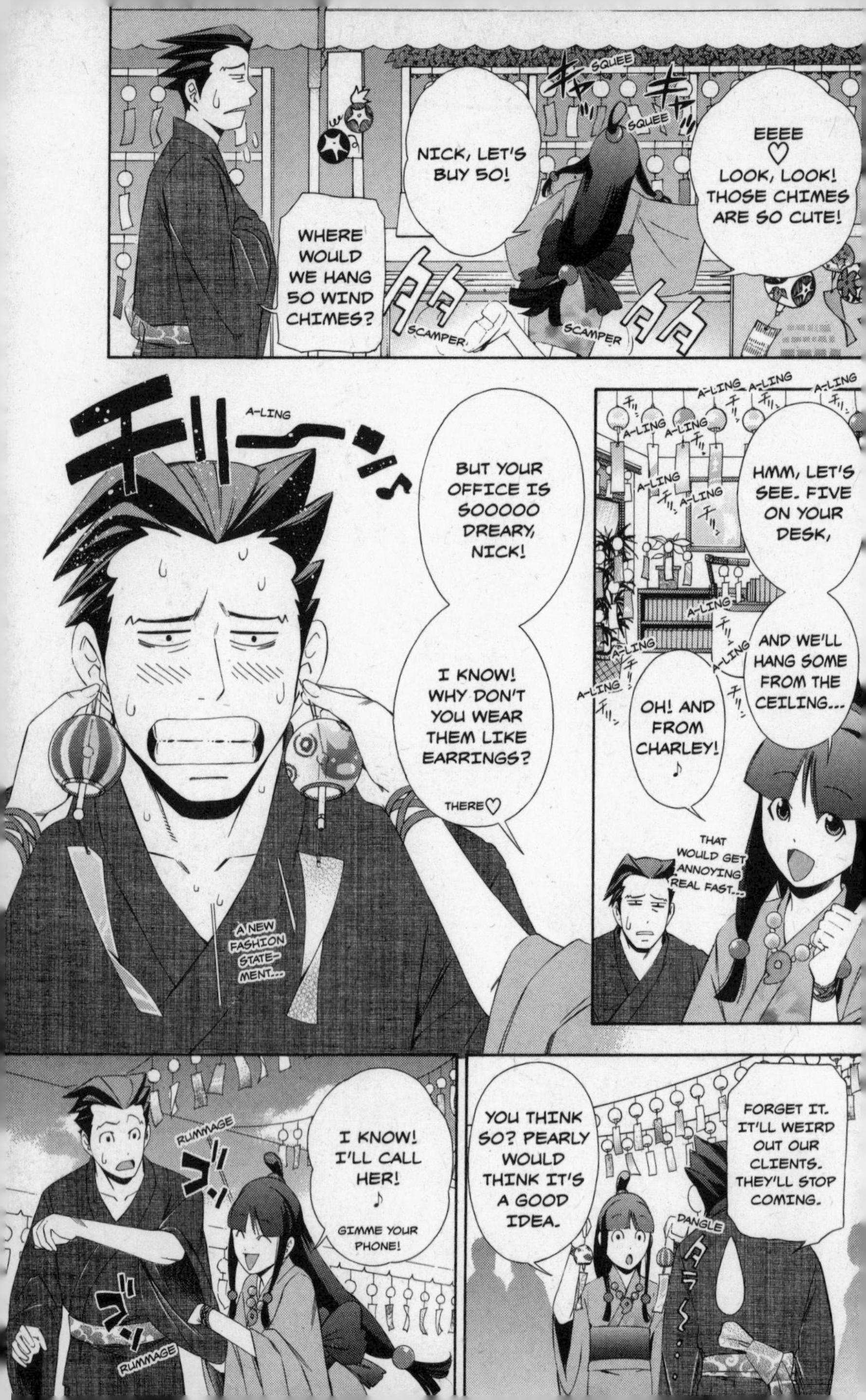
EEEE ♡ LOOK, LOOK! THOSE CHIMES ARE SO CUTE!
SQUEE
SQUEE
NICK, LET'S BUY 50!
WHERE WOULD WE HANG 50 WIND CHIMES?
SCAMPER
SCAMPER
A-LING A-LING A-LING
A-LING A-LING
A-LING A-LING
HMM, LET'S SEE. FIVE ON YOUR DESK,
AND WE'LL HANG SOME FROM THE CEILING...
A-LING A-LING A-LING A-LING
OH! AND FROM CHARLEY! ♪
THAT WOULD GET ANNOYING REAL FAST...
BUT YOUR OFFICE IS SOOOOO DREARY, NICK!
I KNOW! WHY DON'T YOU WEAR THEM LIKE EARRINGS?
THERE♡
A-LING
A NEW FASHION STATEMENT...
FORGET IT. IT'LL WEIRD OUT OUR CLIENTS. THEY'LL STOP COMING.
YOU THINK SO? PEARLY WOULD THINK IT'S A GOOD IDEA.
DANGLE
I KNOW! I'LL CALL HER! ♪
GIMME YOUR PHONE!
RUMMAGE
RUMMAGE

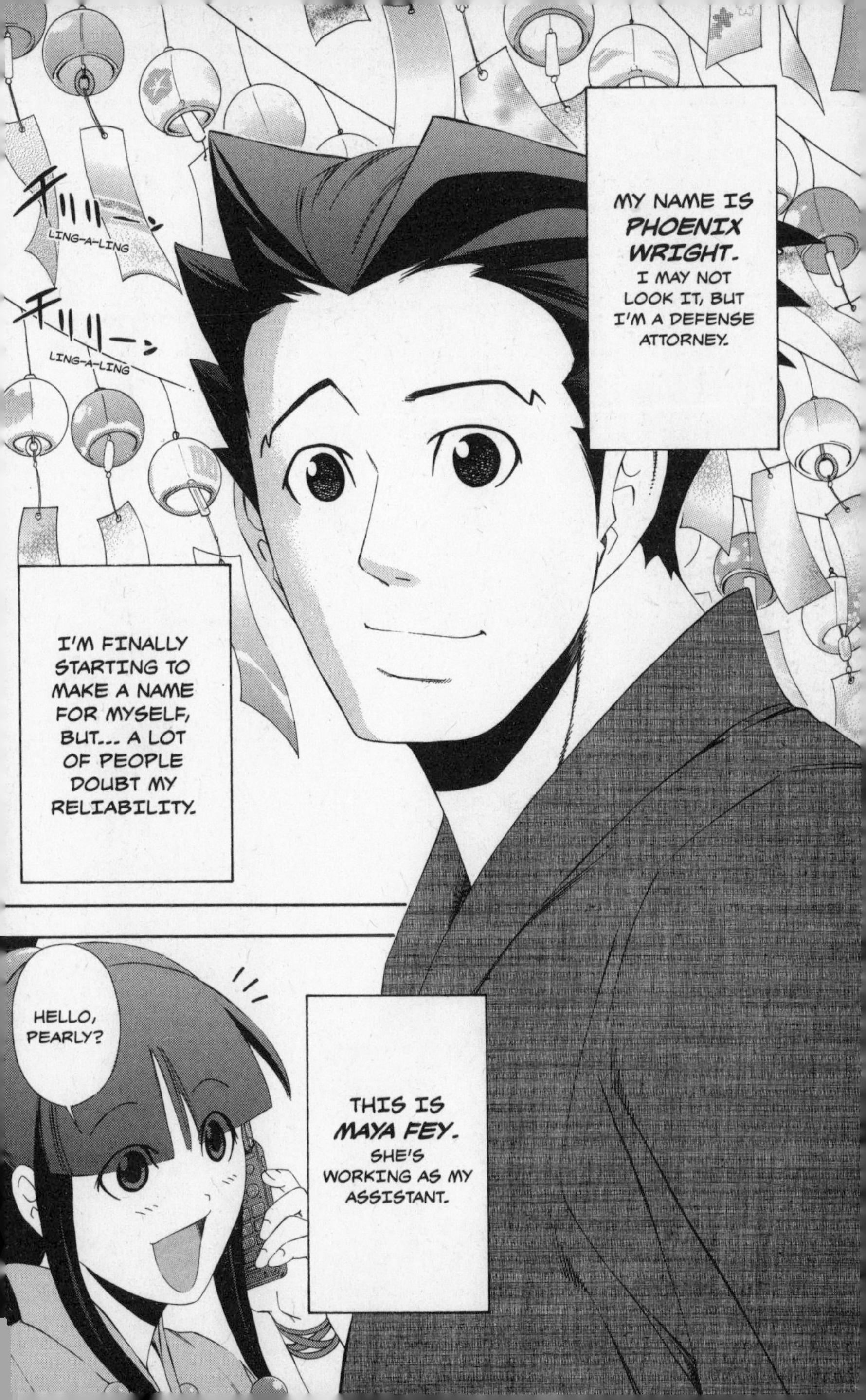

MY NAME IS PHOENIX WRIGHT. I MAY NOT LOOK IT, BUT I'M A DEFENSE ATTORNEY.
LING-A-LING
LING-A-LING
I'M FINALLY STARTING TO MAKE A NAME FOR MYSELF, BUT... A LOT OF PEOPLE DOUBT MY RELIABILITY.
THIS IS MAYA FEY. SHE'S WORKING AS MY ASSISTANT.
HELLO, PEARLY?

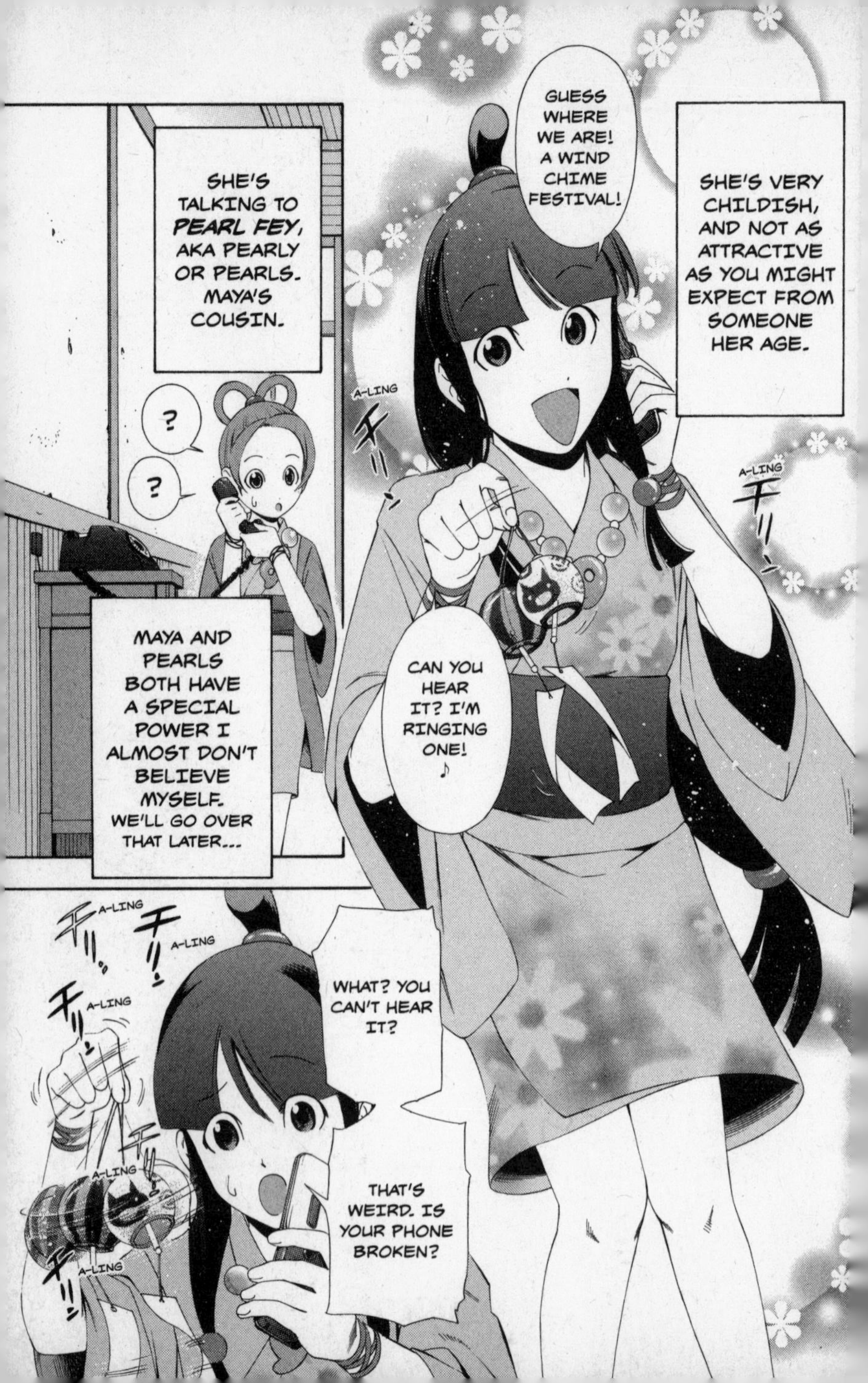

GUESS WHERE WE ARE! A WIND CHIME FESTIVAL!
SHE'S VERY CHILDISH, AND NOT AS ATTRACTIVE AS YOU MIGHT EXPECT FROM SOMEONE HER AGE.
A-LING
A-LING
CAN YOU HEAR IT? I'M RINGING ONE! ♪
SHE'S TALKING TO ***PEARL FEY***, AKA PEARLY OR PEARLS. MAYA'S COUSIN.
?
?
MAYA AND PEARLS BOTH HAVE A SPECIAL POWER I ALMOST DON'T BELIEVE MYSELF. WE'LL GO OVER THAT LATER...
WHAT? YOU CAN'T HEAR IT?
A-LING
A-LING
A-LING
A-LING
A-LING
THAT'S WEIRD. IS YOUR PHONE BROKEN?

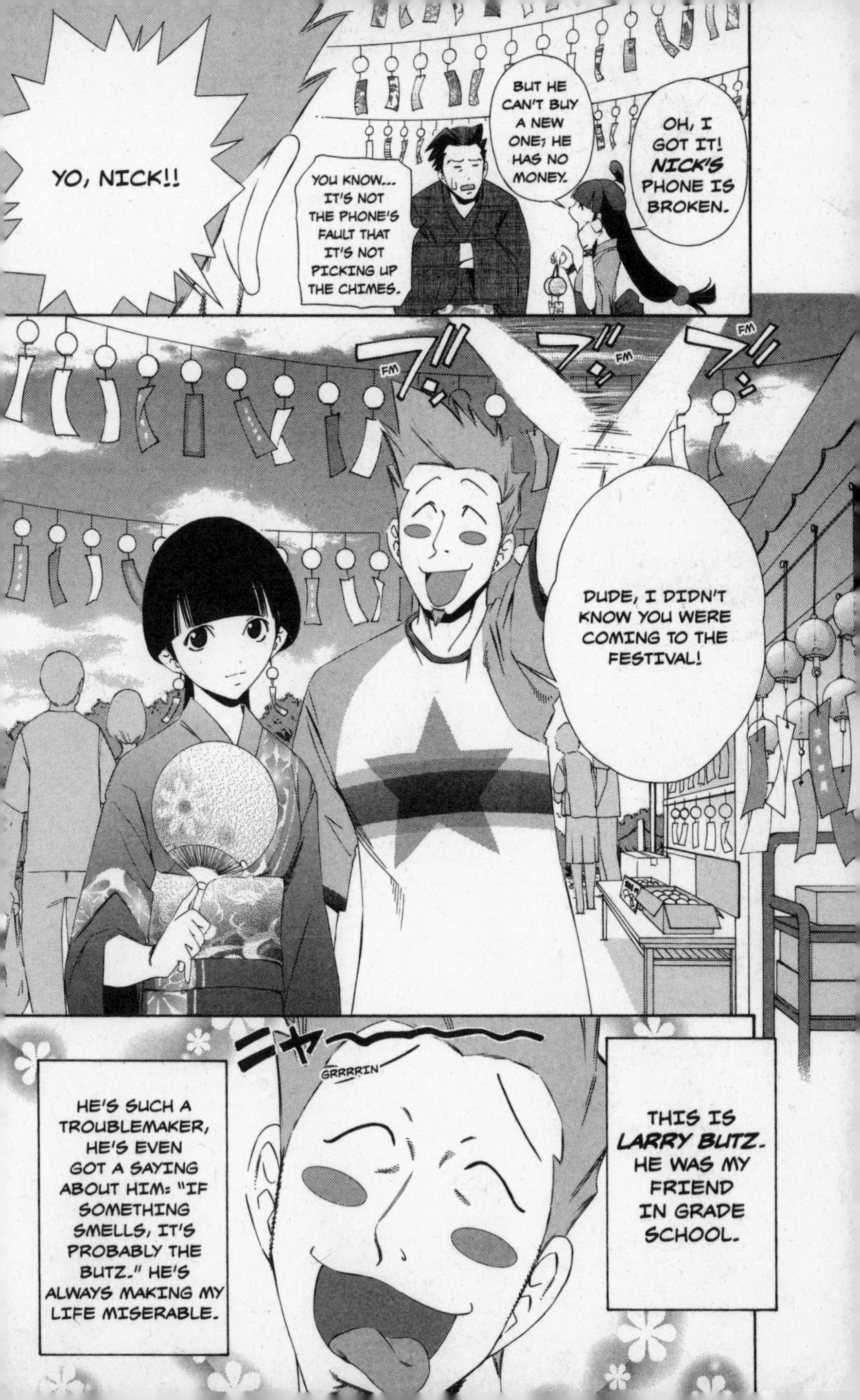
OH, I GOT IT! NICK'S PHONE IS BROKEN.
BUT HE CAN'T BUY A NEW ONE; HE HAS NO MONEY.
YOU KNOW... IT'S NOT THE PHONE'S FAULT THAT IT'S NOT PICKING UP THE CHIMES.
YO, NICK!!
FM
FM
FM
DUDE, I DIDN'T KNOW YOU WERE COMING TO THE FESTIVAL!
THIS IS LARRY BUTZ. HE WAS MY FRIEND IN GRADE SCHOOL.
GRRRRIN
HE'S SUCH A TROUBLEMAKER, HE'S EVEN GOT A SAYING ABOUT HIM: "IF SOMETHING SMELLS, IT'S PROBABLY THE BUTZ." HE'S ALWAYS MAKING MY LIFE MISERABLE.

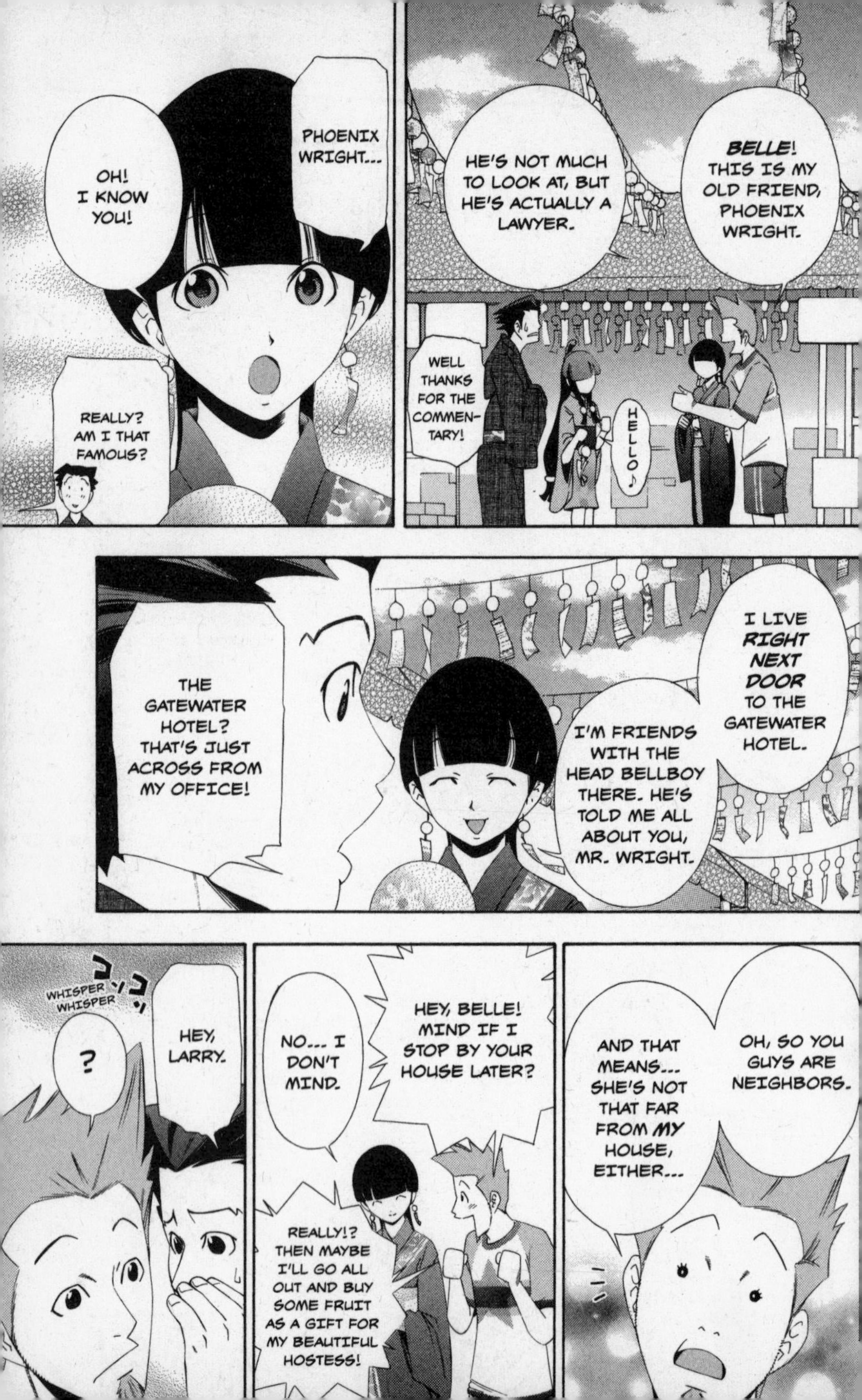
BELLE! THIS IS MY OLD FRIEND, PHOENIX WRIGHT.
HE'S NOT MUCH TO LOOK AT, BUT HE'S ACTUALLY A LAWYER.
HELLO♪
WELL THANKS FOR THE COMMENTARY!
PHOENIX WRIGHT...
OH! I KNOW YOU!
REALLY? AM I THAT FAMOUS?
I LIVE RIGHT NEXT DOOR TO THE GATEWATER HOTEL.
I'M FRIENDS WITH THE HEAD BELLBOY THERE. HE'S TOLD ME ALL ABOUT YOU, MR. WRIGHT.
THE GATEWATER HOTEL? THAT'S JUST ACROSS FROM MY OFFICE!
OH, SO YOU GUYS ARE NEIGHBORS.
AND THAT MEANS... SHE'S NOT THAT FAR FROM MY HOUSE, EITHER...
HEY, BELLE! MIND IF I STOP BY YOUR HOUSE LATER?
NO... I DON'T MIND.
REALLY!? THEN MAYBE I'LL GO ALL OUT AND BUY SOME FRUIT AS A GIFT FOR MY BEAUTIFUL HOSTESS!
HEY, LARRY.
WHISPER WHISPER
?

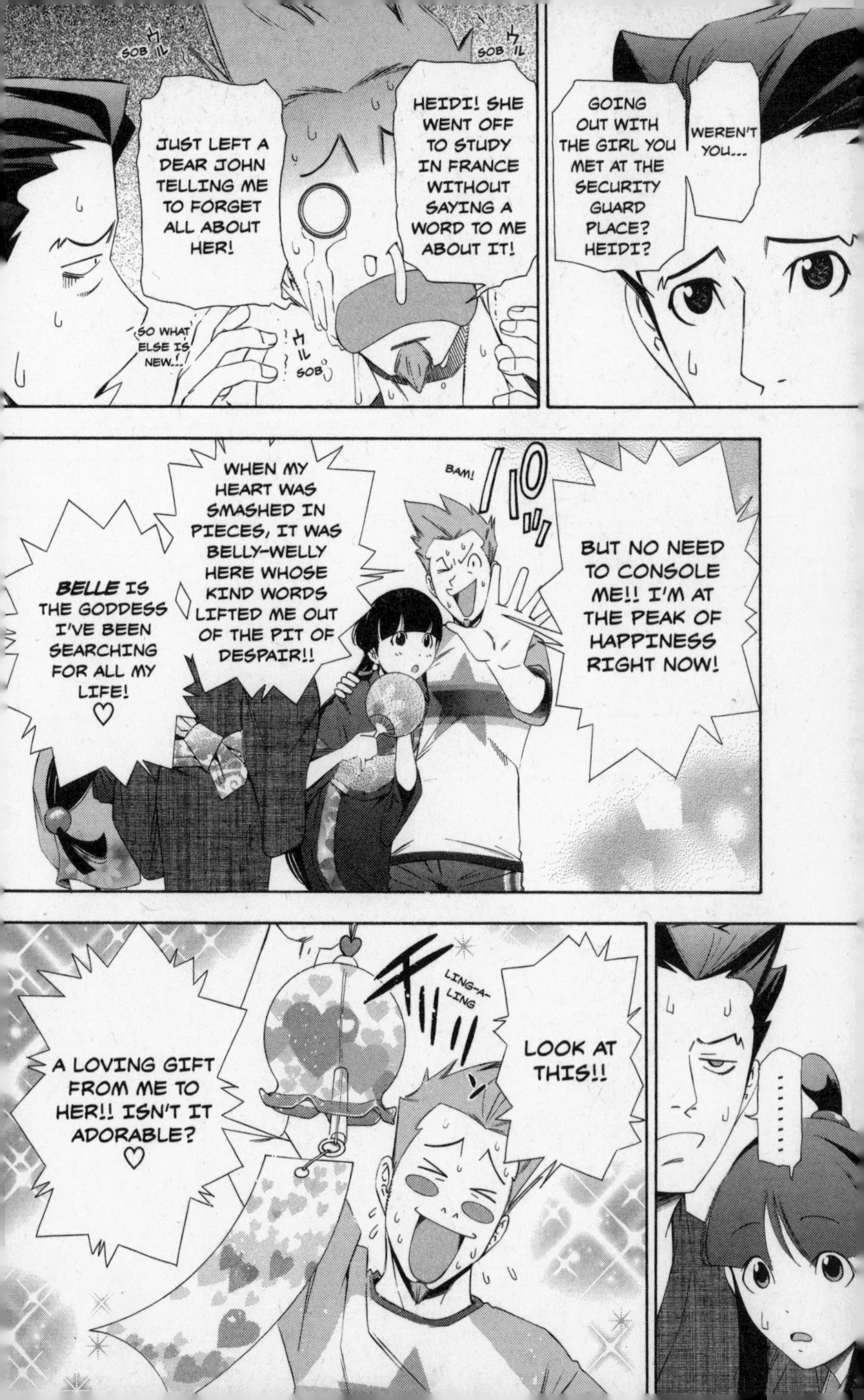
WEREN'T YOU...
GOING OUT WITH THE GIRL YOU MET AT THE SECURITY GUARD PLACE? HEIDI?
SOB
SOB
HEIDI! SHE WENT OFF TO STUDY IN FRANCE WITHOUT SAYING A WORD TO ME ABOUT IT!
JUST LEFT A DEAR JOHN TELLING ME TO FORGET ALL ABOUT HER!
SO WHAT ELSE IS NEW...
SOB
BAM!
BUT NO NEED TO CONSOLE ME!! I'M AT THE PEAK OF HAPPINESS RIGHT NOW!
WHEN MY HEART WAS SMASHED IN PIECES, IT WAS BELLY-WELLY HERE WHOSE KIND WORDS LIFTED ME OUT OF THE PIT OF DESPAIR!!
*BELLE* IS THE GODDESS I'VE BEEN SEARCHING FOR ALL MY LIFE! ♡
......
LING-A-LING
LOOK AT THIS!!
A LOVING GIFT FROM ME TO HER!! ISN'T IT ADORABLE? ♡

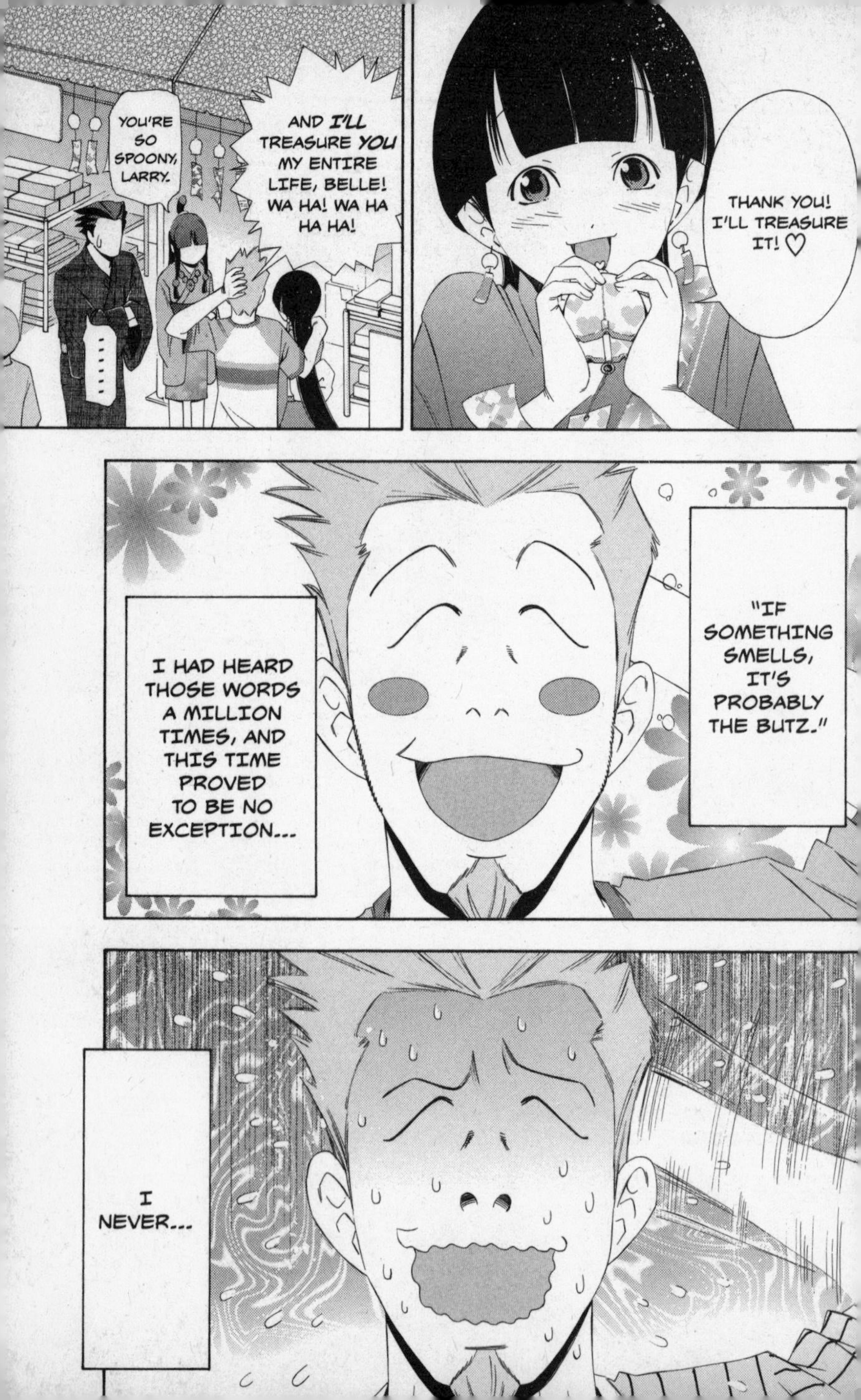
THANK YOU! I'LL TREASURE IT! ♡
AND I'LL TREASURE YOU MY ENTIRE LIFE, BELLE! WA HA! WA HA HA HA!
YOU'RE SO SPOONY, LARRY.
"IF SOMETHING SMELLS, IT'S PROBABLY THE BUTZ."
I HAD HEARD THOSE WORDS A MILLION TIMES, AND THIS TIME PROVED TO BE NO EXCEPTION...
I NEVER...

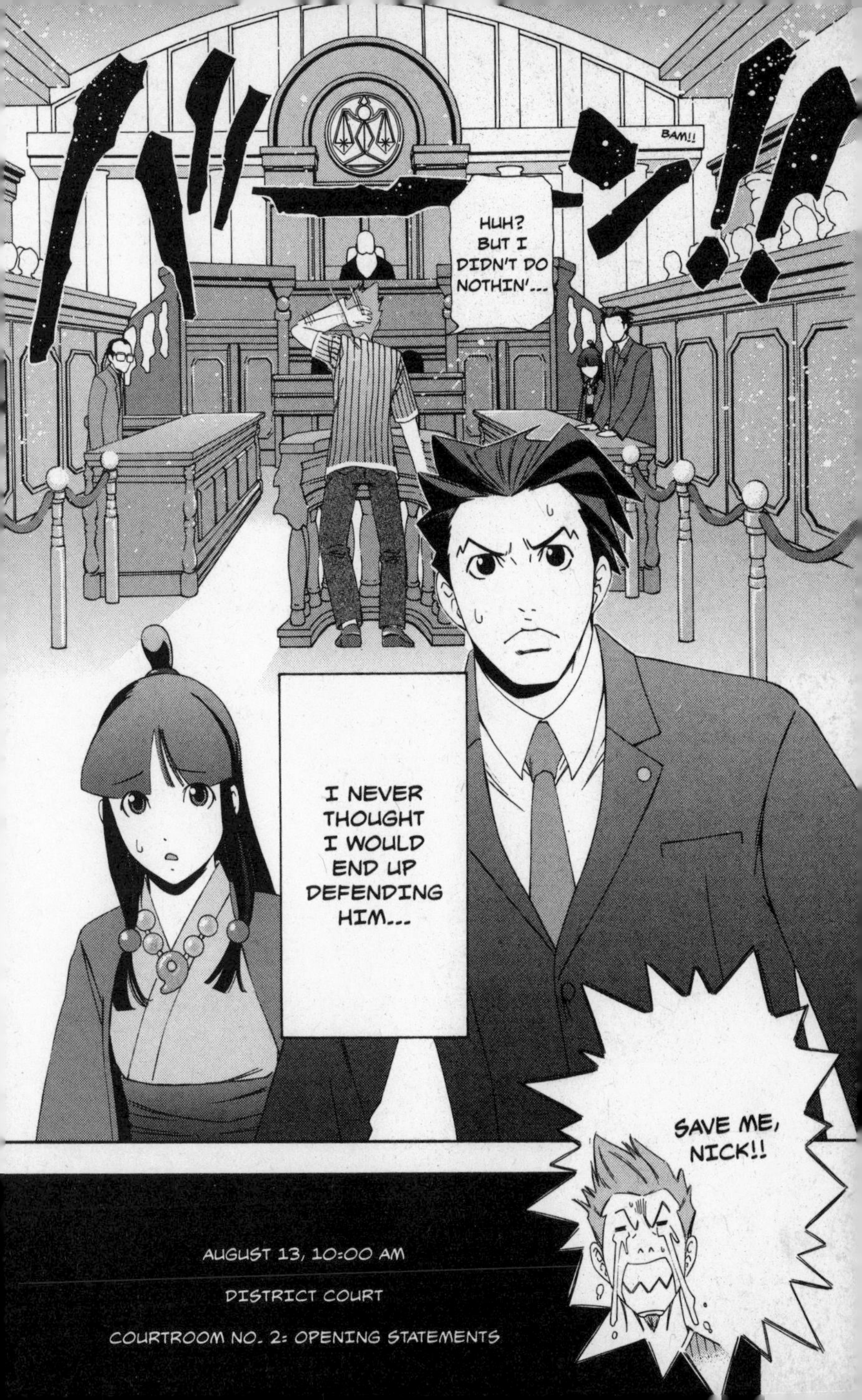
BAM!!
HUH? BUT I DIDN'T DO NOTHIN'...
I NEVER THOUGHT I WOULD END UP DEFENDING HIM...
SAVE ME, NICK!!
AUGUST 13, 10:00 AM
DISTRICT COURT
COURTROOM NO. 2: OPENING STATEMENTS

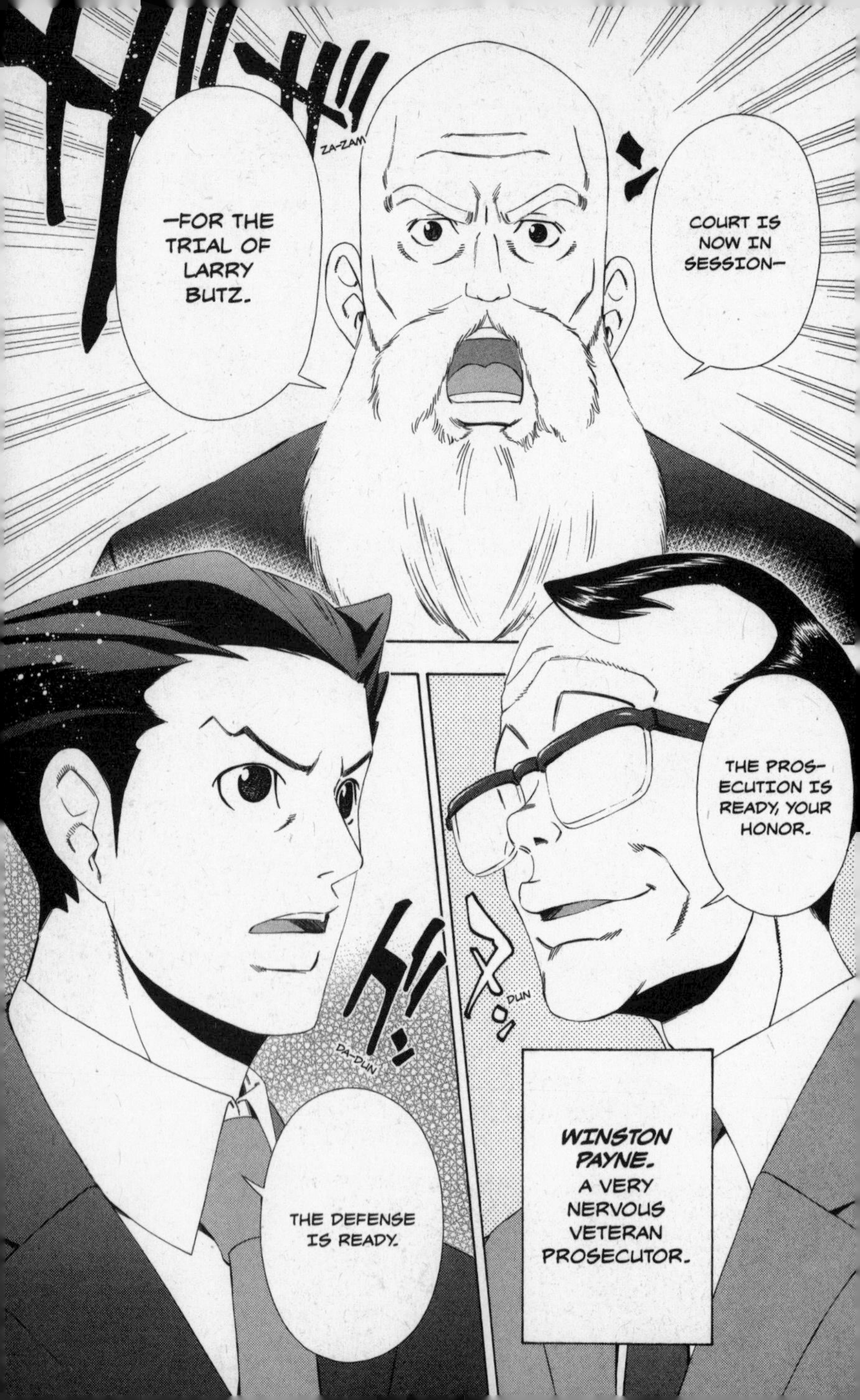
ZA-ZAM
COURT IS NOW IN SESSION—
—FOR THE TRIAL OF LARRY BUTZ.
THE PROS-ECUTION IS READY, YOUR HONOR.
DUN
WINSTON PAYNE. A VERY NERVOUS VETERAN PROSECUTOR.
DA-DUN
THE DEFENSE IS READY.

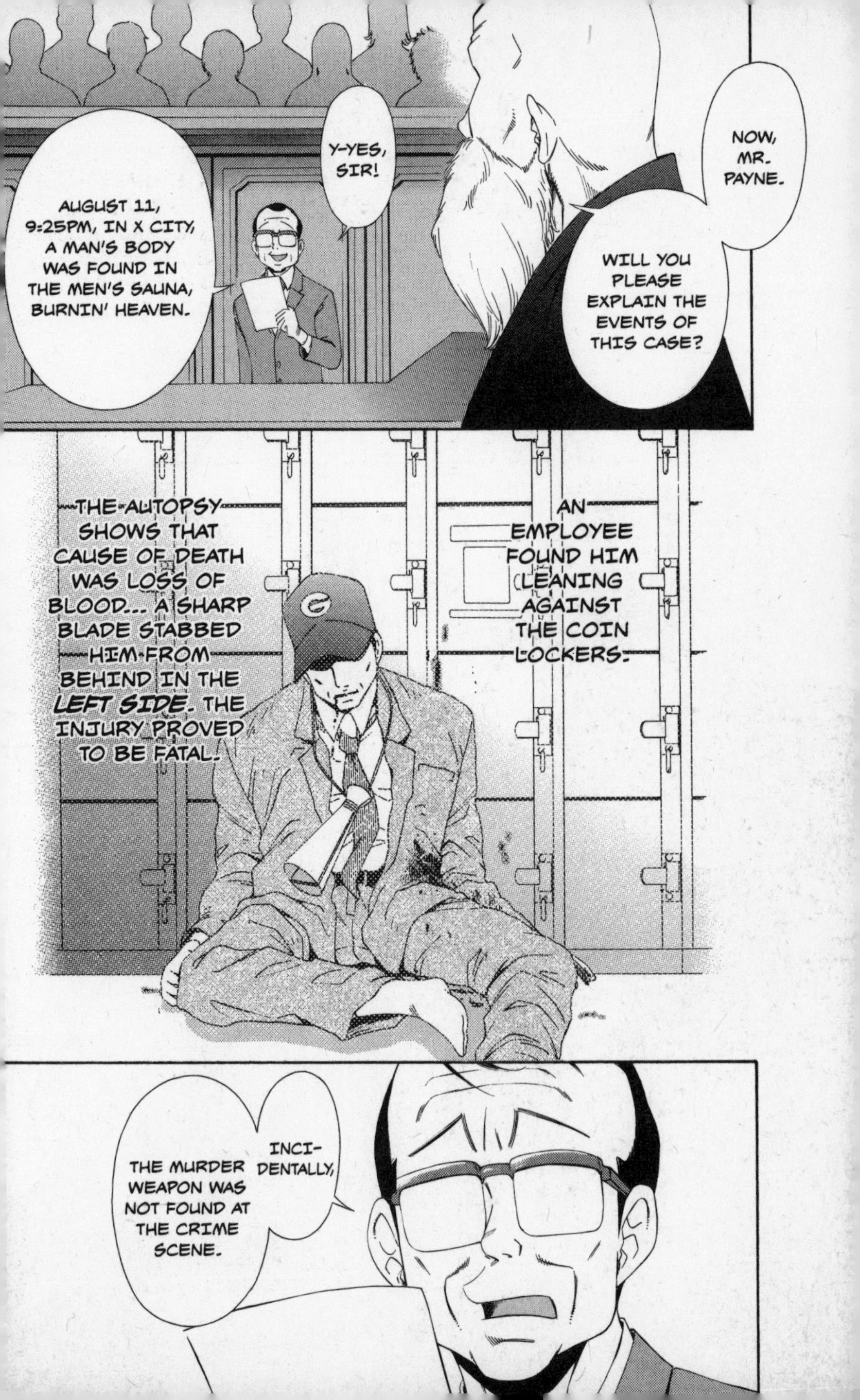
NOW, MR. PAYNE.
WILL YOU PLEASE EXPLAIN THE EVENTS OF THIS CASE?
Y-YES, SIR!
AUGUST 11, 9:25PM, IN X CITY, A MAN'S BODY WAS FOUND IN THE MEN'S SAUNA, BURNIN' HEAVEN.
AN EMPLOYEE FOUND HIM LEANING AGAINST THE COIN LOCKERS.
THE AUTOPSY SHOWS THAT CAUSE OF DEATH WAS LOSS OF BLOOD... A SHARP BLADE STABBED HIM FROM BEHIND IN THE LEFT SIDE. THE INJURY PROVED TO BE FATAL!
INCI- DENTALLY,
THE MURDER WEAPON WAS NOT FOUND AT THE CRIME SCENE.

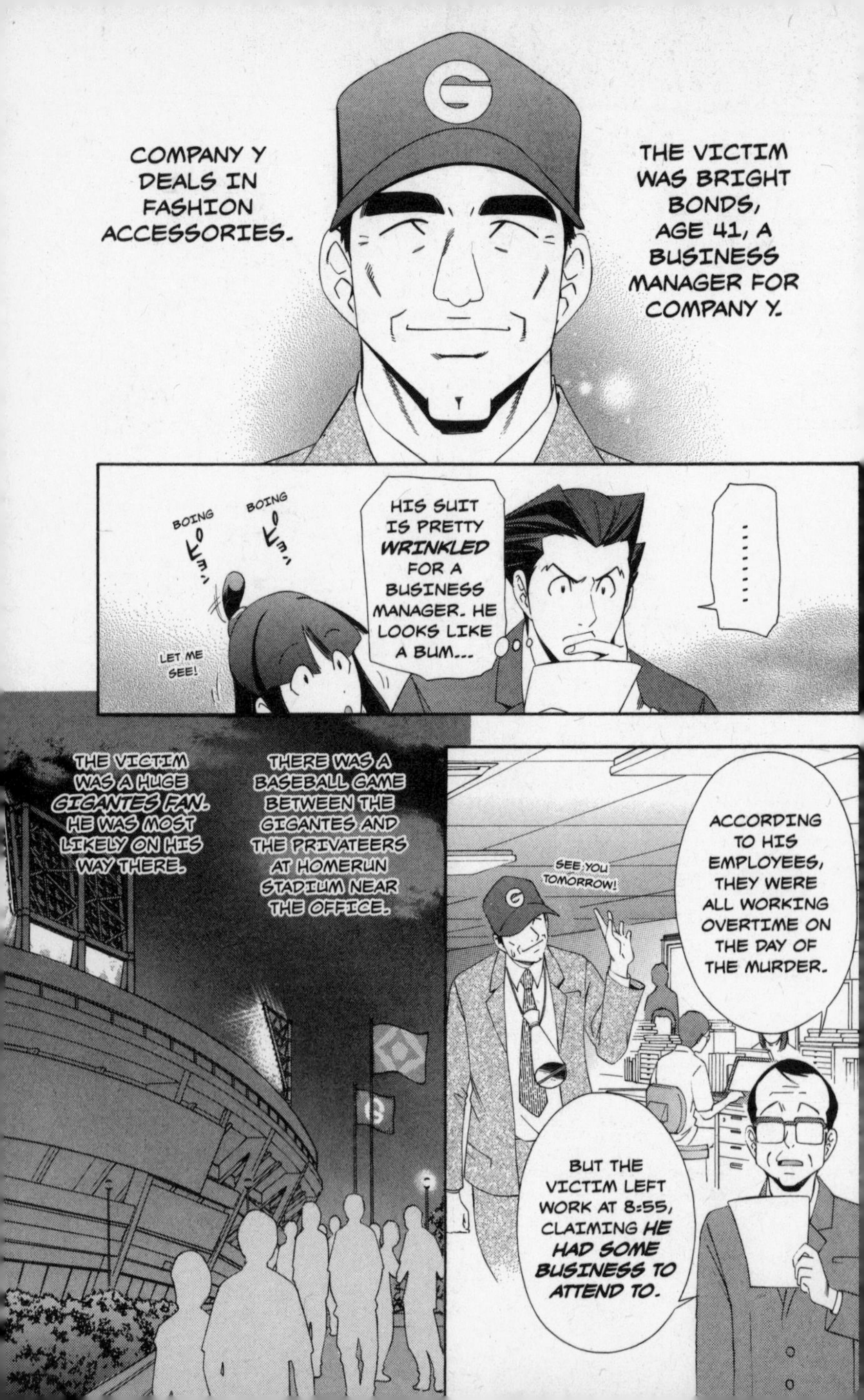
THE VICTIM WAS BRIGHT BONDS, AGE 41, A BUSINESS MANAGER FOR COMPANY Y.
COMPANY Y DEALS IN FASHION ACCESSORIES.
......
HIS SUIT IS PRETTY *WRINKLED* FOR A BUSINESS MANAGER. HE LOOKS LIKE A BUM...
BOING
BOING
LET ME SEE!
ACCORDING TO HIS EMPLOYEES, THEY WERE ALL WORKING OVERTIME ON THE DAY OF THE MURDER.
SEE YOU TOMORROW!
BUT THE VICTIM LEFT WORK AT 8:55, CLAIMING *HE HAD SOME BUSINESS TO ATTEND TO.*
THERE WAS A BASEBALL GAME BETWEEN THE GIGANTES AND THE PRIVATEERS AT HOMERUN STADIUM NEAR THE OFFICE.
THE VICTIM WAS A HUGE *GIGANTES FAN.* HE WAS MOST LIKELY ON HIS WAY THERE.

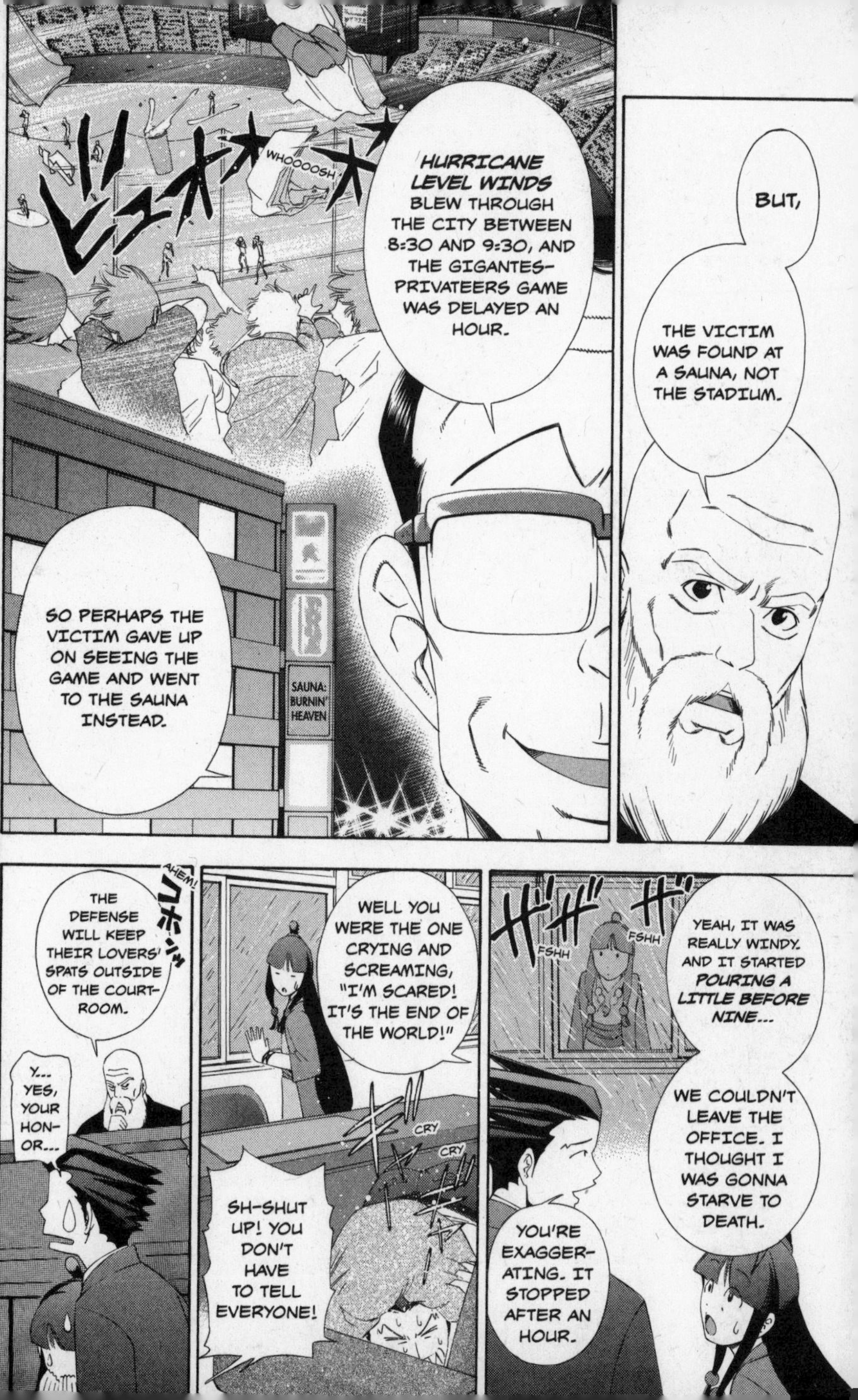

WHOOOOSH
HURRICANE LEVEL WINDS BLEW THROUGH THE CITY BETWEEN 8:30 AND 9:30, AND THE GIGANTES-PRIVATEERS GAME WAS DELAYED AN HOUR.
BUT,
THE VICTIM WAS FOUND AT A SAUNA, NOT THE STADIUM.
SAUNA: BURNIN' HEAVEN
SO PERHAPS THE VICTIM GAVE UP ON SEEING THE GAME AND WENT TO THE SAUNA INSTEAD.
FSHH
FSHH
YEAH, IT WAS REALLY WINDY. AND IT STARTED POURING A LITTLE BEFORE NINE...
WE COULDN'T LEAVE THE OFFICE. I THOUGHT I WAS GONNA STARVE TO DEATH.
YOU'RE EXAGGER-ATING. IT STOPPED AFTER AN HOUR.
WELL YOU WERE THE ONE CRYING AND SCREAMING, "I'M SCARED! IT'S THE END OF THE WORLD!"
CRY
CRY
SH-SHUT UP! YOU DON'T HAVE TO TELL EVERYONE!
AHEM!
THE DEFENSE WILL KEEP THEIR LOVERS' SPATS OUTSIDE OF THE COURT-ROOM.
Y... YES, YOUR HON-OR...

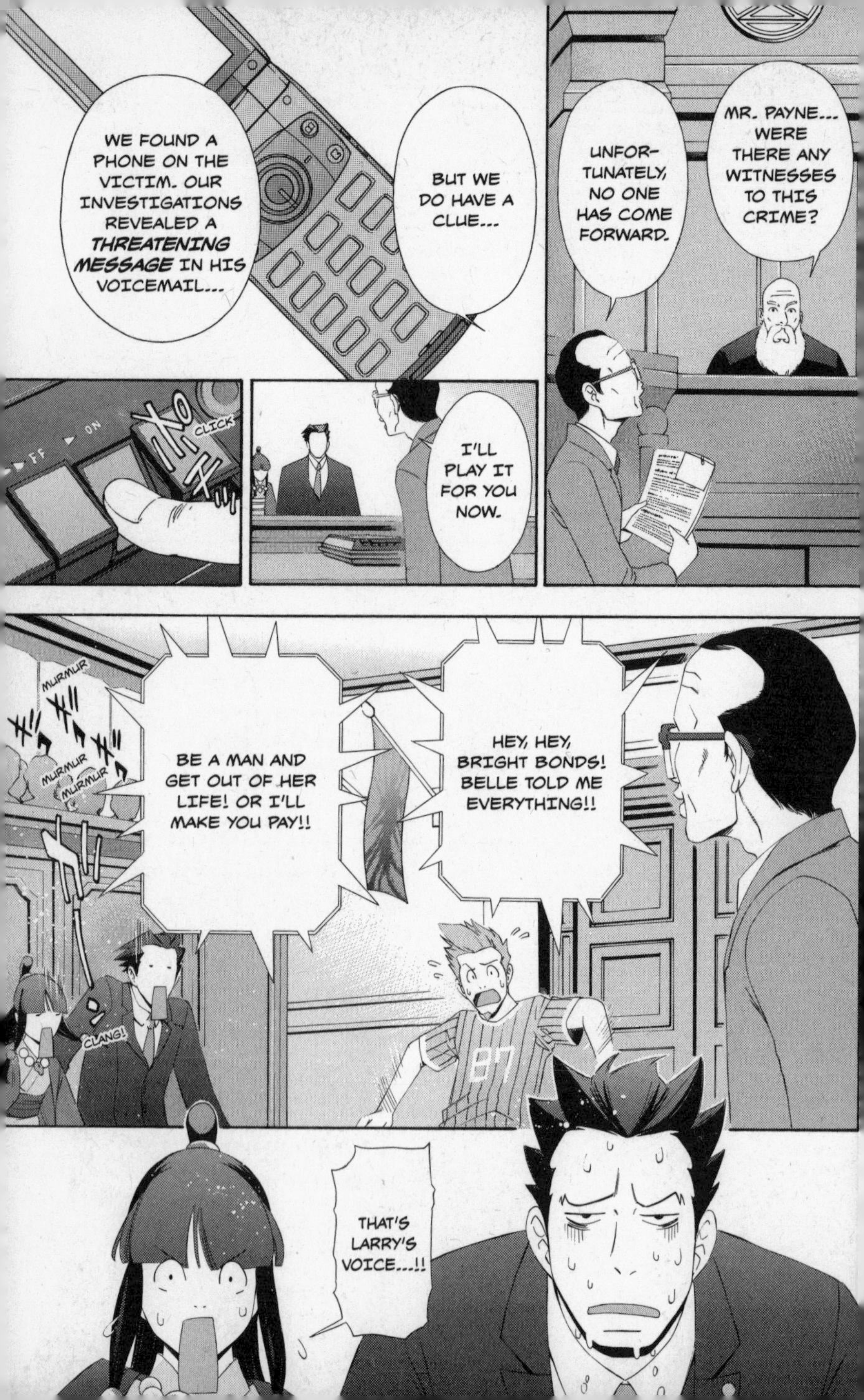
MR. PAYNE... WERE THERE ANY WITNESSES TO THIS CRIME?
UNFORTUNATELY, NO ONE HAS COME FORWARD.
BUT WE DO HAVE A CLUE...
WE FOUND A PHONE ON THE VICTIM. OUR INVESTIGATIONS REVEALED A ***THREATENING MESSAGE*** IN HIS VOICEMAIL...
I'LL PLAY IT FOR YOU NOW.
CLICK
HEY, HEY, BRIGHT BONDS! BELLE TOLD ME EVERYTHING!!
BE A MAN AND GET OUT OF HER LIFE! OR I'LL MAKE YOU PAY!!
MURMUR
MURMUR
MURMUR
CLANG!
THAT'S LARRY'S VOICE...!!

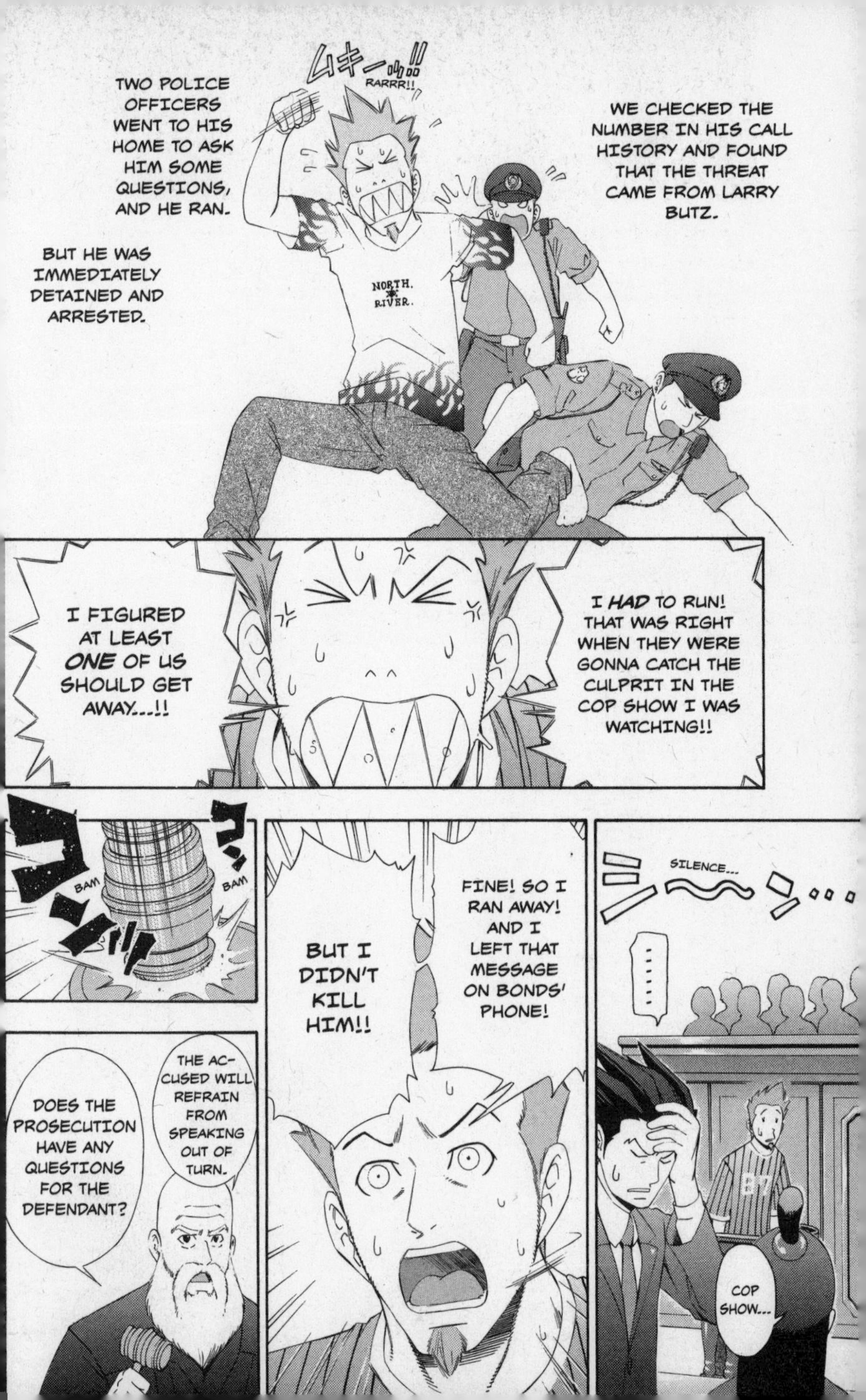
WE CHECKED THE NUMBER IN HIS CALL HISTORY AND FOUND THAT THE THREAT CAME FROM LARRY BUTZ.
TWO POLICE OFFICERS WENT TO HIS HOME TO ASK HIM SOME QUESTIONS, AND HE RAN.
ムキー
RARRR!!
NORTH. RIVER.
BUT HE WAS IMMEDIATELY DETAINED AND ARRESTED.
I *HAD* TO RUN! THAT WAS RIGHT WHEN THEY WERE GONNA CATCH THE CULPRIT IN THE COP SHOW I WAS WATCHING!!
I FIGURED AT LEAST *ONE* OF US SHOULD GET AWAY...!!
SILENCE...
......
COP SHOW...
FINE! SO I RAN AWAY! AND I LEFT THAT MESSAGE ON BONDS' PHONE!
BUT I DIDN'T KILL HIM!!
BAM
BAM
THE ACCUSED WILL REFRAIN FROM SPEAKING OUT OF TURN.
DOES THE PROSECUTION HAVE ANY QUESTIONS FOR THE DEFENDANT?

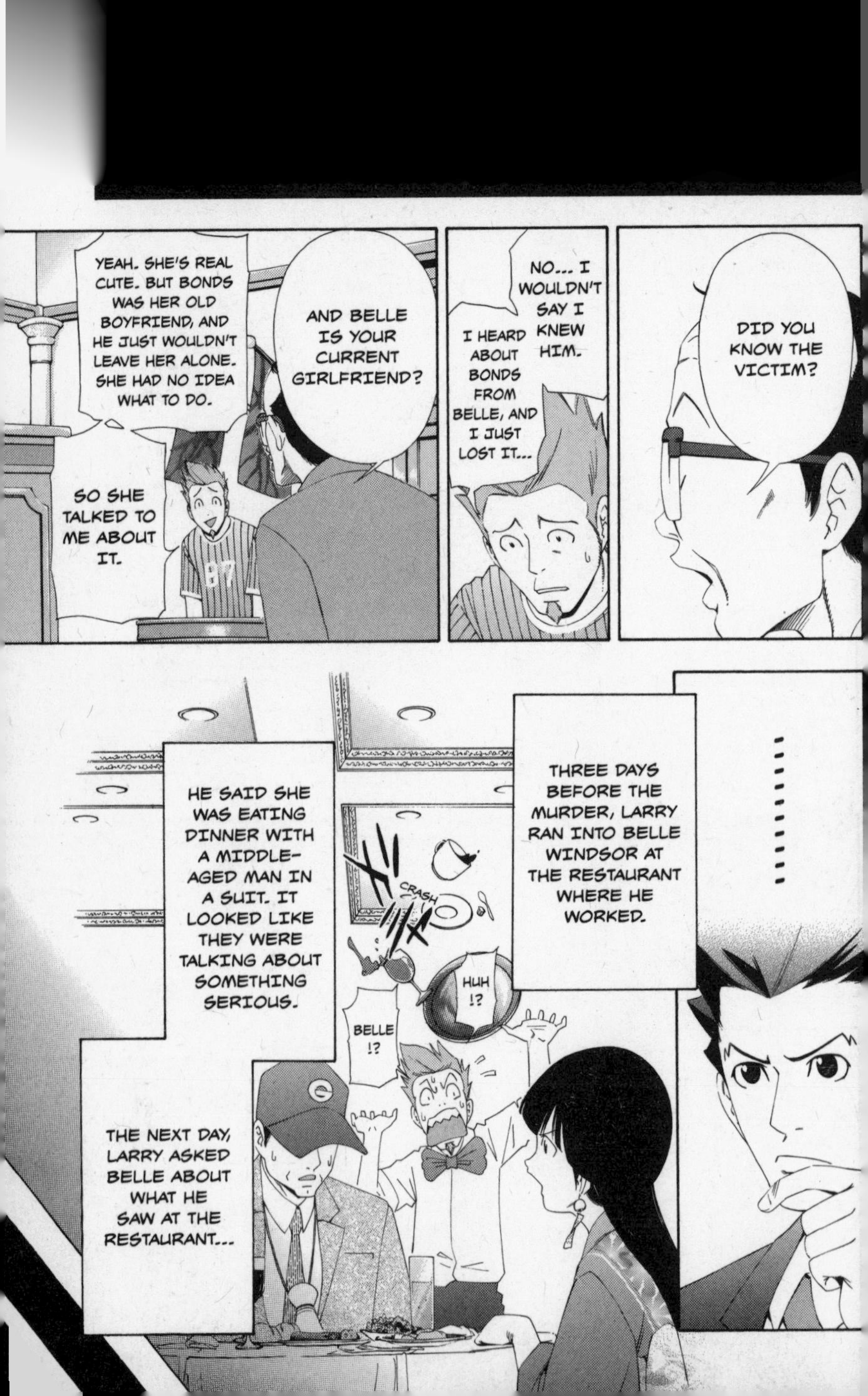
DID YOU KNOW THE VICTIM?
NO... I WOULDN'T SAY I KNEW HIM.
I HEARD ABOUT BONDS FROM BELLE, AND I JUST LOST IT...
AND BELLE IS YOUR CURRENT GIRLFRIEND?
YEAH. SHE'S REAL CUTE. BUT BONDS WAS HER OLD BOYFRIEND, AND HE JUST WOULDN'T LEAVE HER ALONE. SHE HAD NO IDEA WHAT TO DO.
SO SHE TALKED TO ME ABOUT IT.
..........
THREE DAYS BEFORE THE MURDER, LARRY RAN INTO BELLE WINDSOR AT THE RESTAURANT WHERE HE WORKED.
HE SAID SHE WAS EATING DINNER WITH A MIDDLE-AGED MAN IN A SUIT. IT LOOKED LIKE THEY WERE TALKING ABOUT SOMETHING SERIOUS.
CRASH
HUH!?
BELLE!?
THE NEXT DAY, LARRY ASKED BELLE ABOUT WHAT HE SAW AT THE RESTAURANT...

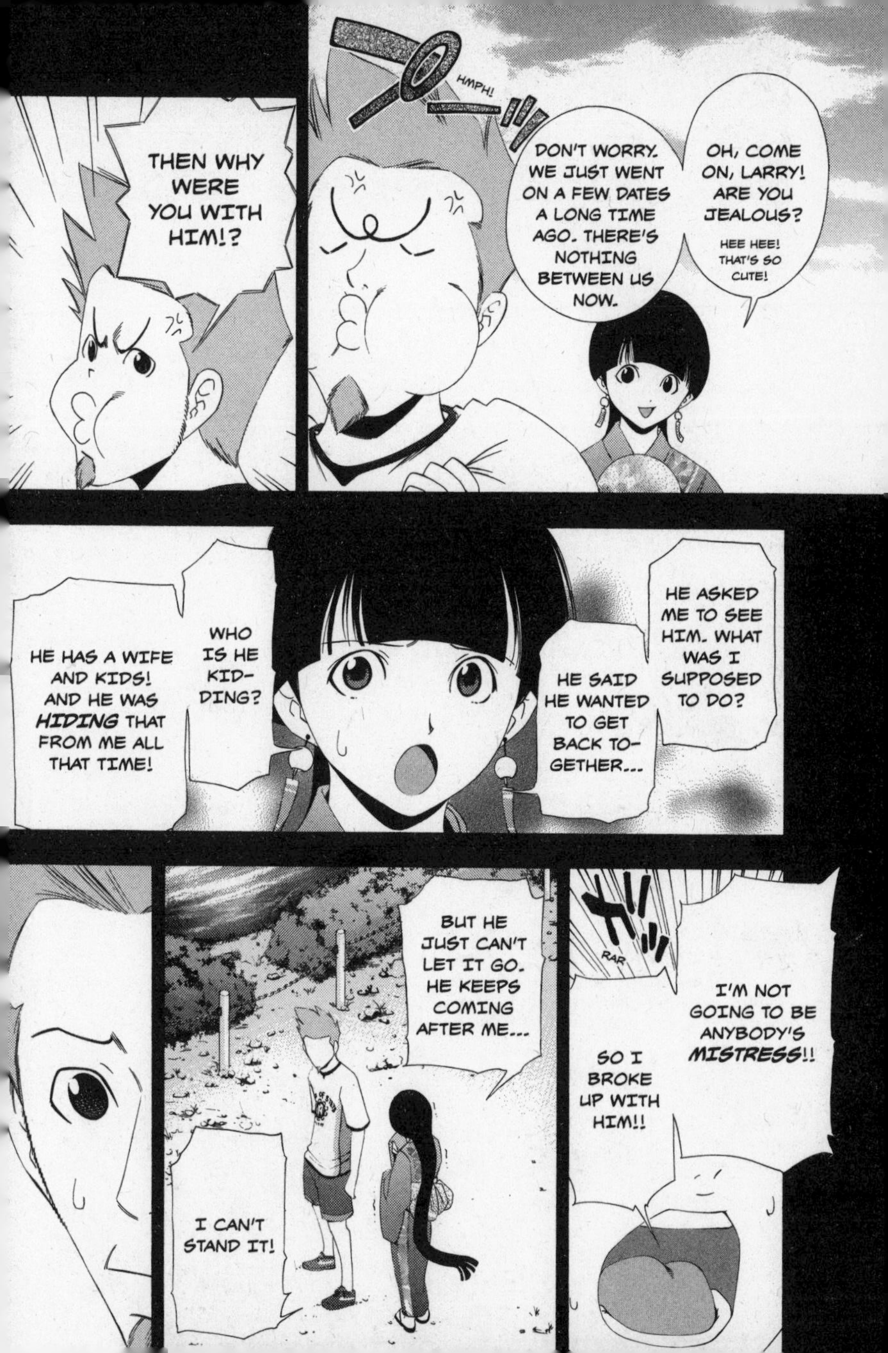
OH, COME ON, LARRY! ARE YOU JEALOUS?
HEE HEE! THAT'S SO CUTE!
DON'T WORRY. WE JUST WENT ON A FEW DATES A LONG TIME AGO. THERE'S NOTHING BETWEEN US NOW.
HMPH!
THEN WHY WERE YOU WITH HIM!?
HE ASKED ME TO SEE HIM. WHAT WAS I SUPPOSED TO DO?
HE SAID HE WANTED TO GET BACK TO-GETHER...
WHO IS HE KID-DING?
HE HAS A WIFE AND KIDS! AND HE WAS *HIDING* THAT FROM ME ALL THAT TIME!
RAR
I'M NOT GOING TO BE ANYBODY'S *MISTRESS*!!
SO I BROKE UP WITH HIM!!
BUT HE JUST CAN'T LET IT GO. HE KEEPS COMING AFTER ME...
I CAN'T STAND IT!

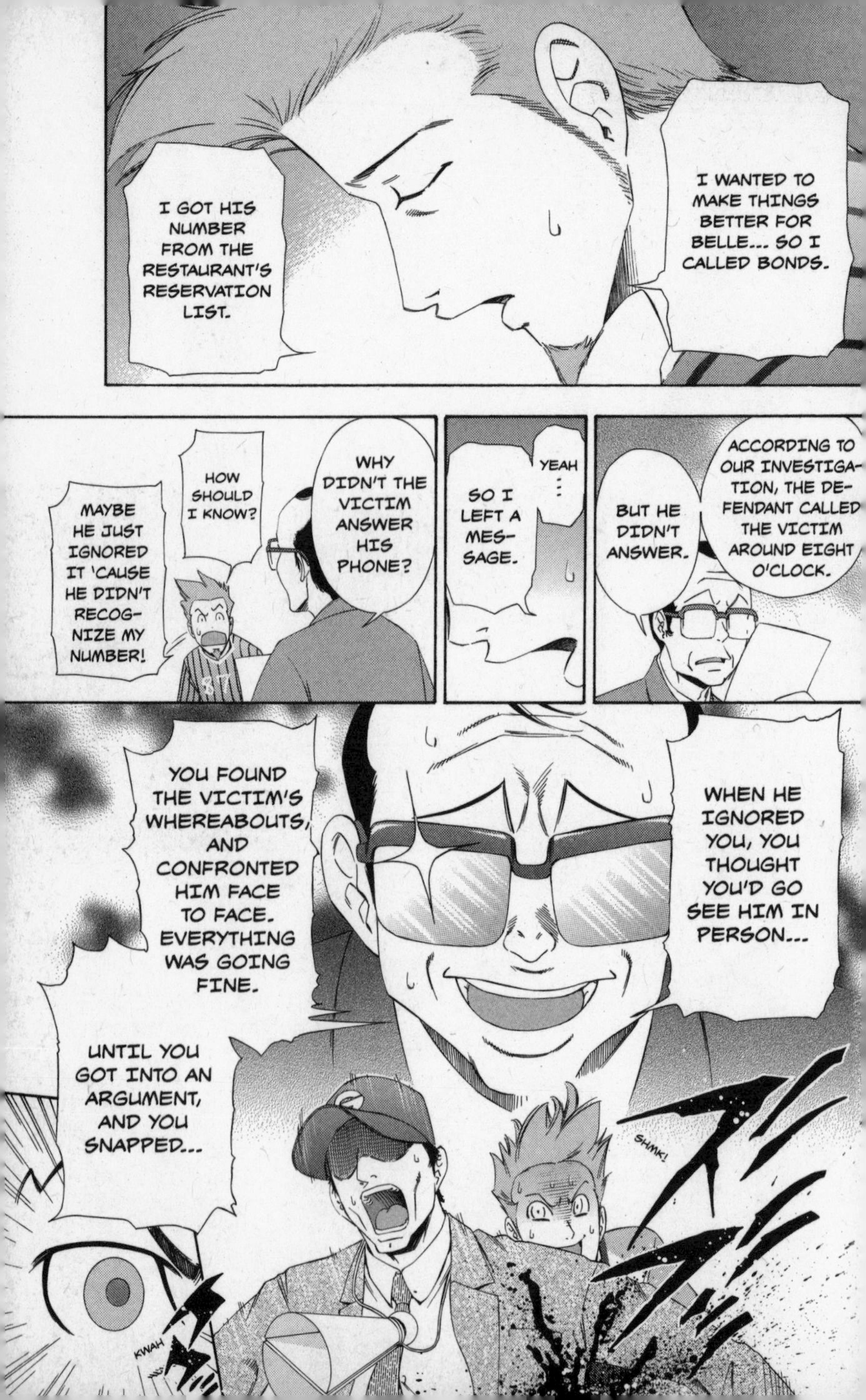

I WANTED TO MAKE THINGS BETTER FOR BELLE... SO I CALLED BONDS.
I GOT HIS NUMBER FROM THE RESTAURANT'S RESERVATION LIST.
ACCORDING TO OUR INVESTIGATION, THE DEFENDANT CALLED THE VICTIM AROUND EIGHT O'CLOCK.
BUT HE DIDN'T ANSWER.
YEAH...
SO I LEFT A MESSAGE.
WHY DIDN'T THE VICTIM ANSWER HIS PHONE?
HOW SHOULD I KNOW?
MAYBE HE JUST IGNORED IT 'CAUSE HE DIDN'T RECOGNIZE MY NUMBER!
WHEN HE IGNORED YOU, YOU THOUGHT YOU'D GO SEE HIM IN PERSON...
YOU FOUND THE VICTIM'S WHEREABOUTS, AND CONFRONTED HIM FACE TO FACE. EVERYTHING WAS GOING FINE.
SHMK!
UNTIL YOU GOT INTO AN ARGUMENT, AND YOU SNAPPED...
KWAH

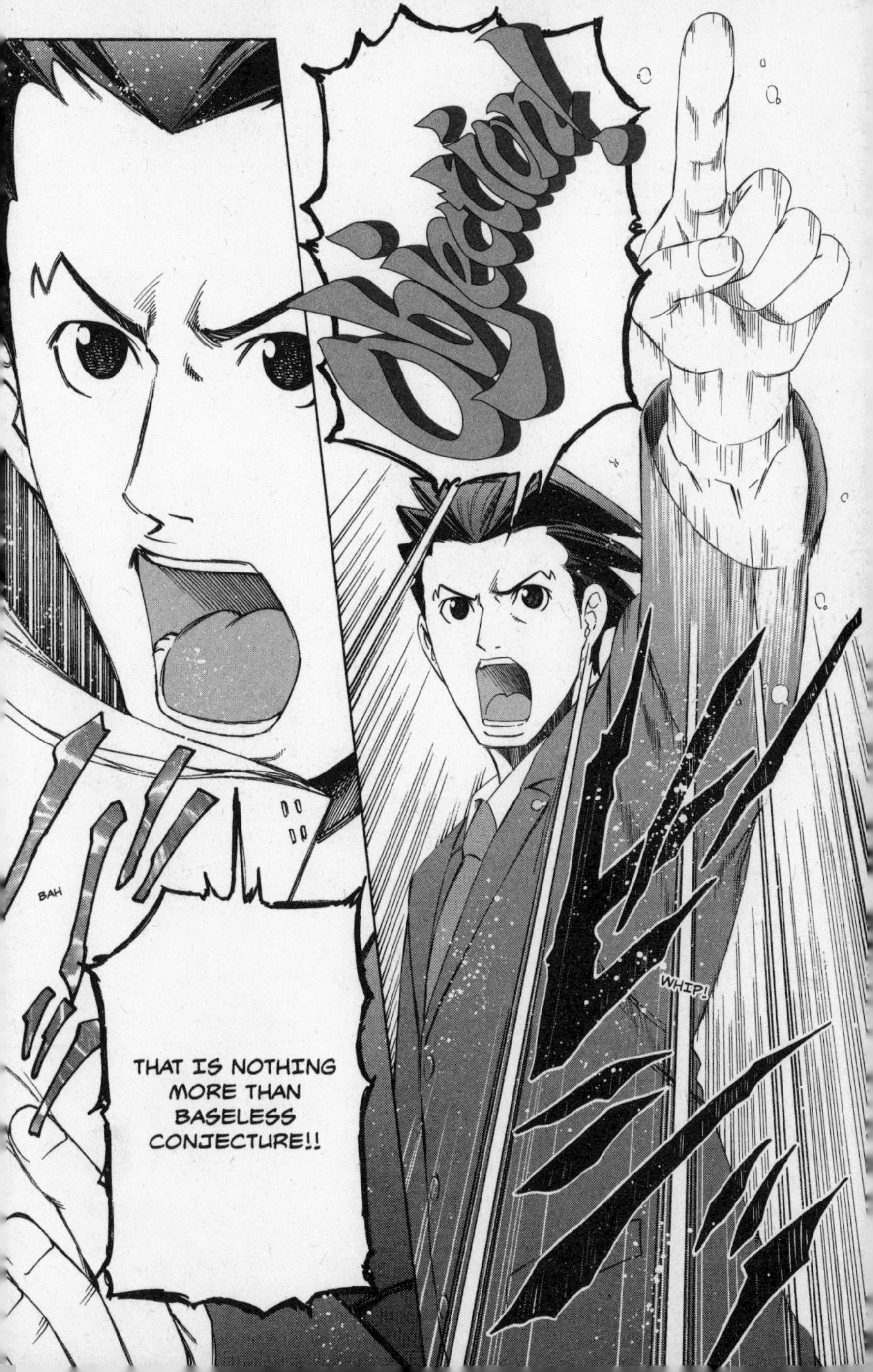
Objection!
WHIP!
BAH
THAT IS NOTHING MORE THAN BASELESS CONJECTURE!!

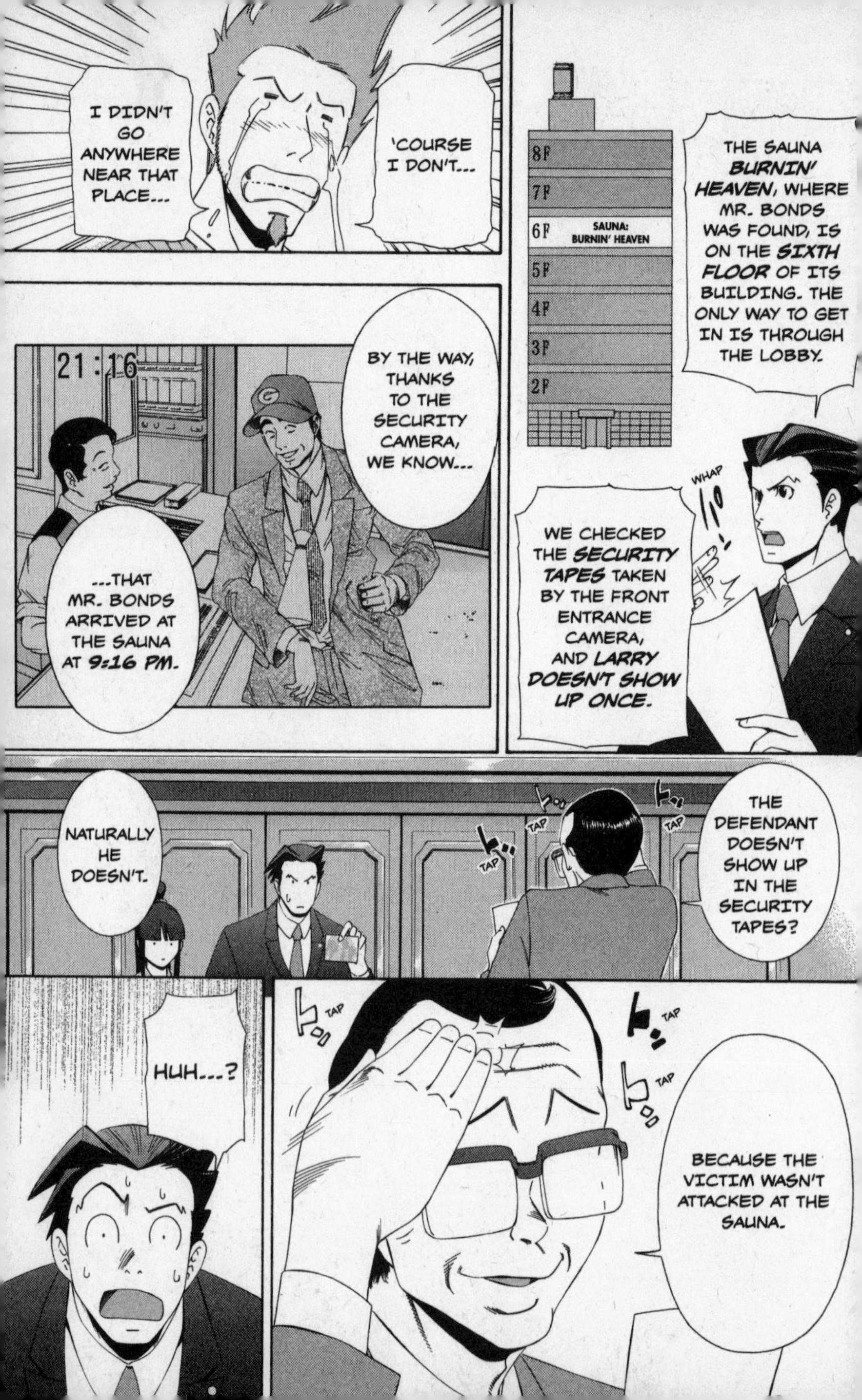
8F
7F
6F
SAUNA: BURNIN' HEAVEN
5F
4F
3F
2F
THE SAUNA BURNIN' HEAVEN, WHERE MR. BONDS WAS FOUND, IS ON THE SIXTH FLOOR OF ITS BUILDING. THE ONLY WAY TO GET IN IS THROUGH THE LOBBY.
WHAP
WE CHECKED THE SECURITY TAPES TAKEN BY THE FRONT ENTRANCE CAMERA, AND LARRY DOESN'T SHOW UP ONCE.
'COURSE I DON'T...
I DIDN'T GO ANYWHERE NEAR THAT PLACE...
21:16
BY THE WAY, THANKS TO THE SECURITY CAMERA, WE KNOW...
...THAT MR. BONDS ARRIVED AT THE SAUNA AT 9:16 PM.
THE DEFENDANT DOESN'T SHOW UP IN THE SECURITY TAPES?
TAP
TAP
TAP
NATURALLY HE DOESN'T.
TAP
TAP
TAP
BECAUSE THE VICTIM WASN'T ATTACKED AT THE SAUNA.
HUH...?

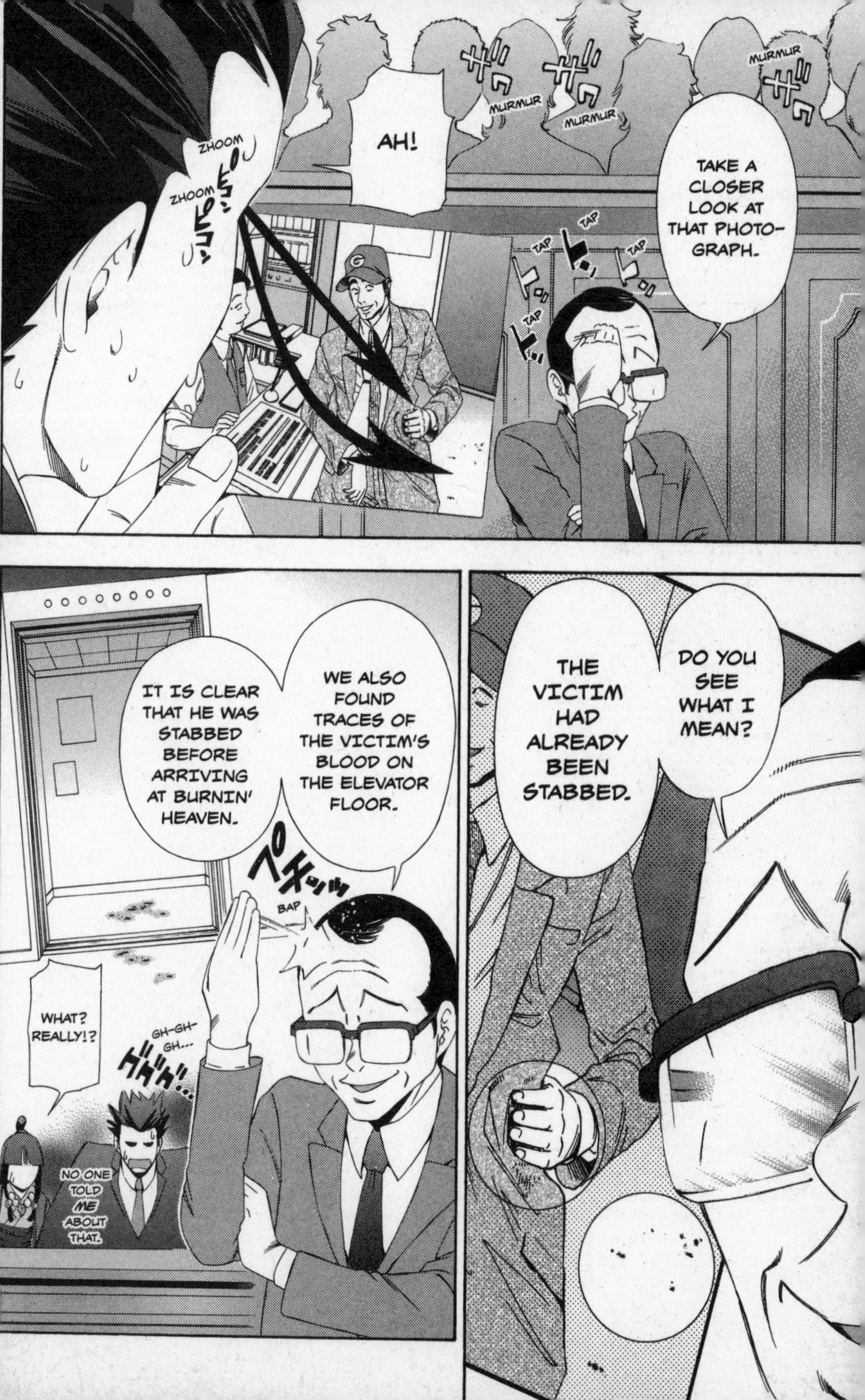
MURMUR
TAKE A CLOSER LOOK AT THAT PHOTO-GRAPH.
TAP TAP
TAP TAP
MURMUR
MURMUR
AH!
ZHOOM
ZHOOM
DO YOU SEE WHAT I MEAN?
THE VICTIM HAD ALREADY BEEN STABBED.
WE ALSO FOUND TRACES OF THE VICTIM'S BLOOD ON THE ELEVATOR FLOOR.
IT IS CLEAR THAT HE WAS STABBED BEFORE ARRIVING AT BURNIN' HEAVEN.
BAP
WHAT? REALLY!?
GH-GH-GH...
NO ONE TOLD ME ABOUT THAT.

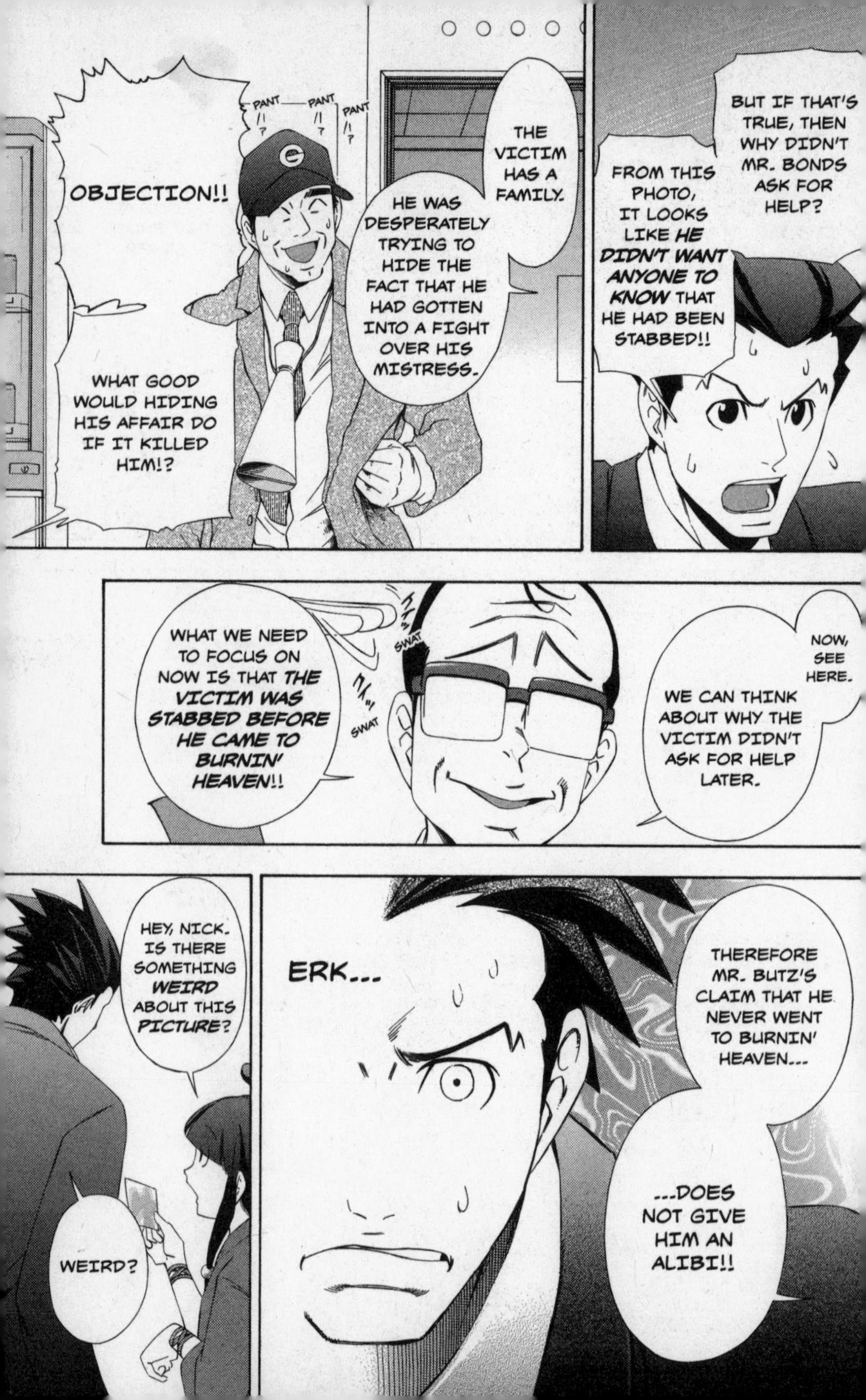
BUT IF THAT'S TRUE, THEN WHY DIDN'T MR. BONDS ASK FOR HELP?
FROM THIS PHOTO, IT LOOKS LIKE *HE DIDN'T WANT ANYONE TO KNOW* THAT HE HAD BEEN STABBED!!
THE VICTIM HAS A FAMILY.
HE WAS DESPERATELY TRYING TO HIDE THE FACT THAT HE HAD GOTTEN INTO A FIGHT OVER HIS MISTRESS.
PANT PANT PANT
OBJECTION!!
WHAT GOOD WOULD HIDING HIS AFFAIR DO IF IT KILLED HIM!?
NOW, SEE HERE.
WE CAN THINK ABOUT WHY THE VICTIM DIDN'T ASK FOR HELP LATER.
SWAT SWAT
WHAT WE NEED TO FOCUS ON NOW IS THAT *THE VICTIM WAS STABBED BEFORE HE CAME TO BURNIN' HEAVEN*!!
THEREFORE MR. BUTZ'S CLAIM THAT HE NEVER WENT TO BURNIN' HEAVEN...
...DOES NOT GIVE HIM AN ALIBI!!
ERK...
HEY, NICK. IS THERE SOMETHING *WEIRD* ABOUT THIS *PICTURE*?
WEIRD?

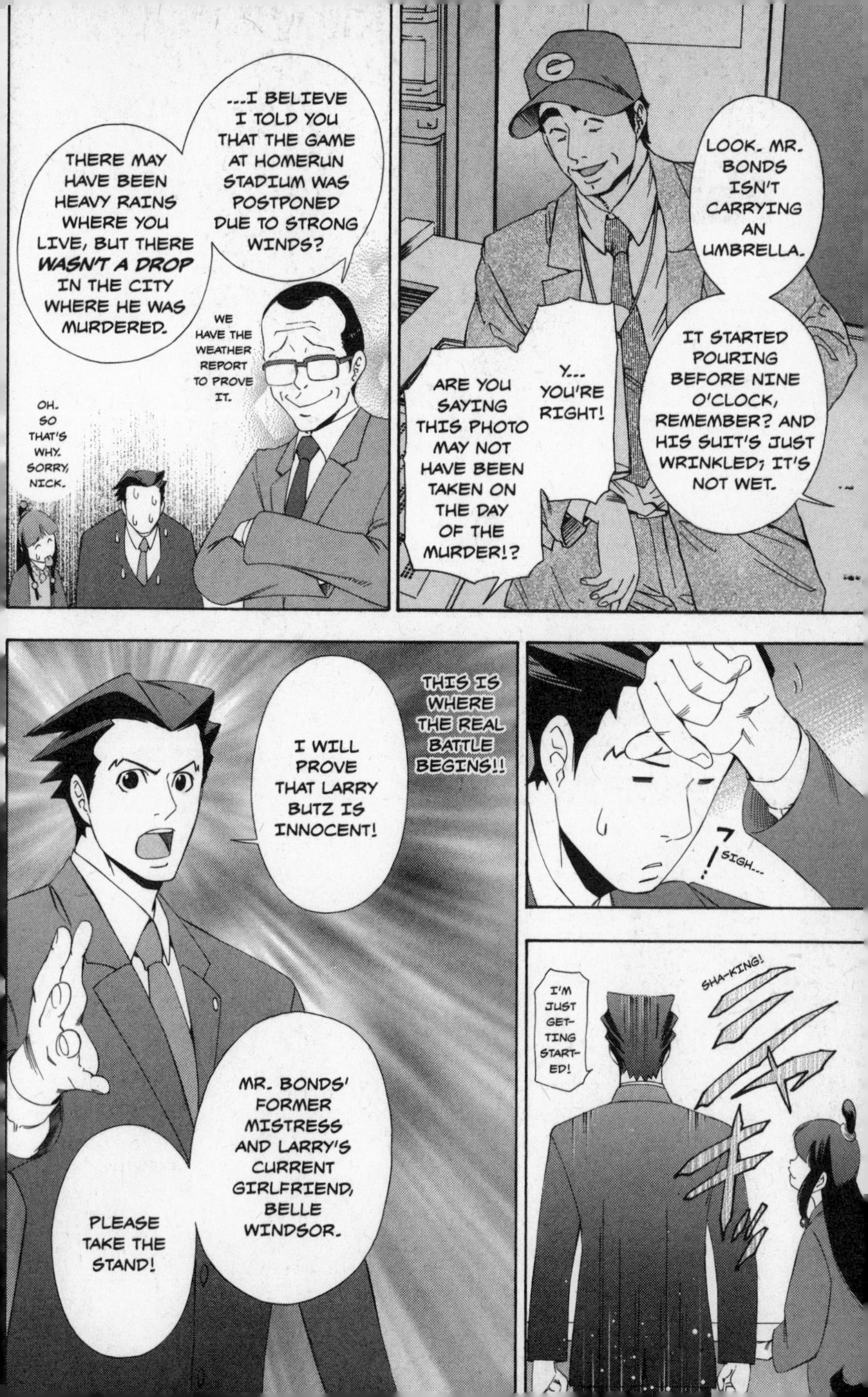
LOOK. MR. BONDS ISN'T CARRYING AN UMBRELLA.
IT STARTED POURING BEFORE NINE O'CLOCK, REMEMBER? AND HIS SUIT'S JUST WRINKLED; IT'S NOT WET.
Y... YOU'RE RIGHT!
ARE YOU SAYING THIS PHOTO MAY NOT HAVE BEEN TAKEN ON THE DAY OF THE MURDER!?
...I BELIEVE I TOLD YOU THAT THE GAME AT HOMERUN STADIUM WAS POSTPONED DUE TO STRONG WINDS?
THERE MAY HAVE BEEN HEAVY RAINS WHERE YOU LIVE, BUT THERE ***WASN'T A DROP*** IN THE CITY WHERE HE WAS MURDERED.
WE HAVE THE WEATHER REPORT TO PROVE IT.
OH. SO THAT'S WHY. SORRY, NICK.
SIGH...
SHA-KING!
I'M JUST GET-TING START-ED!
THIS IS WHERE THE REAL BATTLE BEGINS!!
I WILL PROVE THAT LARRY BUTZ IS INNOCENT!
MR. BONDS' FORMER MISTRESS AND LARRY'S CURRENT GIRLFRIEND, BELLE WINDSOR.
PLEASE TAKE THE STAND!

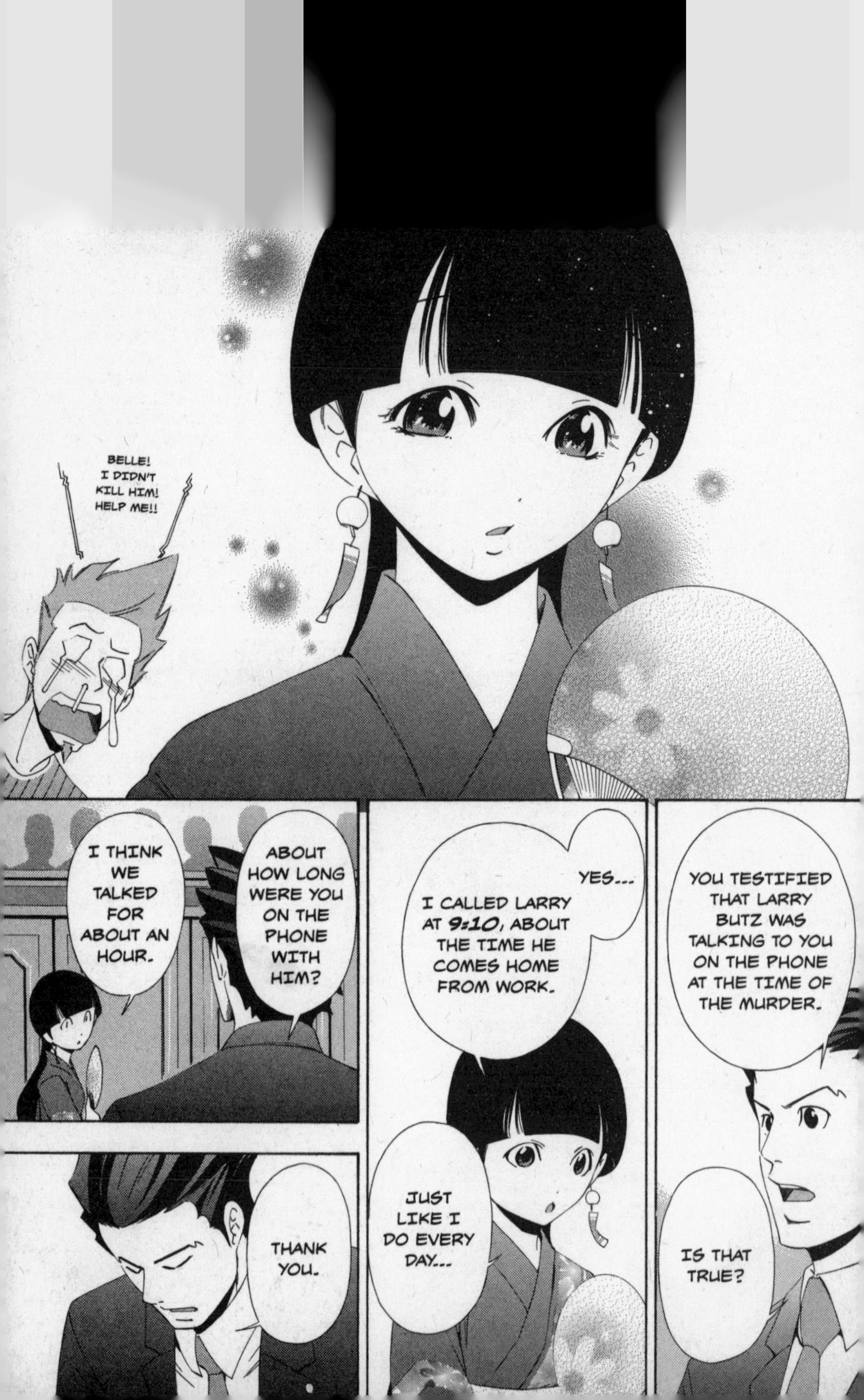
BELLE! I DIDN'T KILL HIM! HELP ME!!
YOU TESTIFIED THAT LARRY BUTZ WAS TALKING TO YOU ON THE PHONE AT THE TIME OF THE MURDER.
IS THAT TRUE?
YES...
I CALLED LARRY AT 9:10, ABOUT THE TIME HE COMES HOME FROM WORK.
JUST LIKE I DO EVERY DAY...
ABOUT HOW LONG WERE YOU ON THE PHONE WITH HIM?
I THINK WE TALKED FOR ABOUT AN HOUR.
THANK YOU.

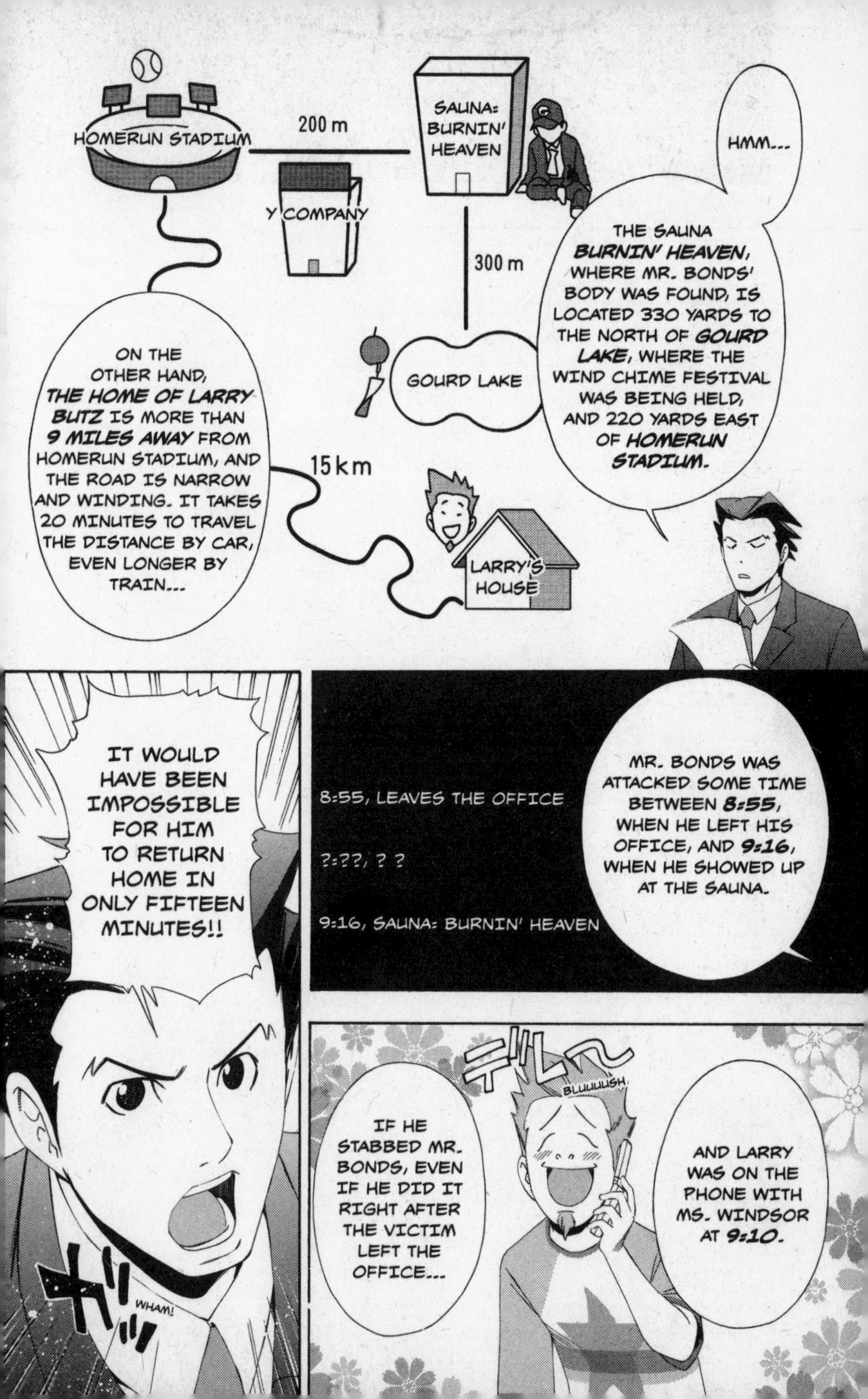
HMM...
THE SAUNA BURNIN' HEAVEN, WHERE MR. BONDS' BODY WAS FOUND, IS LOCATED 330 YARDS TO THE NORTH OF GOURD LAKE, WHERE THE WIND CHIME FESTIVAL WAS BEING HELD, AND 220 YARDS EAST OF HOMERUN STADIUM.
SAUNA: BURNIN' HEAVEN
200 m
HOMERUN STADIUM
Y COMPANY
300 m
GOURD LAKE
LARRY'S HOUSE
15 km
ON THE OTHER HAND, THE HOME OF LARRY BUTZ IS MORE THAN 9 MILES AWAY FROM HOMERUN STADIUM, AND THE ROAD IS NARROW AND WINDING. IT TAKES 20 MINUTES TO TRAVEL THE DISTANCE BY CAR, EVEN LONGER BY TRAIN...
MR. BONDS WAS ATTACKED SOME TIME BETWEEN 8:55, WHEN HE LEFT HIS OFFICE, AND 9:16, WHEN HE SHOWED UP AT THE SAUNA.
8:55, LEAVES THE OFFICE
?:??, ? ?
9:16, SAUNA: BURNIN' HEAVEN
AND LARRY WAS ON THE PHONE WITH MS. WINDSOR AT 9:10.
BLUUUUSH
IF HE STABBED MR. BONDS, EVEN IF HE DID IT RIGHT AFTER THE VICTIM LEFT THE OFFICE...
IT WOULD HAVE BEEN IMPOSSIBLE FOR HIM TO RETURN HOME IN ONLY FIFTEEN MINUTES!!
WHAM!

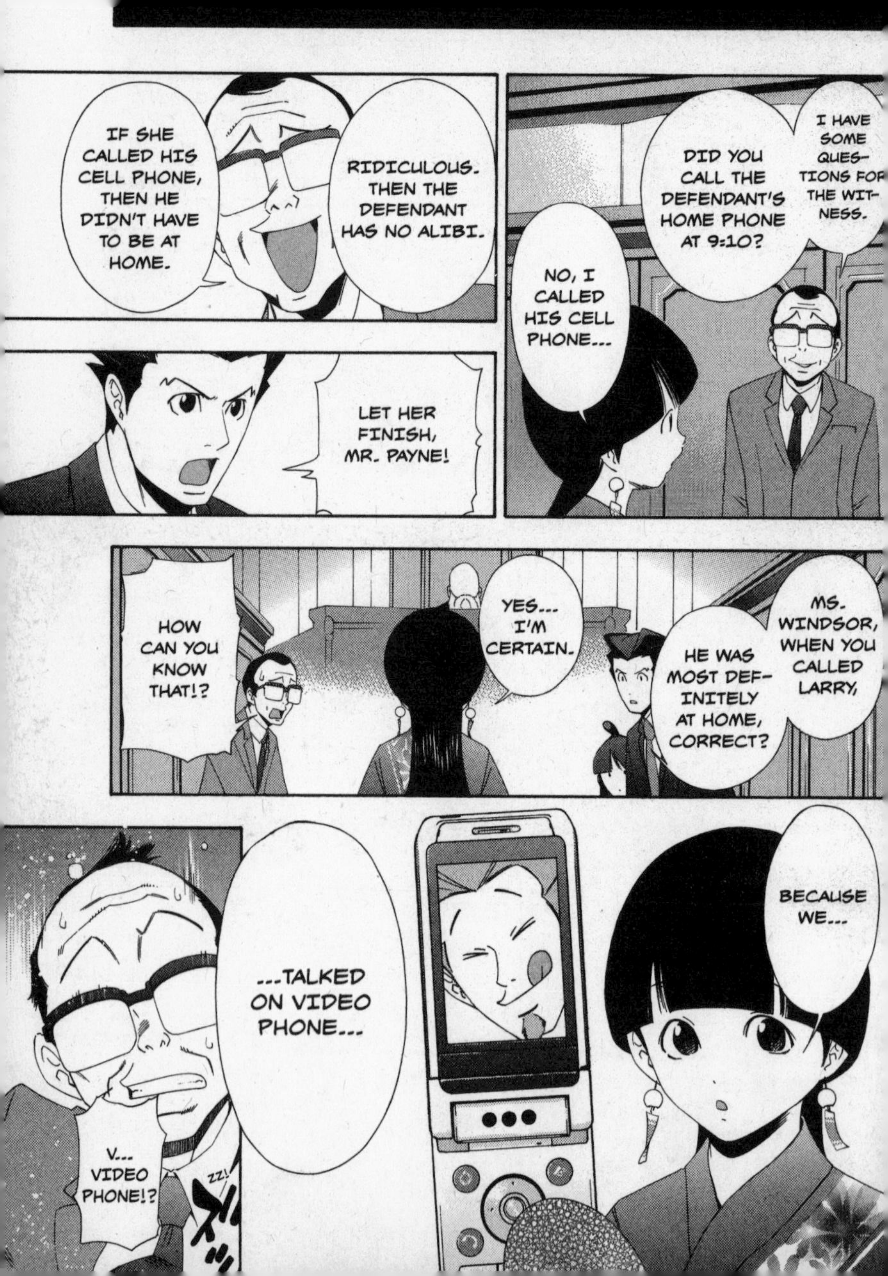
I HAVE SOME QUESTIONS FOR THE WITNESS.
DID YOU CALL THE DEFENDANT'S HOME PHONE AT 9:10?
NO, I CALLED HIS CELL PHONE...
RIDICULOUS. THEN THE DEFENDANT HAS NO ALIBI.
IF SHE CALLED HIS CELL PHONE, THEN HE DIDN'T HAVE TO BE AT HOME.
LET HER FINISH, MR. PAYNE!
MS. WINDSOR, WHEN YOU CALLED LARRY,
HE WAS MOST DEFINITELY AT HOME, CORRECT?
YES... I'M CERTAIN.
HOW CAN YOU KNOW THAT!?
BECAUSE WE...
...TALKED ON VIDEO PHONE...
V... VIDEO PHONE!?
ZZ!

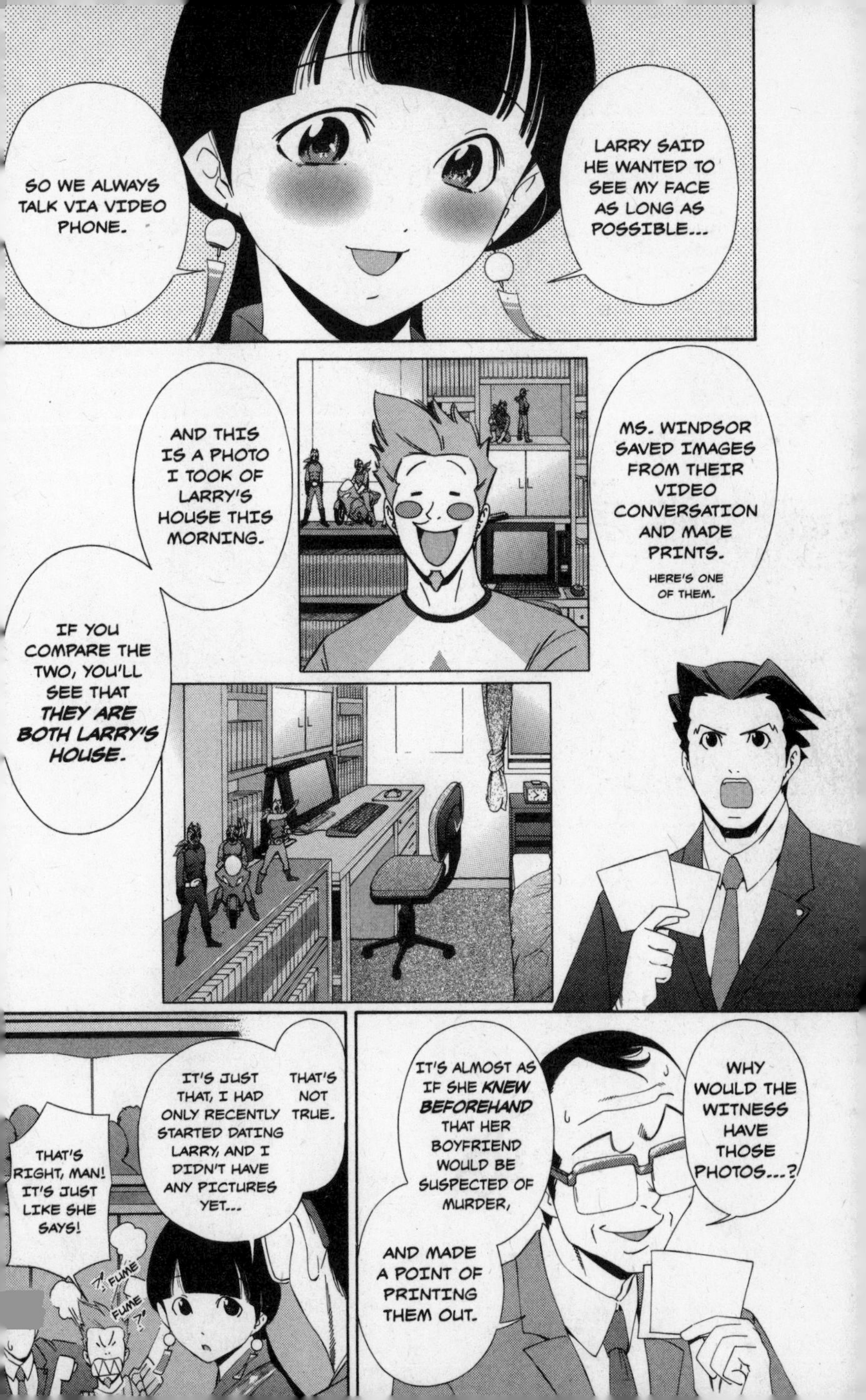
LARRY SAID HE WANTED TO SEE MY FACE AS LONG AS POSSIBLE...
SO WE ALWAYS TALK VIA VIDEO PHONE.
MS. WINDSOR SAVED IMAGES FROM THEIR VIDEO CONVERSATION AND MADE PRINTS.
HERE'S ONE OF THEM.
AND THIS IS A PHOTO I TOOK OF LARRY'S HOUSE THIS MORNING.
IF YOU COMPARE THE TWO, YOU'LL SEE THAT *THEY ARE BOTH LARRY'S HOUSE.*
WHY WOULD THE WITNESS HAVE THOSE PHOTOS...?
IT'S ALMOST AS IF SHE *KNEW BEFOREHAND* THAT HER BOYFRIEND WOULD BE SUSPECTED OF MURDER,
AND MADE A POINT OF PRINTING THEM OUT.
THAT'S NOT TRUE.
IT'S JUST THAT, I HAD ONLY RECENTLY STARTED DATING LARRY, AND I DIDN'T HAVE ANY PICTURES YET...
THAT'S RIGHT, MAN! IT'S JUST LIKE SHE SAYS!
FUME
FUME

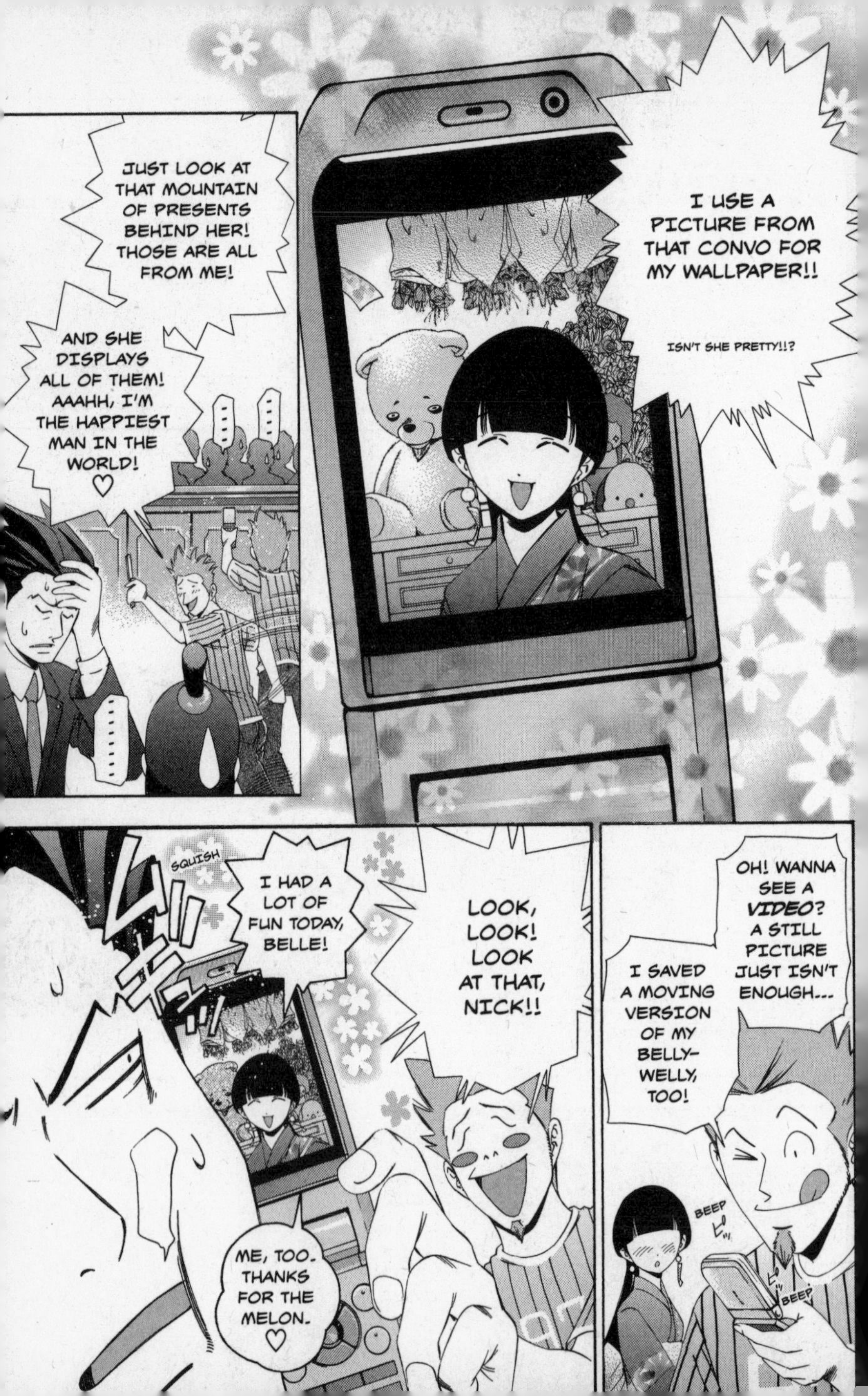
I USE A PICTURE FROM THAT CONVO FOR MY WALLPAPER!!
ISN'T SHE PRETTY!!?
JUST LOOK AT THAT MOUNTAIN OF PRESENTS BEHIND HER! THOSE ARE ALL FROM ME!
AND SHE DISPLAYS ALL OF THEM! AAAHH, I'M THE HAPPIEST MAN IN THE WORLD! ♡
OH! WANNA SEE A *VIDEO*? A STILL PICTURE JUST ISN'T ENOUGH...
I SAVED A MOVING VERSION OF MY BELLY-WELLY, TOO!
BEEP
BEEP
LOOK, LOOK! LOOK AT THAT, NICK!!
I HAD A LOT OF FUN TODAY, BELLE!
SQUISH
ME, TOO. THANKS FOR THE MELON. ♡

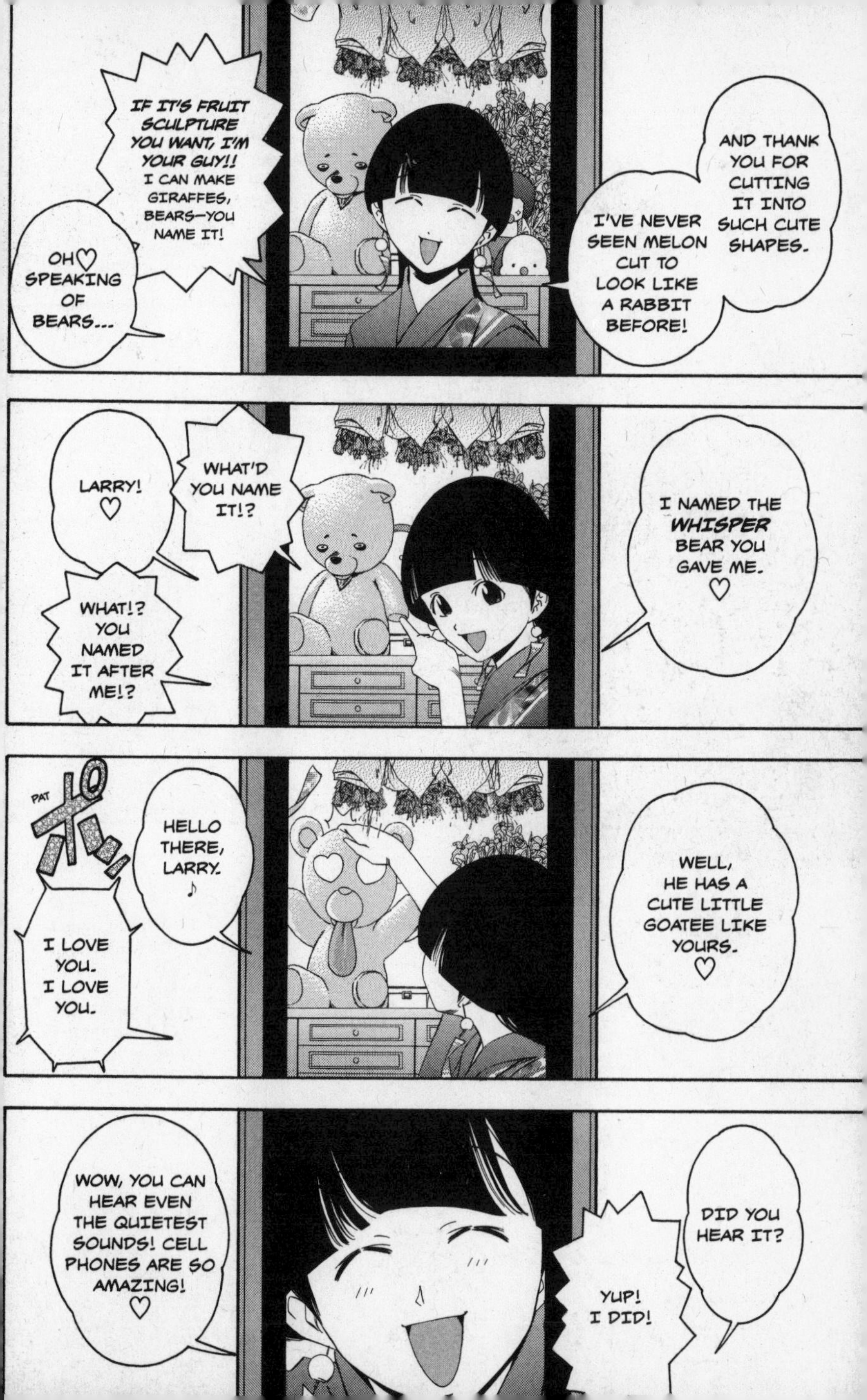
AND THANK YOU FOR CUTTING IT INTO SUCH CUTE SHAPES.
I'VE NEVER SEEN MELON CUT TO LOOK LIKE A RABBIT BEFORE!
IF IT'S FRUIT SCULPTURE YOU WANT, I'M YOUR GUY!! I CAN MAKE GIRAFFES, BEARS—YOU NAME IT!
OH♡ SPEAKING OF BEARS...
I NAMED THE WHISPER BEAR YOU GAVE ME. ♡
WHAT'D YOU NAME IT!?
LARRY! ♡
WHAT!? YOU NAMED IT AFTER ME!?
WELL, HE HAS A CUTE LITTLE GOATEE LIKE YOURS. ♡
HELLO THERE, LARRY. ♪
PAT
I LOVE YOU. I LOVE YOU.
DID YOU HEAR IT?
YUP! I DID!
WOW, YOU CAN HEAR EVEN THE QUIETEST SOUNDS! CELL PHONES ARE SO AMAZING! ♡

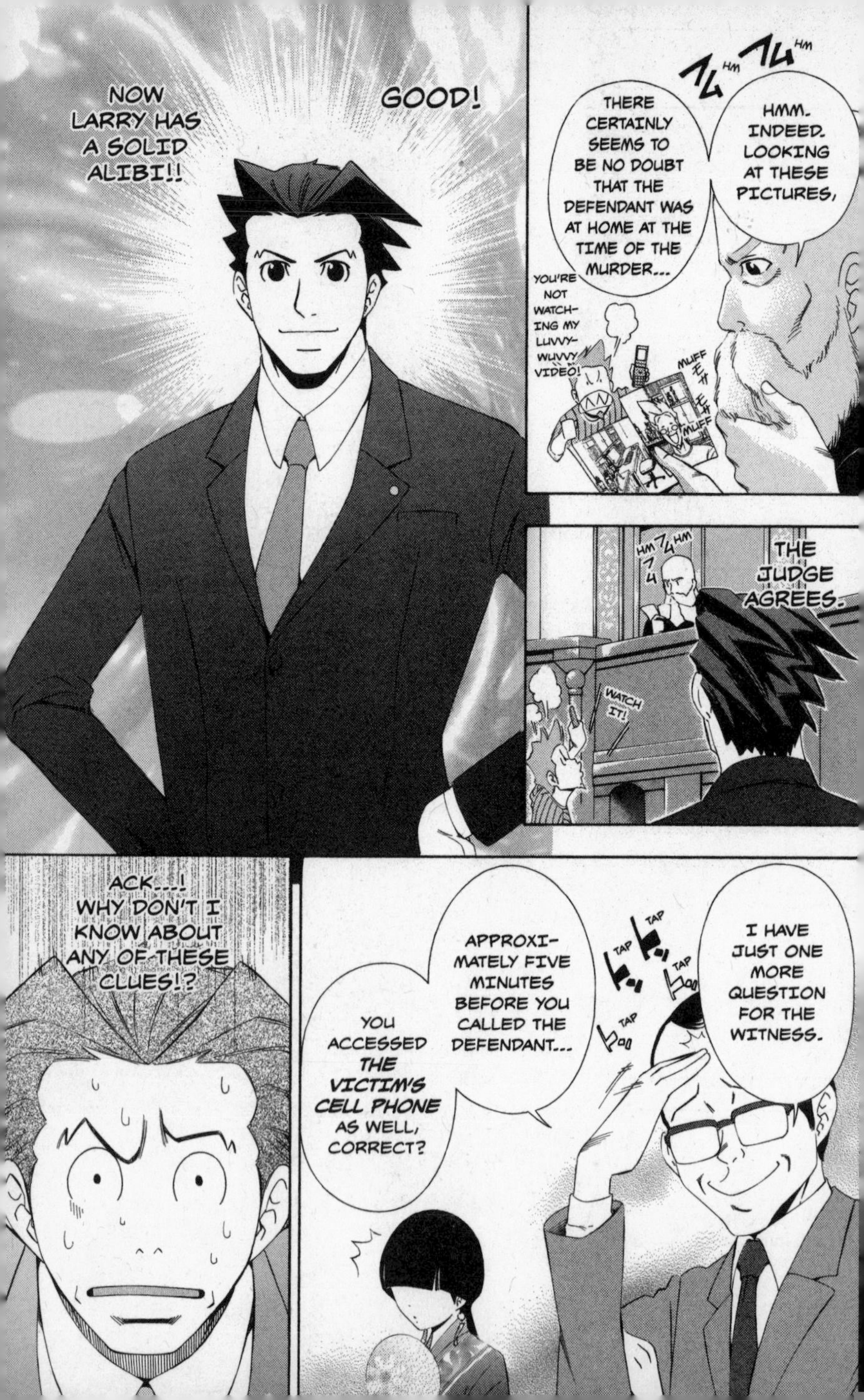
HM HM
HMM. INDEED. LOOKING AT THESE PICTURES,
THERE CERTAINLY SEEMS TO BE NO DOUBT THAT THE DEFENDANT WAS AT HOME AT THE TIME OF THE MURDER...
MUFF MUFF
YOU'RE NOT WATCHING MY LUVVY-WUVVY VIDEO!
HM HM
THE JUDGE AGREES.
WATCH IT!
GOOD!
NOW LARRY HAS A SOLID ALIBI!!
I HAVE JUST ONE MORE QUESTION FOR THE WITNESS.
TAP TAP TAP TAP
APPROXIMATELY FIVE MINUTES BEFORE YOU CALLED THE DEFENDANT...
YOU ACCESSED THE VICTIM'S CELL PHONE AS WELL, CORRECT?
ACK...! WHY DON'T I KNOW ABOUT ANY OF THESE CLUES!?

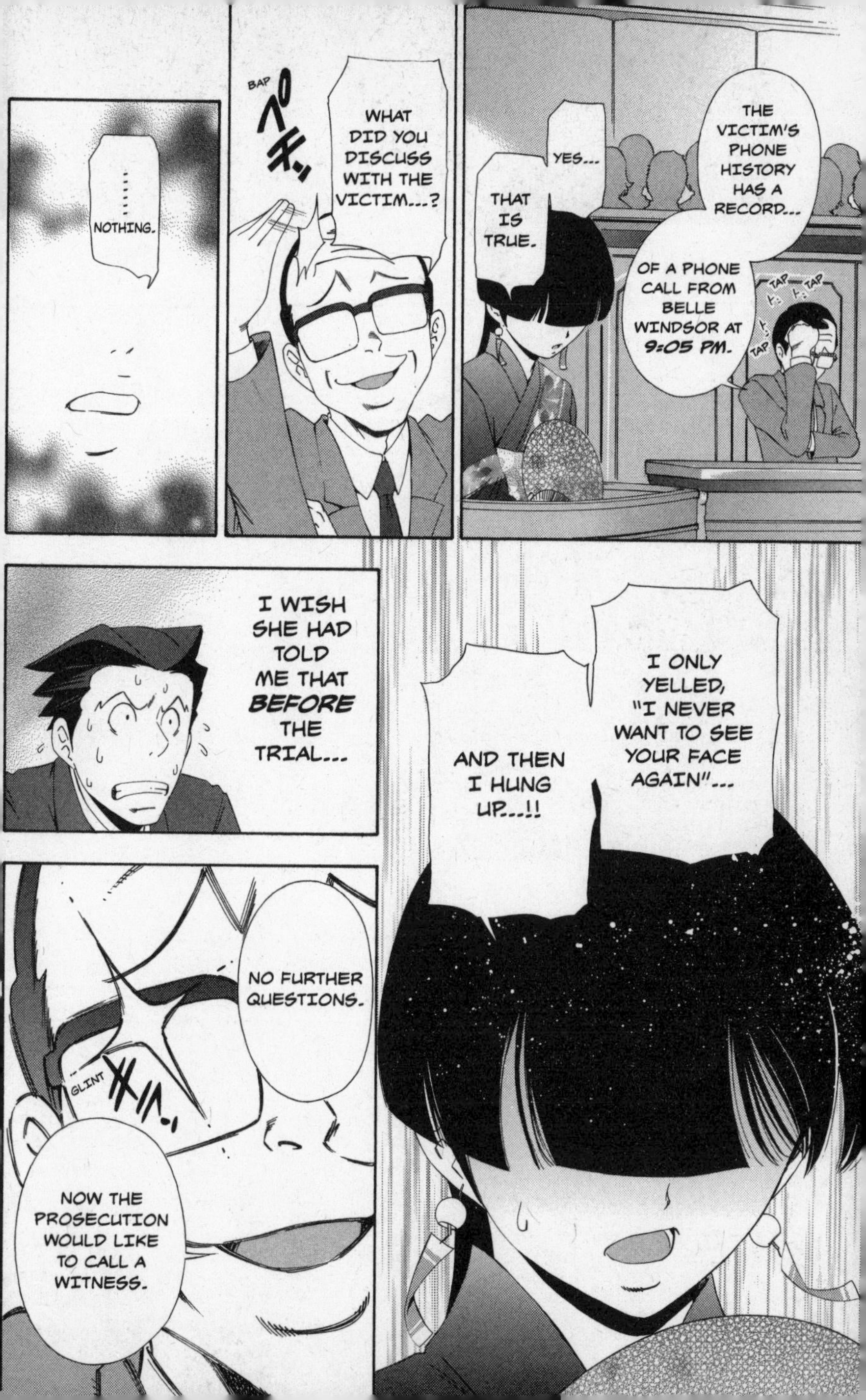
THE VICTIM'S PHONE HISTORY HAS A RECORD...
OF A PHONE CALL FROM BELLE WINDSOR AT 9:05 PM.
TAP TAP TAP TAP
YES...
THAT IS TRUE.
BAP
WHAT DID YOU DISCUSS WITH THE VICTIM...?
...... NOTHING.
I ONLY YELLED, "I NEVER WANT TO SEE YOUR FACE AGAIN"...
AND THEN I HUNG UP...!!
I WISH SHE HAD TOLD ME THAT *BEFORE* THE TRIAL...
NO FURTHER QUESTIONS.
GLINT
NOW THE PROSECUTION WOULD LIKE TO CALL A WITNESS.

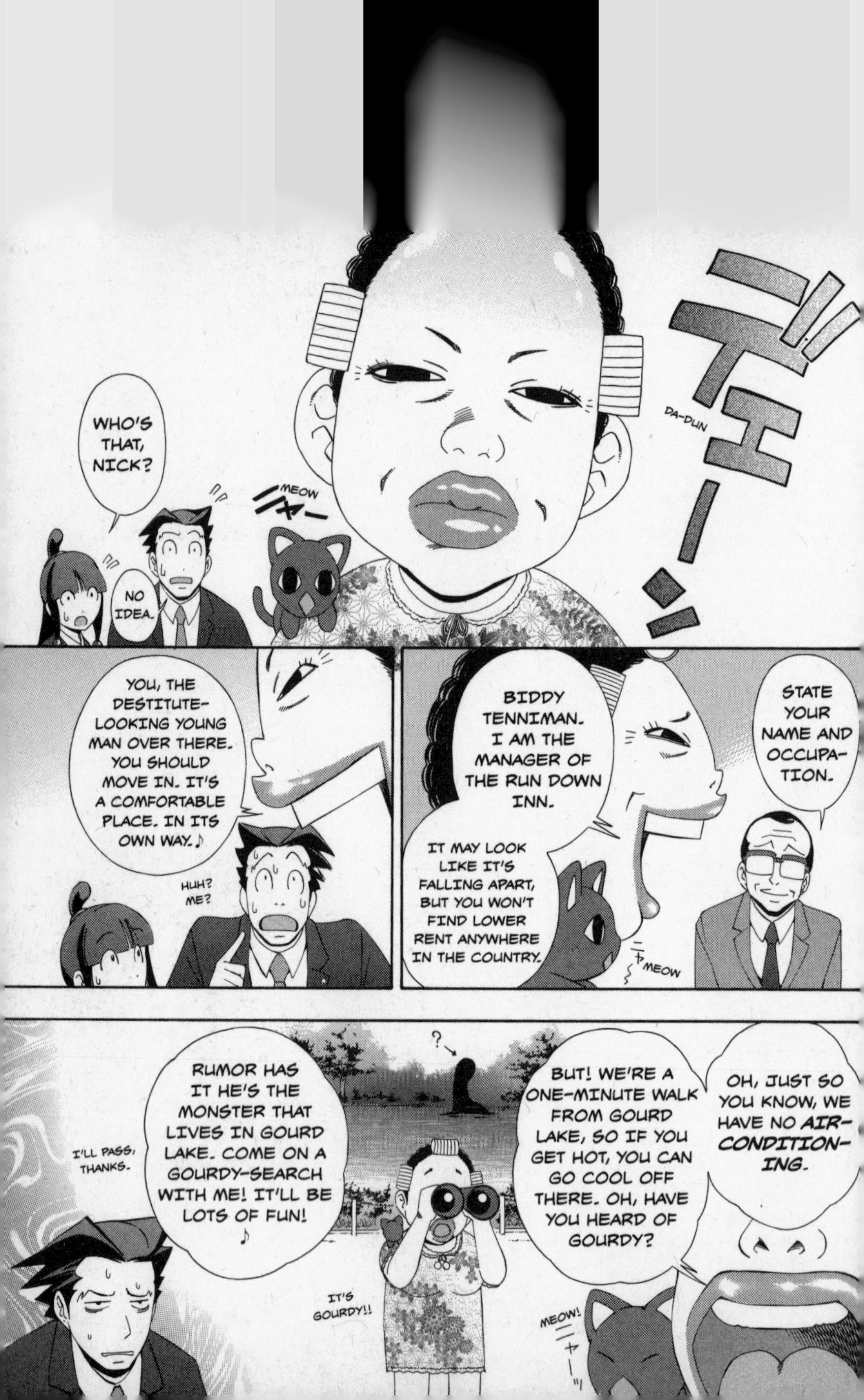
DA-DUN
MEOW
WHO'S THAT, NICK?
NO IDEA.
STATE YOUR NAME AND OCCUPA-TION.
BIDDY TENNIMAN. I AM THE MANAGER OF THE RUN DOWN INN.
IT MAY LOOK LIKE IT'S FALLING APART, BUT YOU WON'T FIND LOWER RENT ANYWHERE IN THE COUNTRY.
MEOW
YOU, THE DESTITUTE-LOOKING YOUNG MAN OVER THERE. YOU SHOULD MOVE IN. IT'S A COMFORTABLE PLACE. IN ITS OWN WAY.♪
HUH? ME?
OH, JUST SO YOU KNOW, WE HAVE NO AIR-CONDITION-ING.
BUT! WE'RE A ONE-MINUTE WALK FROM GOURD LAKE, SO IF YOU GET HOT, YOU CAN GO COOL OFF THERE. OH, HAVE YOU HEARD OF GOURDY?
RUMOR HAS IT HE'S THE MONSTER THAT LIVES IN GOURD LAKE. COME ON A GOURDY-SEARCH WITH ME! IT'LL BE LOTS OF FUN! ♪
MEOW!
IT'S GOURDY!!
I'LL PASS, THANKS.

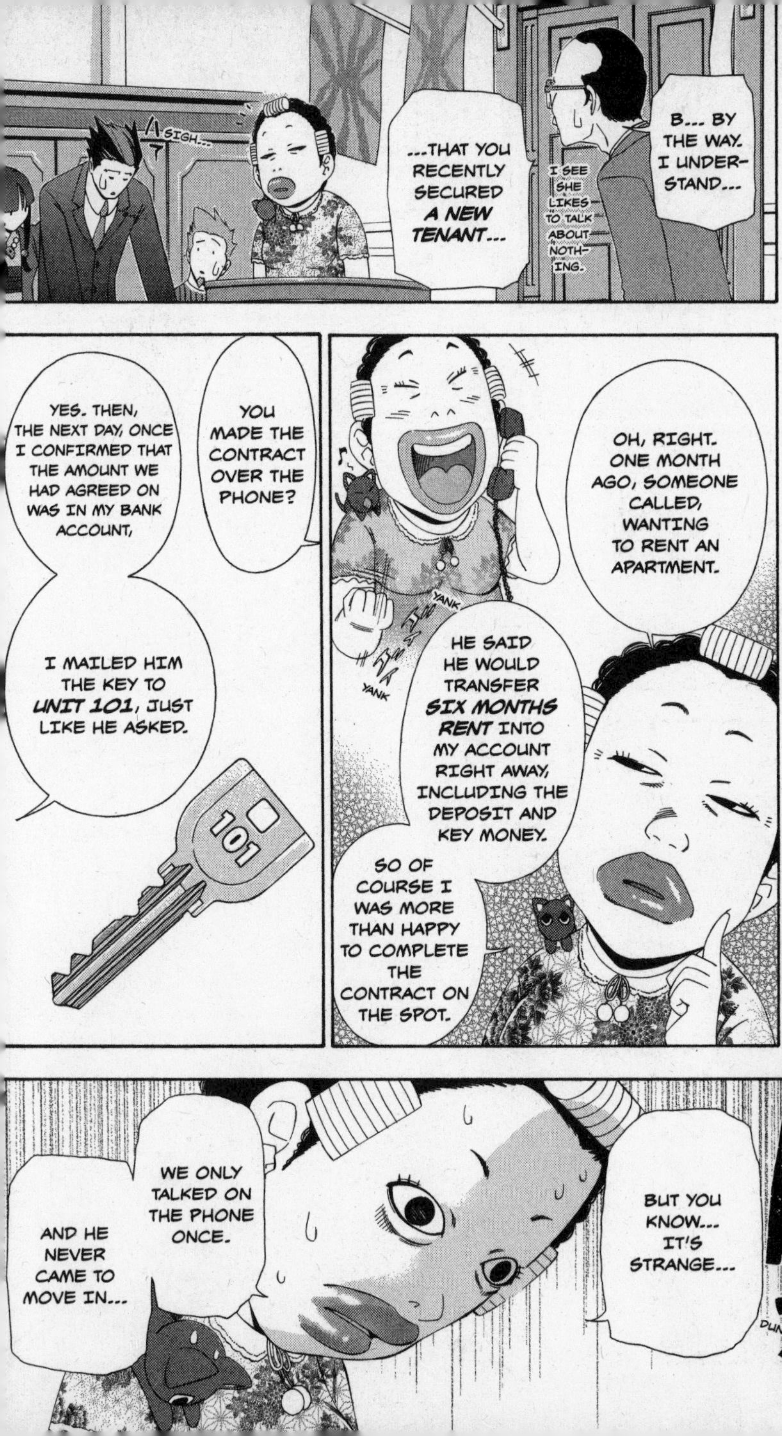
B... BY THE WAY. I UNDERSTAND...
I SEE SHE LIKES TO TALK ABOUT NOTHING.
...THAT YOU RECENTLY SECURED *A NEW TENANT*...
SIGH...
OH, RIGHT. ONE MONTH AGO, SOMEONE CALLED, WANTING TO RENT AN APARTMENT.
YANK
YANK
HE SAID HE WOULD TRANSFER *SIX MONTHS RENT* INTO MY ACCOUNT RIGHT AWAY, INCLUDING THE DEPOSIT AND KEY MONEY.
SO OF COURSE I WAS MORE THAN HAPPY TO COMPLETE THE CONTRACT ON THE SPOT.
YOU MADE THE CONTRACT OVER THE PHONE?
YES. THEN, THE NEXT DAY, ONCE I CONFIRMED THAT THE AMOUNT WE HAD AGREED ON WAS IN MY BANK ACCOUNT,
I MAILED HIM THE KEY TO *UNIT 101*, JUST LIKE HE ASKED.
101
BUT YOU KNOW... IT'S STRANGE...
DUN!
WE ONLY TALKED ON THE PHONE ONCE.
AND HE NEVER CAME TO MOVE IN...

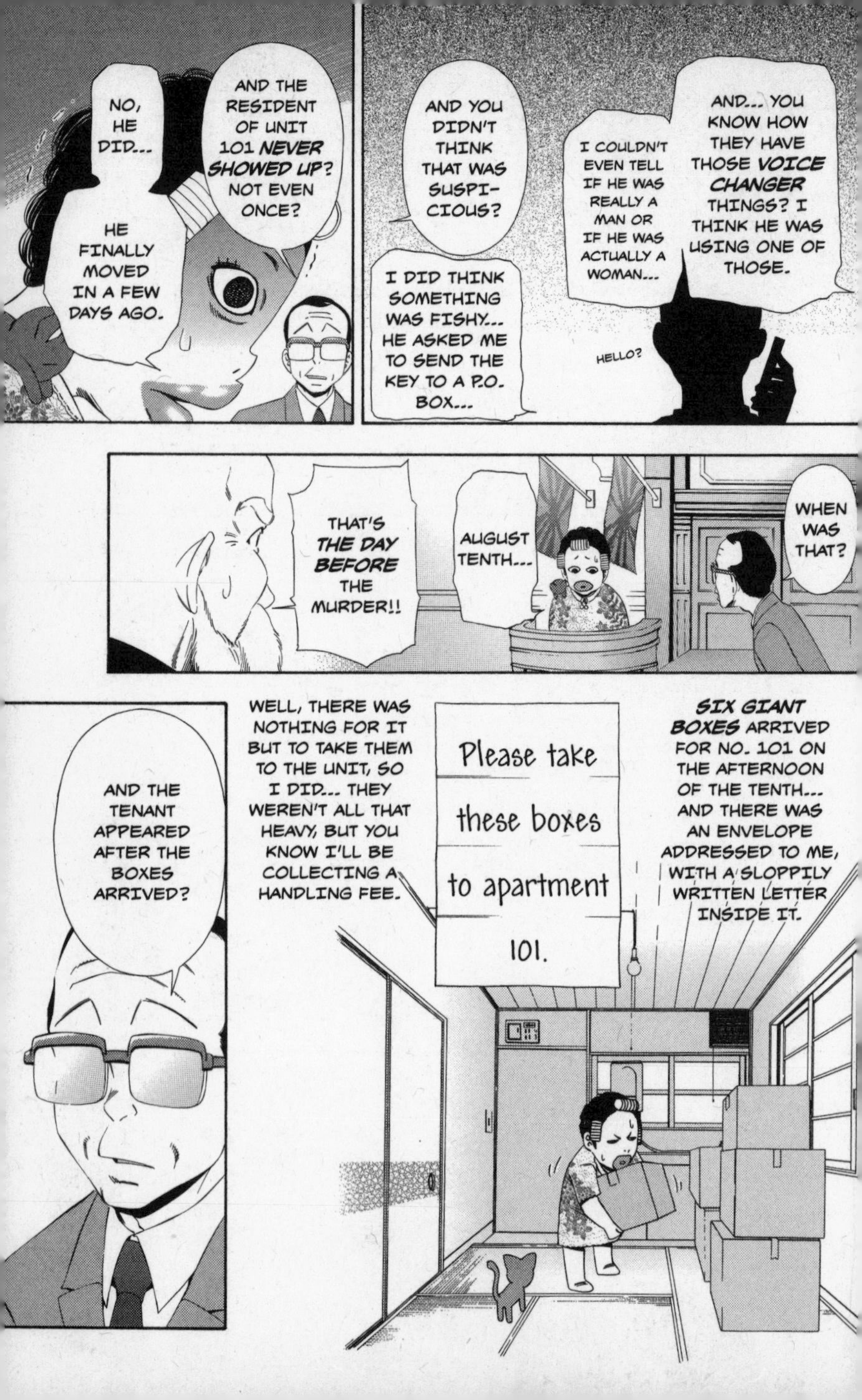
AND... YOU KNOW HOW THEY HAVE THOSE VOICE CHANGER THINGS? I THINK HE WAS USING ONE OF THOSE.
I COULDN'T EVEN TELL IF HE WAS REALLY A MAN OR IF HE WAS ACTUALLY A WOMAN...
AND YOU DIDN'T THINK THAT WAS SUSPICIOUS?
HELLO?
I DID THINK SOMETHING WAS FISHY... HE ASKED ME TO SEND THE KEY TO A P.O. BOX...
AND THE RESIDENT OF UNIT 101 NEVER SHOWED UP? NOT EVEN ONCE?
NO, HE DID...
HE FINALLY MOVED IN A FEW DAYS AGO.
WHEN WAS THAT?
AUGUST TENTH...
THAT'S THE DAY BEFORE THE MURDER!!
SIX GIANT BOXES ARRIVED FOR NO. 101 ON THE AFTERNOON OF THE TENTH... AND THERE WAS AN ENVELOPE ADDRESSED TO ME, WITH A SLOPPILY WRITTEN LETTER INSIDE IT.
Please take these boxes to apartment 101.
WELL, THERE WAS NOTHING FOR IT BUT TO TAKE THEM TO THE UNIT, SO I DID... THEY WEREN'T ALL THAT HEAVY, BUT YOU KNOW I'LL BE COLLECTING A HANDLING FEE.
AND THE TENANT APPEARED AFTER THE BOXES ARRIVED?

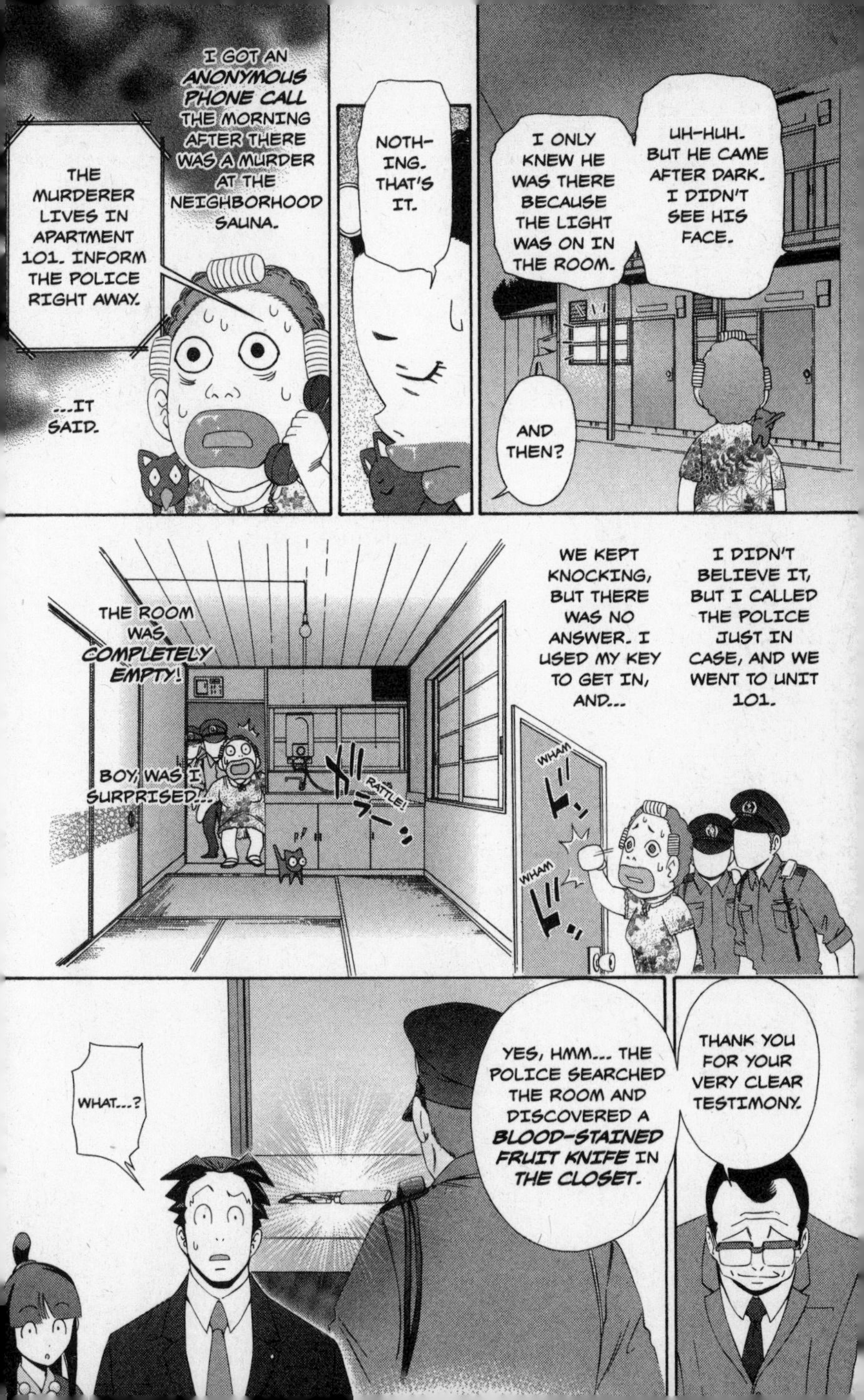
UH-HUH. BUT HE CAME AFTER DARK. I DIDN'T SEE HIS FACE.
I ONLY KNEW HE WAS THERE BECAUSE THE LIGHT WAS ON IN THE ROOM.
AND THEN?
NOTH-ING. THAT'S IT.
I GOT AN ANONYMOUS PHONE CALL THE MORNING AFTER THERE WAS A MURDER AT THE NEIGHBORHOOD SAUNA.
THE MURDERER LIVES IN APARTMENT 101. INFORM THE POLICE RIGHT AWAY.
...IT SAID.
I DIDN'T BELIEVE IT, BUT I CALLED THE POLICE JUST IN CASE, AND WE WENT TO UNIT 101.
WE KEPT KNOCKING, BUT THERE WAS NO ANSWER. I USED MY KEY TO GET IN, AND...
WHAM
WHAM
THE ROOM WAS COMPLETELY EMPTY!
RATTLE!
BOY, WAS I SURPRISED...
THANK YOU FOR YOUR VERY CLEAR TESTIMONY.
YES, HMM... THE POLICE SEARCHED THE ROOM AND DISCOVERED A BLOOD-STAINED FRUIT KNIFE IN THE CLOSET.
WHAT...?

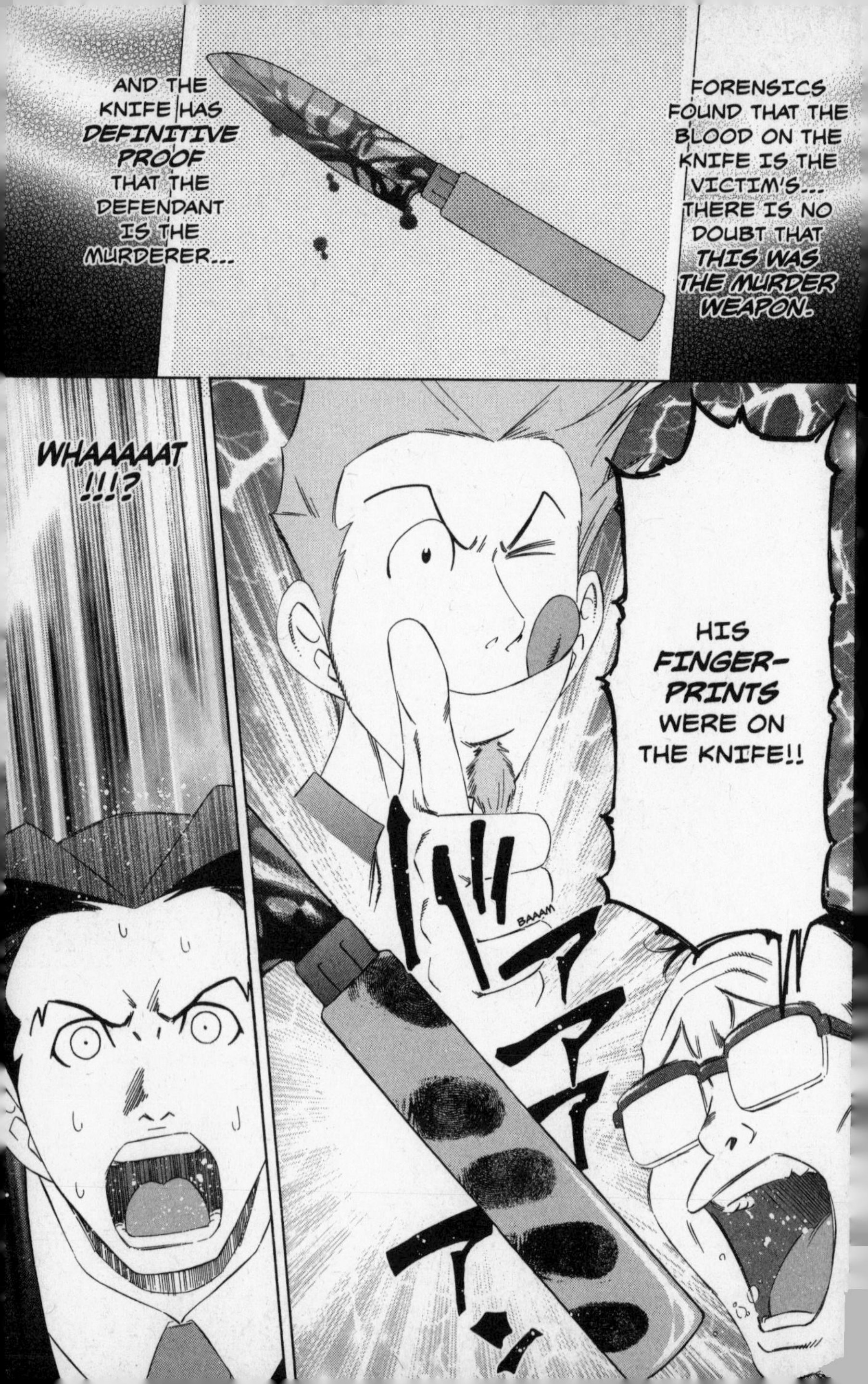
FORENSICS FOUND THAT THE BLOOD ON THE KNIFE IS THE VICTIM'S... THERE IS NO DOUBT THAT THIS WAS THE MURDER WEAPON.
AND THE KNIFE HAS DEFINITIVE PROOF THAT THE DEFENDANT IS THE MURDERER...
HIS FINGER-PRINTS WERE ON THE KNIFE!!
BAAAM
WHAAAAAT !!!?

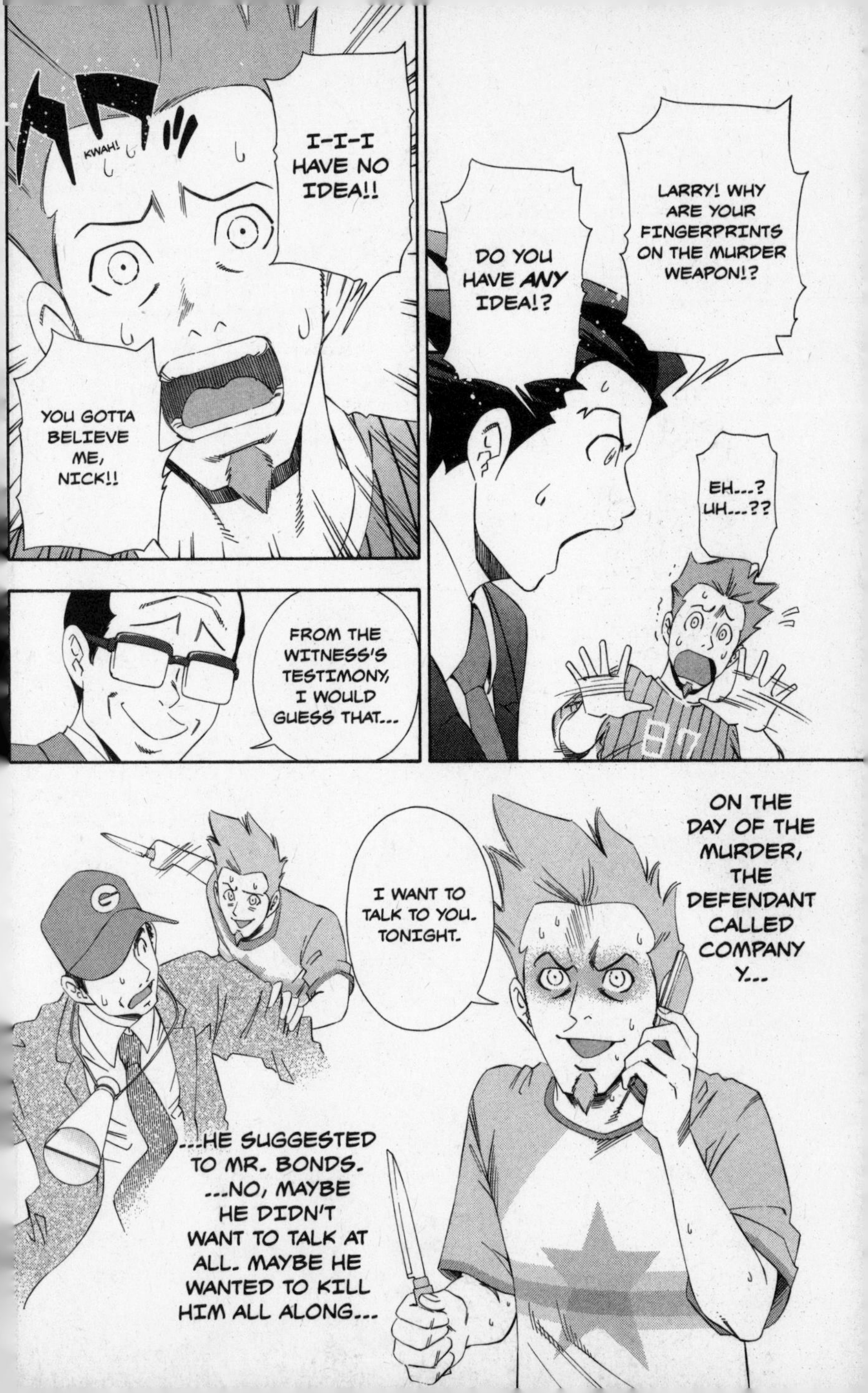
LARRY! WHY ARE YOUR FINGERPRINTS ON THE MURDER WEAPON!?
DO YOU HAVE ANY IDEA!?
EH...? UH...??
I-I-I HAVE NO IDEA!!
KWAH!
YOU GOTTA BELIEVE ME, NICK!!
FROM THE WITNESS'S TESTIMONY, I WOULD GUESS THAT...
ON THE DAY OF THE MURDER, THE DEFENDANT CALLED COMPANY Y...
I WANT TO TALK TO YOU. TONIGHT.
...HE SUGGESTED TO MR. BONDS. ...NO, MAYBE HE DIDN'T WANT TO TALK AT ALL. MAYBE HE WANTED TO KILL HIM ALL ALONG...

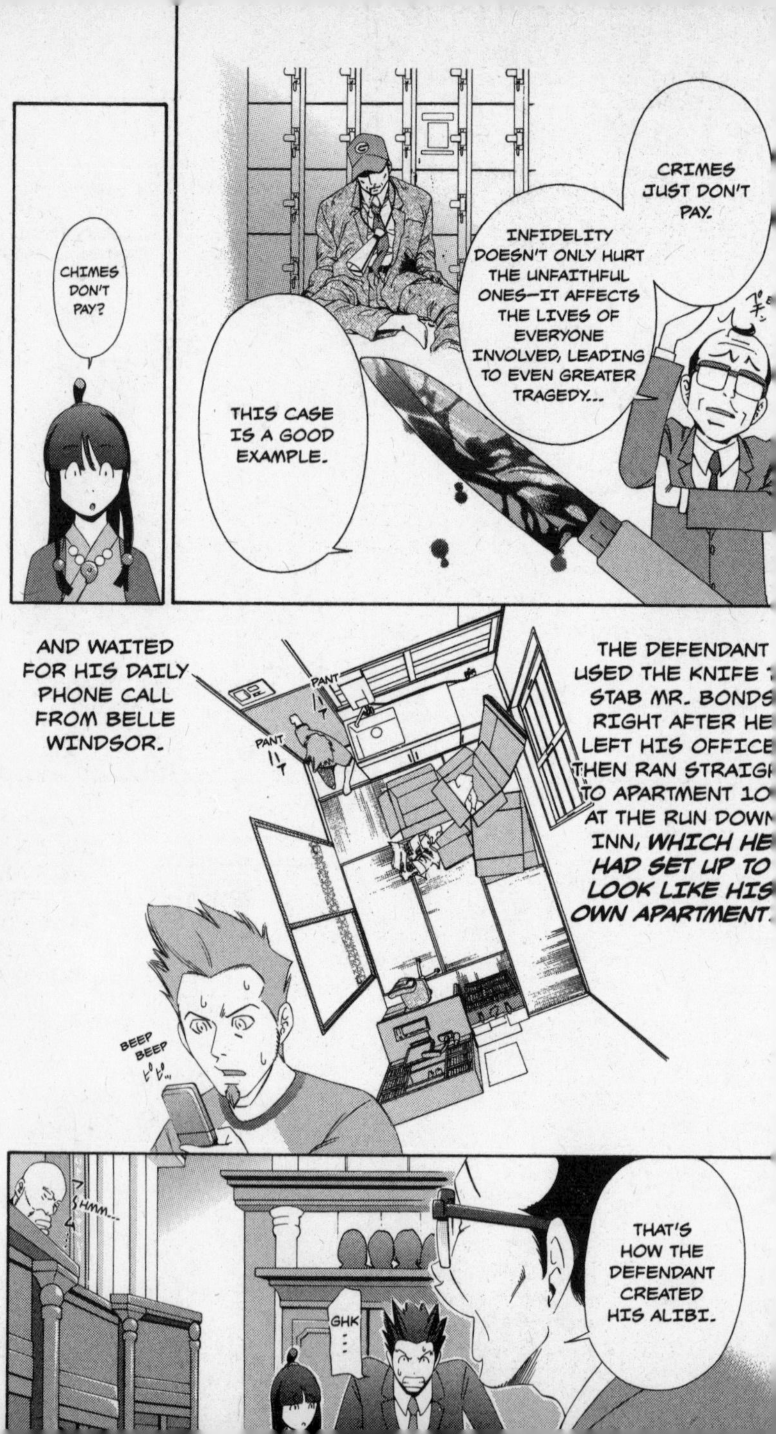
CRIMES JUST DON'T PAY.
INFIDELITY DOESN'T ONLY HURT THE UNFAITHFUL ONES—IT AFFECTS THE LIVES OF EVERYONE INVOLVED, LEADING TO EVEN GREATER TRAGEDY...
THIS CASE IS A GOOD EXAMPLE.
CHIMES DON'T PAY?
THE DEFENDANT USED THE KNIFE T STAB MR. BONDS RIGHT AFTER HE LEFT HIS OFFICE THEN RAN STRAIGH TO APARTMENT 10 AT THE RUN DOWN INN, WHICH HE HAD SET UP TO LOOK LIKE HIS OWN APARTMENT.
PANT
PANT
AND WAITED FOR HIS DAILY PHONE CALL FROM BELLE WINDSOR.
BEEP BEEP
THAT'S HOW THE DEFENDANT CREATED HIS ALIBI.
GHK...
HMM...

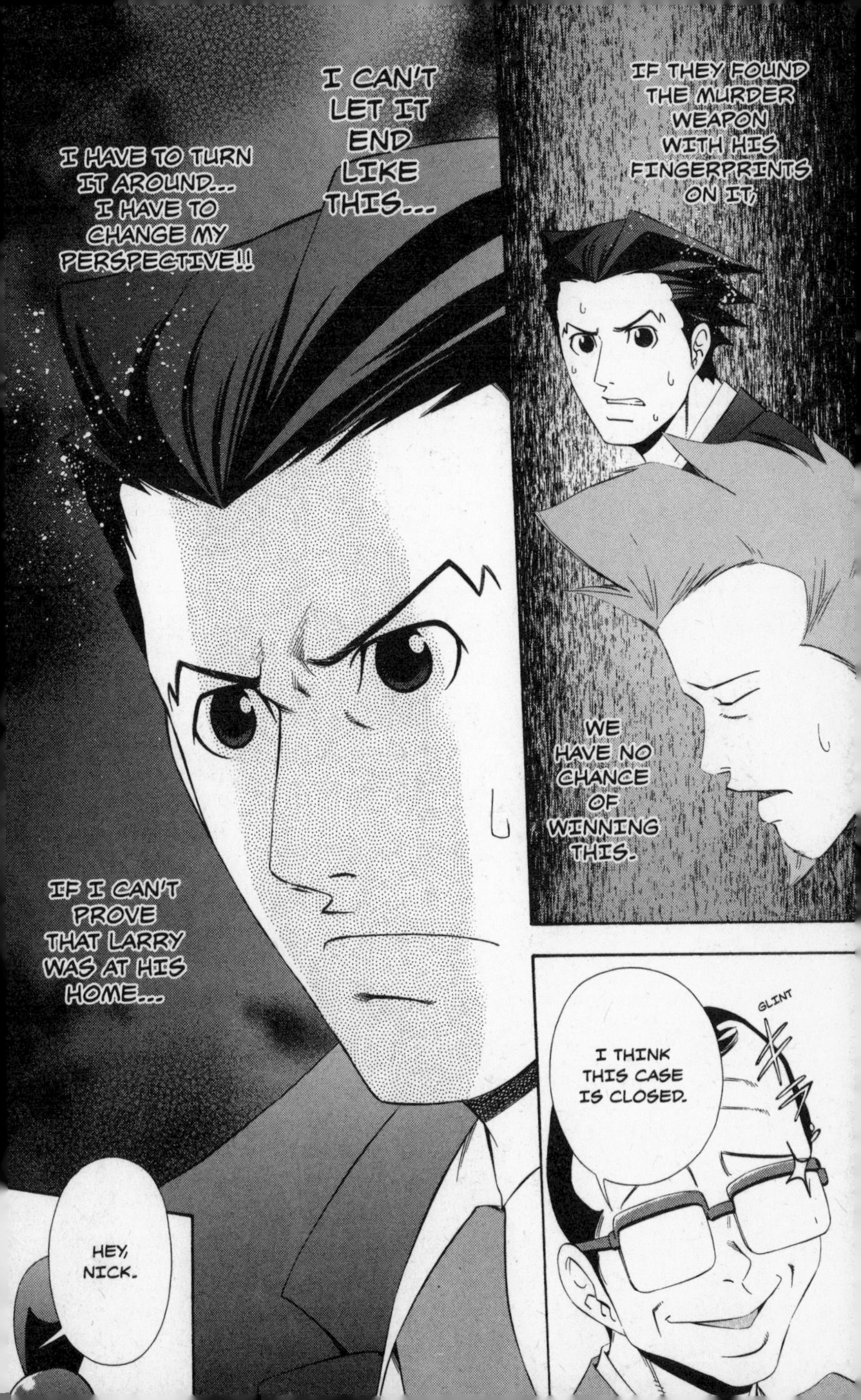
IF THEY FOUND THE MURDER WEAPON WITH HIS FINGERPRINTS ON IT,
WE HAVE NO CHANCE OF WINNING THIS.
GLINT
I THINK THIS CASE IS CLOSED.
I CAN'T LET IT END LIKE THIS...
I HAVE TO TURN IT AROUND... I HAVE TO CHANGE MY PERSPECTIVE!!
IF I CAN'T PROVE THAT LARRY WAS AT HIS HOME...
HEY, NICK.

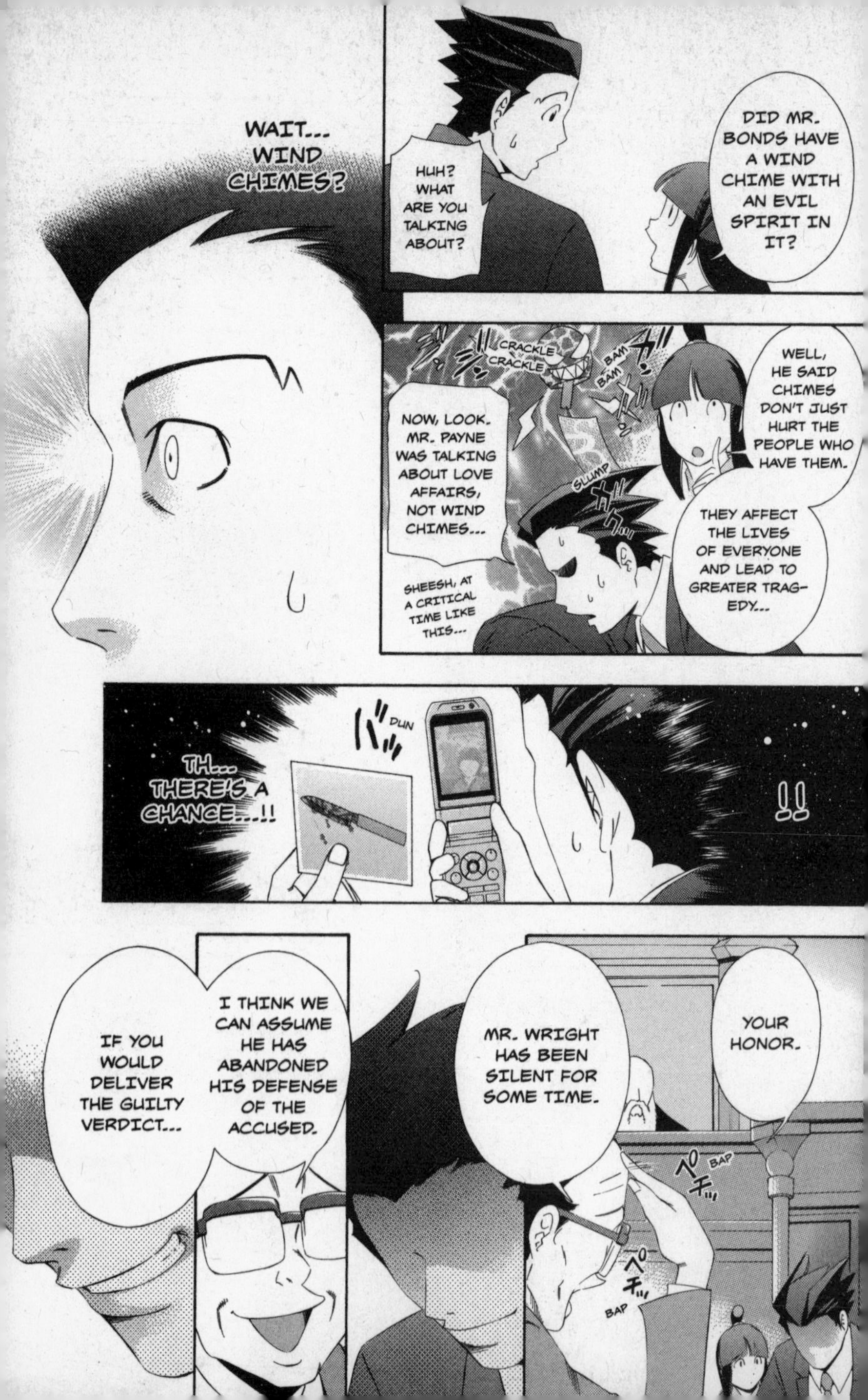
DID MR. BONDS HAVE A WIND CHIME WITH AN EVIL SPIRIT IN IT?
HUH? WHAT ARE YOU TALKING ABOUT?
WELL, HE SAID CHIMES DON'T JUST HURT THE PEOPLE WHO HAVE THEM.
BAM BAM
CRACKLE CRACKLE
THEY AFFECT THE LIVES OF EVERYONE AND LEAD TO GREATER TRAG-EDY...
NOW, LOOK. MR. PAYNE WAS TALKING ABOUT LOVE AFFAIRS, NOT WIND CHIMES...
SLUMP
SHEESH, AT A CRITICAL TIME LIKE THIS...
WAIT... WIND CHIMES?
!!
DUN
TH... THERE'S A CHANCE...!!
YOUR HONOR.
MR. WRIGHT HAS BEEN SILENT FOR SOME TIME.
BAP
BAP
I THINK WE CAN ASSUME HE HAS ABANDONED HIS DEFENSE OF THE ACCUSED.
IF YOU WOULD DELIVER THE GUILTY VERDICT...

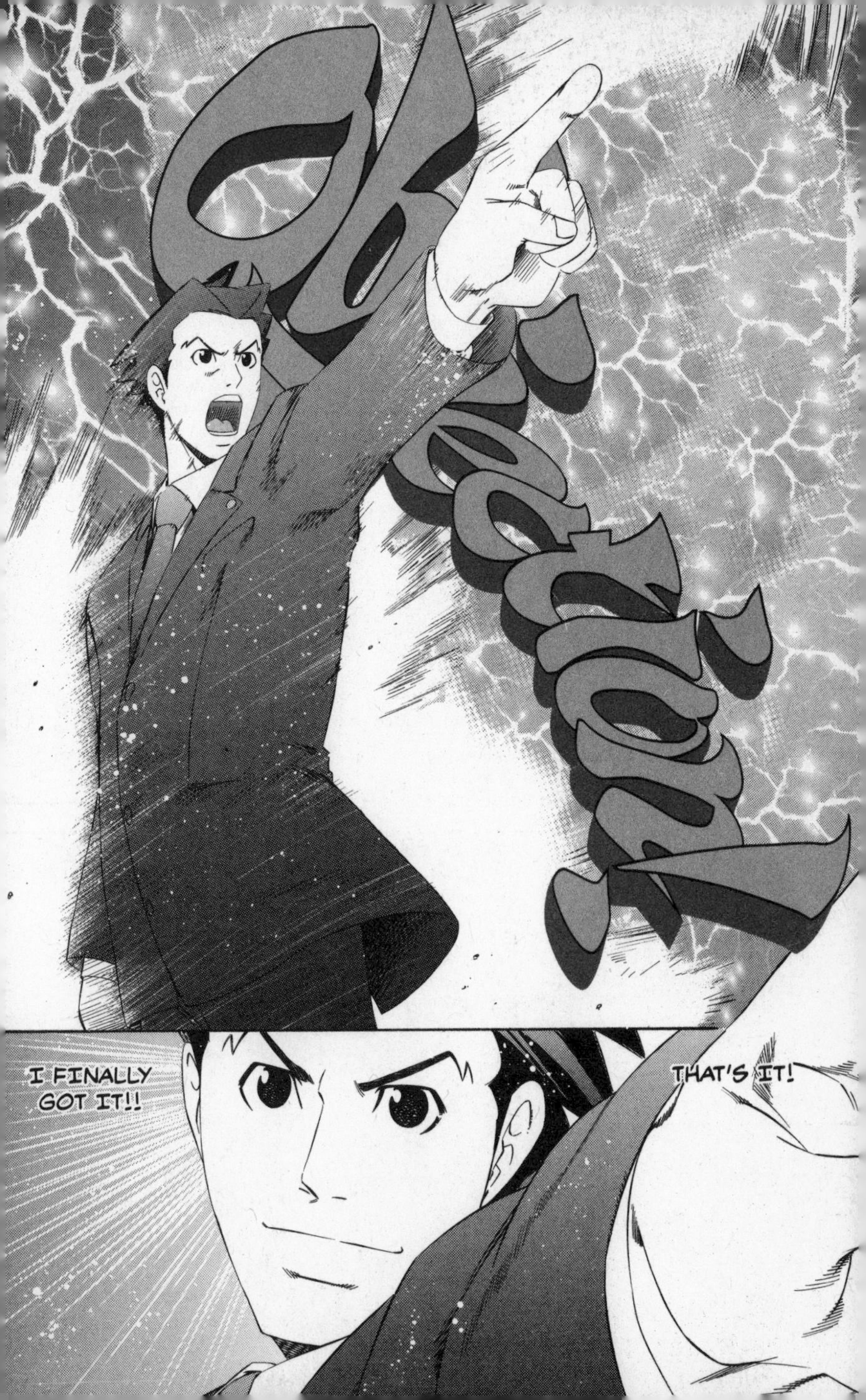
Objection!
THAT'S IT!
I FINALLY GOT IT!!

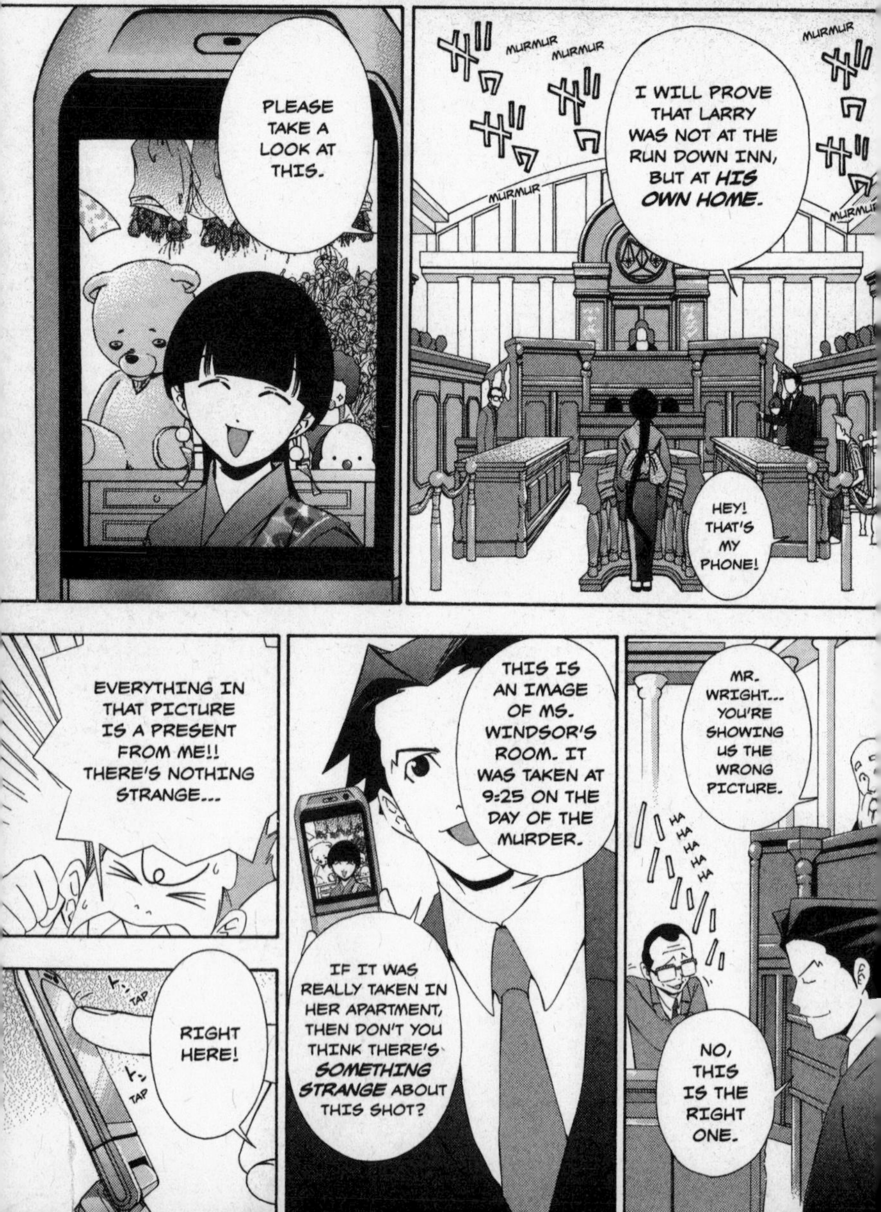
MURMUR
MURMUR
MURMUR
I WILL PROVE THAT LARRY WAS NOT AT THE RUN DOWN INN, BUT AT **HIS OWN HOME**.
MURMUR
MURMUR
HEY! THAT'S MY PHONE!
PLEASE TAKE A LOOK AT THIS.
MR. WRIGHT... YOU'RE SHOWING US THE WRONG PICTURE.
HA HA HA HA HA HA
NO, THIS IS THE RIGHT ONE.
THIS IS AN IMAGE OF MS. WINDSOR'S ROOM. IT WAS TAKEN AT 9:25 ON THE DAY OF THE MURDER.
IF IT WAS REALLY TAKEN IN HER APARTMENT, THEN DON'T YOU THINK THERE'S *SOMETHING STRANGE* ABOUT THIS SHOT?
EVERYTHING IN THAT PICTURE IS A PRESENT FROM ME!! THERE'S NOTHING STRANGE...
TAP
TAP
RIGHT HERE!

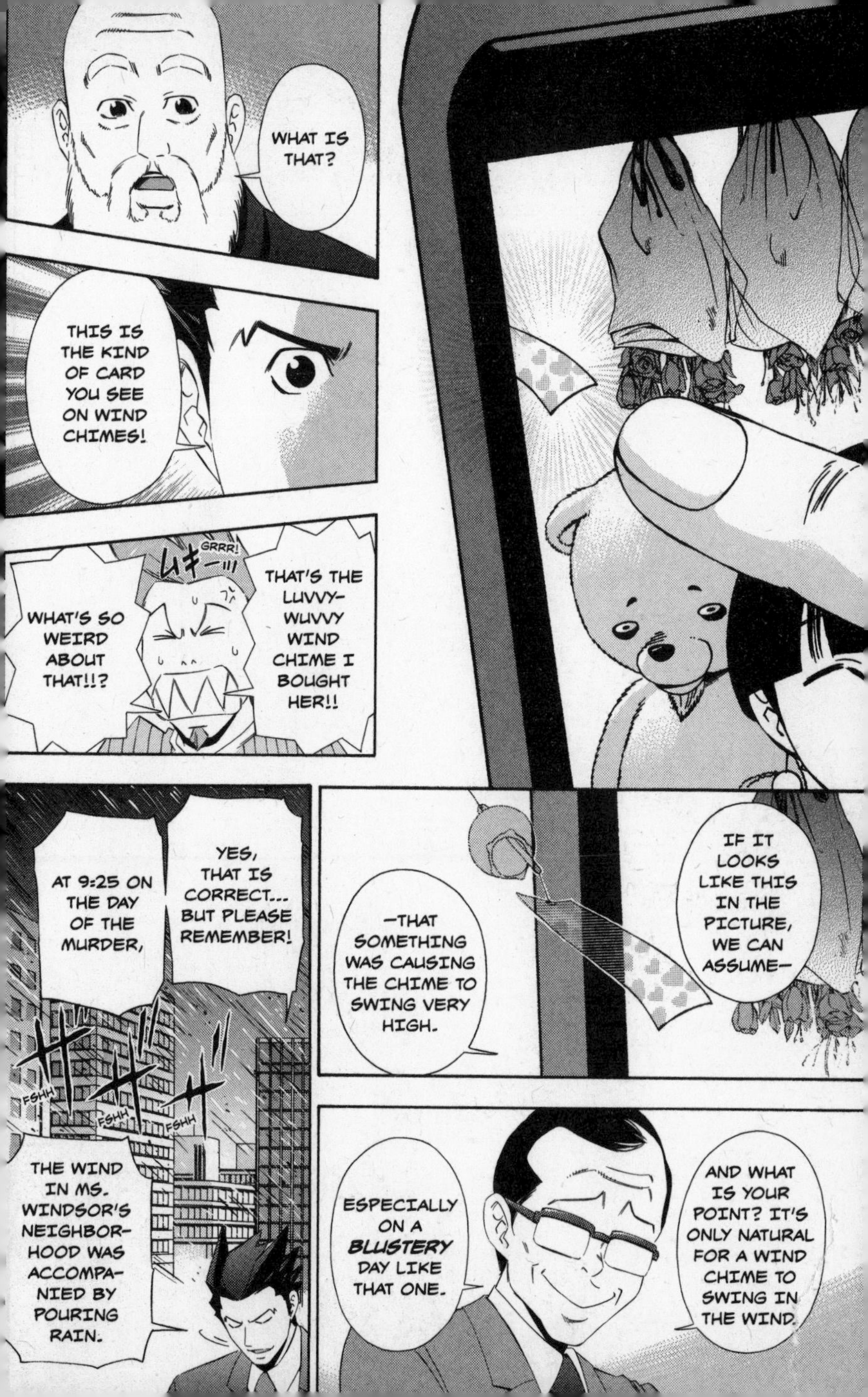
WHAT IS THAT?
THIS IS THE KIND OF CARD YOU SEE ON WIND CHIMES!
GRRR!
THAT'S THE LUVVY-WUVVY WIND CHIME I BOUGHT HER!!
WHAT'S SO WEIRD ABOUT THAT!!?
IF IT LOOKS LIKE THIS IN THE PICTURE, WE CAN ASSUME—
—THAT SOMETHING WAS CAUSING THE CHIME TO SWING VERY HIGH.
AND WHAT IS YOUR POINT? IT'S ONLY NATURAL FOR A WIND CHIME TO SWING IN THE WIND.
ESPECIALLY ON A *BLUSTERY* DAY LIKE THAT ONE.
YES, THAT IS CORRECT... BUT PLEASE REMEMBER!
AT 9:25 ON THE DAY OF THE MURDER,
FSHH
FSHH
FSHH
THE WIND IN MS. WINDSOR'S NEIGHBORHOOD WAS ACCOMPANIED BY POURING RAIN.

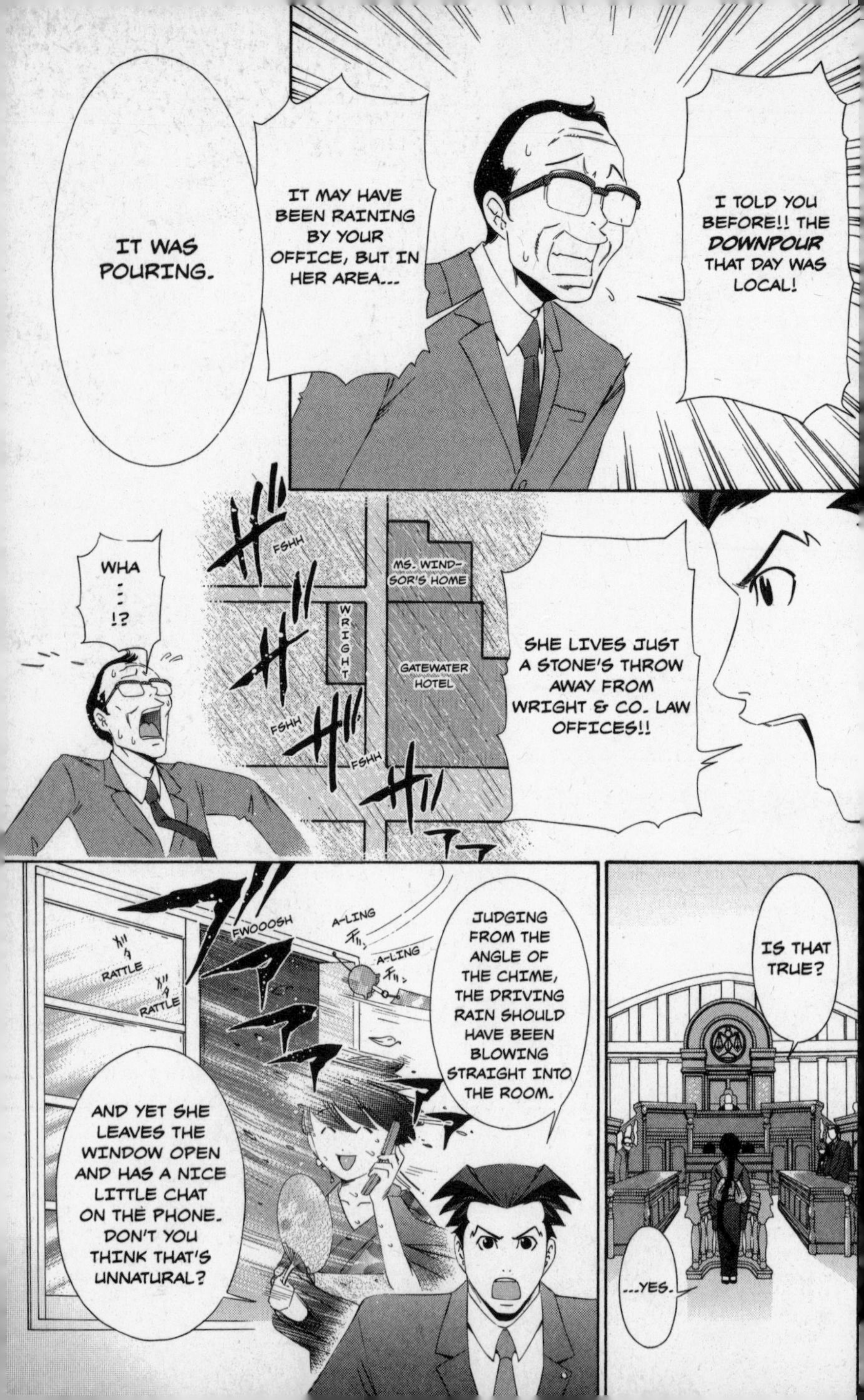
I TOLD YOU BEFORE!! THE DOWNPOUR THAT DAY WAS LOCAL!
IT MAY HAVE BEEN RAINING BY YOUR OFFICE, BUT IN HER AREA...
IT WAS POURING.
SHE LIVES JUST A STONE'S THROW AWAY FROM WRIGHT & CO. LAW OFFICES!!
MS. WINDSOR'S HOME
WRIGHT
GATEWATER HOTEL
FSHH
FSHH
FSHH
WHA ...!?
IS THAT TRUE?
...YES.
JUDGING FROM THE ANGLE OF THE CHIME, THE DRIVING RAIN SHOULD HAVE BEEN BLOWING STRAIGHT INTO THE ROOM.
A-LING
A-LING
FWOOOSH
RATTLE
RATTLE
AND YET SHE LEAVES THE WINDOW OPEN AND HAS A NICE LITTLE CHAT ON THE PHONE. DON'T YOU THINK THAT'S UNNATURAL?

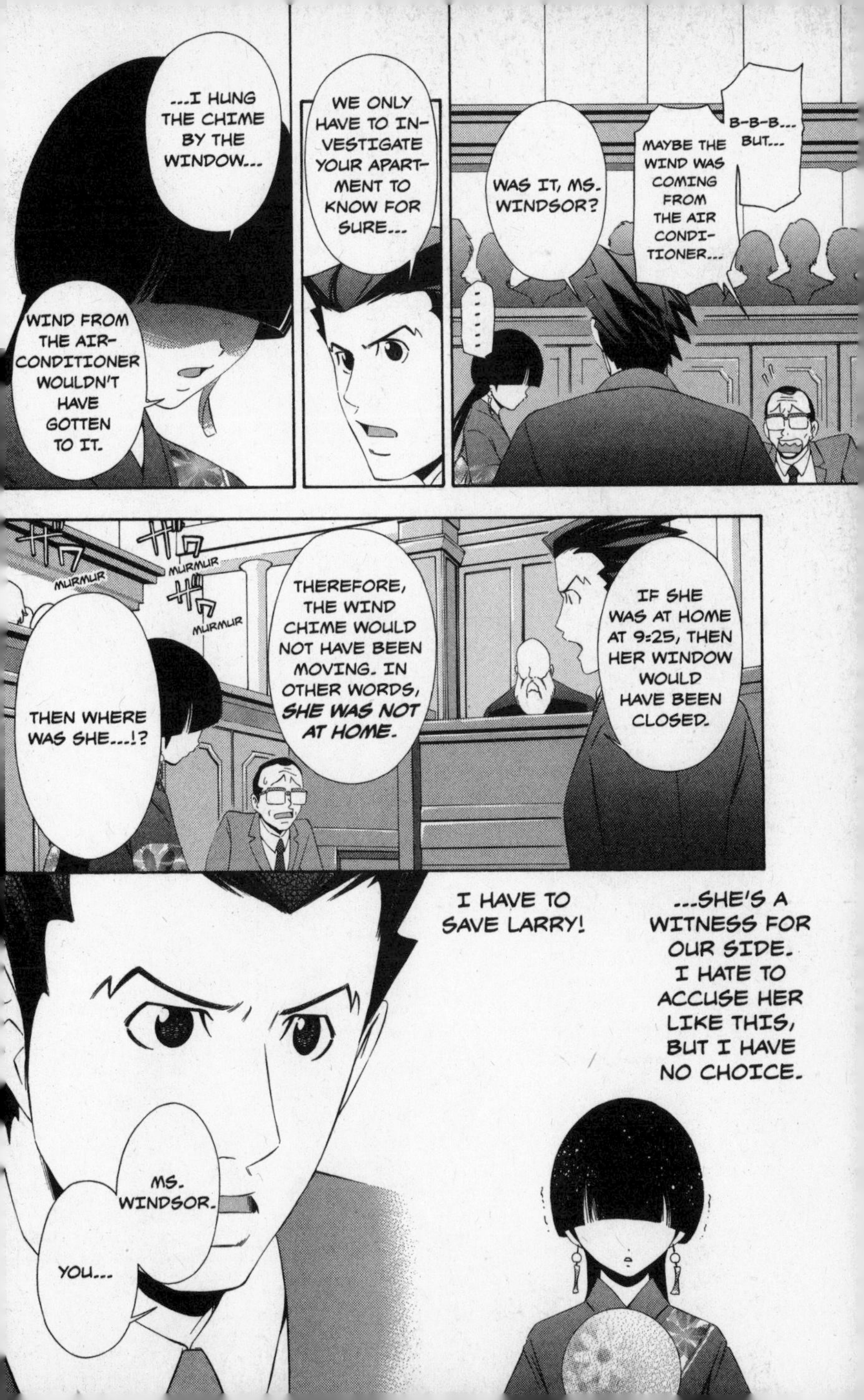
B-B-B... BUT...
MAYBE THE WIND WAS COMING FROM THE AIR CONDITIONER...
WAS IT, MS. WINDSOR?
......
WE ONLY HAVE TO INVESTIGATE YOUR APARTMENT TO KNOW FOR SURE...
...I HUNG THE CHIME BY THE WINDOW...
WIND FROM THE AIR-CONDITIONER WOULDN'T HAVE GOTTEN TO IT.
IF SHE WAS AT HOME AT 9:25, THEN HER WINDOW WOULD HAVE BEEN CLOSED.
THEREFORE, THE WIND CHIME WOULD NOT HAVE BEEN MOVING. IN OTHER WORDS, SHE WAS NOT AT HOME.
MURMUR
MURMUR
MURMUR
THEN WHERE WAS SHE...!?
...SHE'S A WITNESS FOR OUR SIDE. I HATE TO ACCUSE HER LIKE THIS, BUT I HAVE NO CHOICE.
I HAVE TO SAVE LARRY!
MS. WINDSOR.
YOU...

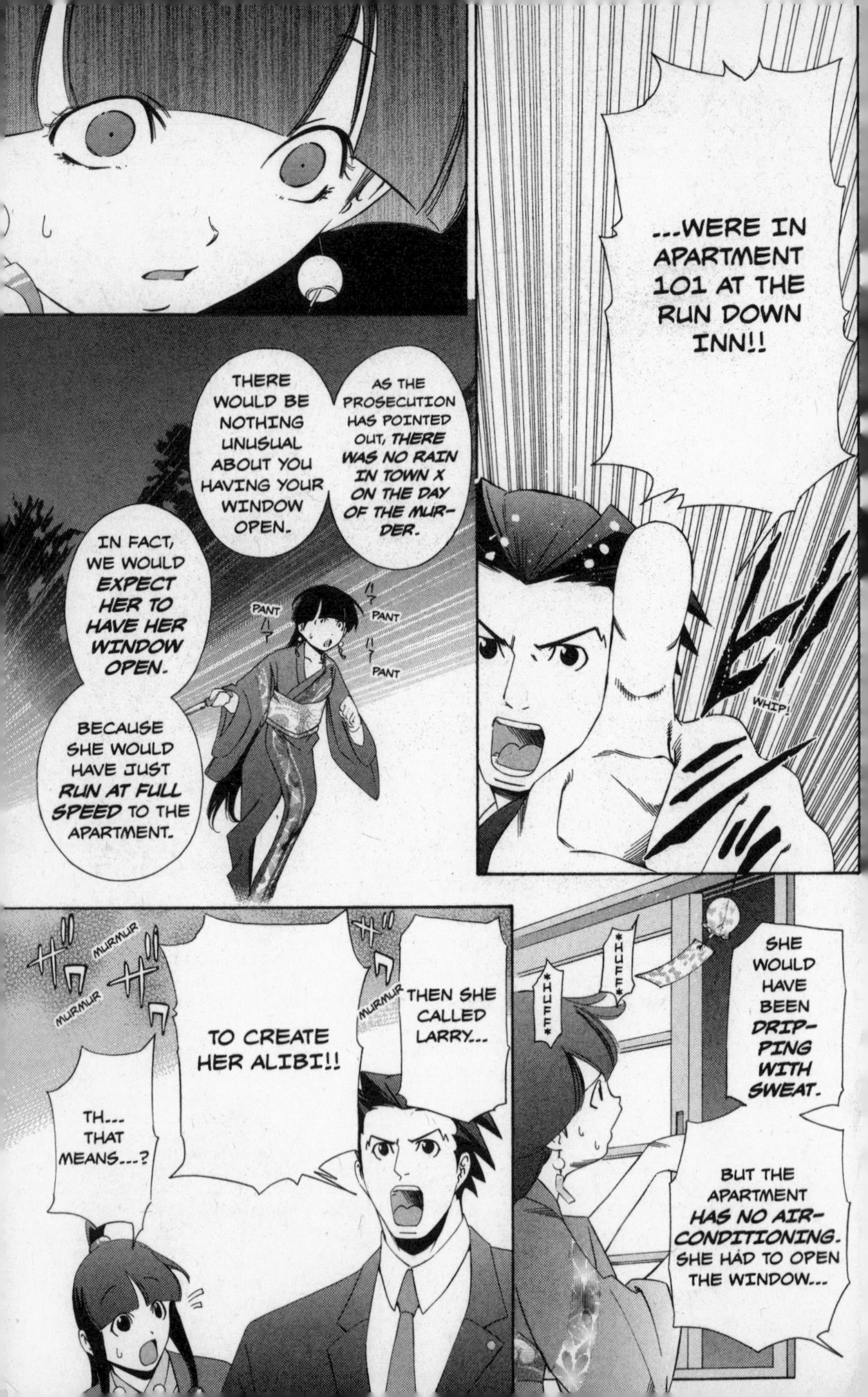

...WERE IN APARTMENT 101 AT THE RUN DOWN INN!!
WHIP!
AS THE PROSECUTION HAS POINTED OUT, *THERE WAS NO RAIN IN TOWN X ON THE DAY OF THE MUR-DER.*
THERE WOULD BE NOTHING UNUSUAL ABOUT YOU HAVING YOUR WINDOW OPEN.
IN FACT, WE WOULD *EXPECT HER TO HAVE HER WINDOW OPEN.*
PANT PANT PANT
BECAUSE SHE WOULD HAVE JUST *RUN AT FULL SPEED* TO THE APARTMENT.
SHE WOULD HAVE BEEN *DRIP-PING WITH SWEAT.*
*HUFF*
*HUFF*
BUT THE APARTMENT *HAS NO AIR-CONDITIONING.* SHE HAD TO OPEN THE WINDOW...
THEN SHE CALLED LARRY...
TO CREATE HER ALIBI!!
MURMUR
MURMUR
MURMUR
TH... THAT MEANS...?

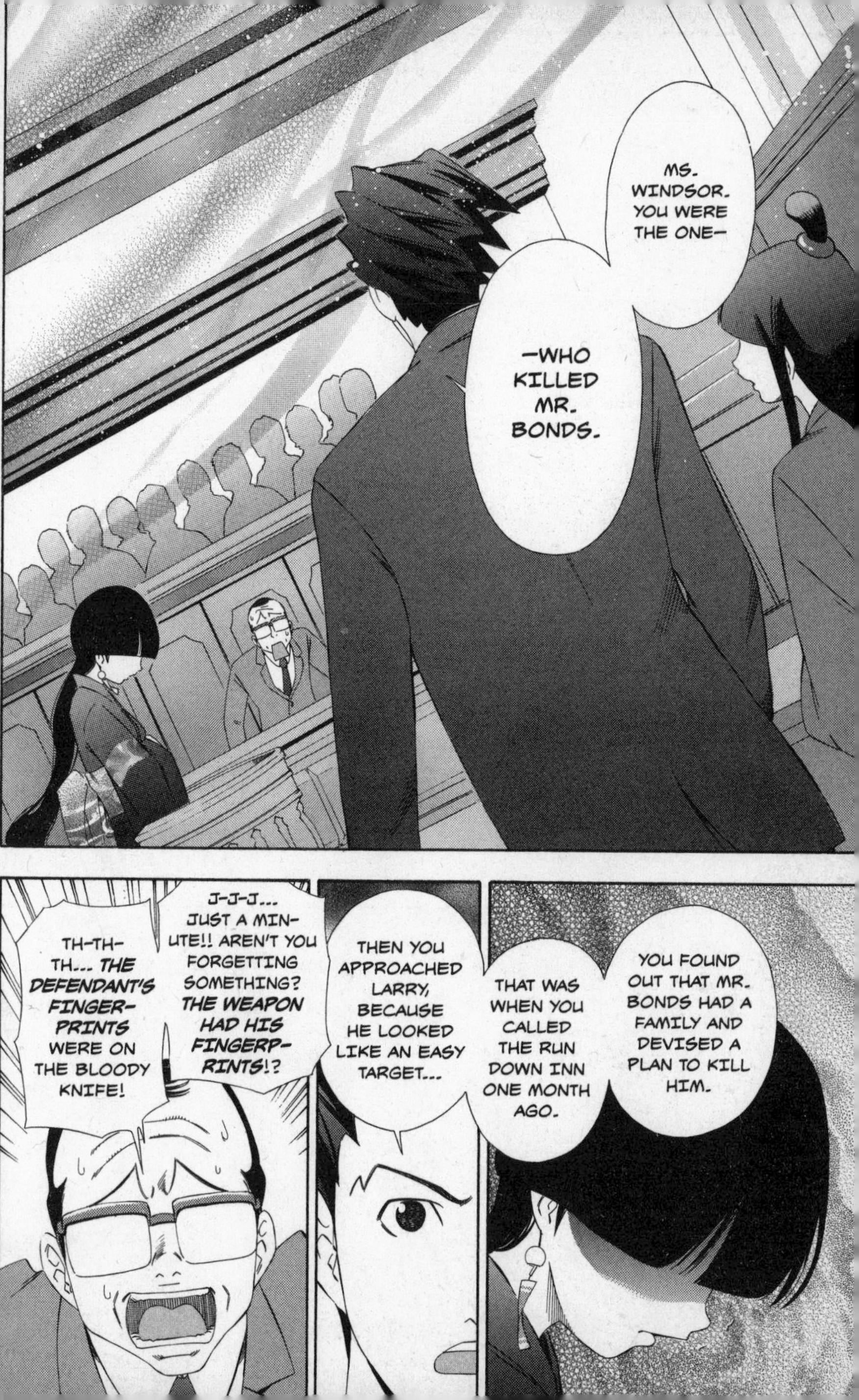
MS. WINDSOR. YOU WERE THE ONE—
—WHO KILLED MR. BONDS.
YOU FOUND OUT THAT MR. BONDS HAD A FAMILY AND DEVISED A PLAN TO KILL HIM.
THAT WAS WHEN YOU CALLED THE RUN DOWN INN ONE MONTH AGO.
THEN YOU APPROACHED LARRY, BECAUSE HE LOOKED LIKE AN EASY TARGET...
J-J-J... JUST A MIN-UTE!! AREN'T YOU FORGETTING SOMETHING? *THE WEAPON HAD HIS FINGERP-RINTS!?*
TH-TH-TH... *THE DEFENDANT'S FINGER-PRINTS* WERE ON THE BLOODY KNIFE!

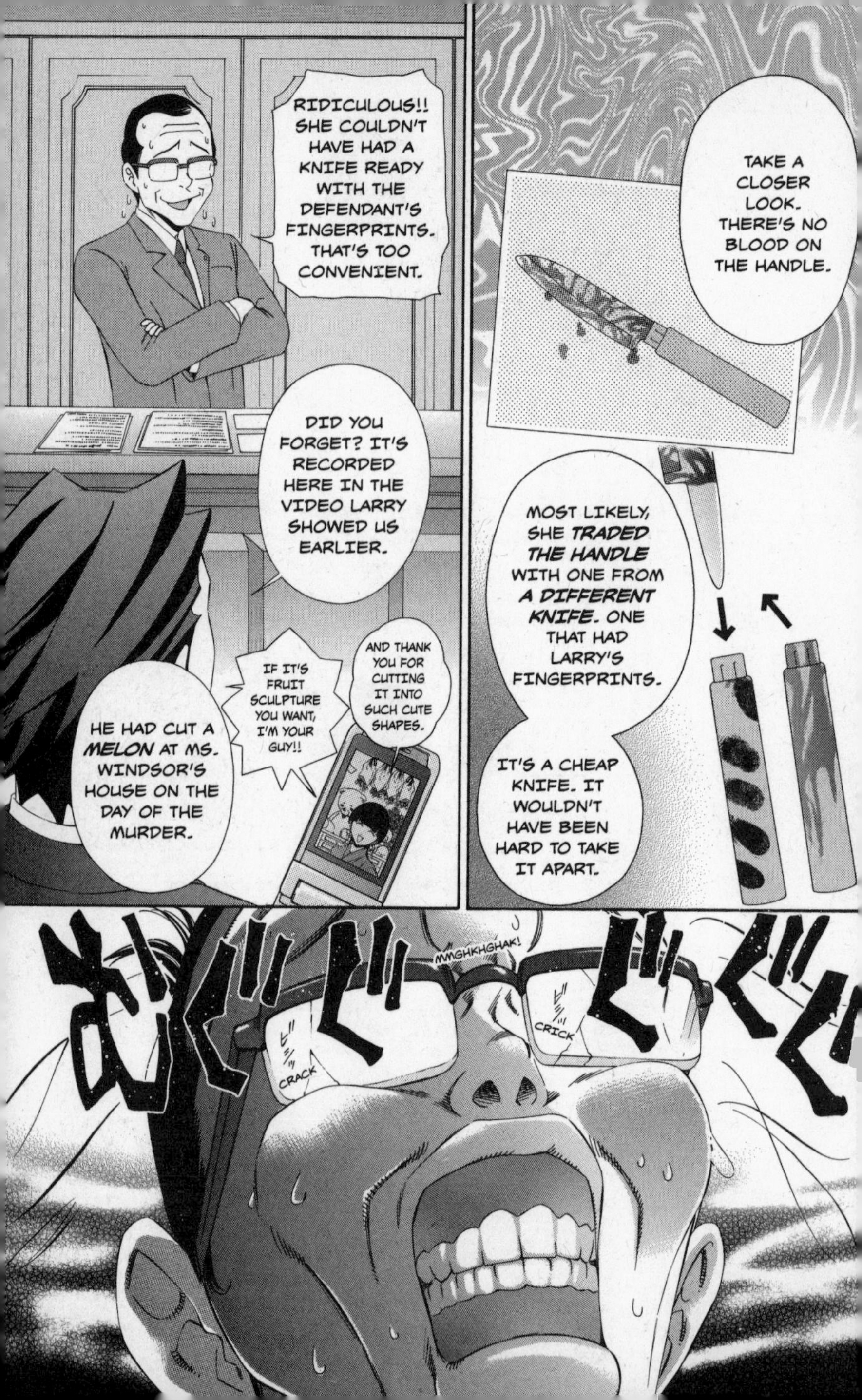
TAKE A CLOSER LOOK. THERE'S NO BLOOD ON THE HANDLE.
MOST LIKELY, SHE *TRADED THE HANDLE* WITH ONE FROM *A DIFFERENT KNIFE*. ONE THAT HAD LARRY'S FINGERPRINTS.
IT'S A CHEAP KNIFE. IT WOULDN'T HAVE BEEN HARD TO TAKE IT APART.
RIDICULOUS!! SHE COULDN'T HAVE HAD A KNIFE READY WITH THE DEFENDANT'S FINGERPRINTS. THAT'S TOO CONVENIENT.
DID YOU FORGET? IT'S RECORDED HERE IN THE VIDEO LARRY SHOWED US EARLIER.
AND THANK YOU FOR CUTTING IT INTO SUCH CUTE SHAPES.
IF IT'S FRUIT SCULPTURE YOU WANT, I'M YOUR GUY!!
HE HAD CUT A *MELON* AT MS. WINDSOR'S HOUSE ON THE DAY OF THE MURDER.
MMGHKHGHAK!
CRICK
CRACK

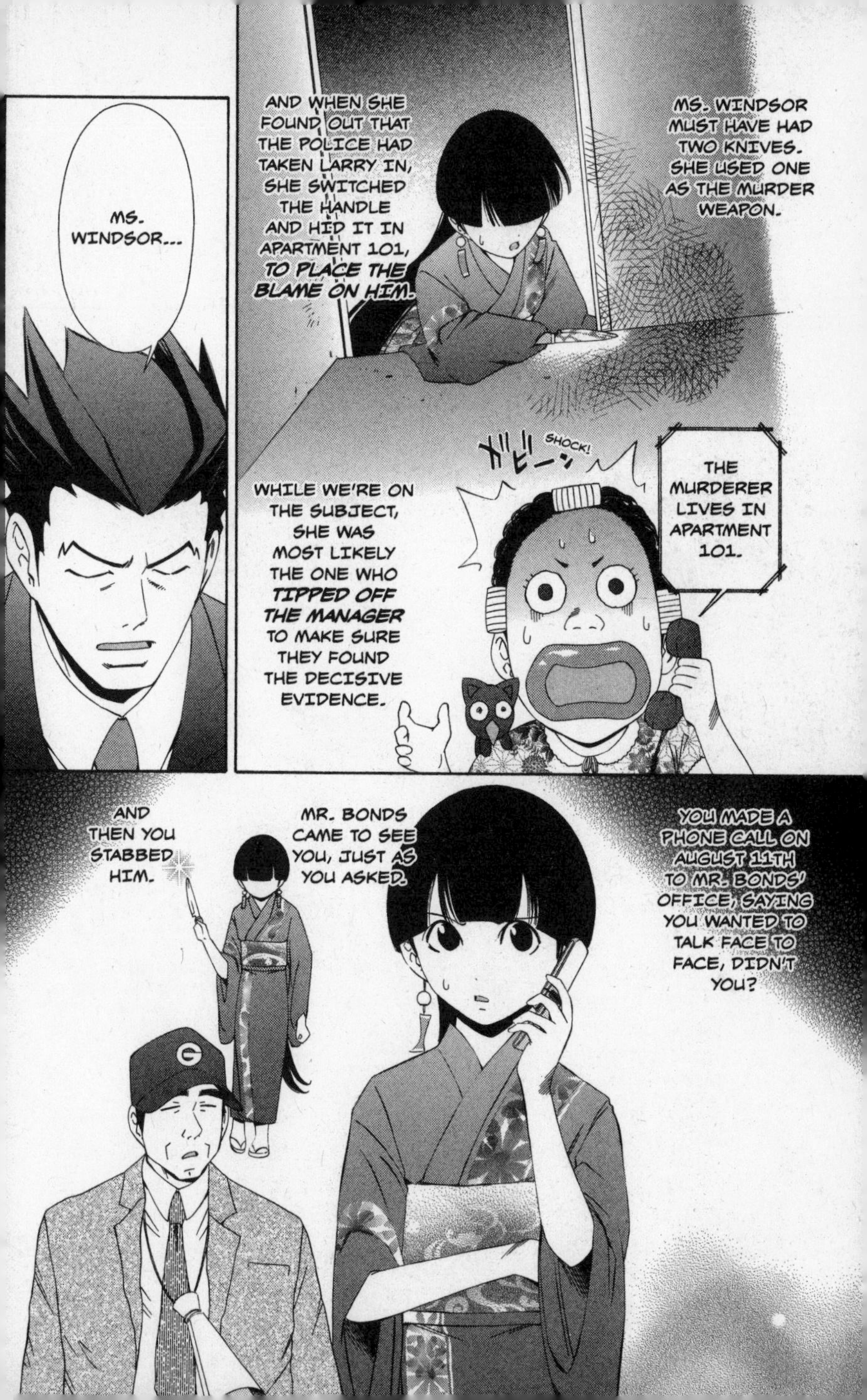
MS. WINDSOR MUST HAVE HAD TWO KNIVES. SHE USED ONE AS THE MURDER WEAPON.
AND WHEN SHE FOUND OUT THAT THE POLICE HAD TAKEN LARRY IN, SHE SWITCHED THE HANDLE AND HID IT IN APARTMENT 101, *TO PLACE THE BLAME ON HIM.*
THE MURDERER LIVES IN APARTMENT 101.
ガビーン
SHOCK!
WHILE WE'RE ON THE SUBJECT, SHE WAS MOST LIKELY THE ONE WHO *TIPPED OFF THE MANAGER* TO MAKE SURE THEY FOUND THE DECISIVE EVIDENCE.
MS. WINDSOR...
YOU MADE A PHONE CALL ON AUGUST 11TH TO MR. BONDS' OFFICE, SAYING YOU WANTED TO TALK FACE TO FACE, DIDN'T YOU?
MR. BONDS CAME TO SEE YOU, JUST AS YOU ASKED.
AND THEN YOU STABBED HIM.

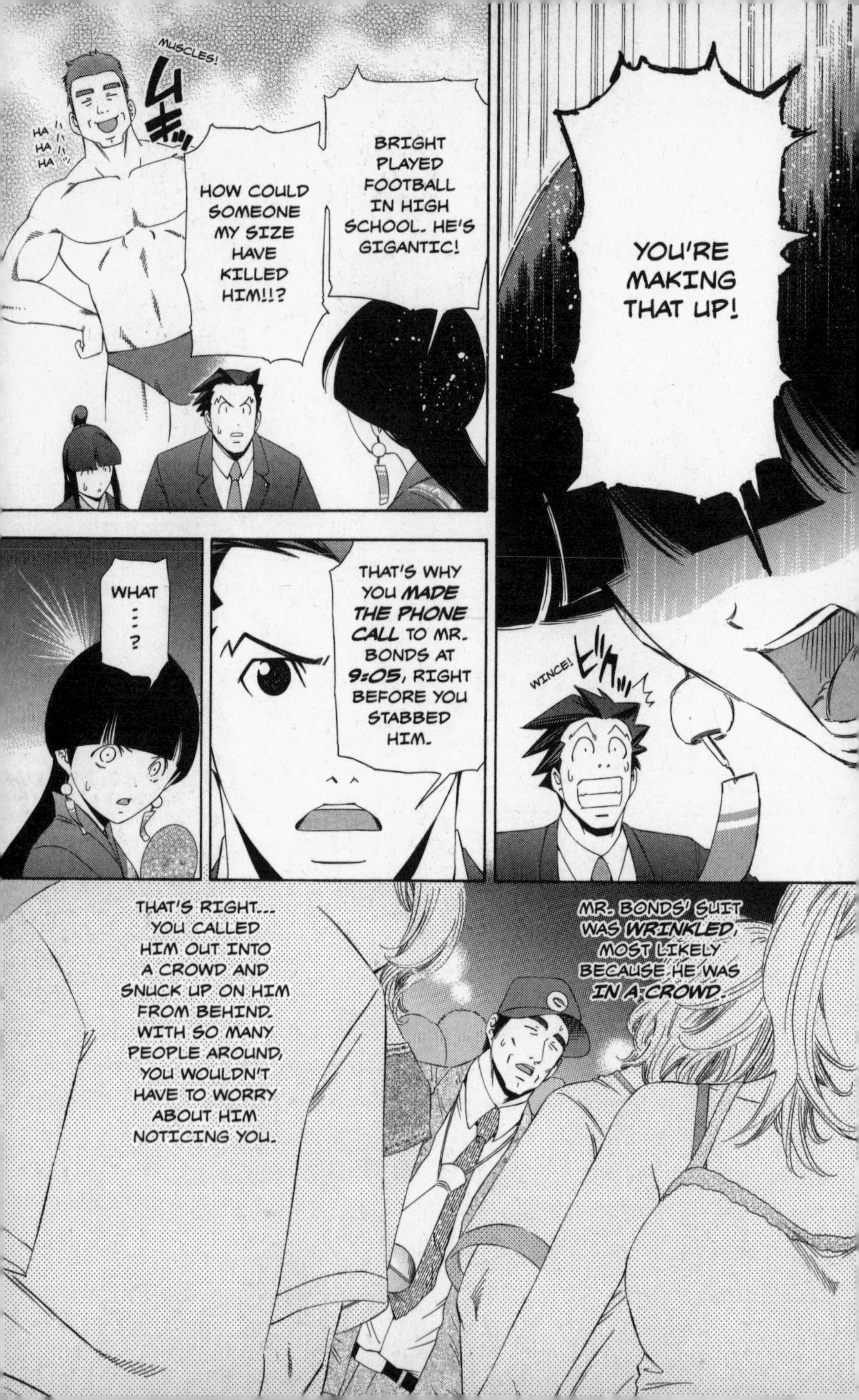
YOU'RE MAKING THAT UP!
WINCE!
BRIGHT PLAYED FOOTBALL IN HIGH SCHOOL. HE'S GIGANTIC!
HOW COULD SOMEONE MY SIZE HAVE KILLED HIM!!?
MUSCLES!
HA HA HA
THAT'S WHY YOU MADE THE PHONE CALL TO MR. BONDS AT 9:05, RIGHT BEFORE YOU STABBED HIM.
WHAT ...?
MR. BONDS' SUIT WAS WRINKLED, MOST LIKELY BECAUSE HE WAS IN A CROWD.
THAT'S RIGHT... YOU CALLED HIM OUT INTO A CROWD AND SNUCK UP ON HIM FROM BEHIND. WITH SO MANY PEOPLE AROUND, YOU WOULDN'T HAVE TO WORRY ABOUT HIM NOTICING YOU.

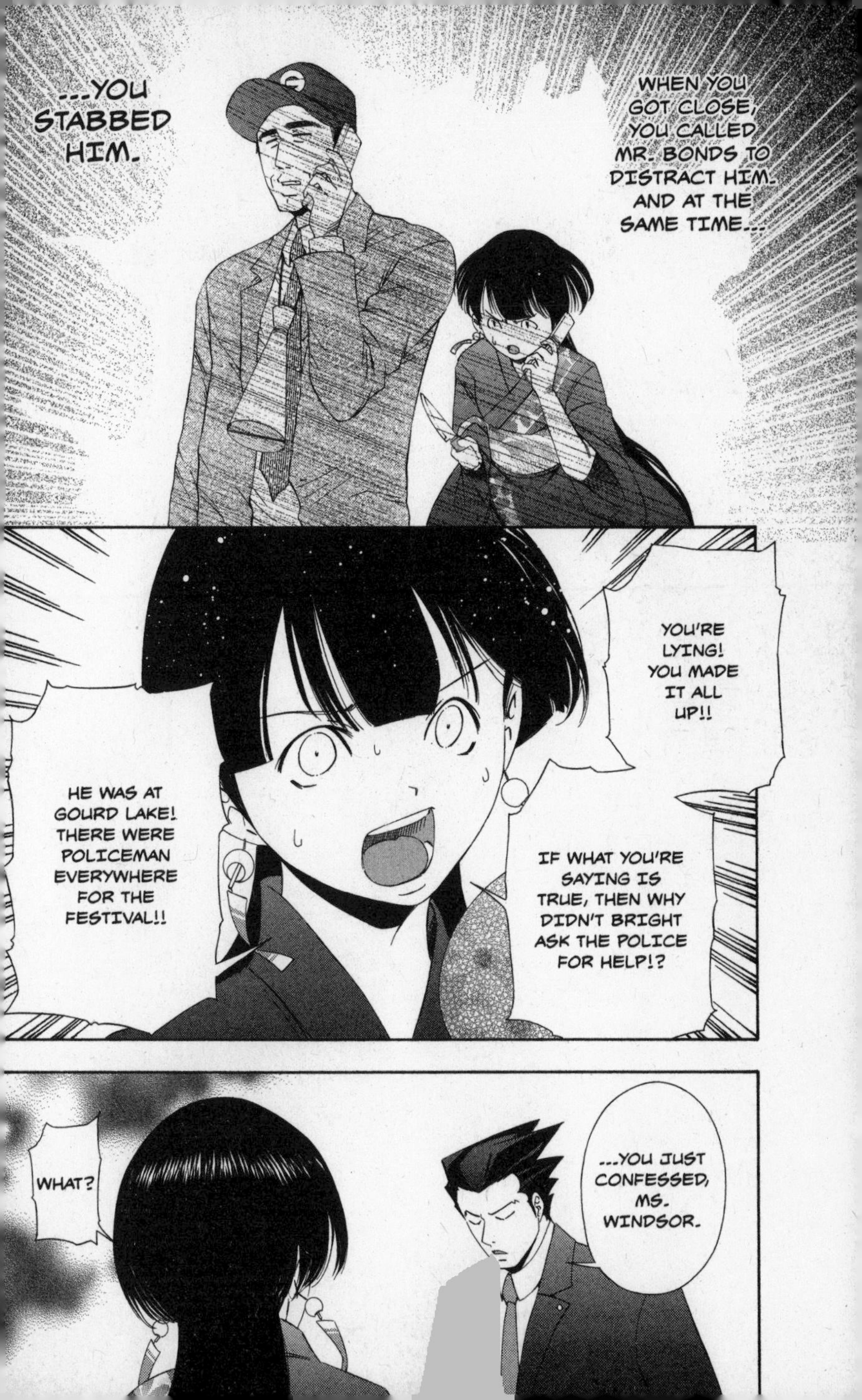
WHEN YOU GOT CLOSE, YOU CALLED MR. BONDS TO DISTRACT HIM. AND AT THE SAME TIME...
...YOU STABBED HIM.
YOU'RE LYING! YOU MADE IT ALL UP!!
IF WHAT YOU'RE SAYING IS TRUE, THEN WHY DIDN'T BRIGHT ASK THE POLICE FOR HELP!?
HE WAS AT GOURD LAKE! THERE WERE POLICEMAN EVERYWHERE FOR THE FESTIVAL!!
...YOU JUST CONFESSED, MS. WINDSOR.
WHAT?

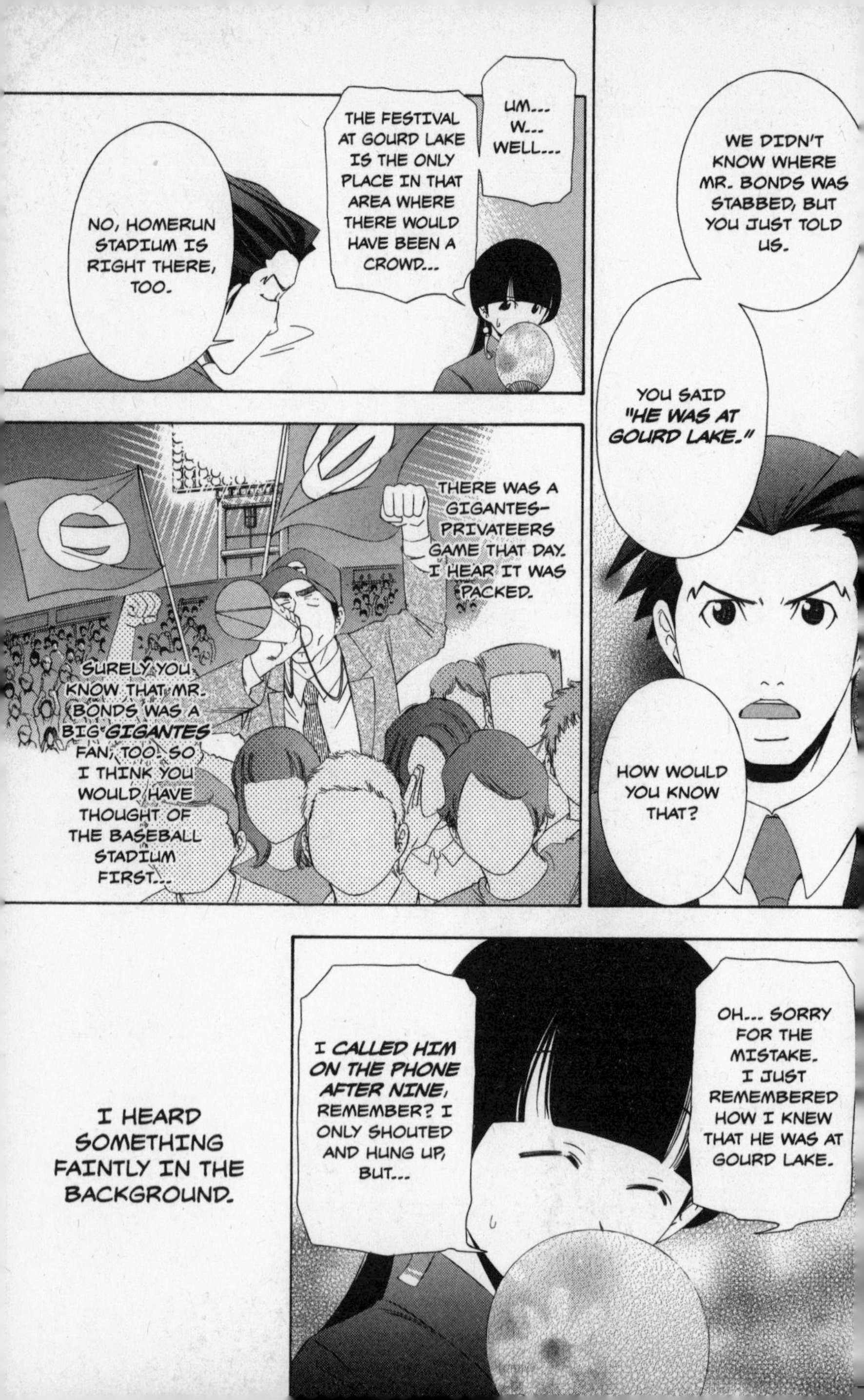
WE DIDN'T KNOW WHERE MR. BONDS WAS STABBED, BUT YOU JUST TOLD US.
YOU SAID "HE WAS AT GOURD LAKE."
HOW WOULD YOU KNOW THAT?
UM... W... WELL...
THE FESTIVAL AT GOURD LAKE IS THE ONLY PLACE IN THAT AREA WHERE THERE WOULD HAVE BEEN A CROWD...
NO, HOMERUN STADIUM IS RIGHT THERE, TOO.
THERE WAS A GIGANTES-PRIVATEERS GAME THAT DAY. I HEAR IT WAS PACKED.
SURELY YOU KNOW THAT MR. BONDS WAS A BIG GIGANTES FAN, TOO. SO I THINK YOU WOULD HAVE THOUGHT OF THE BASEBALL STADIUM FIRST...
OH... SORRY FOR THE MISTAKE. I JUST REMEMBERED HOW I KNEW THAT HE WAS AT GOURD LAKE.
I CALLED HIM ON THE PHONE AFTER NINE, REMEMBER? I ONLY SHOUTED AND HUNG UP, BUT...
I HEARD SOMETHING FAINTLY IN THE BACKGROUND.

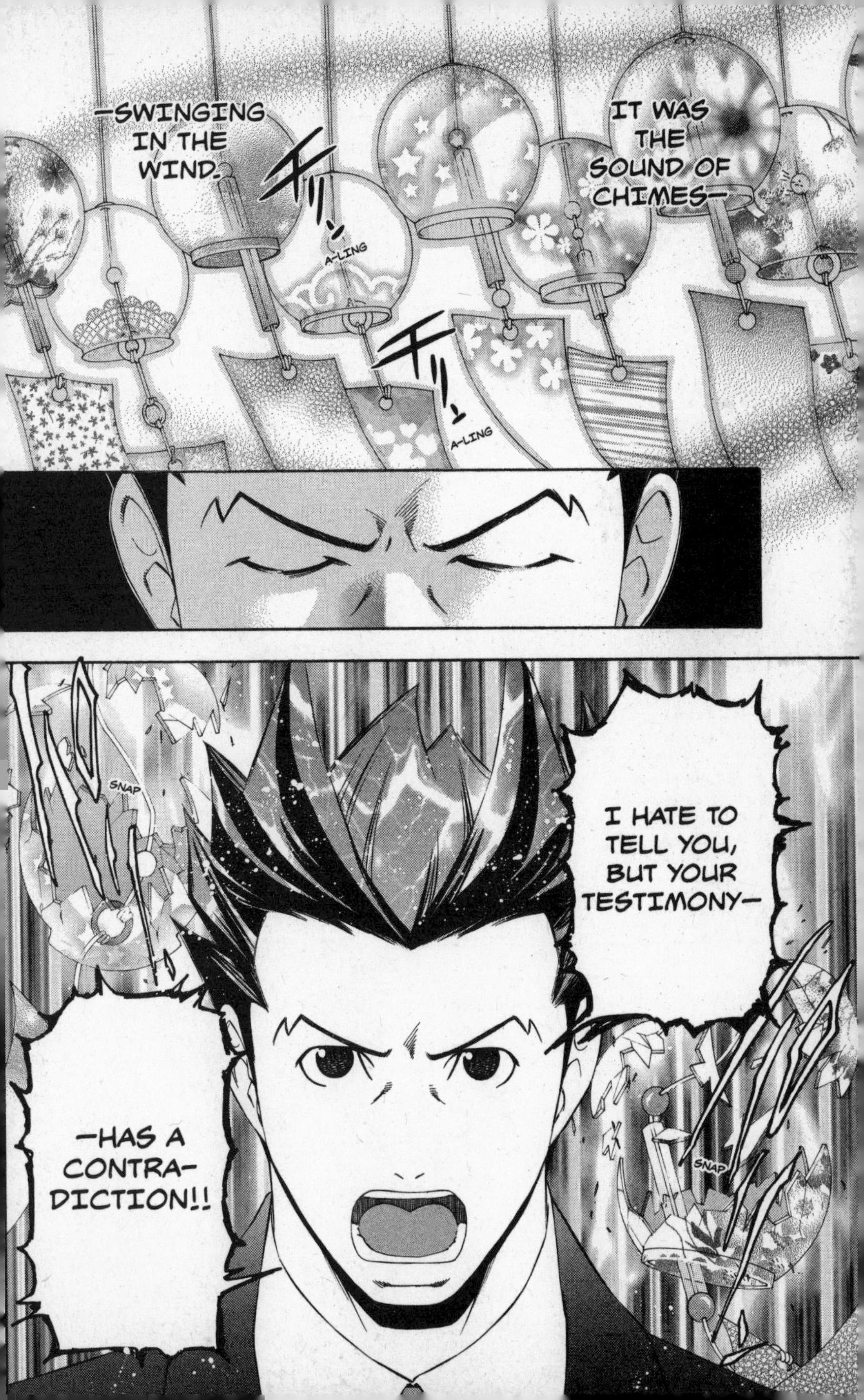
IT WAS THE SOUND OF CHIMES—
A-LING
—SWINGING IN THE WIND.
A-LING
I HATE TO TELL YOU, BUT YOUR TESTIMONY—
SNAP
SNAP
—HAS A CONTRA-DICTION!!

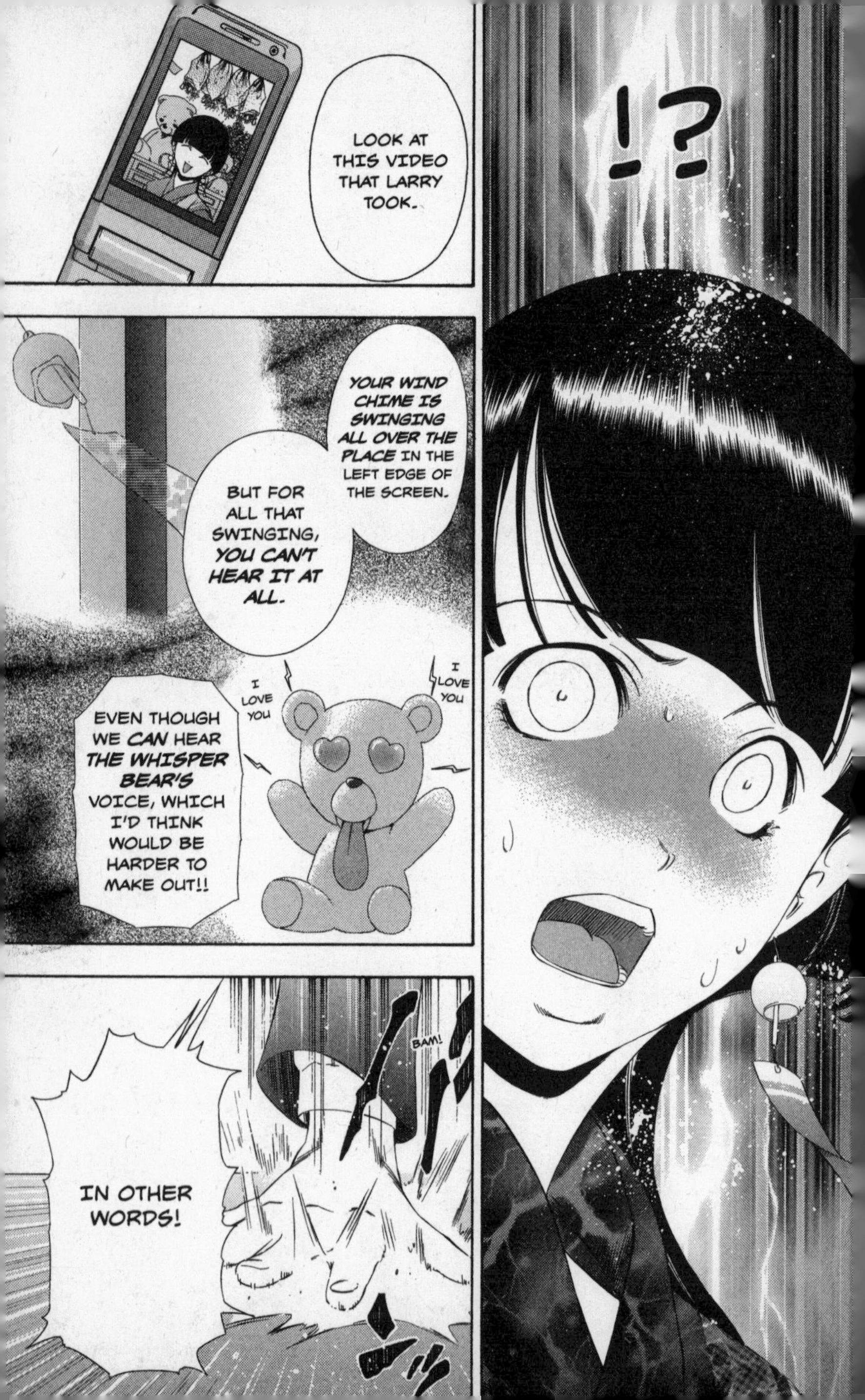
!?
LOOK AT THIS VIDEO THAT LARRY TOOK.
YOUR WIND CHIME IS SWINGING ALL OVER THE PLACE IN THE LEFT EDGE OF THE SCREEN.
BUT FOR ALL THAT SWINGING, YOU CAN'T HEAR IT AT ALL.
I LOVE YOU
I LOVE YOU
EVEN THOUGH WE CAN HEAR THE WHISPER BEAR'S VOICE, WHICH I'D THINK WOULD BE HARDER TO MAKE OUT!!
BAM!
IN OTHER WORDS!

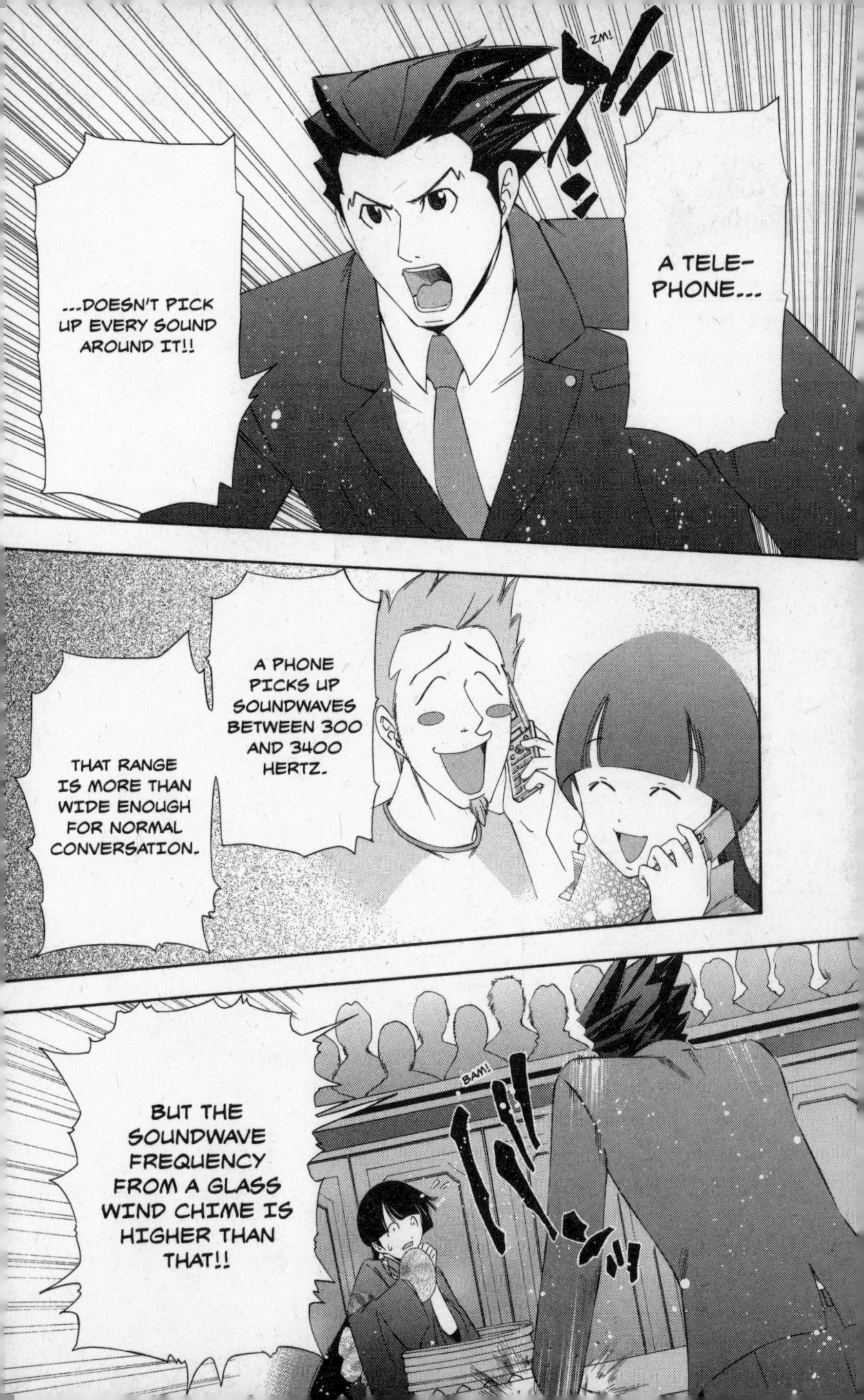
ZM!
A TELE-PHONE...
...DOESN'T PICK UP EVERY SOUND AROUND IT!!
A PHONE PICKS UP SOUNDWAVES BETWEEN 300 AND 3400 HERTZ.
THAT RANGE IS MORE THAN WIDE ENOUGH FOR NORMAL CONVERSATION.
BAM!
BUT THE SOUNDWAVE FREQUENCY FROM A GLASS WIND CHIME IS HIGHER THAN THAT!!

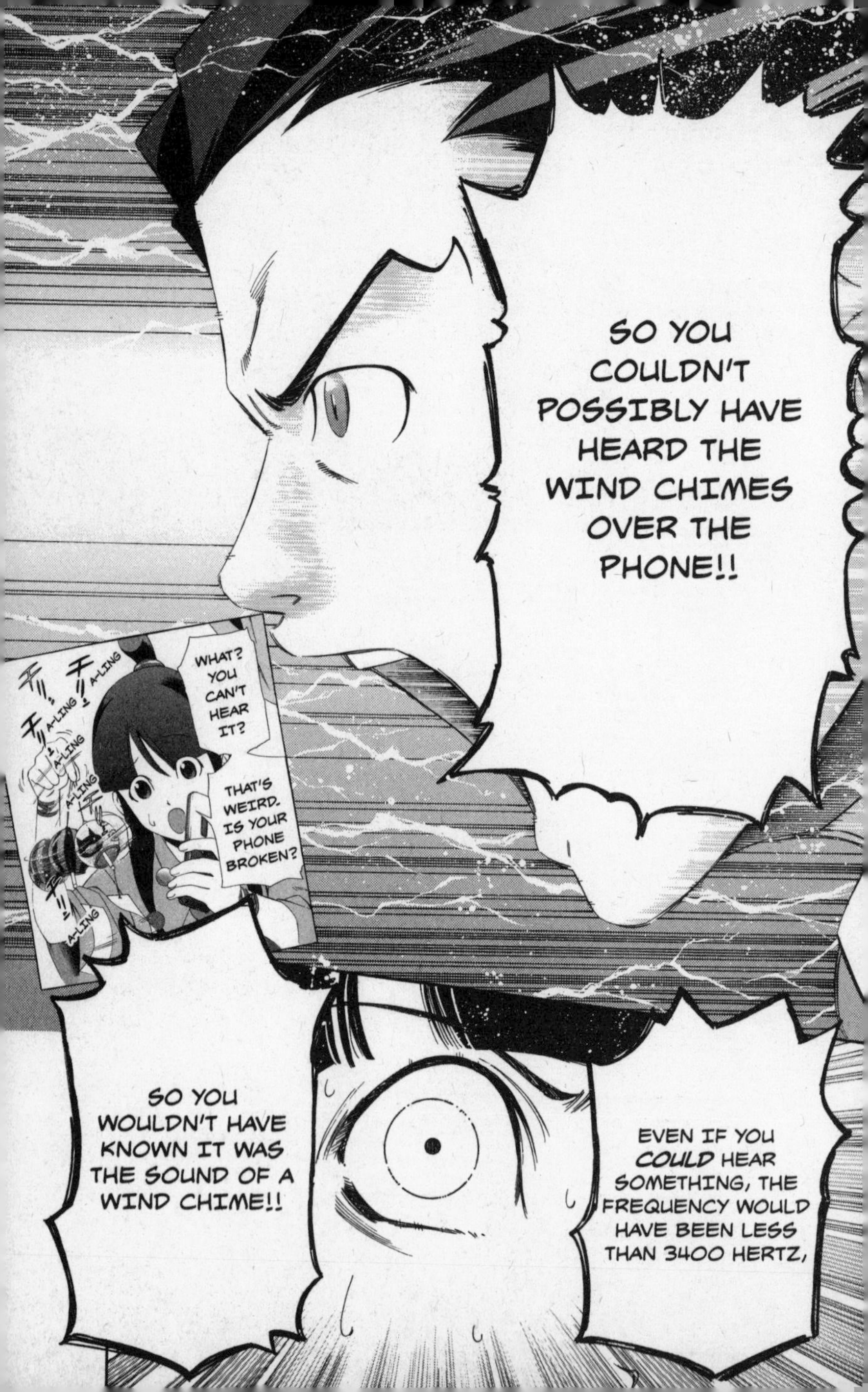
SO YOU COULDN'T POSSIBLY HAVE HEARD THE WIND CHIMES OVER THE PHONE!!
WHAT? YOU CAN'T HEAR IT?
THAT'S WEIRD. IS YOUR PHONE BROKEN?
A-LING
A-LING
A-LING
A-LING
A-LING
EVEN IF YOU COULD HEAR SOMETHING, THE FREQUENCY WOULD HAVE BEEN LESS THAN 3400 HERTZ,
SO YOU WOULDN'T HAVE KNOWN IT WAS THE SOUND OF A WIND CHIME!!

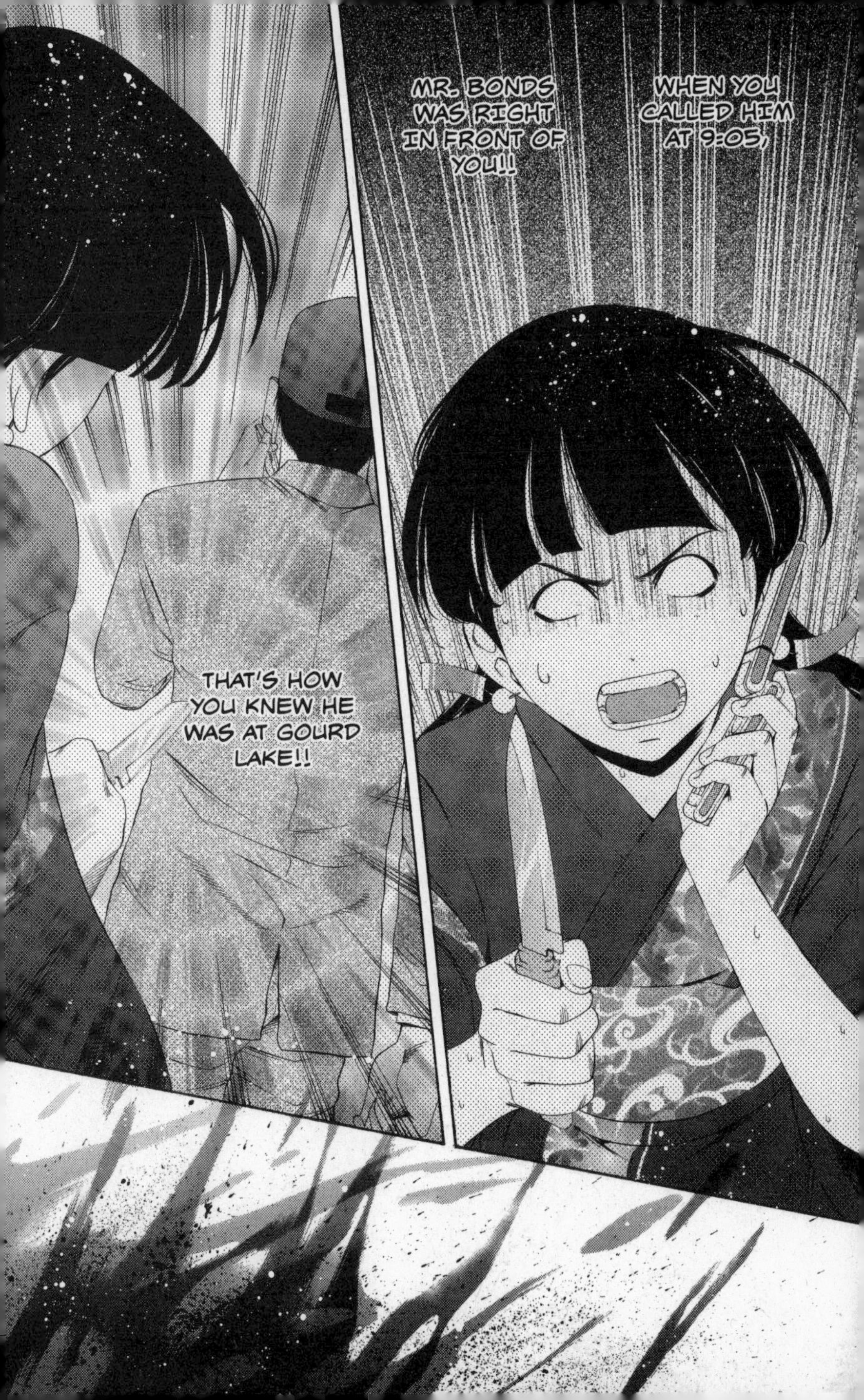
WHEN YOU CALLED HIM AT 9:05,
MR. BONDS WAS RIGHT IN FRONT OF YOU!!
THAT'S HOW YOU KNEW HE WAS AT GOURD LAKE!!

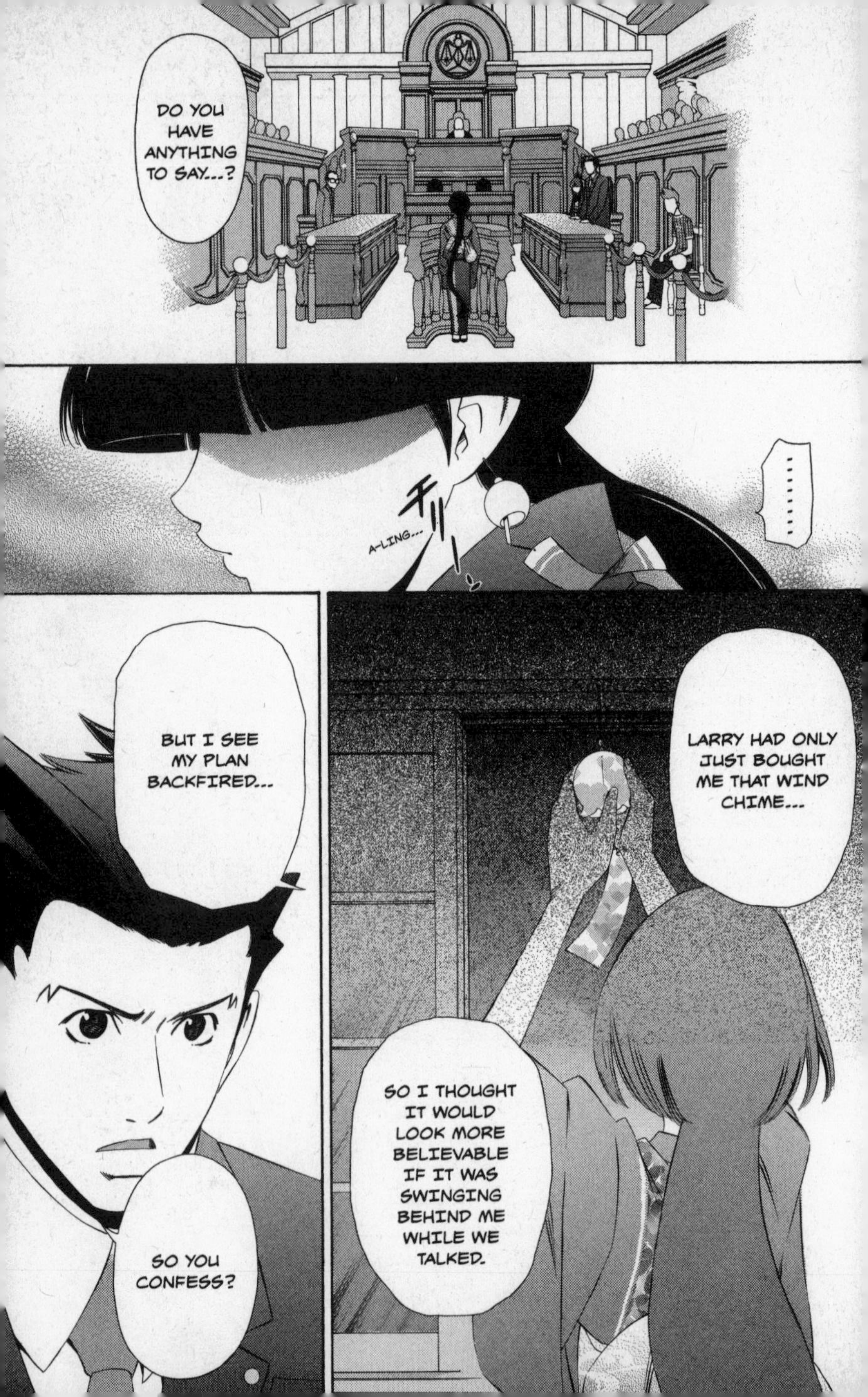
DO YOU HAVE ANYTHING TO SAY...?
........
A-LING...
LARRY HAD ONLY JUST BOUGHT ME THAT WIND CHIME...
SO I THOUGHT IT WOULD LOOK MORE BELIEVABLE IF IT WAS SWINGING BEHIND ME WHILE WE TALKED.
BUT I SEE MY PLAN BACKFIRED...
SO YOU CONFESS?

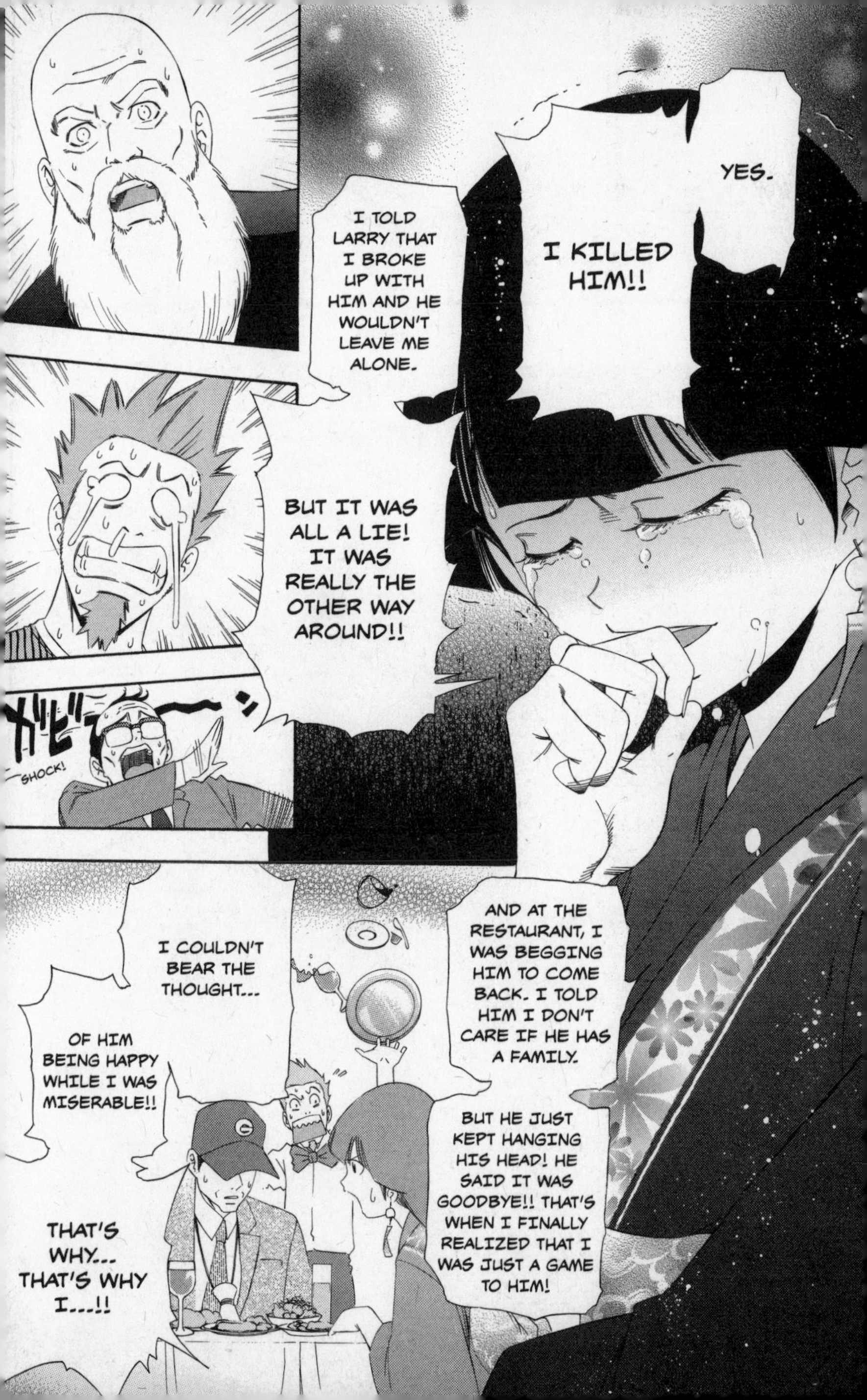
YES.
I KILLED HIM!!
I TOLD LARRY THAT I BROKE UP WITH HIM AND HE WOULDN'T LEAVE ME ALONE.
BUT IT WAS ALL A LIE! IT WAS REALLY THE OTHER WAY AROUND!!
ガビーン
SHOCK!
AND AT THE RESTAURANT, I WAS BEGGING HIM TO COME BACK. I TOLD HIM I DON'T CARE IF HE HAS A FAMILY.
BUT HE JUST KEPT HANGING HIS HEAD! HE SAID IT WAS GOODBYE!! THAT'S WHEN I FINALLY REALIZED THAT I WAS JUST A GAME TO HIM!
I COULDN'T BEAR THE THOUGHT...
OF HIM BEING HAPPY WHILE I WAS MISERABLE!!
THAT'S WHY... THAT'S WHY I...!!

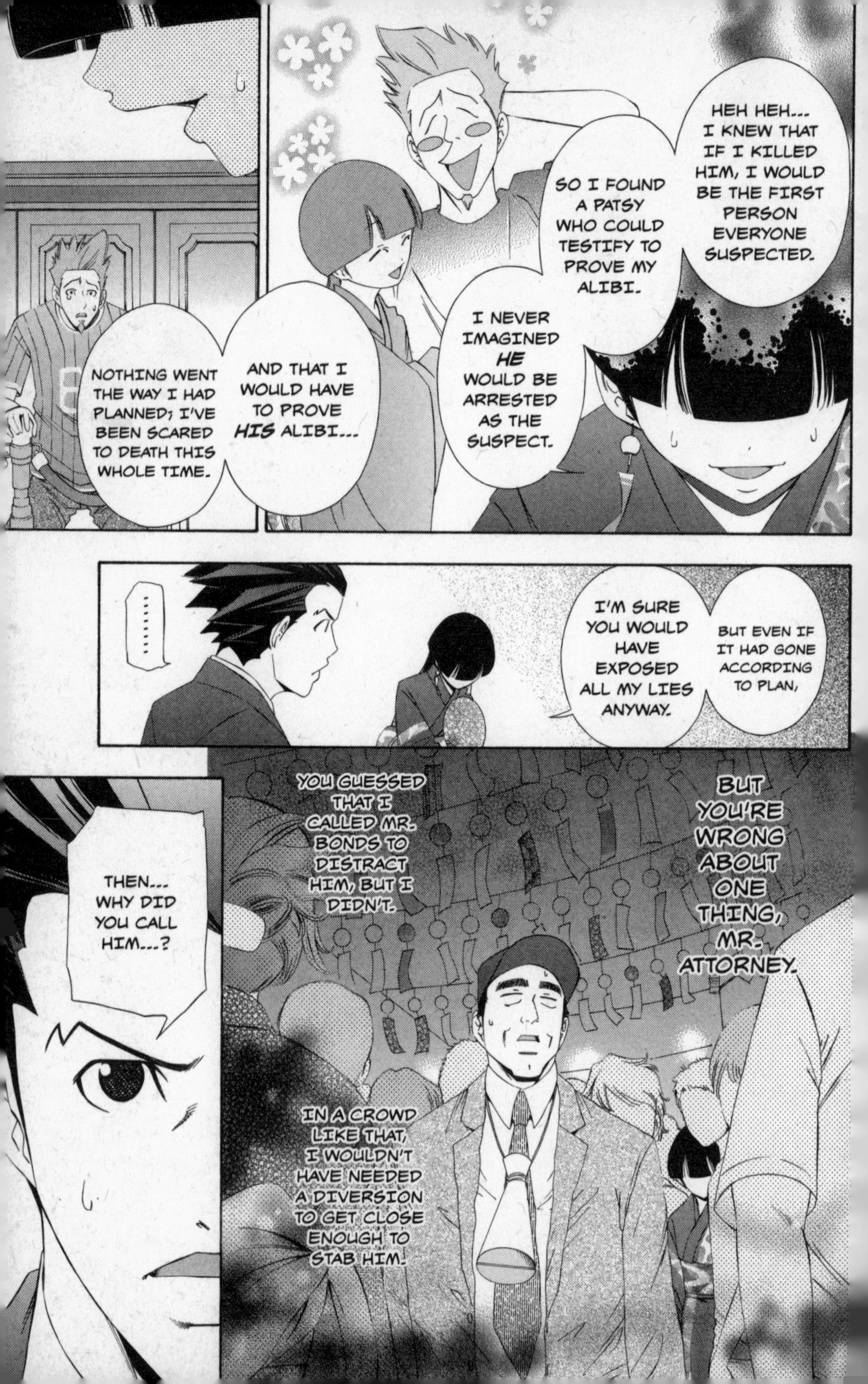

HEH HEH... I KNEW THAT IF I KILLED HIM, I WOULD BE THE FIRST PERSON EVERYONE SUSPECTED.
SO I FOUND A PATSY WHO COULD TESTIFY TO PROVE MY ALIBI.
I NEVER IMAGINED *HE* WOULD BE ARRESTED AS THE SUSPECT.
AND THAT I WOULD HAVE TO PROVE *HIS* ALIBI...
NOTHING WENT THE WAY I HAD PLANNED; I'VE BEEN SCARED TO DEATH THIS WHOLE TIME.
BUT EVEN IF IT HAD GONE ACCORDING TO PLAN,
I'M SURE YOU WOULD HAVE EXPOSED ALL MY LIES ANYWAY.
.......
BUT YOU'RE WRONG ABOUT ONE THING, MR. ATTORNEY.
YOU GUESSED THAT I CALLED MR. BONDS TO DISTRACT HIM, BUT I DIDN'T.
IN A CROWD LIKE THAT, I WOULDN'T HAVE NEEDED A DIVERSION TO GET CLOSE ENOUGH TO STAB HIM.
THEN... WHY DID YOU CALL HIM...?

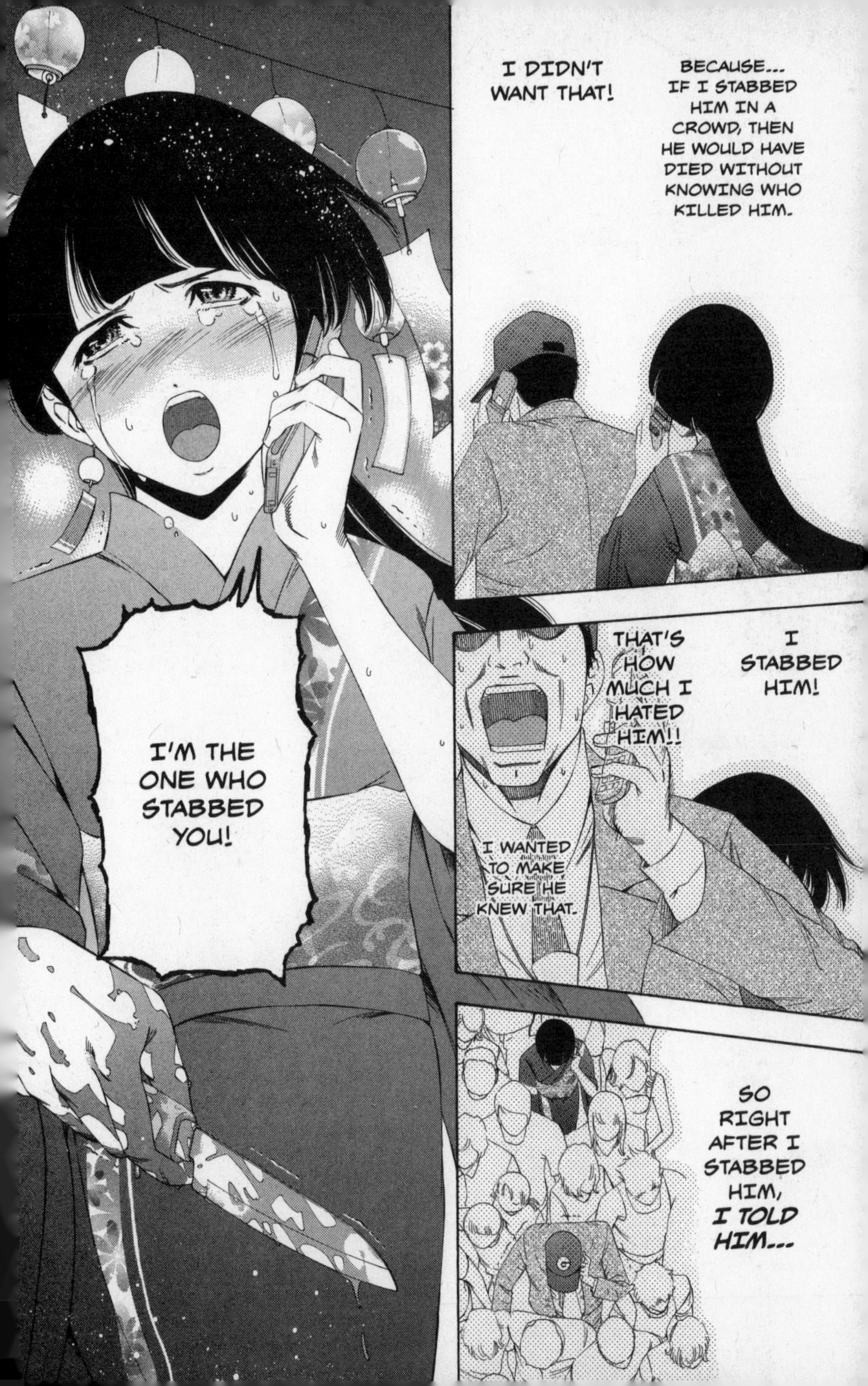
BECAUSE... IF I STABBED HIM IN A CROWD, THEN HE WOULD HAVE DIED WITHOUT KNOWING WHO KILLED HIM.
I DIDN'T WANT THAT!
I STABBED HIM!
THAT'S HOW MUCH I HATED HIM!!
I WANTED TO MAKE SURE HE KNEW THAT.
SO RIGHT AFTER I STABBED HIM, *I TOLD HIM...*
I'M THE ONE WHO STABBED YOU!

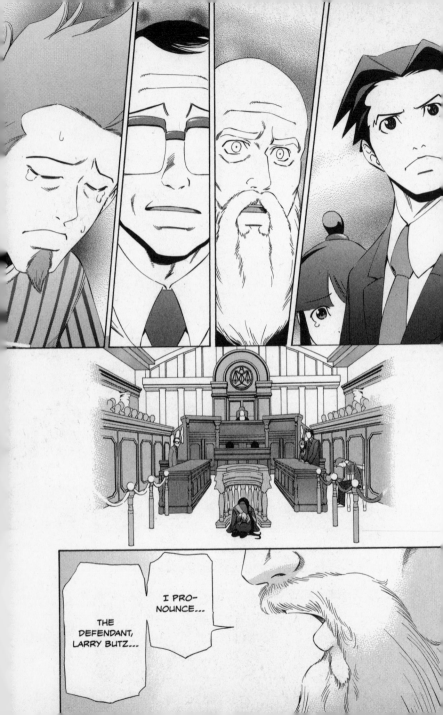

I PRO-NOUNCE...

THE DEFENDANT, LARRY BUTZ...

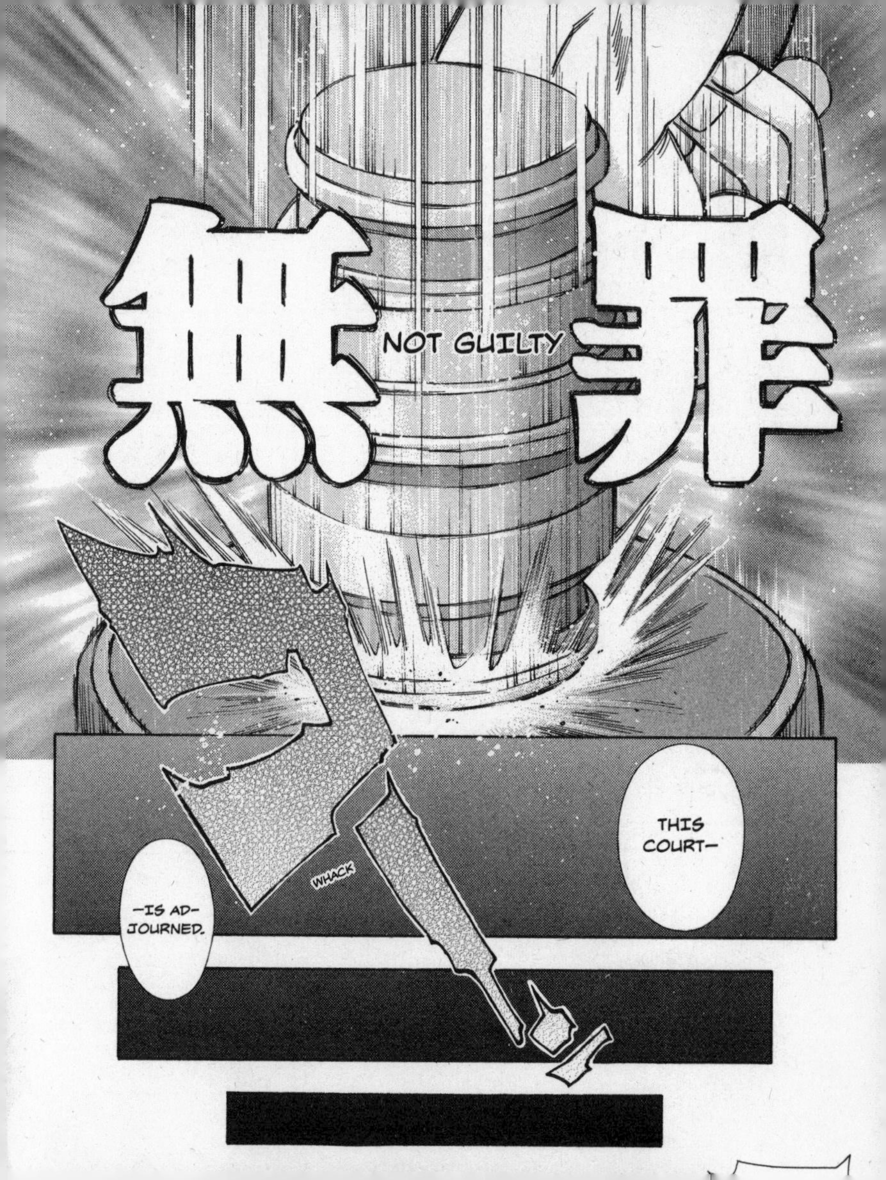
無罪
NOT GUILTY
WHACK
THIS COURT—
—IS AD-JOURNED.

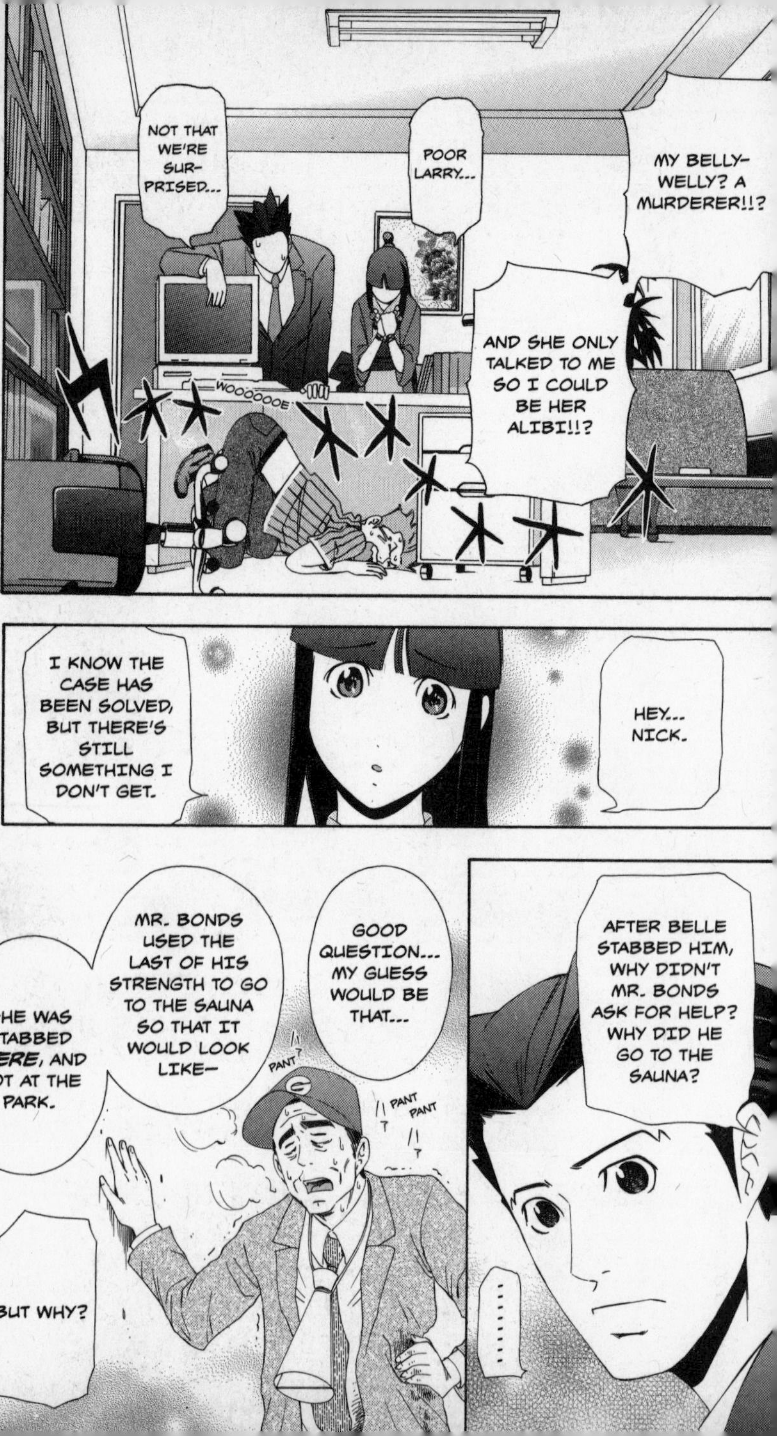
MY BELLY-WELLY? A MURDERER!!?
AND SHE ONLY TALKED TO ME SO I COULD BE HER ALIBI!!?
POOR LARRY...
NOT THAT WE'RE SUR-PRISED...
WOOOOOOE
HEY... NICK.
I KNOW THE CASE HAS BEEN SOLVED, BUT THERE'S STILL SOMETHING I DON'T GET.
AFTER BELLE STABBED HIM, WHY DIDN'T MR. BONDS ASK FOR HELP? WHY DID HE GO TO THE SAUNA?
......
GOOD QUESTION... MY GUESS WOULD BE THAT...
MR. BONDS USED THE LAST OF HIS STRENGTH TO GO TO THE SAUNA SO THAT IT WOULD LOOK LIKE—
—HE WAS STABBED *THERE*, AND NOT AT THE PARK.
PANT
PANT
PANT
BUT WHY?

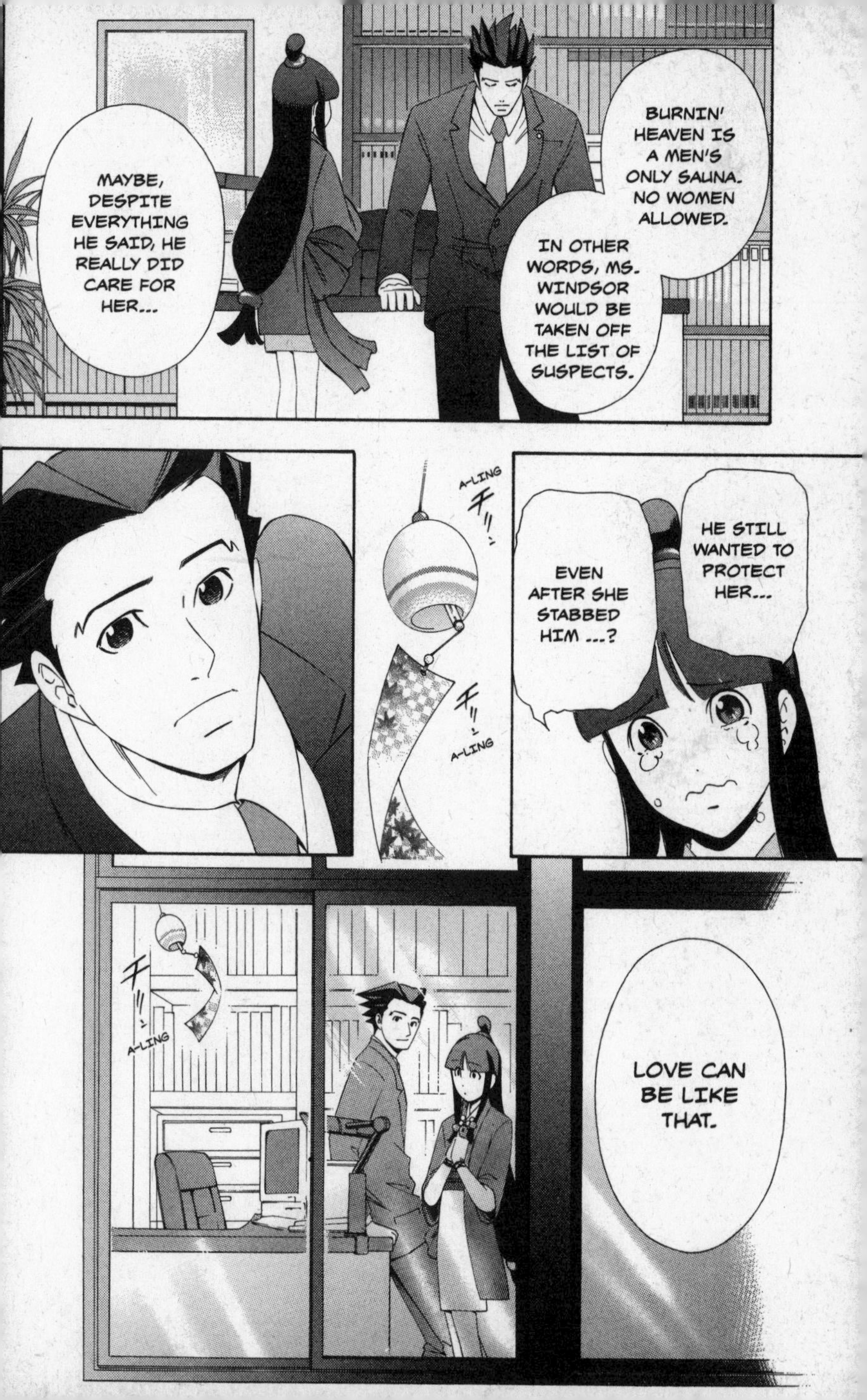
BURNIN' HEAVEN IS A MEN'S ONLY SAUNA. NO WOMEN ALLOWED.
IN OTHER WORDS, MS. WINDSOR WOULD BE TAKEN OFF THE LIST OF SUSPECTS.
MAYBE, DESPITE EVERYTHING HE SAID, HE REALLY DID CARE FOR HER...
HE STILL WANTED TO PROTECT HER...
EVEN AFTER SHE STABBED HIM ...?
A-LING
A-LING
LOVE CAN BE LIKE THAT.
A-LING

Ace Phoenix Wright
Attorney™

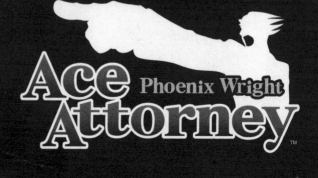

## SCRIPT: KENJI KURODA

Pleased to meet you, everyone. I'm Kuroda, a mystery writer. This was a new experience for me—I'd never written an original story using existing characters, or written the script for a manga before. My heart was pounding the whole time—I had no idea how it was going to work out. But Ms. Kazuo Maekawa draws such a wonderful world, and I think that we've made something pretty entertaining. I'm very satisfied with how it turned out. Please continue to support this Ace Attorney series forever, along with all of the games.

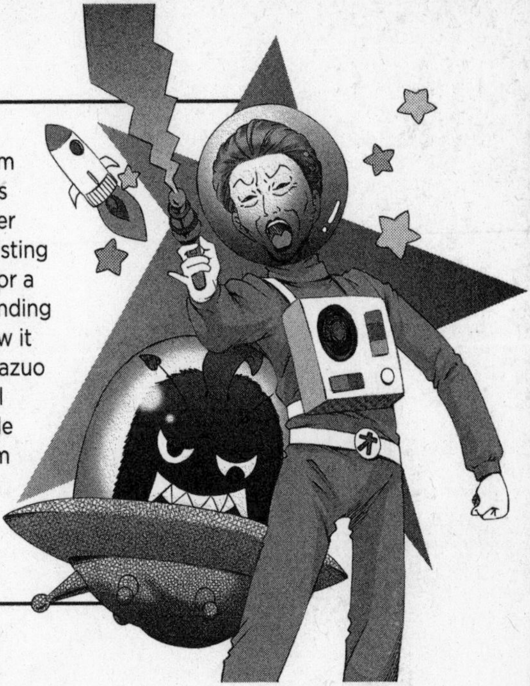

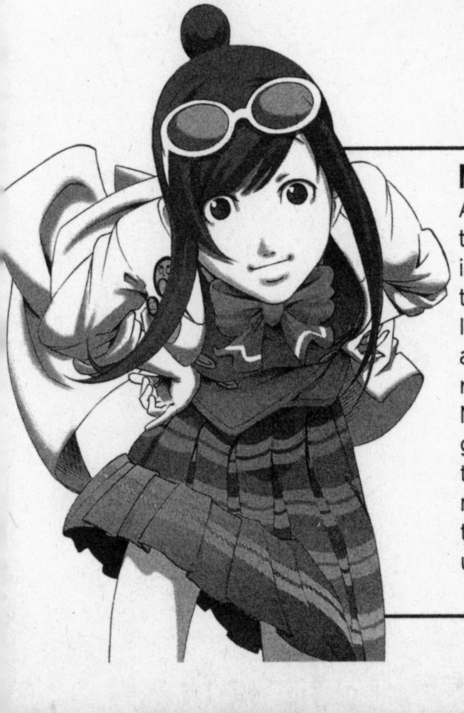

## MANGA: KAZUO MAEKAWA

After I beat Ace Attorney (the game), the story and characters were so interesting, I thought, "I wanna make this a manga!!" A few years after that, I really did get put in charge of the art for the manga version!! Wishes really do come true! I'm so happy!! My favorite character from the game is Ema Skye, from "Rise from the Ashes." If I wish reeeeally hard, maybe I can put her in the manga, too? (But the way I'd draw her, she'd upstage Phoenix!)

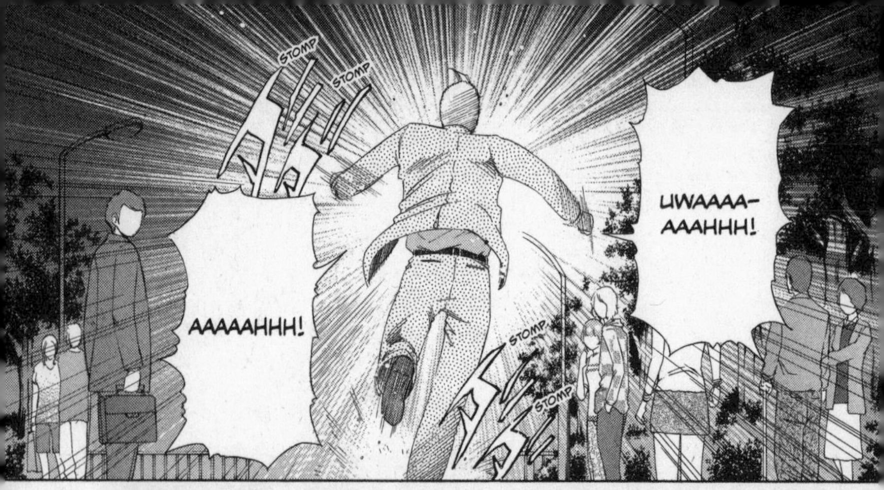
UWAAAA-AAAHHH!
STOMP
STOMP
STOMP
STOMP
AAAAAHHH!

0

SEPTEMBER 6, 10:25 PM

EXPOSÉ PARK

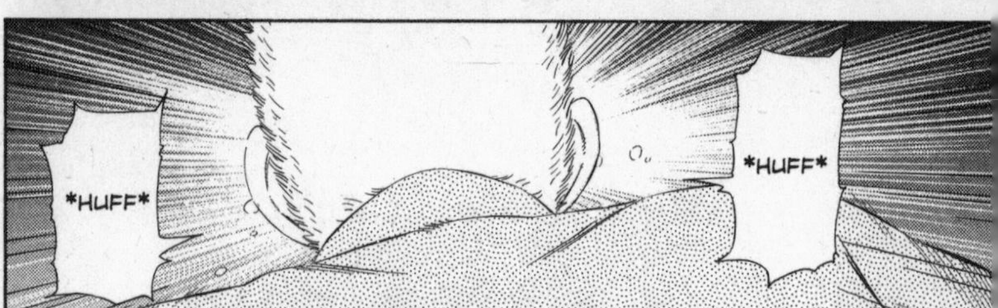
*HUFF*
*HUFF*

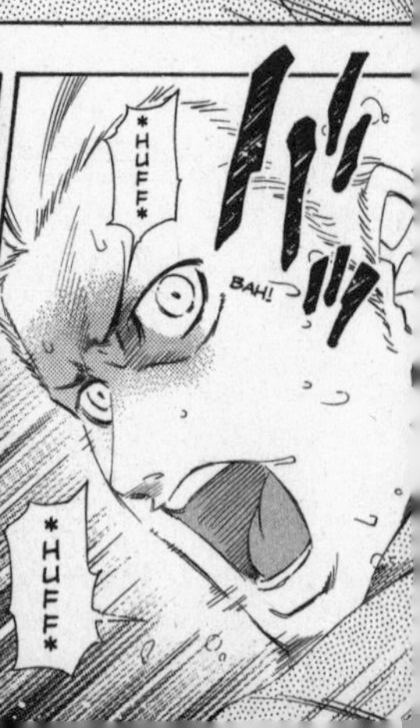
*HUFF*
BAH!
*HUFF*

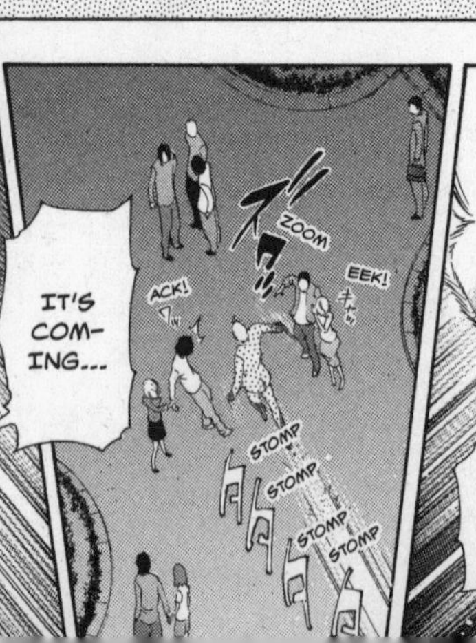
ZOOM
EEK!
ACK!
IT'S COM-ING...
STOMP
STOMP
STOMP
STOMP

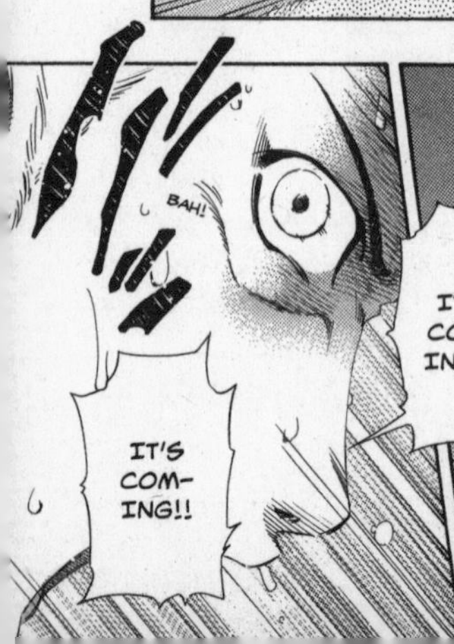
BAH!
IT'S COM-ING!!

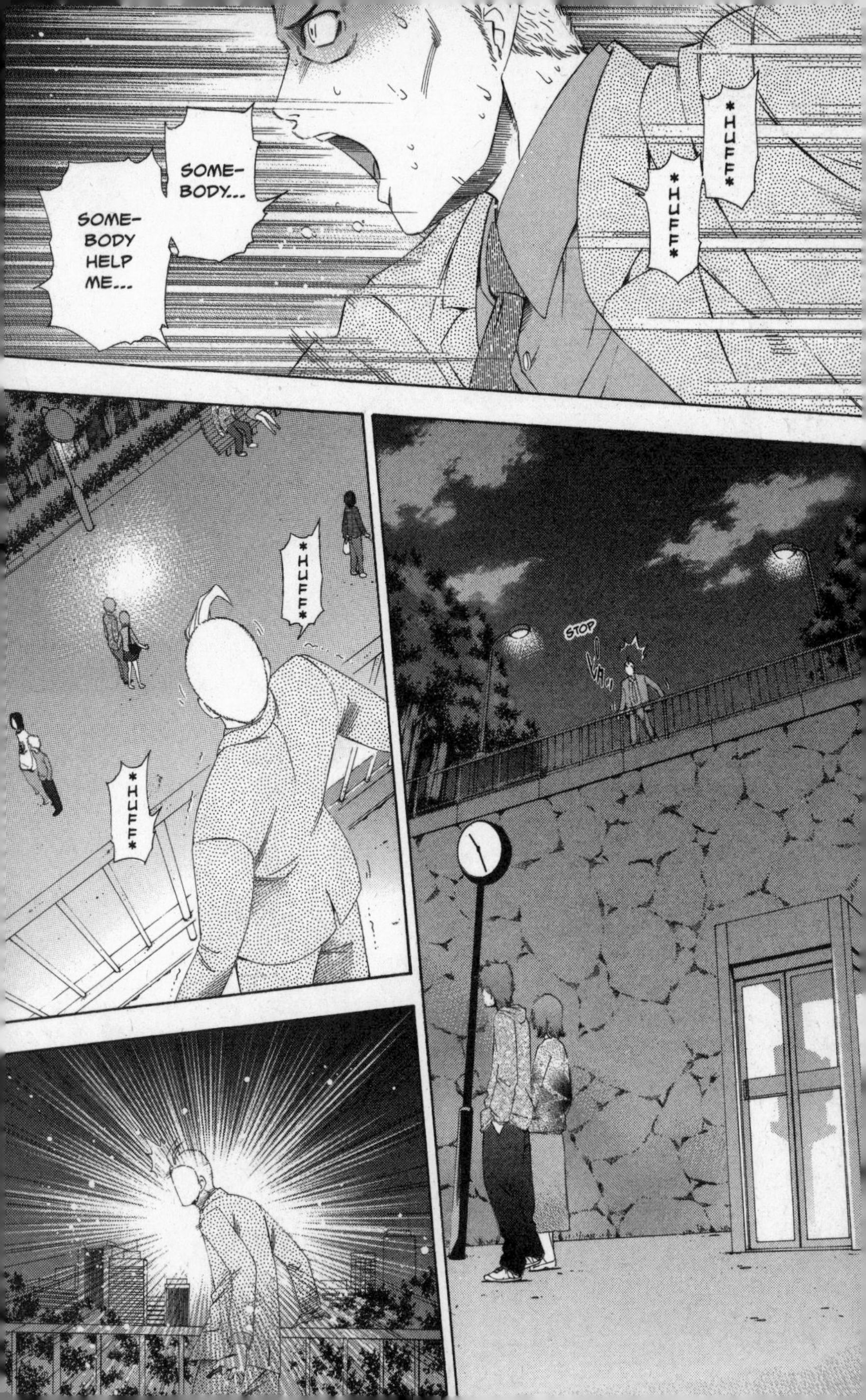
*HUFF*
*HUFF*
SOME-BODY...
SOME-BODY HELP ME...
STOP
*HUFF*
*HUFF*

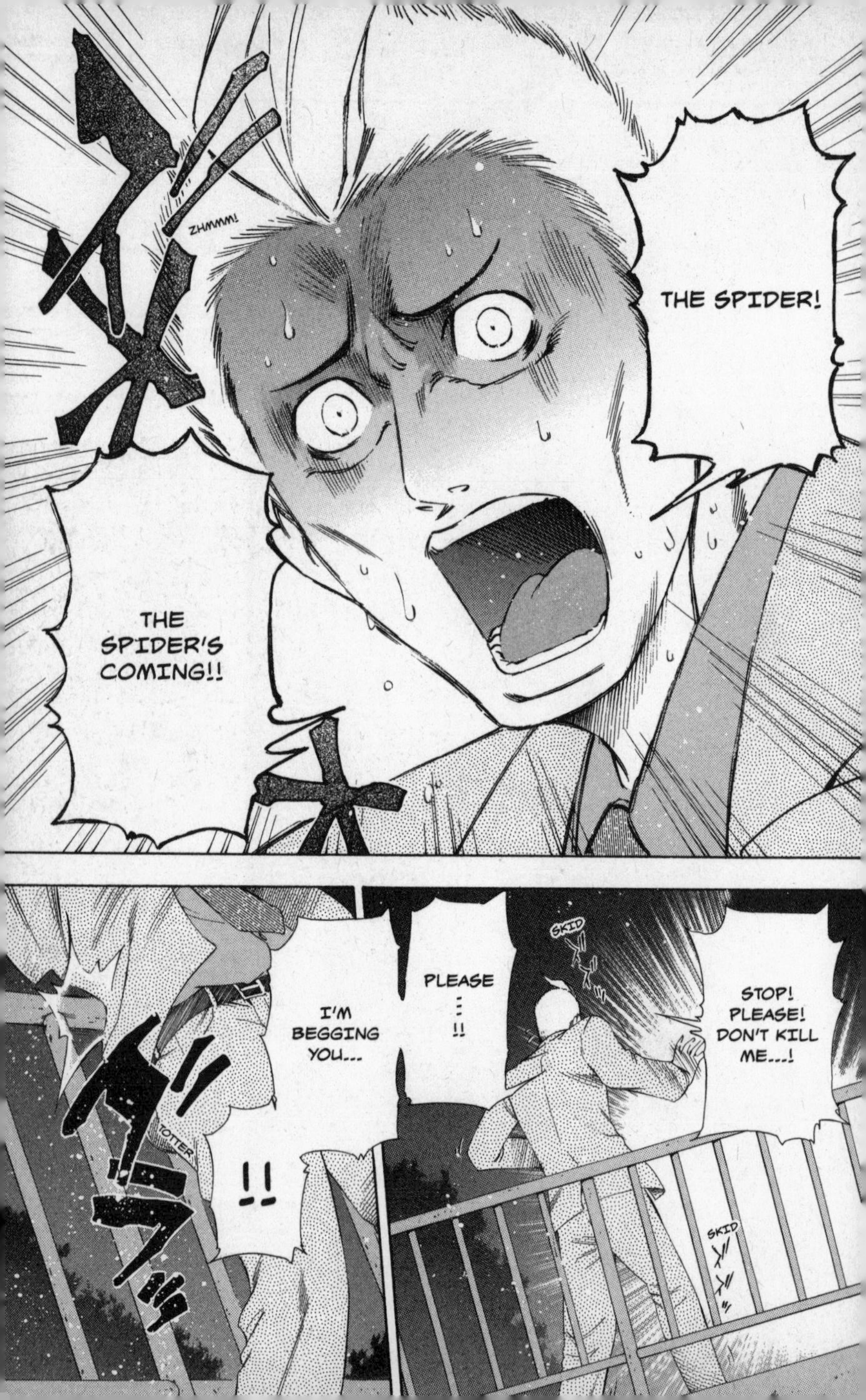
THE SPIDER!
ZHMMM!
THE SPIDER'S COMING!!
SKID
STOP! PLEASE! DON'T KILL ME...!
SKID
PLEASE...!!
I'M BEGGING YOU...
!!
TOTTER

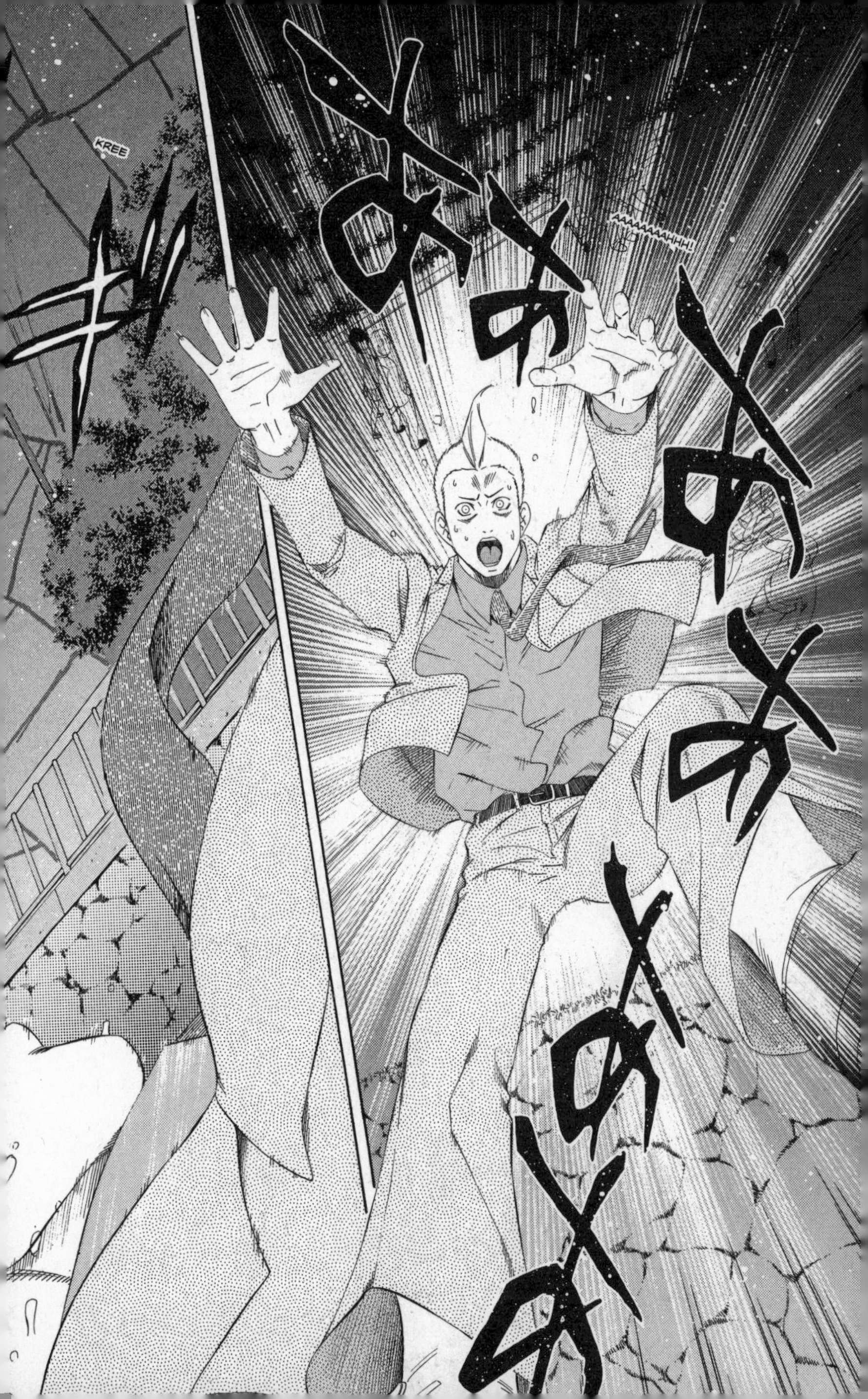
AAAAAAAAAAHHHH!
KREE

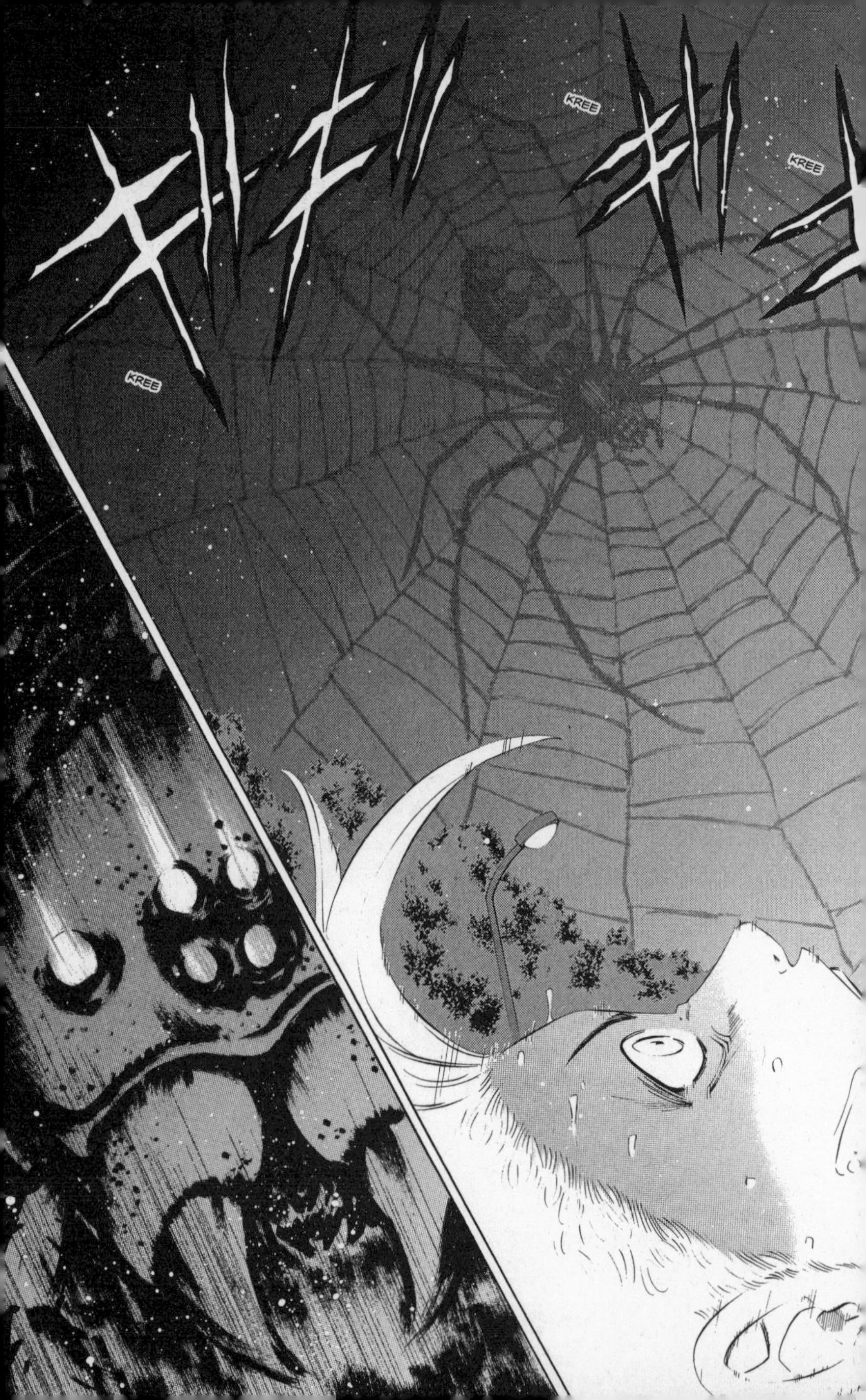
KREE
KREE
KREE

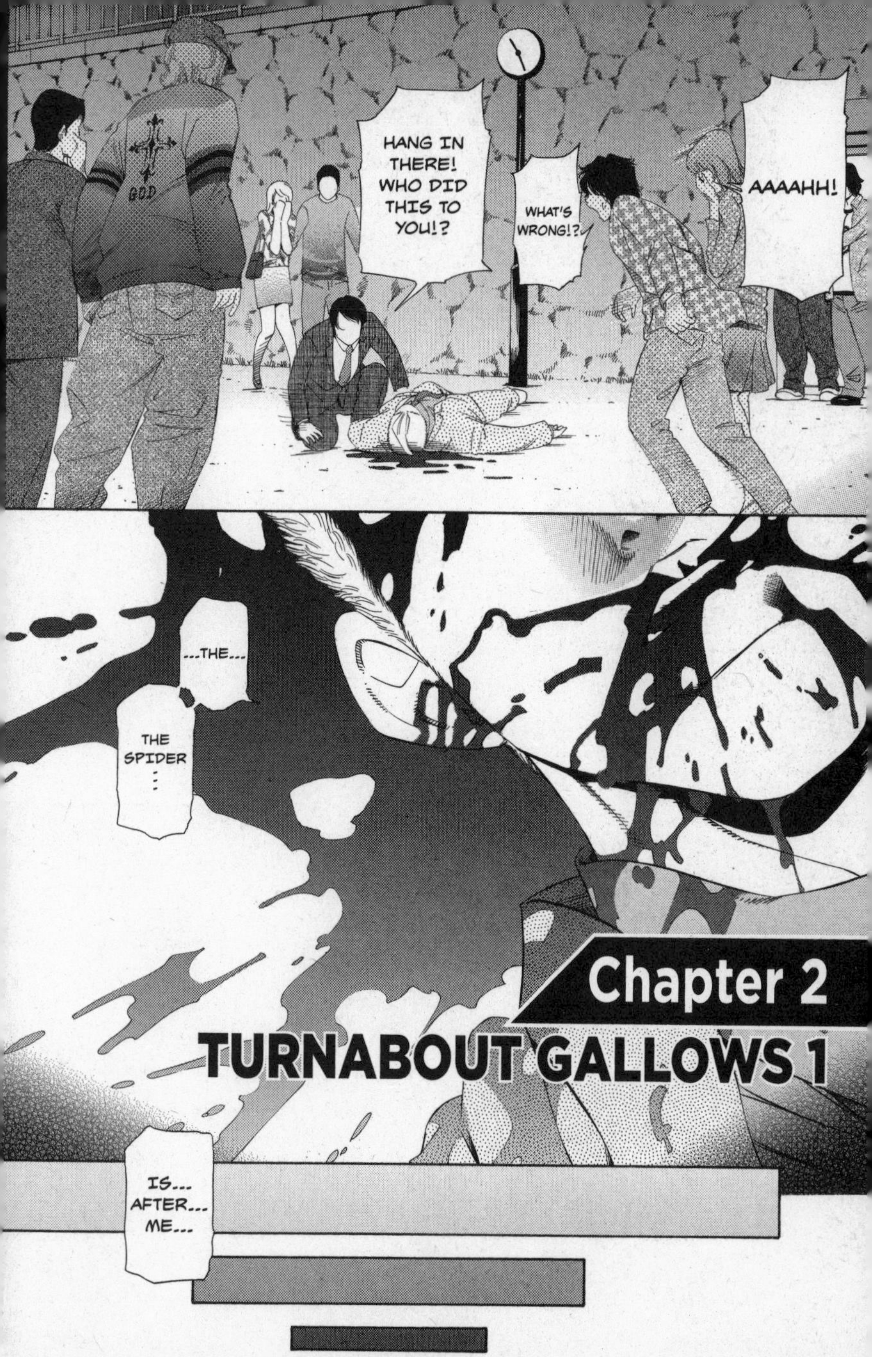
AAAAHH!
WHAT'S WRONG!?
HANG IN THERE! WHO DID THIS TO YOU!?
...THE...
THE SPIDER...
Chapter 2
TURNABOUT GALLOWS 1
IS... AFTER... ME...

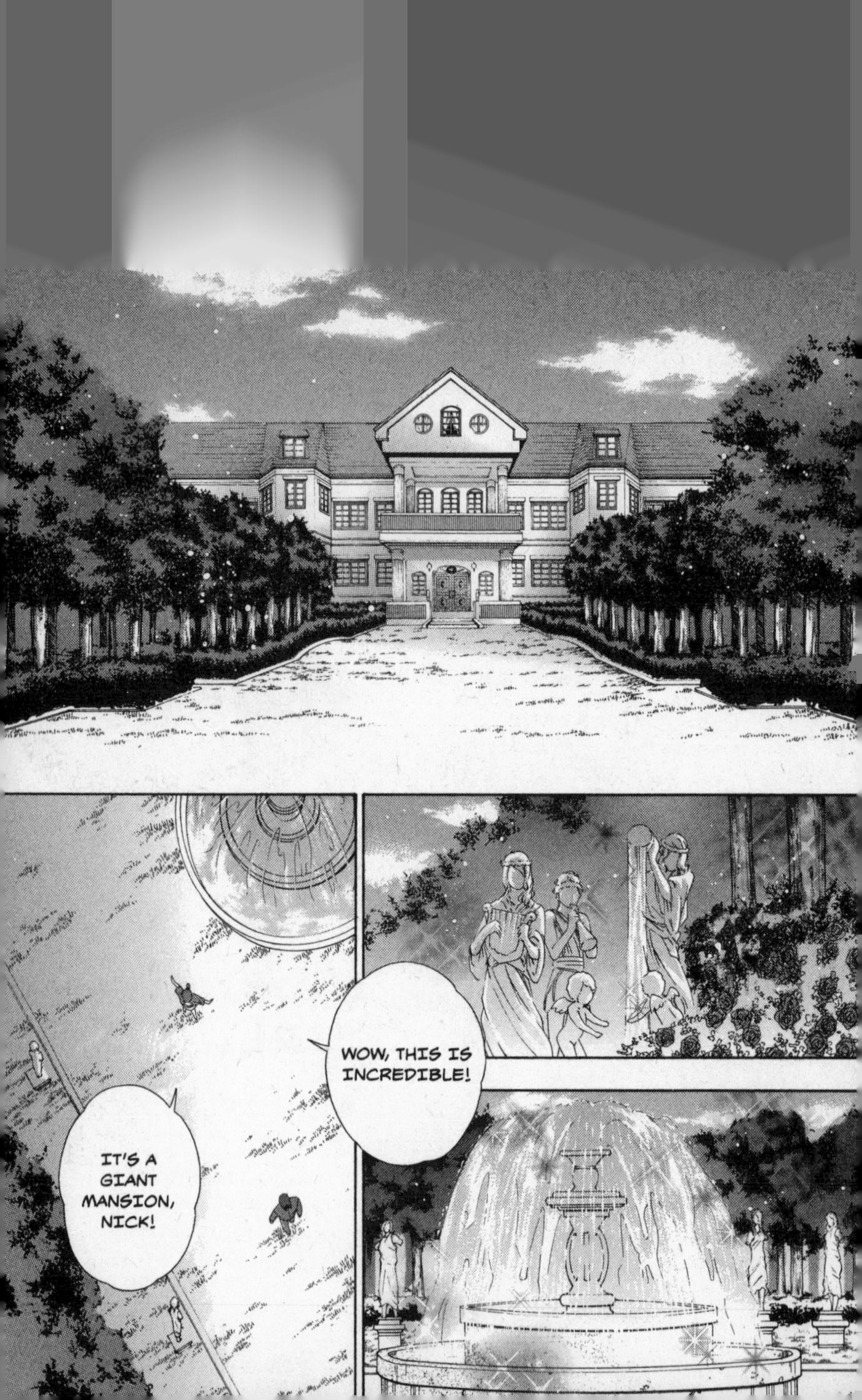
WOW, THIS IS INCREDIBLE!
IT'S A GIANT MANSION, NICK!

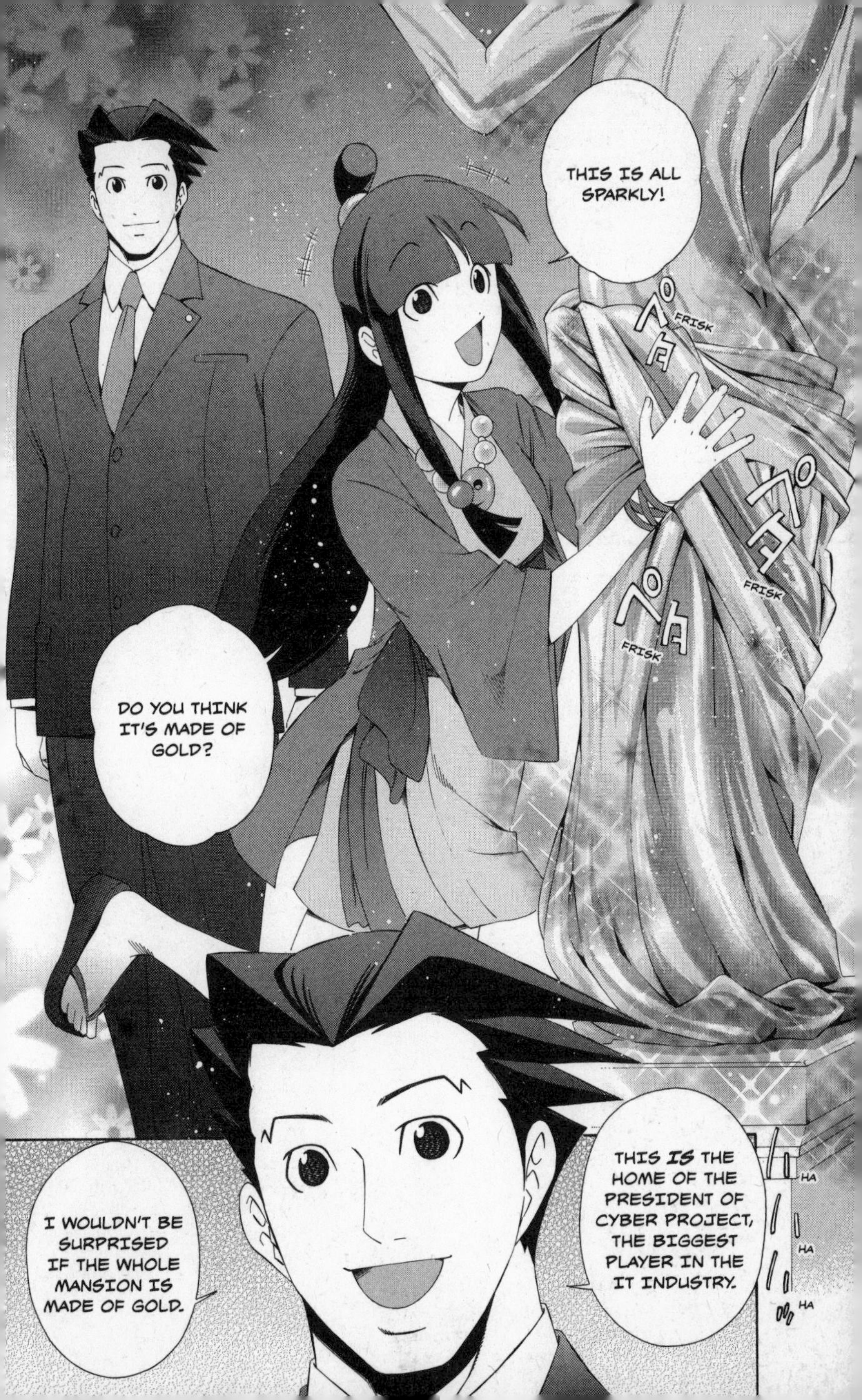
THIS IS ALL SPARKLY!
ペタ FRISK
ペタ FRISK
ペタ FRISK
DO YOU THINK IT'S MADE OF GOLD?
THIS *IS* THE HOME OF THE PRESIDENT OF CYBER PROJECT, THE BIGGEST PLAYER IN THE IT INDUSTRY.
HA
HA
HA
I WOULDN'T BE SURPRISED IF THE WHOLE MANSION IS MADE OF GOLD.

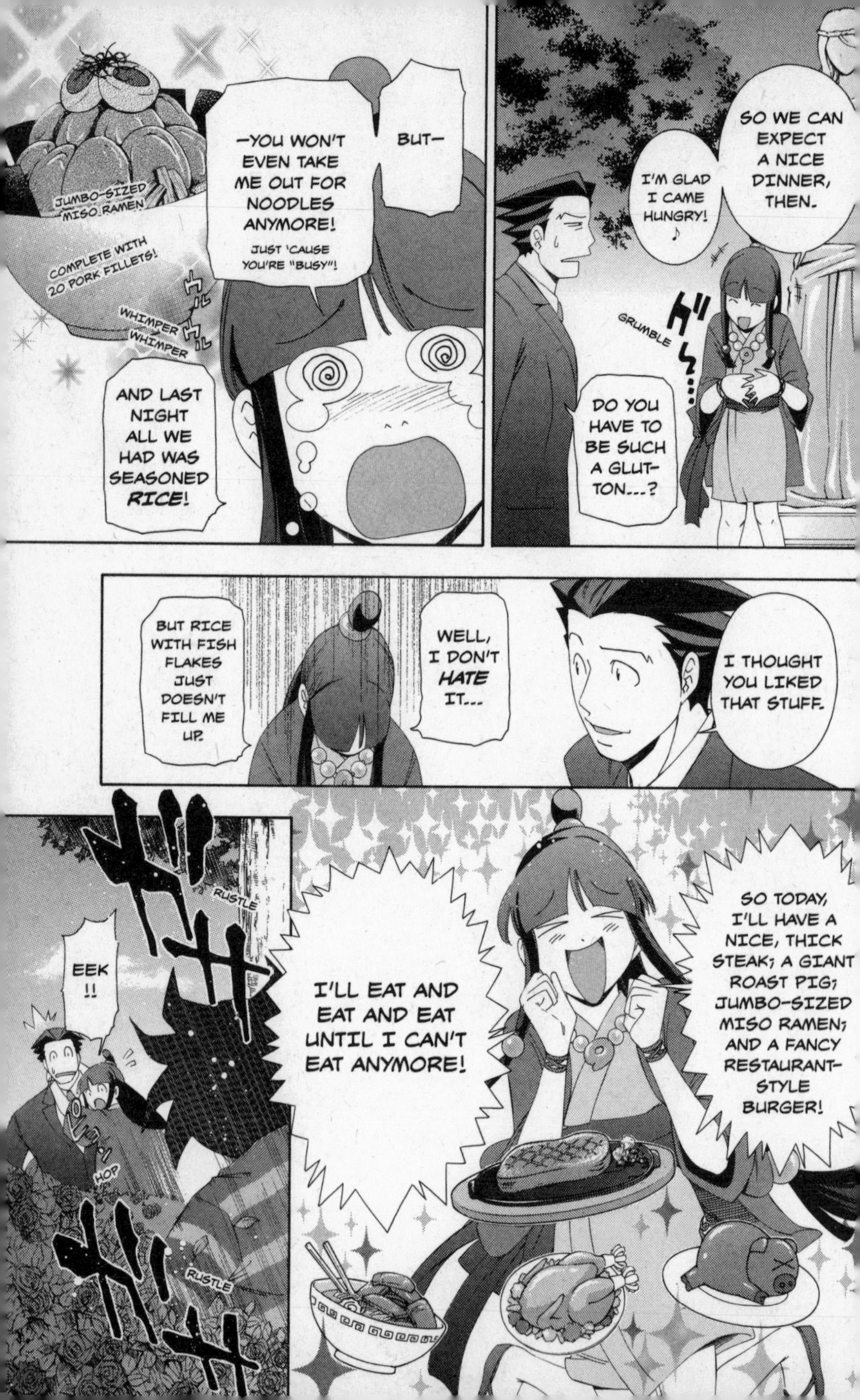
SO WE CAN EXPECT A NICE DINNER, THEN.
I'M GLAD I CAME HUNGRY! ♪
GRUMBLE
DO YOU HAVE TO BE SUCH A GLUT-TON...?
BUT—
—YOU WON'T EVEN TAKE ME OUT FOR NOODLES ANYMORE!
JUST 'CAUSE YOU'RE "BUSY"!
JUMBO-SIZED MISO RAMEN
COMPLETE WITH 20 PORK FILLETS!
WHIMPER WHIMPER
AND LAST NIGHT ALL WE HAD WAS SEASONED *RICE*!
I THOUGHT YOU LIKED THAT STUFF.
WELL, I DON'T *HATE* IT...
BUT RICE WITH FISH FLAKES JUST DOESN'T FILL ME UP.
SO TODAY, I'LL HAVE A NICE, THICK STEAK; A GIANT ROAST PIG; JUMBO-SIZED MISO RAMEN; AND A FANCY RESTAURANT-STYLE BURGER!
I'LL EAT AND EAT AND EAT UNTIL I CAN'T EAT ANYMORE!
RUSTLE
EEK !!
HOP
RUSTLE

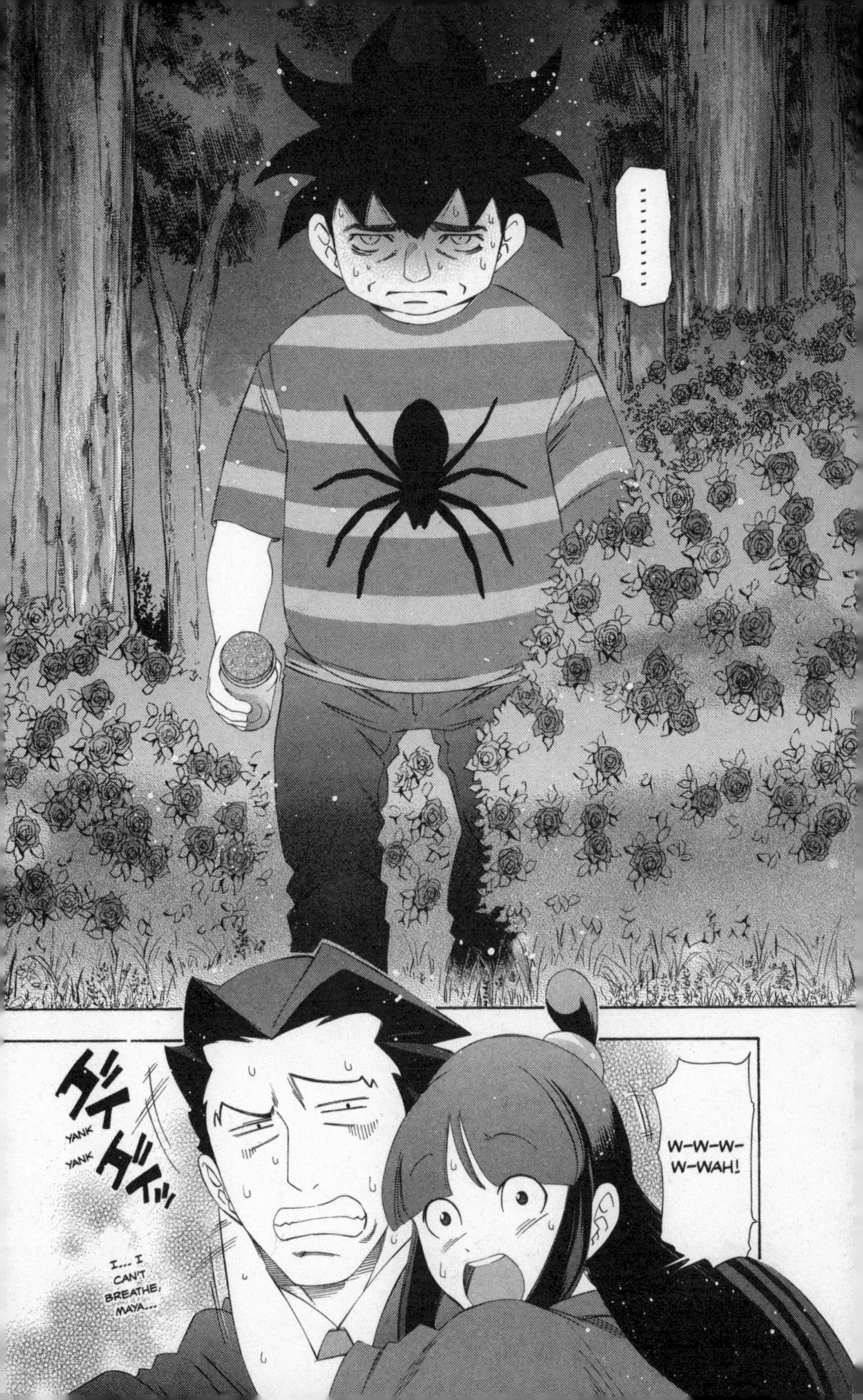
......
W-W-W-W-WAH!
YANK YANK
I... I CAN'T BREATHE, MAYA...

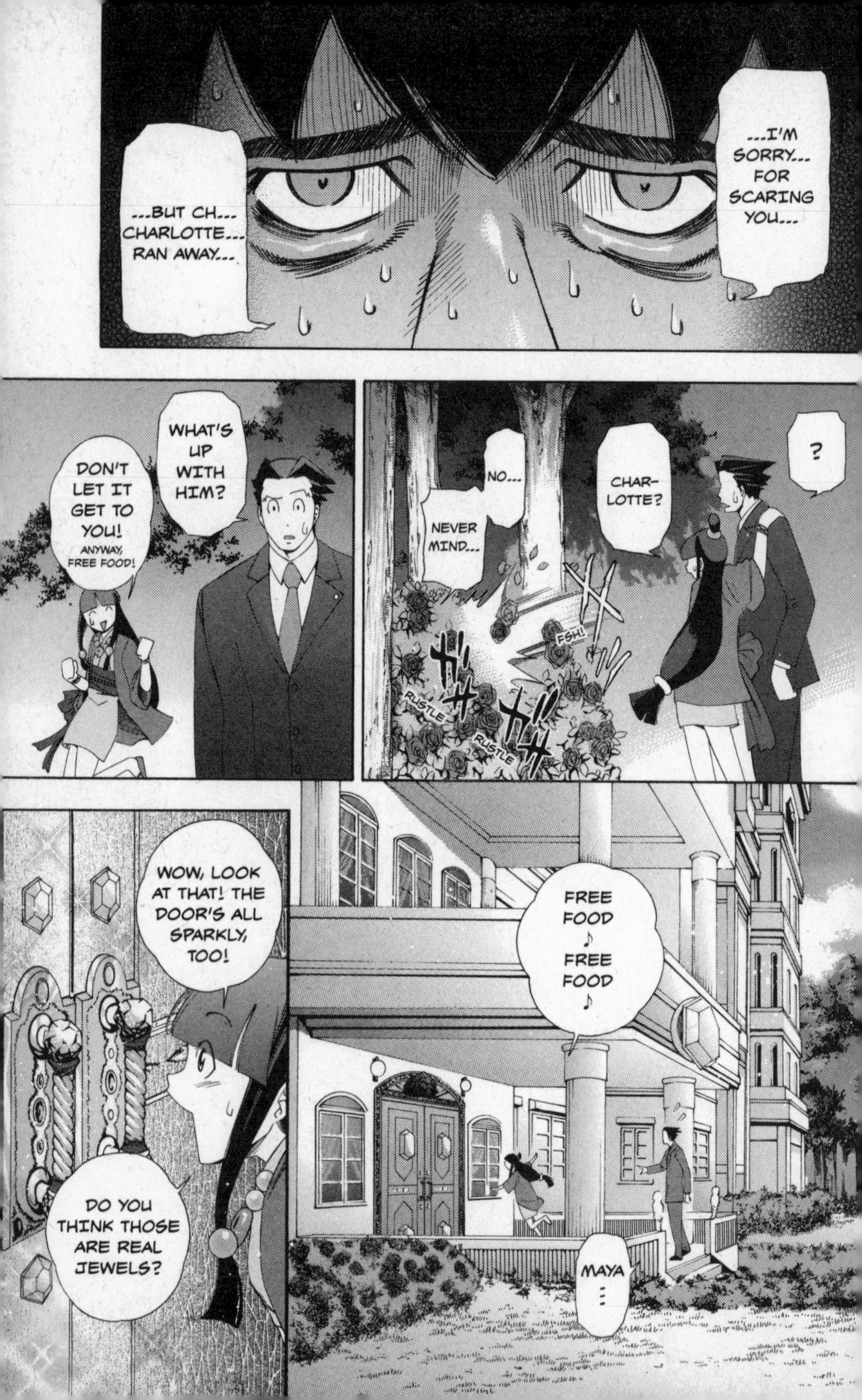
...I'M SORRY... FOR SCARING YOU...
...BUT CH... CHARLOTTE... RAN AWAY...
?
CHAR-LOTTE?
NO...
NEVER MIND...
FSH!
RUSTLE
RUSTLE
WHAT'S UP WITH HIM?
DON'T LET IT GET TO YOU!
ANYWAY, FREE FOOD!
FREE FOOD ♪ FREE FOOD ♪
MAYA ...
WOW, LOOK AT THAT! THE DOOR'S ALL SPARKLY, TOO!
DO YOU THINK THOSE ARE REAL JEWELS?

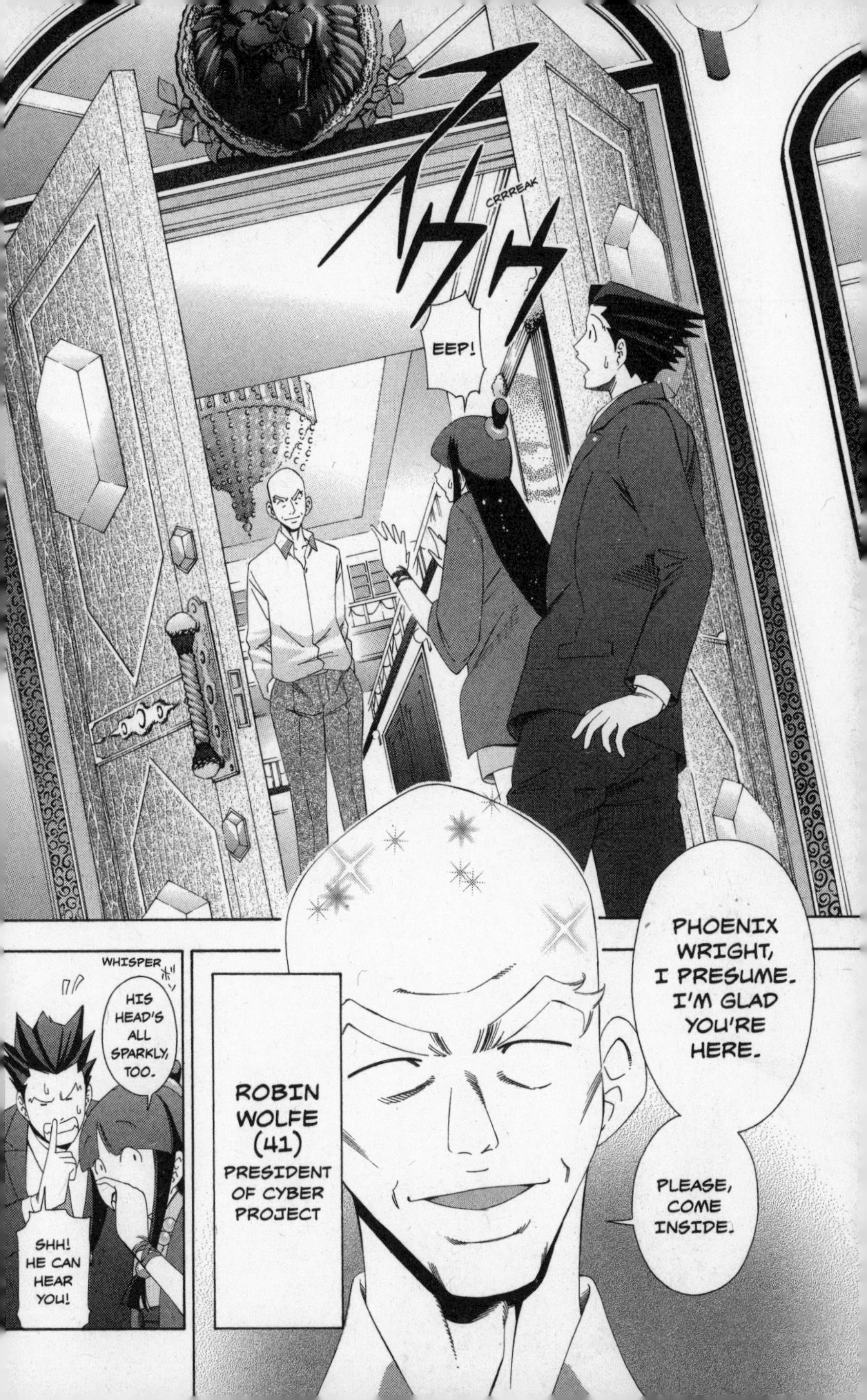
CRRREAK
EEP!
PHOENIX WRIGHT, I PRESUME. I'M GLAD YOU'RE HERE.
PLEASE, COME INSIDE.
ROBIN WOLFE (41) PRESIDENT OF CYBER PROJECT
WHISPER
HIS HEAD'S ALL SPARKLY, TOO.
SHH! HE CAN HEAR YOU!

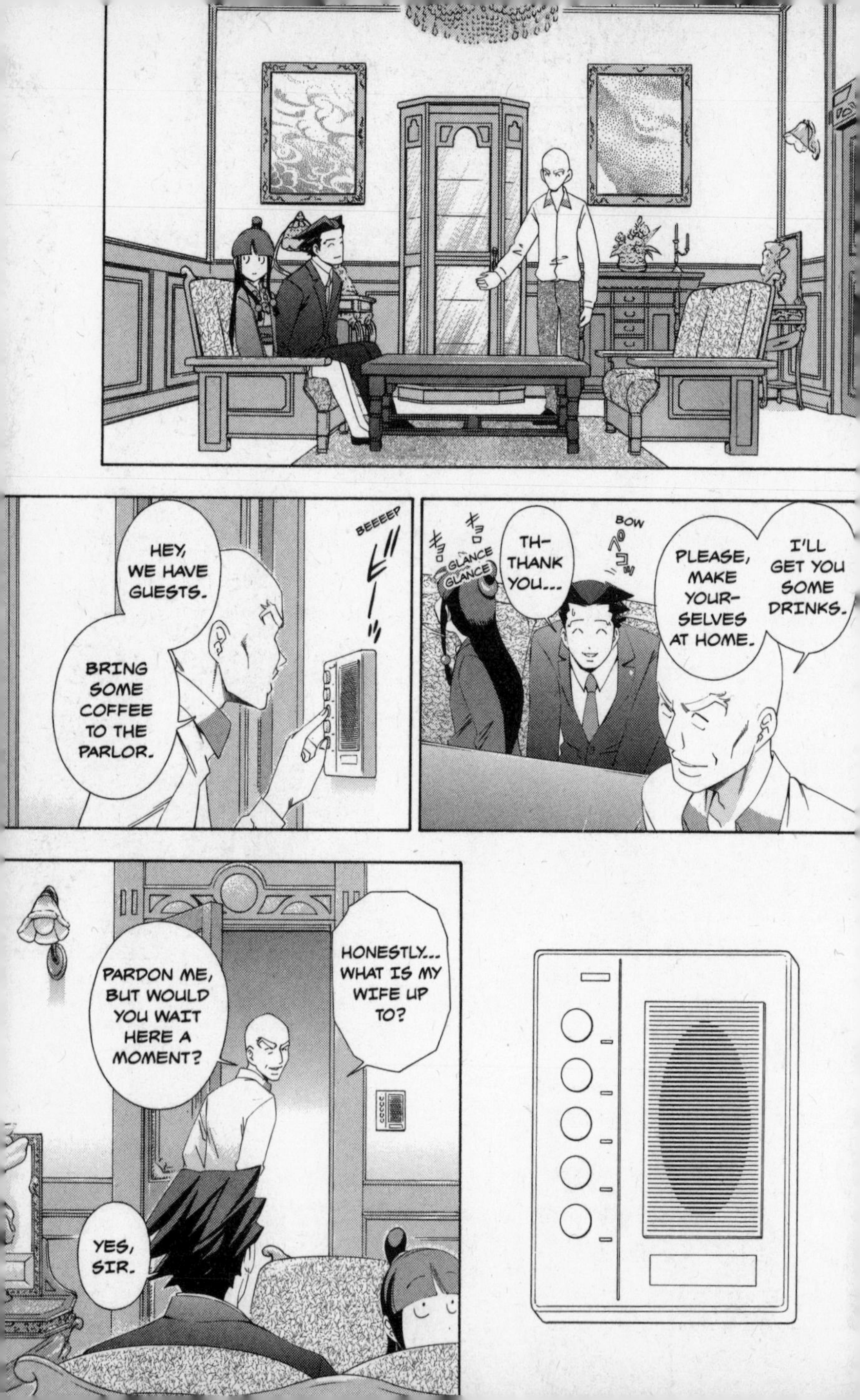
I'LL GET YOU SOME DRINKS.
PLEASE, MAKE YOUR-SELVES AT HOME.
BOW
TH-THANK YOU...
GLANCE GLANCE
BEEEEP
HEY, WE HAVE GUESTS.
BRING SOME COFFEE TO THE PARLOR.
HONESTLY... WHAT IS MY WIFE UP TO?
PARDON ME, BUT WOULD YOU WAIT HERE A MOMENT?
YES, SIR.

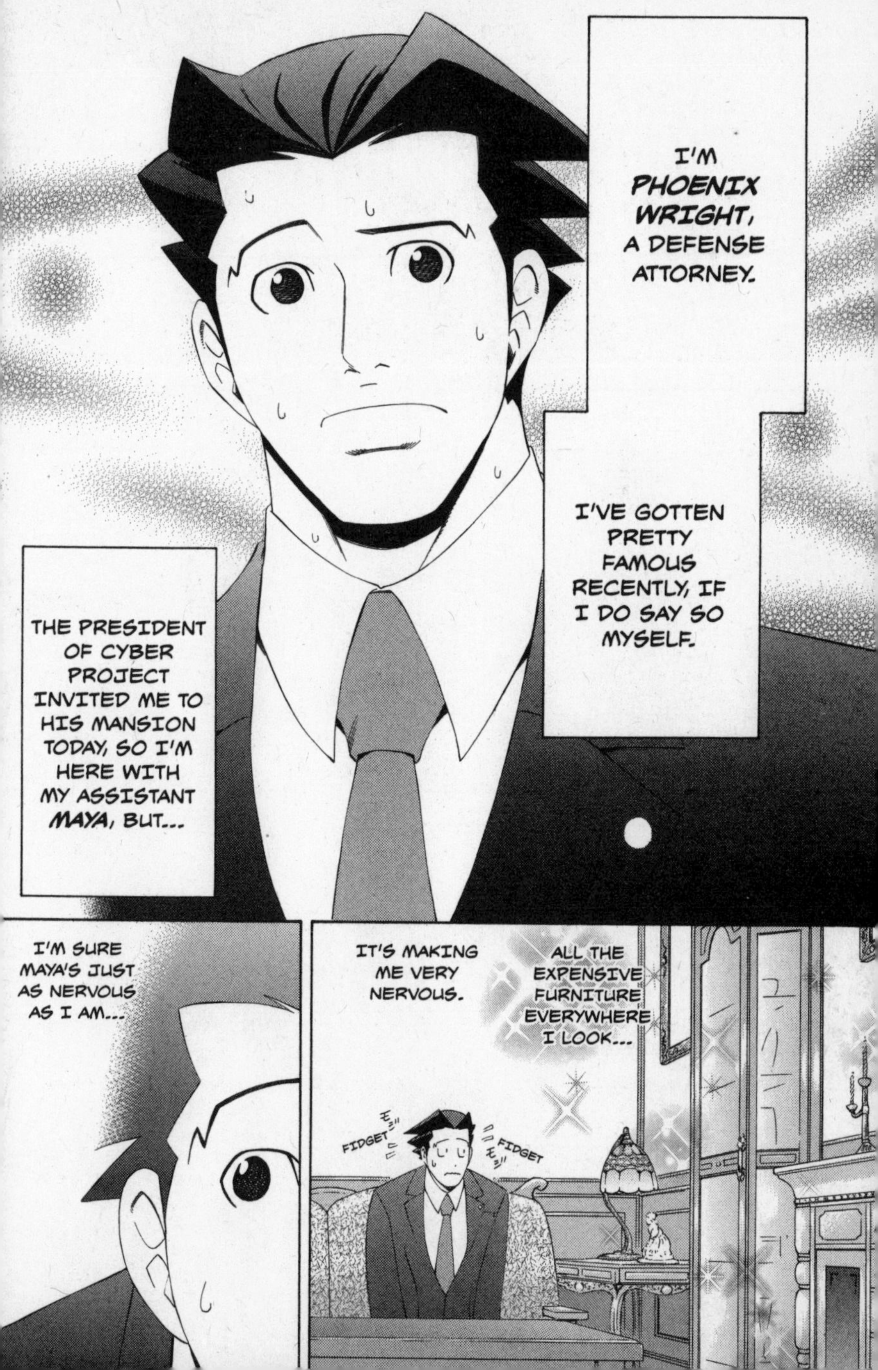
I'M PHOENIX WRIGHT, A DEFENSE ATTORNEY.
I'VE GOTTEN PRETTY FAMOUS RECENTLY, IF I DO SAY SO MYSELF.
THE PRESIDENT OF CYBER PROJECT INVITED ME TO HIS MANSION TODAY, SO I'M HERE WITH MY ASSISTANT MAYA, BUT...
ALL THE EXPENSIVE FURNITURE EVERYWHERE I LOOK...
IT'S MAKING ME VERY NERVOUS.
FIDGET
FIDGET
I'M SURE MAYA'S JUST AS NERVOUS AS I AM...

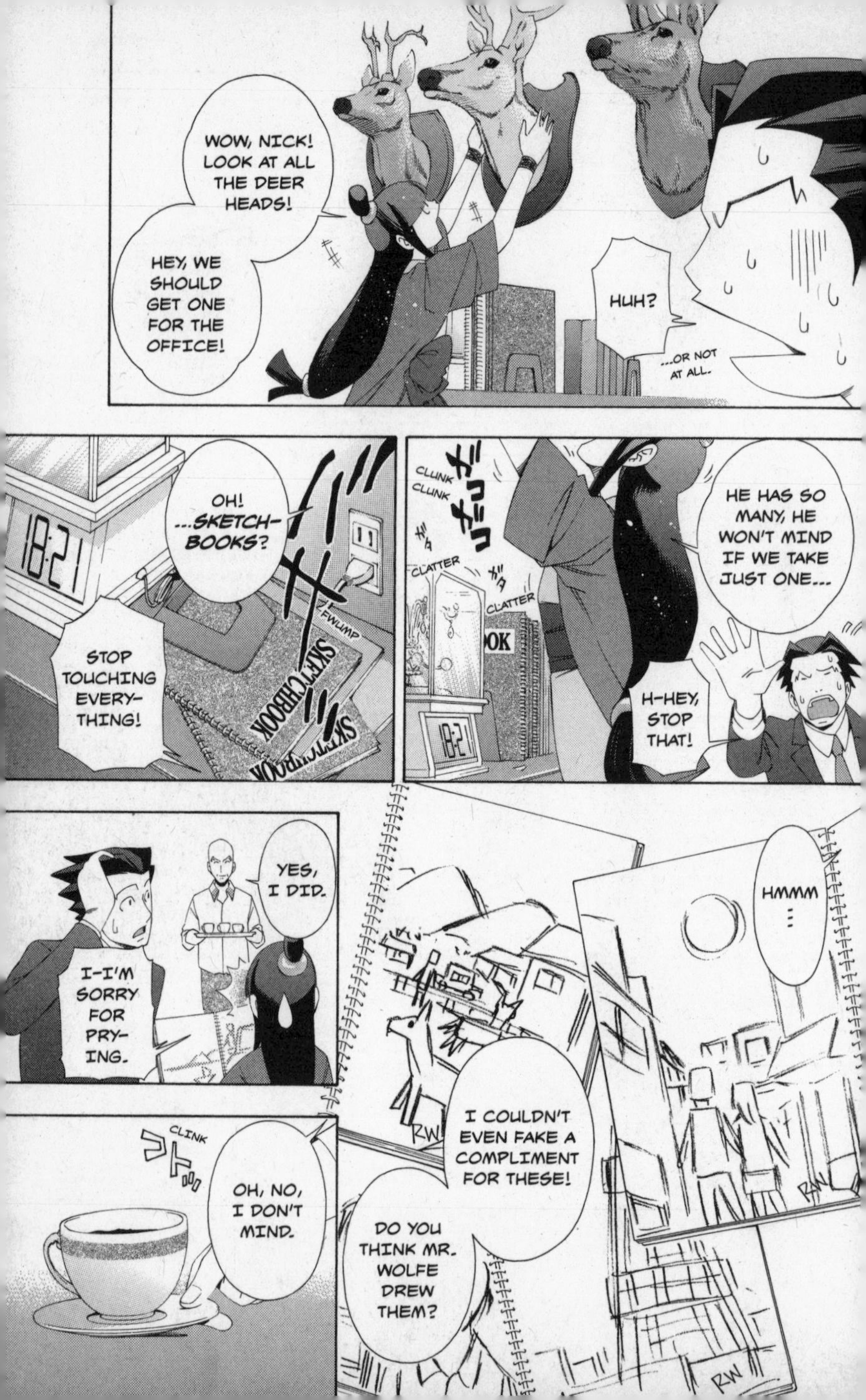
WOW, NICK! LOOK AT ALL THE DEER HEADS!
HEY, WE SHOULD GET ONE FOR THE OFFICE!
HUH?
...OR NOT AT ALL.
CLUNK
CLUNK
CLATTER
CLATTER
HE HAS SO MANY, HE WON'T MIND IF WE TAKE JUST ONE...
H-HEY, STOP THAT!
OH! ...SKETCHBOOKS?
FWUMP
STOP TOUCHING EVERYTHING!
SKETCHBOOK
SKETCHBOOK
HMMM...
I COULDN'T EVEN FAKE A COMPLIMENT FOR THESE!
DO YOU THINK MR. WOLFE DREW THEM?
I-I'M SORRY FOR PRYING.
YES, I DID.
CLINK
OH, NO, I DON'T MIND.

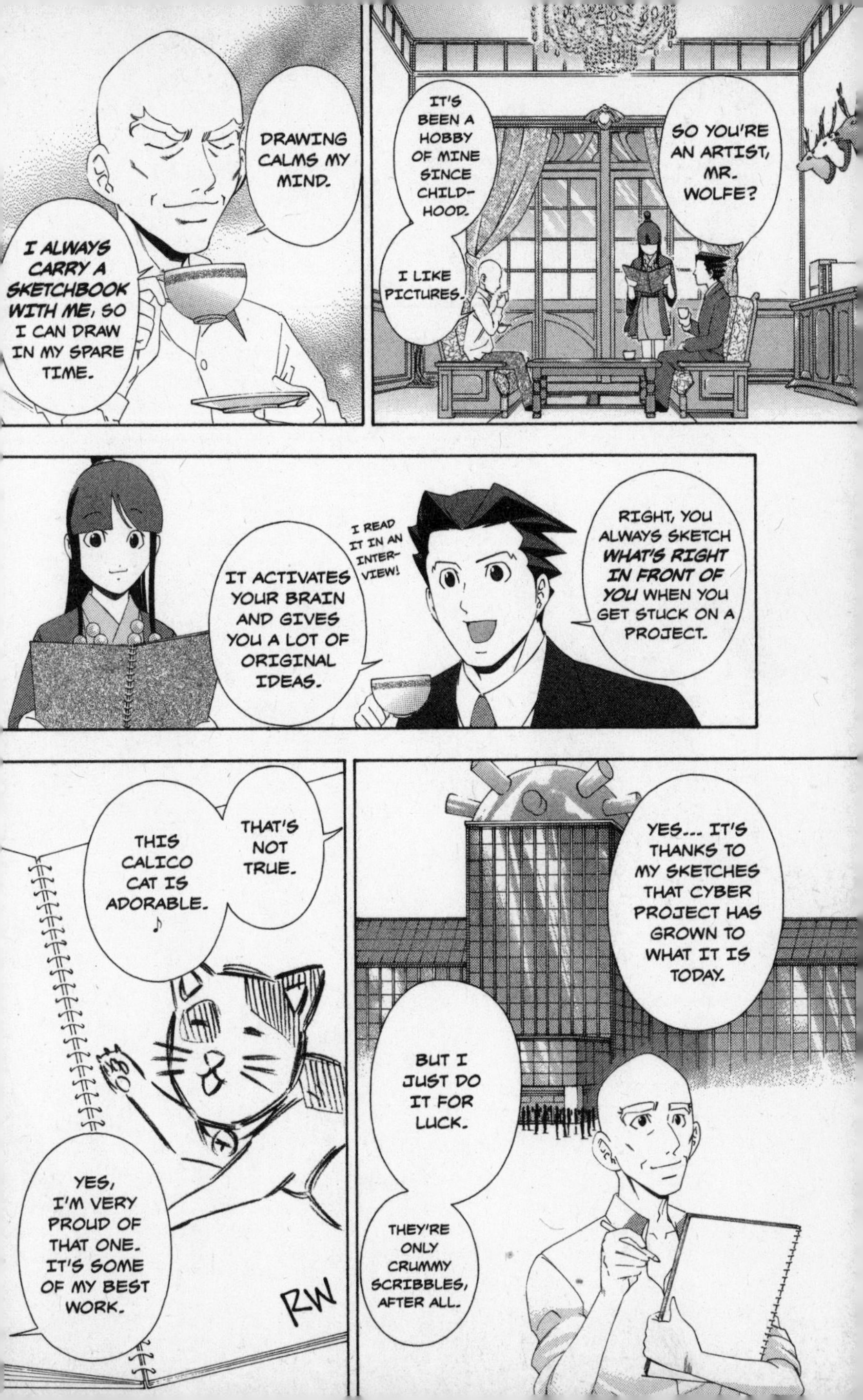
SO YOU'RE AN ARTIST, MR. WOLFE?
IT'S BEEN A HOBBY OF MINE SINCE CHILDHOOD.
I LIKE PICTURES.
DRAWING CALMS MY MIND.
I ALWAYS CARRY A SKETCHBOOK WITH ME, SO I CAN DRAW IN MY SPARE TIME.
RIGHT, YOU ALWAYS SKETCH WHAT'S RIGHT IN FRONT OF YOU WHEN YOU GET STUCK ON A PROJECT.
I READ IT IN AN INTERVIEW!
IT ACTIVATES YOUR BRAIN AND GIVES YOU A LOT OF ORIGINAL IDEAS.
YES... IT'S THANKS TO MY SKETCHES THAT CYBER PROJECT HAS GROWN TO WHAT IT IS TODAY.
BUT I JUST DO IT FOR LUCK.
THEY'RE ONLY CRUMMY SCRIBBLES, AFTER ALL.
THAT'S NOT TRUE.
THIS CALICO CAT IS ADORABLE. ♪
YES, I'M VERY PROUD OF THAT ONE. IT'S SOME OF MY BEST WORK.
RW

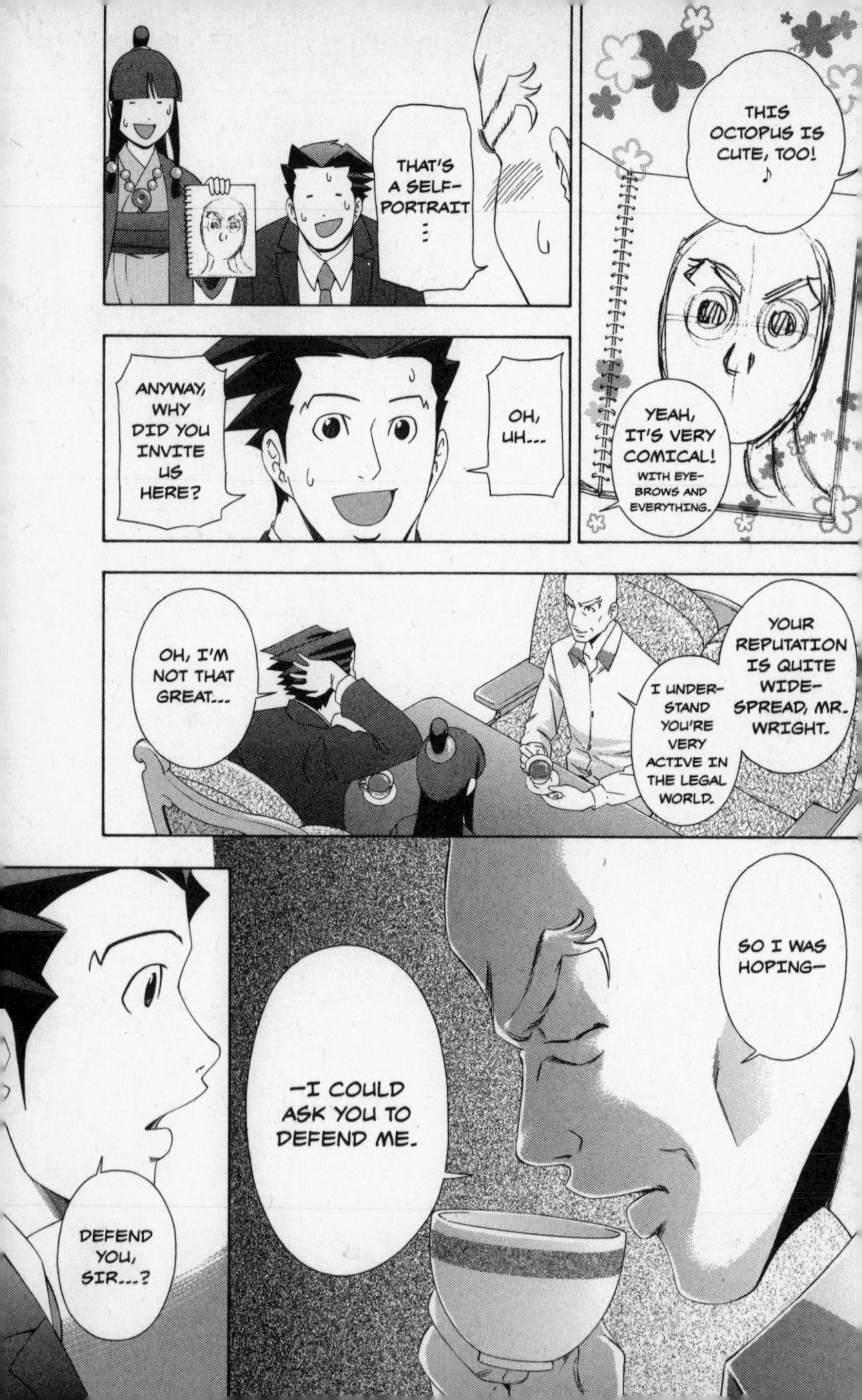
THIS OCTOPUS IS CUTE, TOO! ♪
YEAH, IT'S VERY COMICAL! WITH EYEBROWS AND EVERYTHING.
THAT'S A SELF-PORTRAIT...
OH, UH...
ANYWAY, WHY DID YOU INVITE US HERE?
YOUR REPUTATION IS QUITE WIDESPREAD, MR. WRIGHT.
I UNDERSTAND YOU'RE VERY ACTIVE IN THE LEGAL WORLD.
OH, I'M NOT THAT GREAT...
SO I WAS HOPING—
—I COULD ASK YOU TO DEFEND ME.
DEFEND YOU, SIR...?

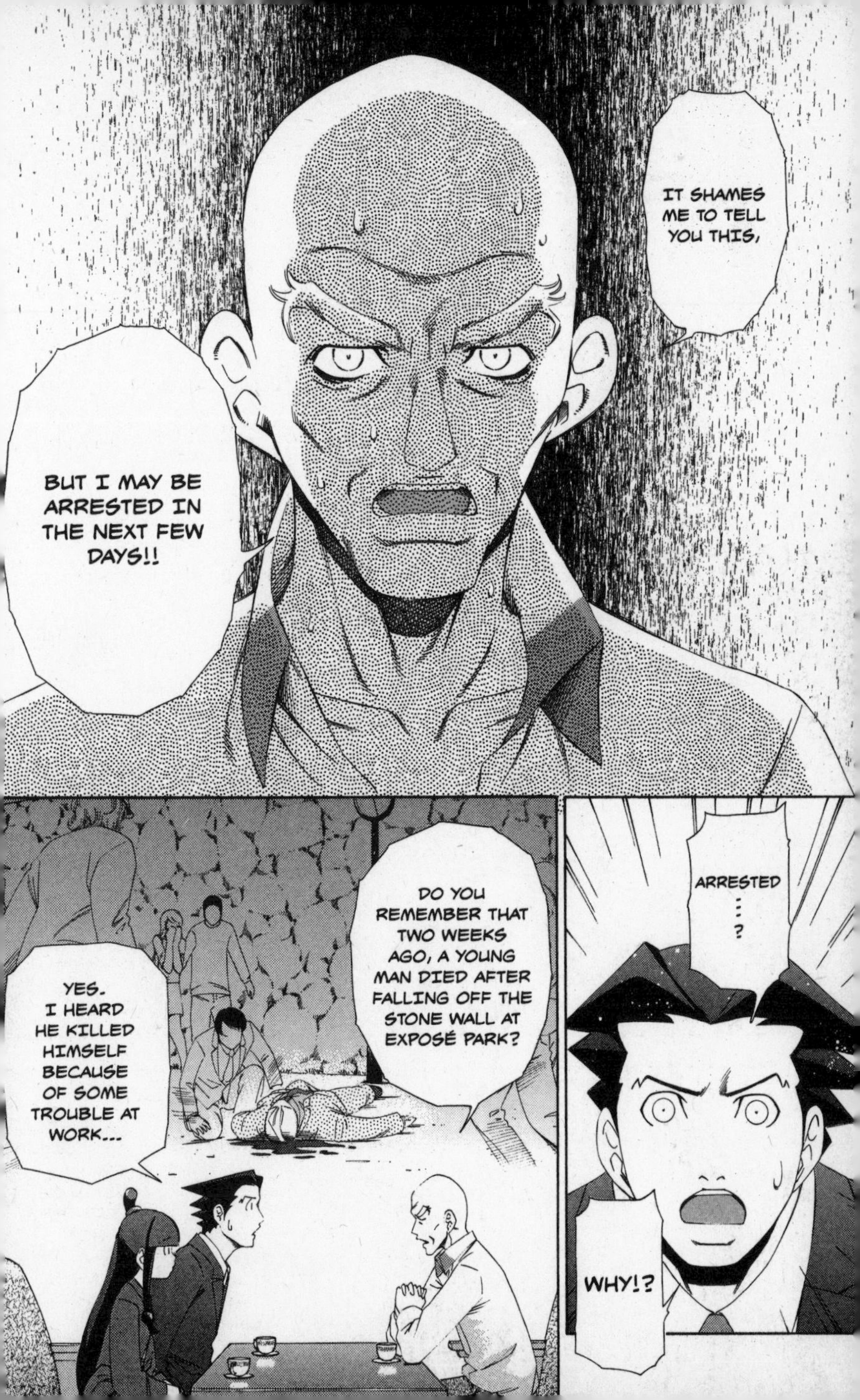
IT SHAMES ME TO TELL YOU THIS,
BUT I MAY BE ARRESTED IN THE NEXT FEW DAYS!!
ARRESTED ...?
WHY!?
DO YOU REMEMBER THAT TWO WEEKS AGO, A YOUNG MAN DIED AFTER FALLING OFF THE STONE WALL AT EXPOSÉ PARK?
YES. I HEARD HE KILLED HIMSELF BECAUSE OF SOME TROUBLE AT WORK...

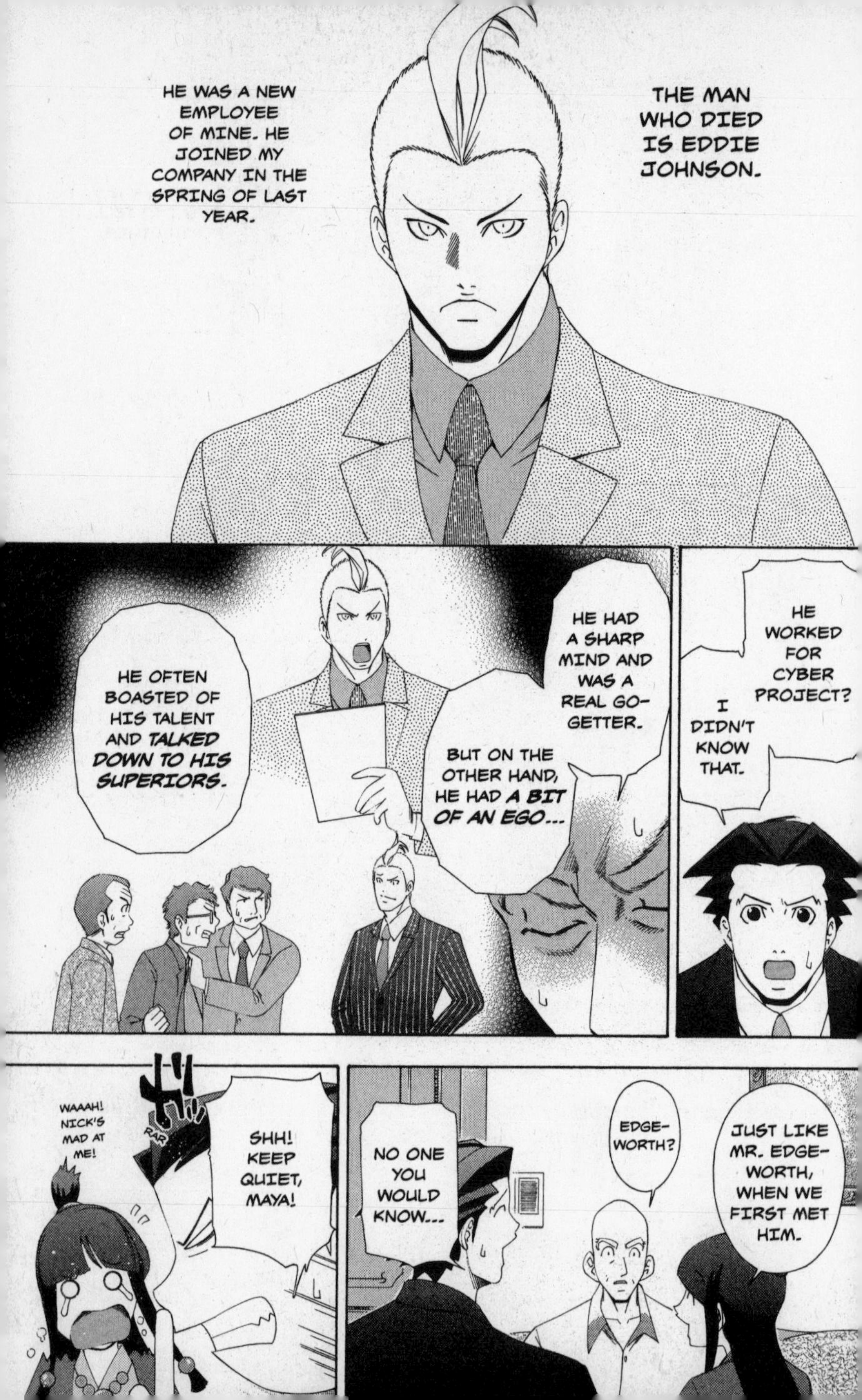
THE MAN WHO DIED IS EDDIE JOHNSON.
HE WAS A NEW EMPLOYEE OF MINE. HE JOINED MY COMPANY IN THE SPRING OF LAST YEAR.
HE WORKED FOR CYBER PROJECT?
I DIDN'T KNOW THAT.
HE HAD A SHARP MIND AND WAS A REAL GO-GETTER.
BUT ON THE OTHER HAND, HE HAD A BIT OF AN EGO...
HE OFTEN BOASTED OF HIS TALENT AND TALKED DOWN TO HIS SUPERIORS.
JUST LIKE MR. EDGE-WORTH, WHEN WE FIRST MET HIM.
EDGE-WORTH?
NO ONE YOU WOULD KNOW...
SHH! KEEP QUIET, MAYA!
RAR
WAAAH! NICK'S MAD AT ME!

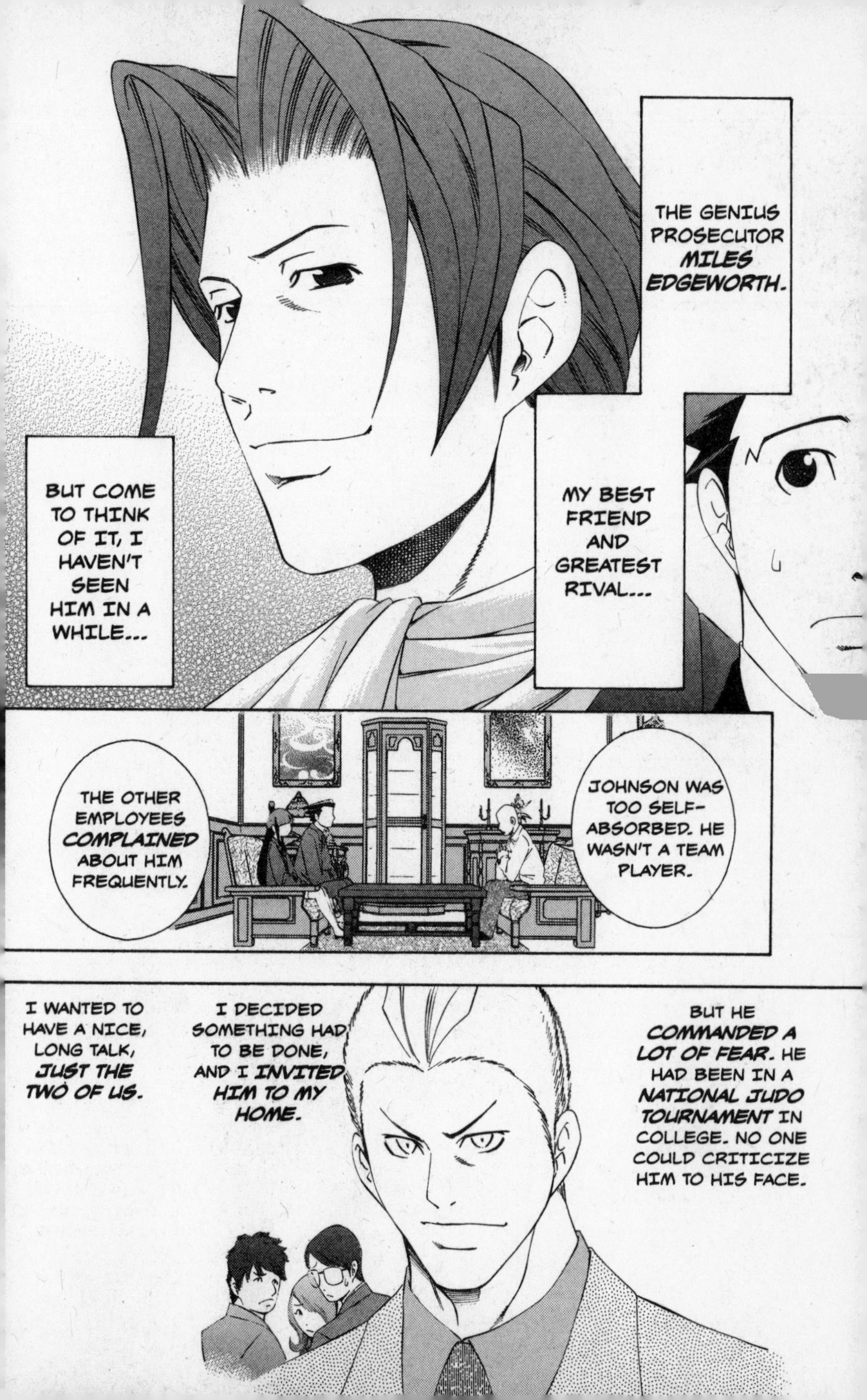
THE GENIUS PROSECUTOR MILES EDGEWORTH.
MY BEST FRIEND AND GREATEST RIVAL...
BUT COME TO THINK OF IT, I HAVEN'T SEEN HIM IN A WHILE...
JOHNSON WAS TOO SELF-ABSORBED. HE WASN'T A TEAM PLAYER.
THE OTHER EMPLOYEES COMPLAINED ABOUT HIM FREQUENTLY.
BUT HE COMMANDED A LOT OF FEAR. HE HAD BEEN IN A NATIONAL JUDO TOURNAMENT IN COLLEGE. NO ONE COULD CRITICIZE HIM TO HIS FACE.
I DECIDED SOMETHING HAD TO BE DONE, AND I INVITED HIM TO MY HOME.
I WANTED TO HAVE A NICE, LONG TALK, JUST THE TWO OF US.

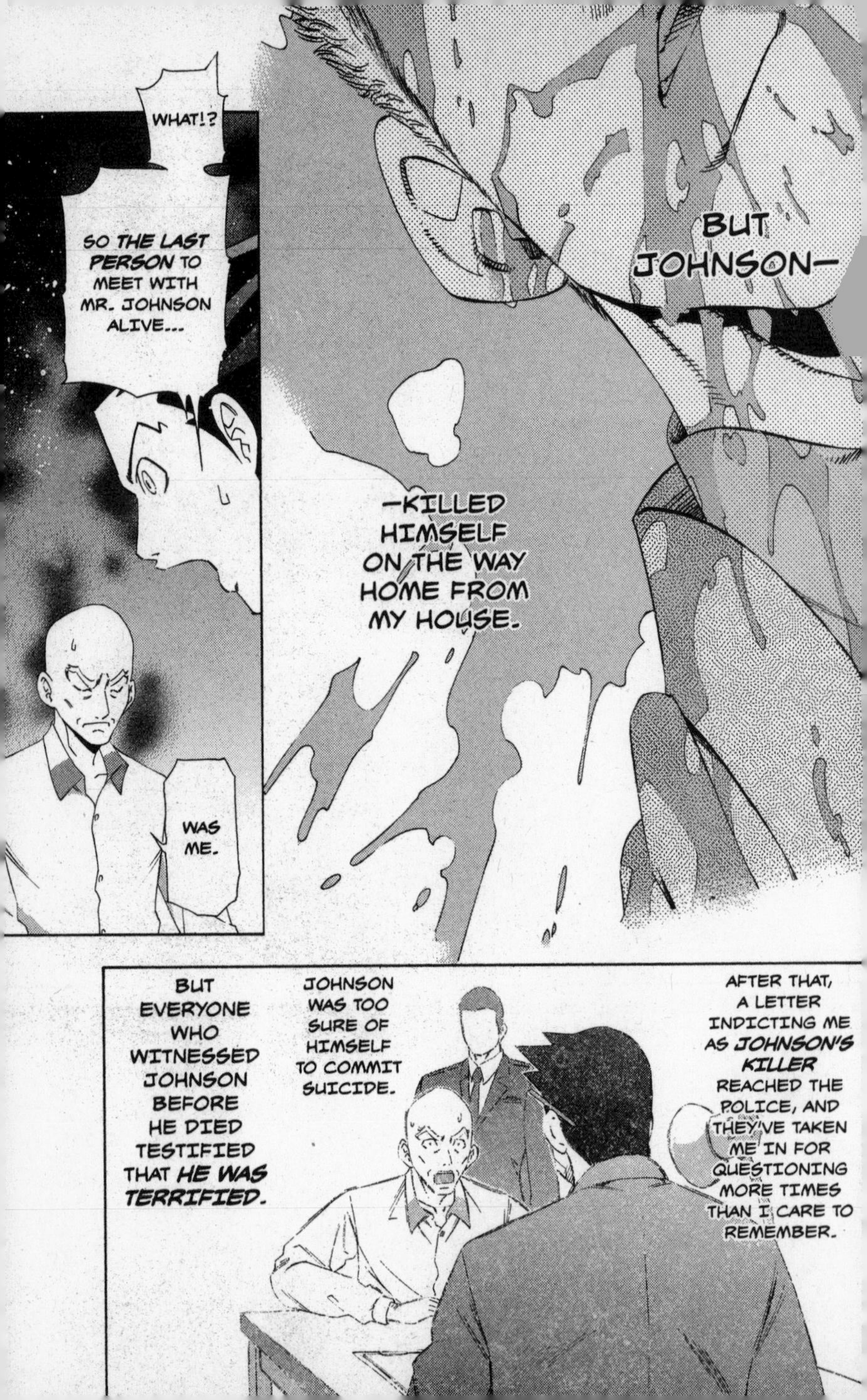
BUT JOHNSON—
—KILLED HIMSELF ON THE WAY HOME FROM MY HOUSE.
WHAT!?
SO THE LAST PERSON TO MEET WITH MR. JOHNSON ALIVE...
WAS ME.
AFTER THAT, A LETTER INDICTING ME AS JOHNSON'S KILLER REACHED THE POLICE, AND THEY'VE TAKEN ME IN FOR QUESTIONING MORE TIMES THAN I CARE TO REMEMBER.
JOHNSON WAS TOO SURE OF HIMSELF TO COMMIT SUICIDE.
BUT EVERYONE WHO WITNESSED JOHNSON BEFORE HE DIED TESTIFIED THAT HE WAS TERRIFIED.

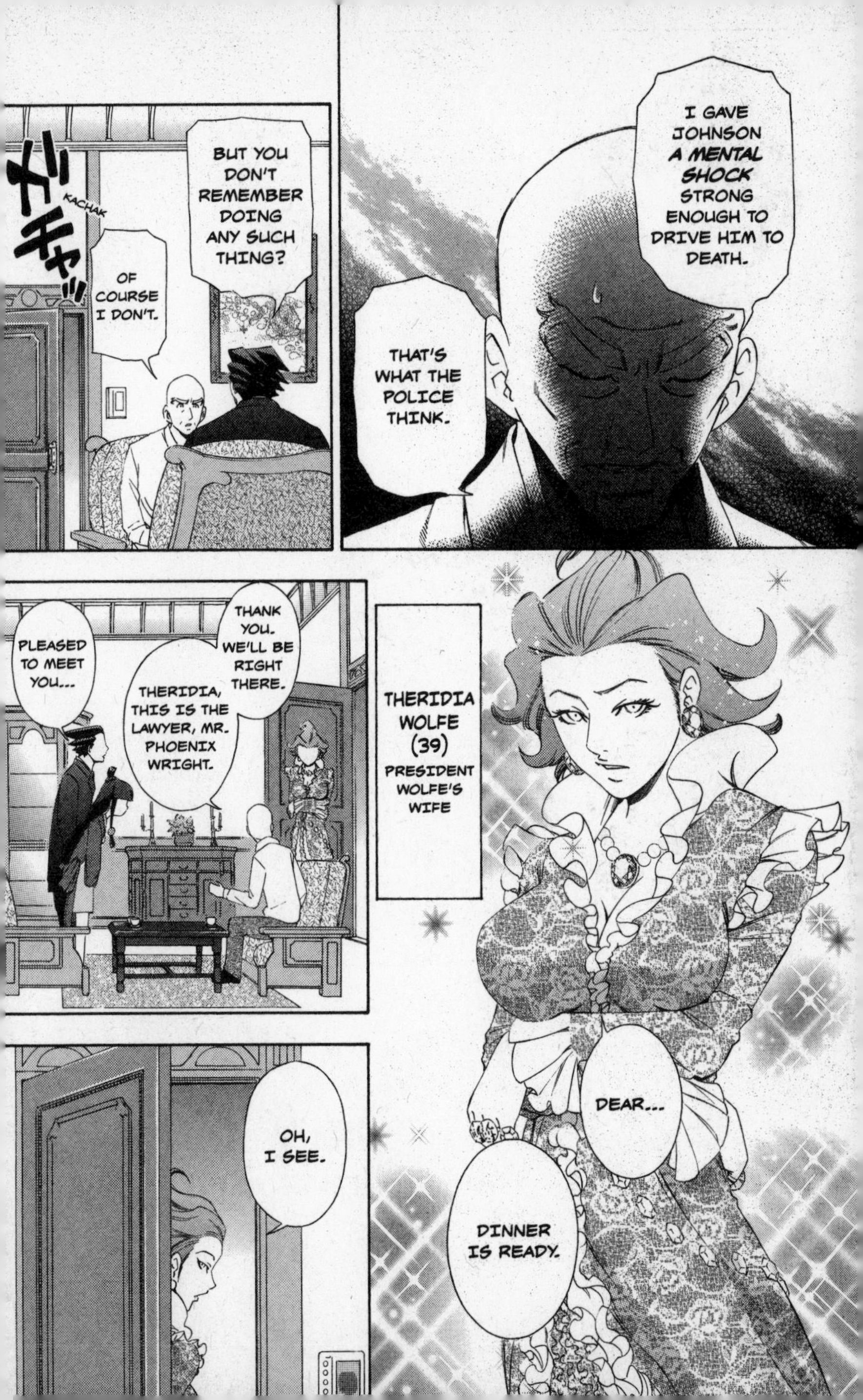
I GAVE JOHNSON A MENTAL SHOCK STRONG ENOUGH TO DRIVE HIM TO DEATH.
THAT'S WHAT THE POLICE THINK.
BUT YOU DON'T REMEMBER DOING ANY SUCH THING?
ガチャッ
KACHAK
OF COURSE I DON'T.
THERIDIA WOLFE (39) PRESIDENT WOLFE'S WIFE
DEAR...
DINNER IS READY.
THANK YOU. WE'LL BE RIGHT THERE.
THERIDIA, THIS IS THE LAWYER, MR. PHOENIX WRIGHT.
PLEASED TO MEET YOU...
OH, I SEE.

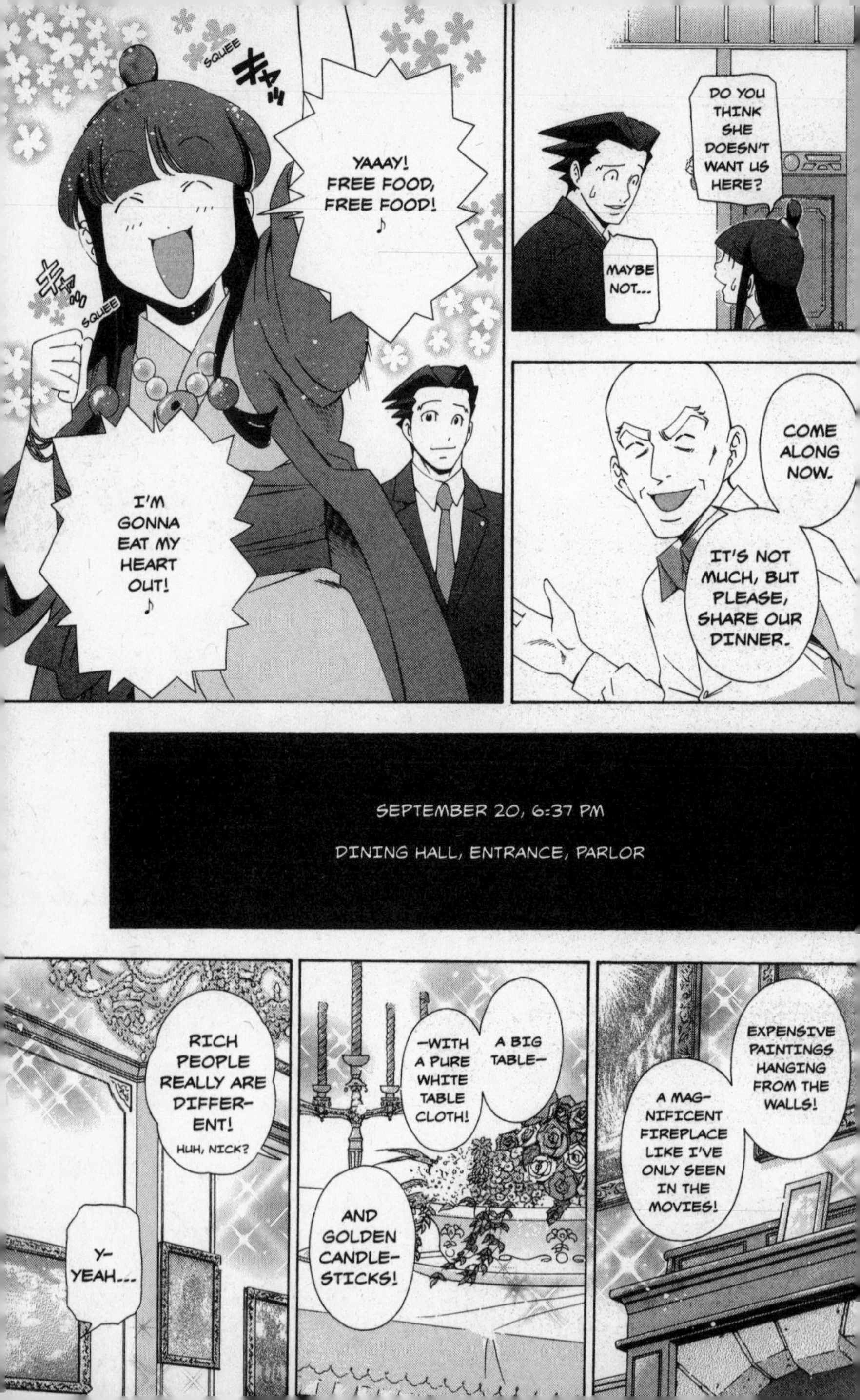
DO YOU THINK SHE DOESN'T WANT US HERE?
MAYBE NOT...
COME ALONG NOW.
IT'S NOT MUCH, BUT PLEASE, SHARE OUR DINNER.
SQUEE
YAAAY! FREE FOOD, FREE FOOD! ♪
SQUEE
I'M GONNA EAT MY HEART OUT! ♪
SEPTEMBER 20, 6:37 PM
DINING HALL, ENTRANCE, PARLOR
EXPENSIVE PAINTINGS HANGING FROM THE WALLS!
A MAGNIFICENT FIREPLACE LIKE I'VE ONLY SEEN IN THE MOVIES!
A BIG TABLE—
—WITH A PURE WHITE TABLECLOTH!
AND GOLDEN CANDLESTICKS!
RICH PEOPLE REALLY ARE DIFFERENT! HUH, NICK?
Y-YEAH...

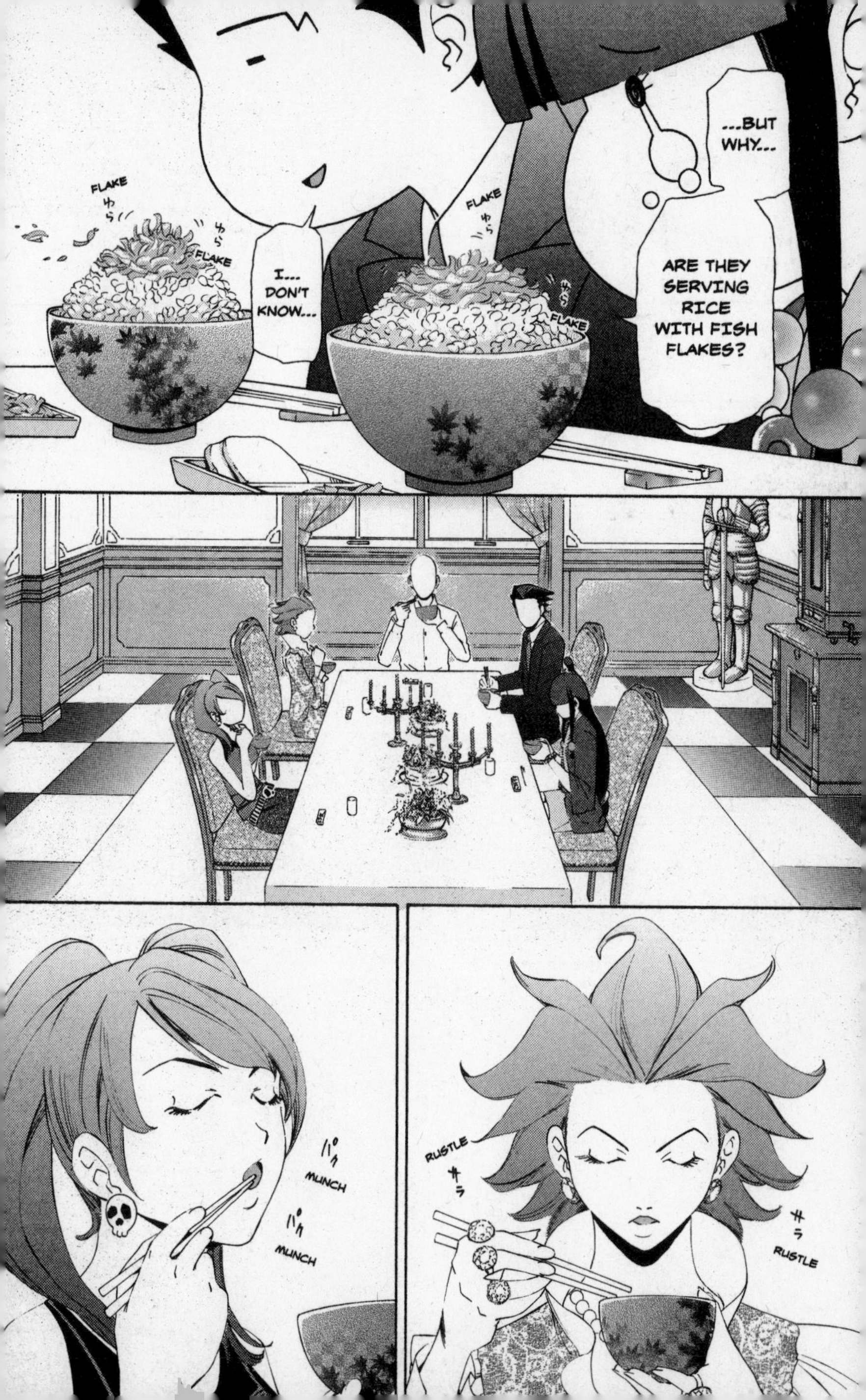

...BUT WHY...
ARE THEY SERVING RICE WITH FISH FLAKES?
FLAKE
ゆら
FLAKE
I... DON'T KNOW...
FLAKE
ゆら
FLAKE
RUSTLE
サラ
RUSTLE
サラ
パク
MUNCH
パク
MUNCH

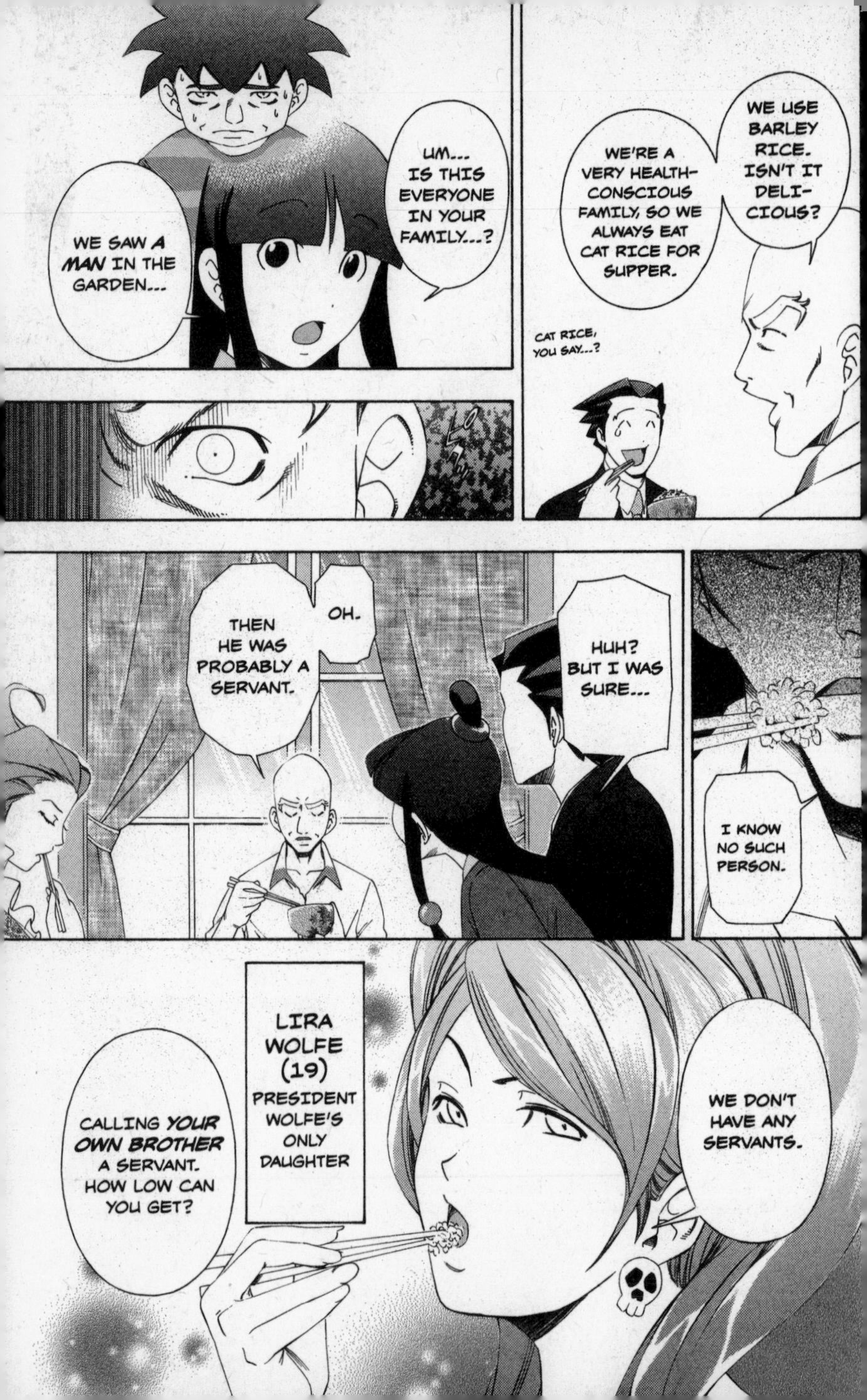
WE USE BARLEY RICE. ISN'T IT DELI-CIOUS?
WE'RE A VERY HEALTH-CONSCIOUS FAMILY, SO WE ALWAYS EAT CAT RICE FOR SUPPER.
CAT RICE, YOU SAY...?
UM... IS THIS EVERYONE IN YOUR FAMILY...?
WE SAW A *MAN* IN THE GARDEN...
I KNOW NO SUCH PERSON.
HUH? BUT I WAS SURE...
OH.
THEN HE WAS PROBABLY A SERVANT.
WE DON'T HAVE ANY SERVANTS.
LIRA WOLFE (19) PRESIDENT WOLFE'S ONLY DAUGHTER
CALLING *YOUR OWN BROTHER* A SERVANT. HOW LOW CAN YOU GET?

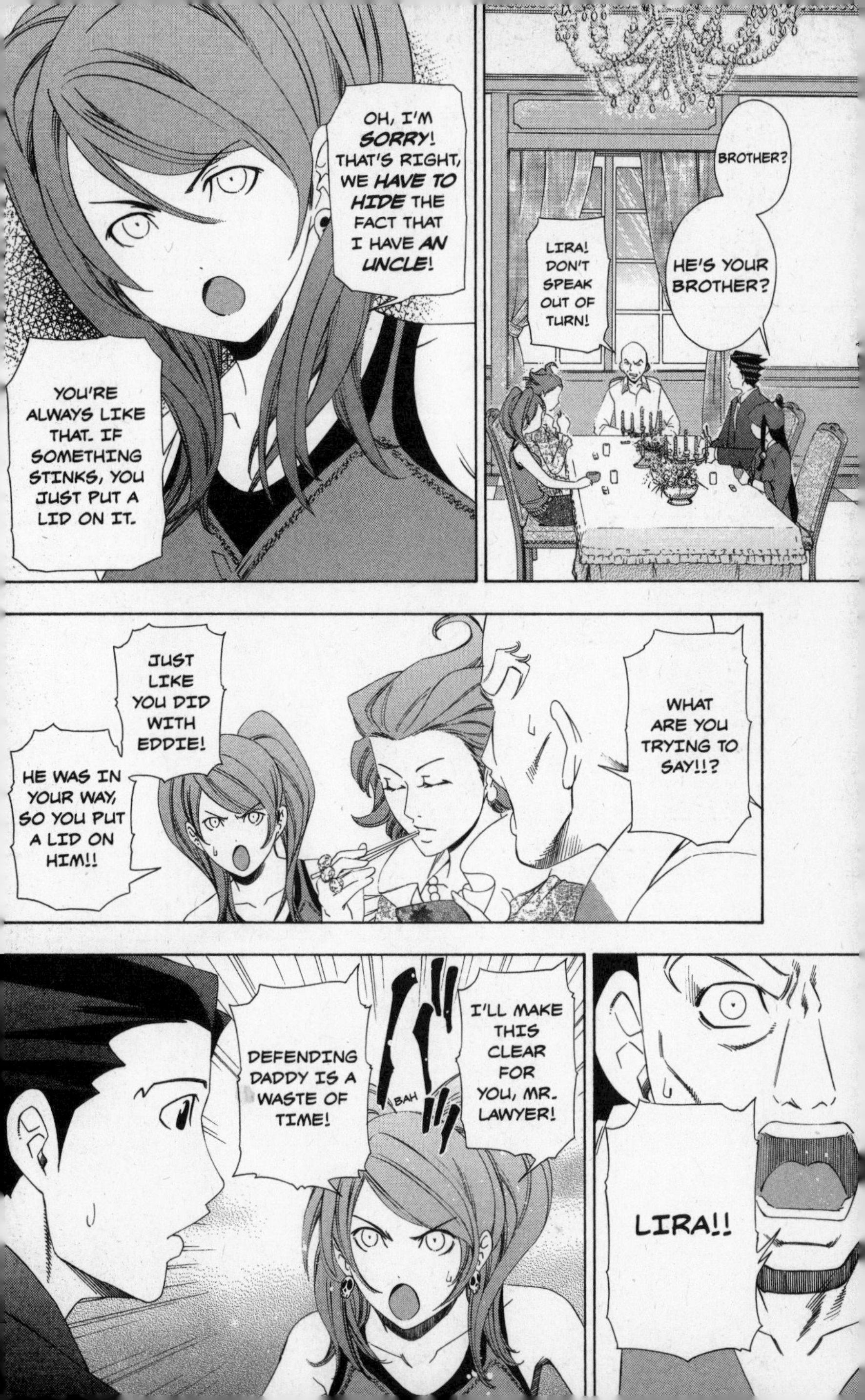
BROTHER?
HE'S YOUR BROTHER?
LIRA! DON'T SPEAK OUT OF TURN!
OH, I'M SORRY! THAT'S RIGHT, WE HAVE TO HIDE THE FACT THAT I HAVE AN UNCLE!
YOU'RE ALWAYS LIKE THAT. IF SOMETHING STINKS, YOU JUST PUT A LID ON IT.
WHAT ARE YOU TRYING TO SAY!!?
JUST LIKE YOU DID WITH EDDIE!
HE WAS IN YOUR WAY, SO YOU PUT A LID ON HIM!!
LIRA!!
I'LL MAKE THIS CLEAR FOR YOU, MR. LAWYER!
BAH
DEFENDING DADDY IS A WASTE OF TIME!

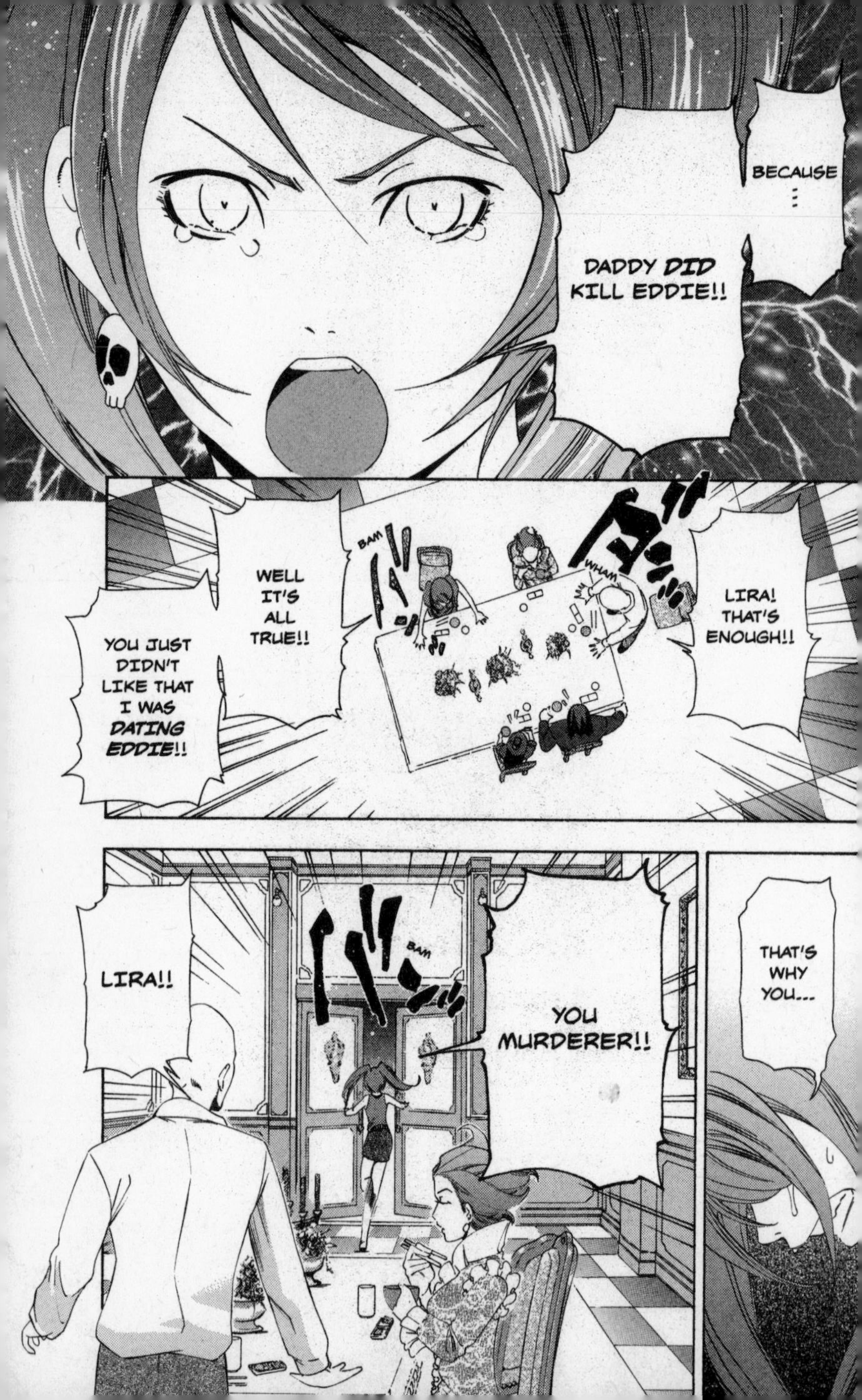
BECAUSE…
DADDY DID KILL EDDIE!!
LIRA! THAT'S ENOUGH!!
WHAM
BAM
WELL IT'S ALL TRUE!!
YOU JUST DIDN'T LIKE THAT I WAS DATING EDDIE!!
THAT'S WHY YOU...
YOU MURDERER!!
BAM
LIRA!!

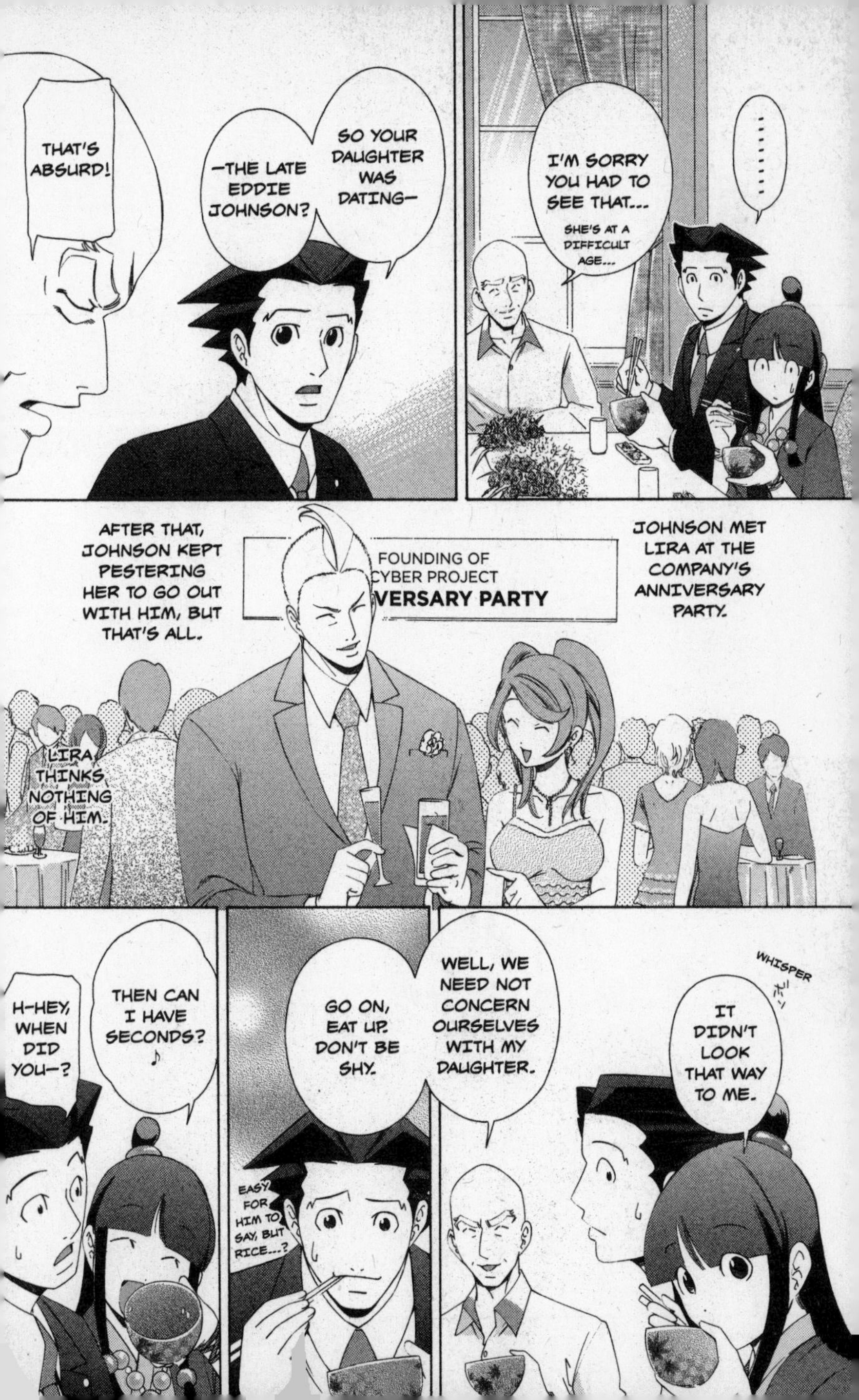
......
I'M SORRY YOU HAD TO SEE THAT...
SHE'S AT A DIFFICULT AGE...
SO YOUR DAUGHTER WAS DATING—
—THE LATE EDDIE JOHNSON?
THAT'S ABSURD!
JOHNSON MET LIRA AT THE COMPANY'S ANNIVERSARY PARTY.
FOUNDING OF CYBER PROJECT VERSARY PARTY
AFTER THAT, JOHNSON KEPT PESTERING HER TO GO OUT WITH HIM, BUT THAT'S ALL.
LIRA THINKS NOTHING OF HIM.
WHISPER
IT DIDN'T LOOK THAT WAY TO ME.
WELL, WE NEED NOT CONCERN OURSELVES WITH MY DAUGHTER.
GO ON, EAT UP. DON'T BE SHY.
EASY FOR HIM TO SAY, BUT RICE...?
THEN CAN I HAVE SECONDS? ♪
H-HEY, WHEN DID YOU—?

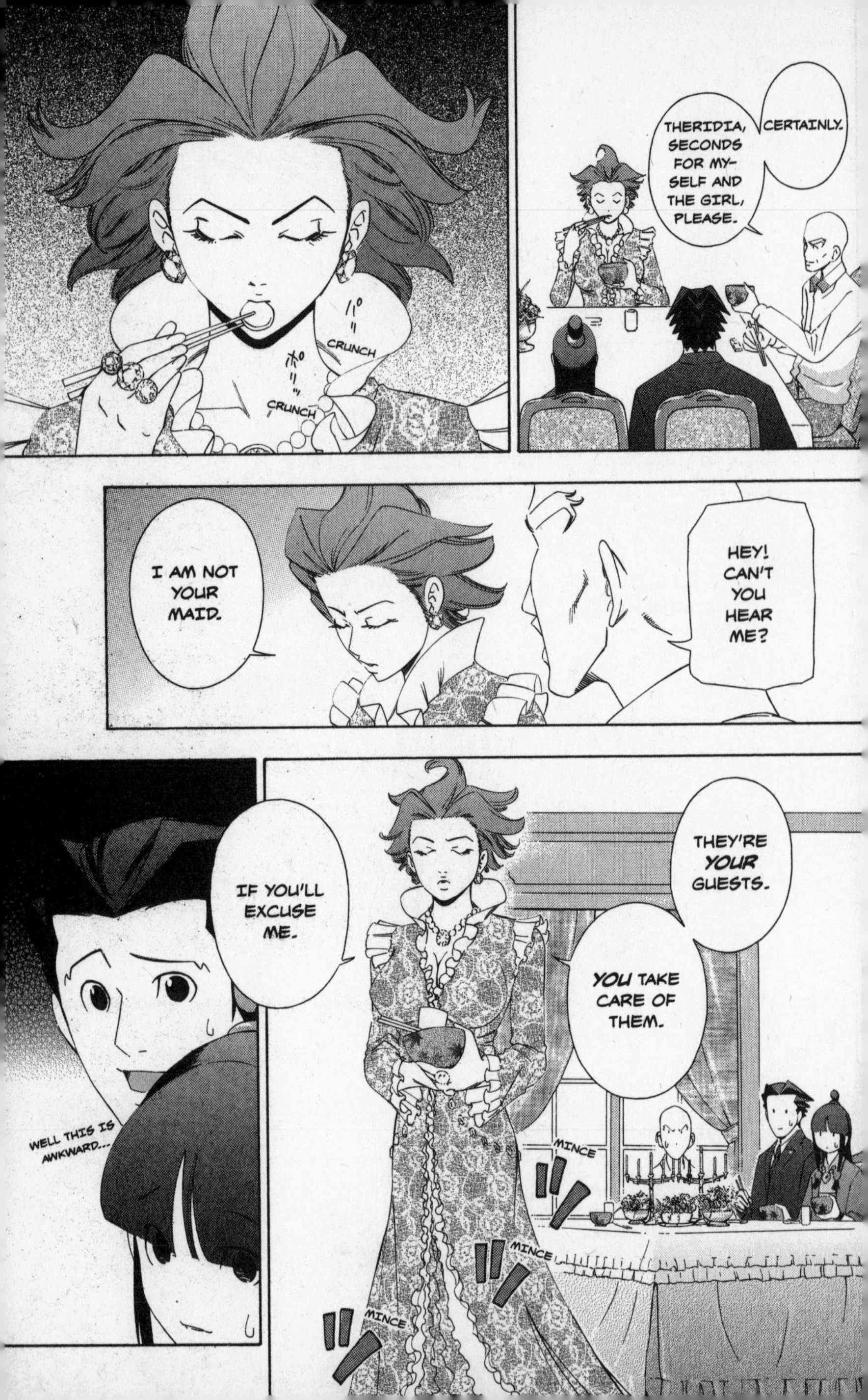

CERTAINLY.
THERIDIA, SECONDS FOR MY-SELF AND THE GIRL, PLEASE.
パリ
CRUNCH
ポリ
CRUNCH
HEY! CAN'T YOU HEAR ME?
I AM NOT YOUR MAID.
THEY'RE YOUR GUESTS.
YOU TAKE CARE OF THEM.
IF YOU'LL EXCUSE ME.
MINCE
MINCE
MINCE
WELL THIS IS AWKWARD...

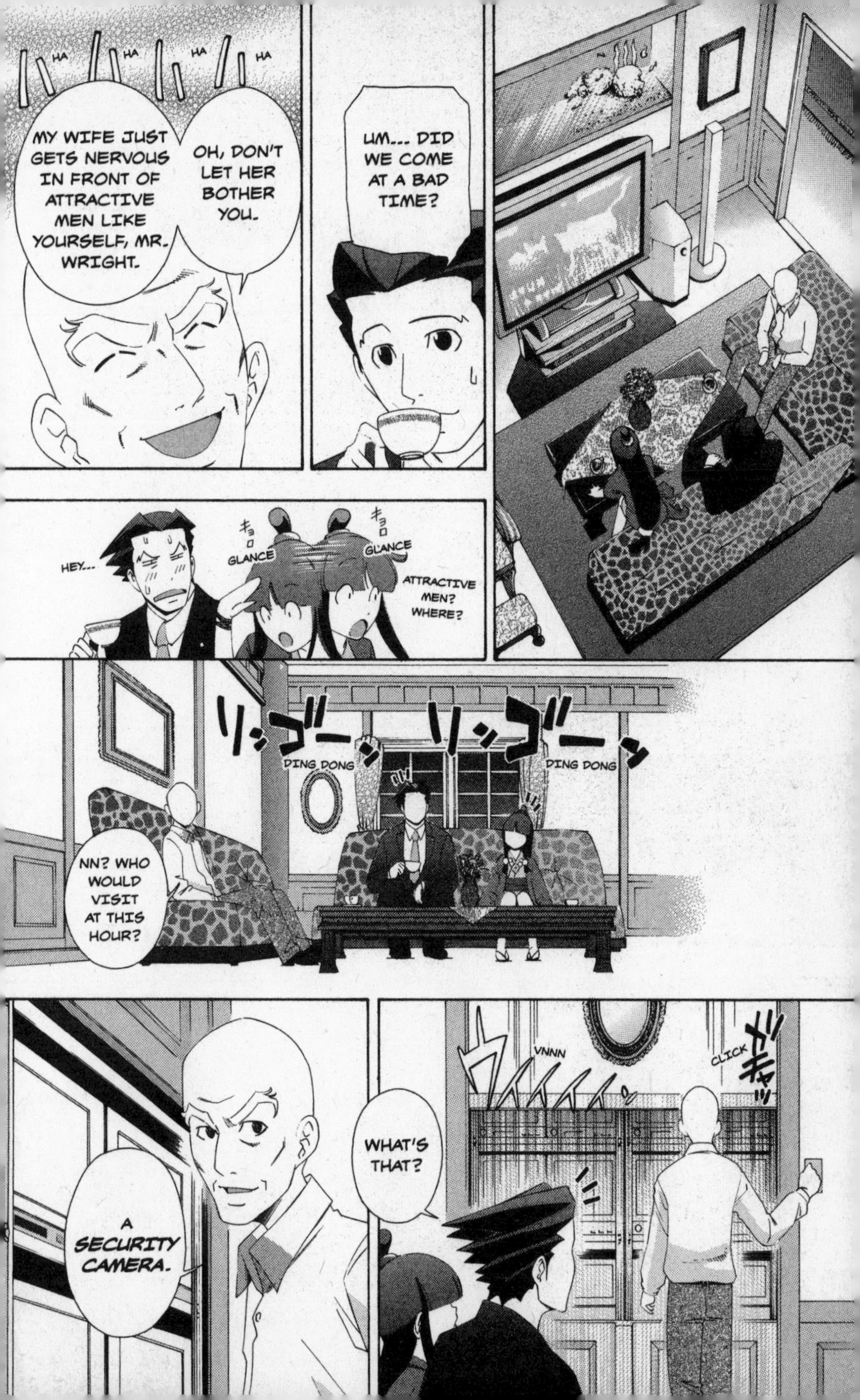
UM... DID WE COME AT A BAD TIME?
HA HA HA HA
OH, DON'T LET HER BOTHER YOU.
MY WIFE JUST GETS NERVOUS IN FRONT OF ATTRACTIVE MEN LIKE YOURSELF, MR. WRIGHT.
ATTRACTIVE MEN? WHERE?
キョロ GLANCE
キョロ GLANCE
HEY...
リッゴーッ DING DONG
リッゴーッ DING DONG
NN? WHO WOULD VISIT AT THIS HOUR?
ガチャッ CLICK
ウィィィィン VNNN
WHAT'S THAT?
A SECURITY CAMERA.

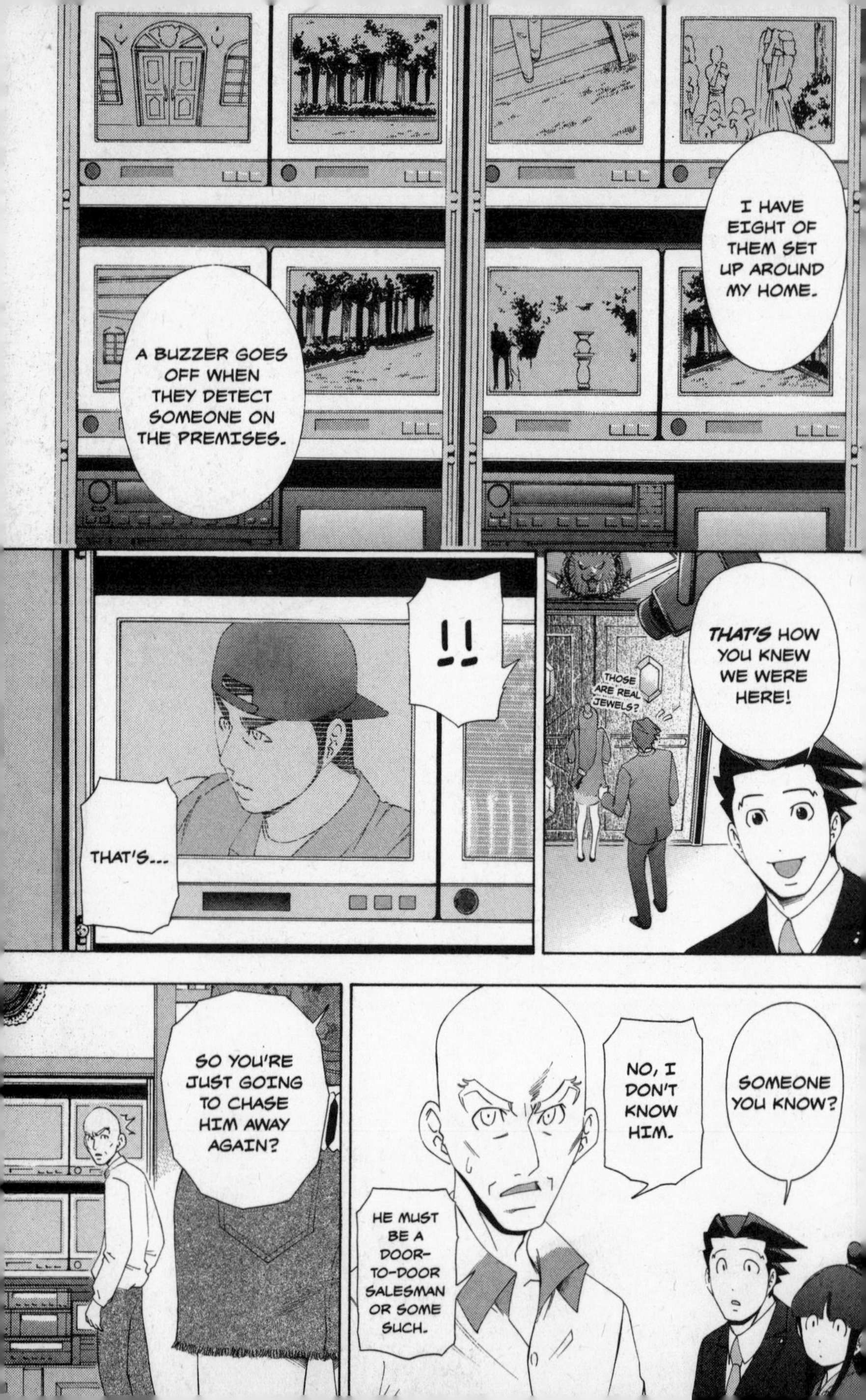
I HAVE EIGHT OF THEM SET UP AROUND MY HOME.
A BUZZER GOES OFF WHEN THEY DETECT SOMEONE ON THE PREMISES.
*THAT'S* HOW YOU KNEW WE WERE HERE!
THOSE ARE REAL JEWELS?
!!
THAT'S...
SOMEONE YOU KNOW?
NO, I DON'T KNOW HIM.
HE MUST BE A DOOR-TO-DOOR SALESMAN OR SOME SUCH.
SO YOU'RE JUST GOING TO CHASE HIM AWAY AGAIN?

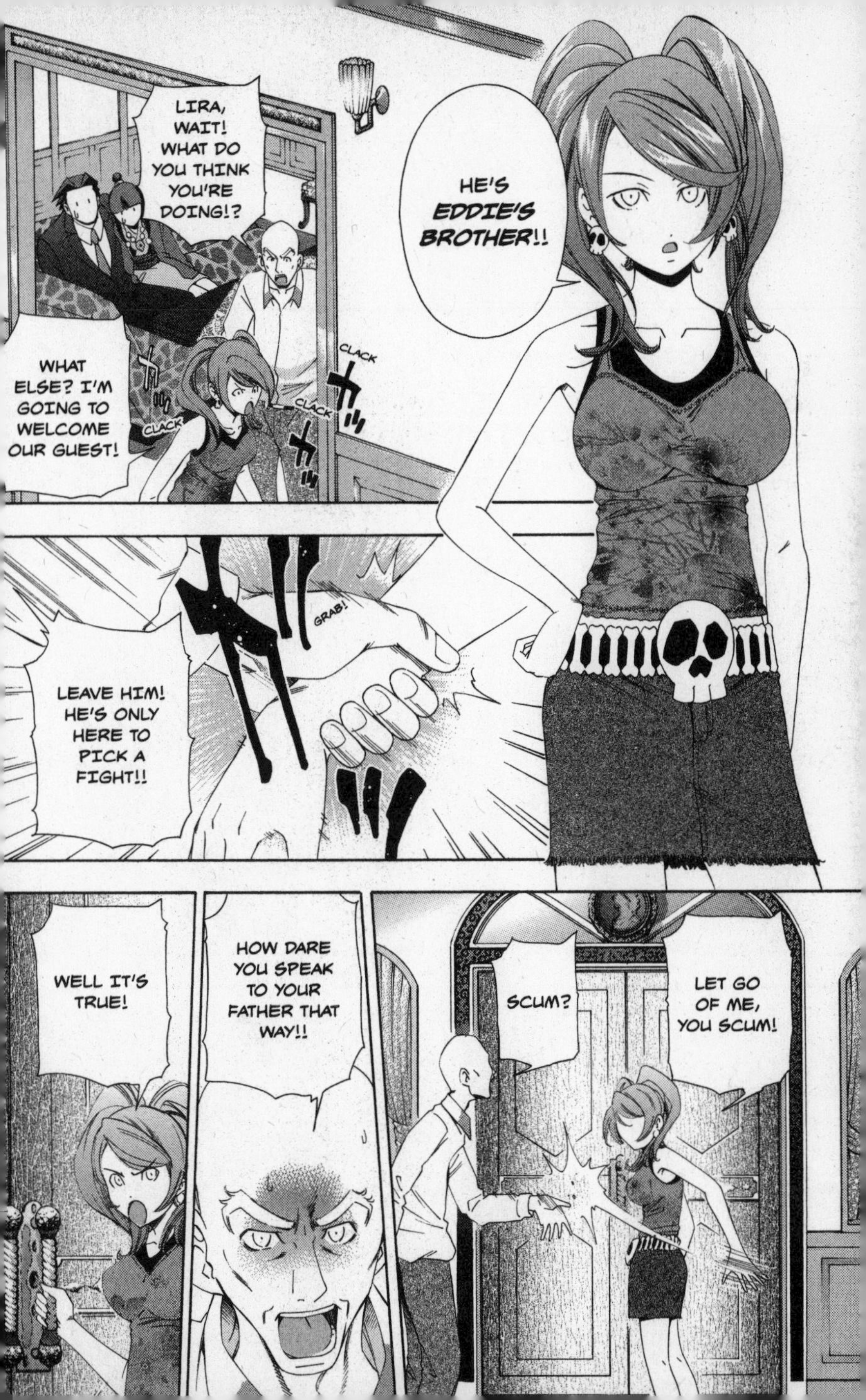
HE'S EDDIE'S BROTHER!!
LIRA, WAIT! WHAT DO YOU THINK YOU'RE DOING!?
CLACK
CLACK
CLACK
WHAT ELSE? I'M GOING TO WELCOME OUR GUEST!
GRAB!
LEAVE HIM! HE'S ONLY HERE TO PICK A FIGHT!!
LET GO OF ME, YOU SCUM!
SCUM?
HOW DARE YOU SPEAK TO YOUR FATHER THAT WAY!!
WELL IT'S TRUE!

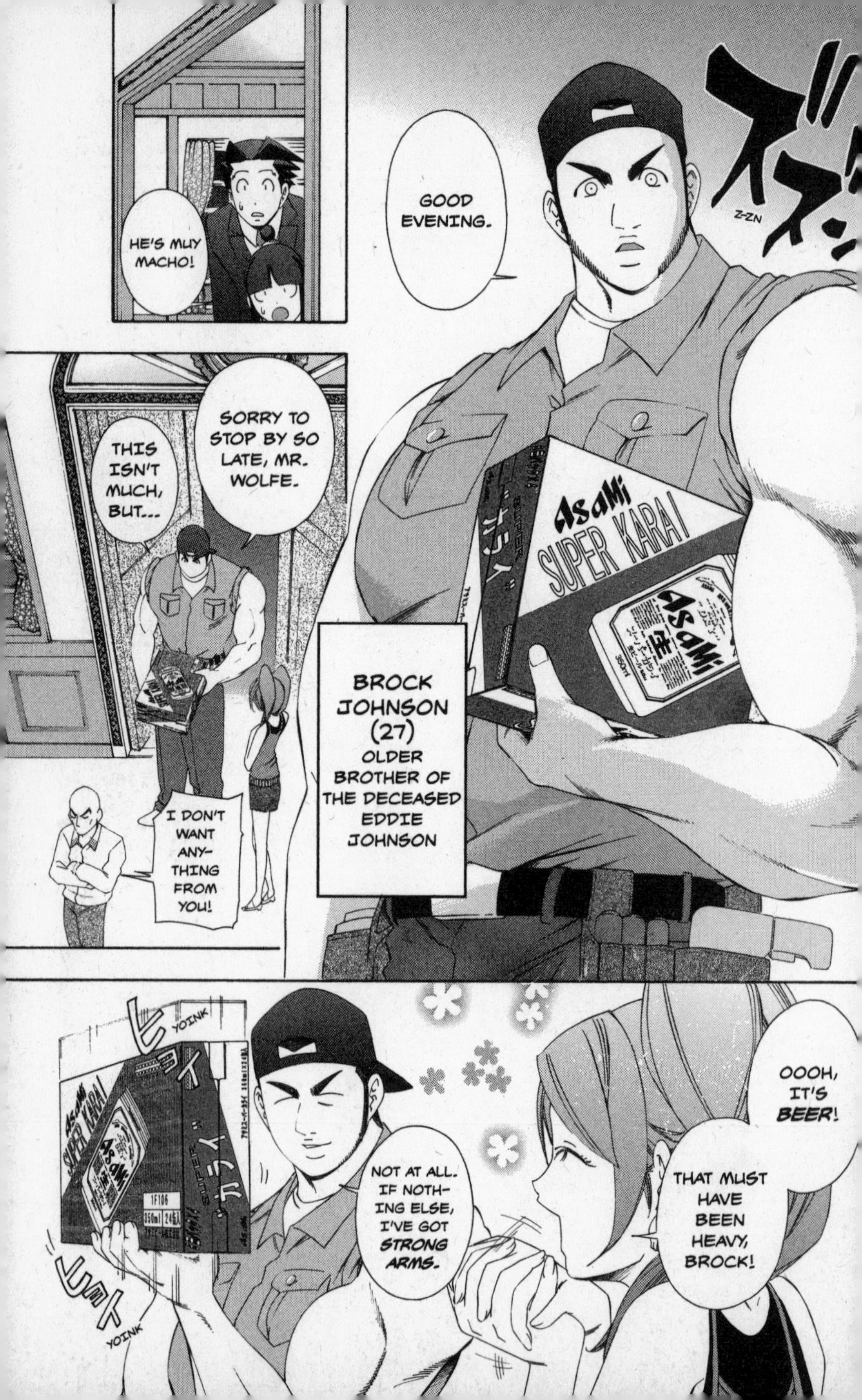
Z-ZN
GOOD EVENING.
BROCK JOHNSON (27) OLDER BROTHER OF THE DECEASED EDDIE JOHNSON
HE'S MUY MACHO!
SORRY TO STOP BY SO LATE, MR. WOLFE.
THIS ISN'T MUCH, BUT...
I DON'T WANT ANYTHING FROM YOU!
OOOH, IT'S BEER!
THAT MUST HAVE BEEN HEAVY, BROCK!
NOT AT ALL. IF NOTHING ELSE, I'VE GOT STRONG ARMS.
YOINK
YOINK

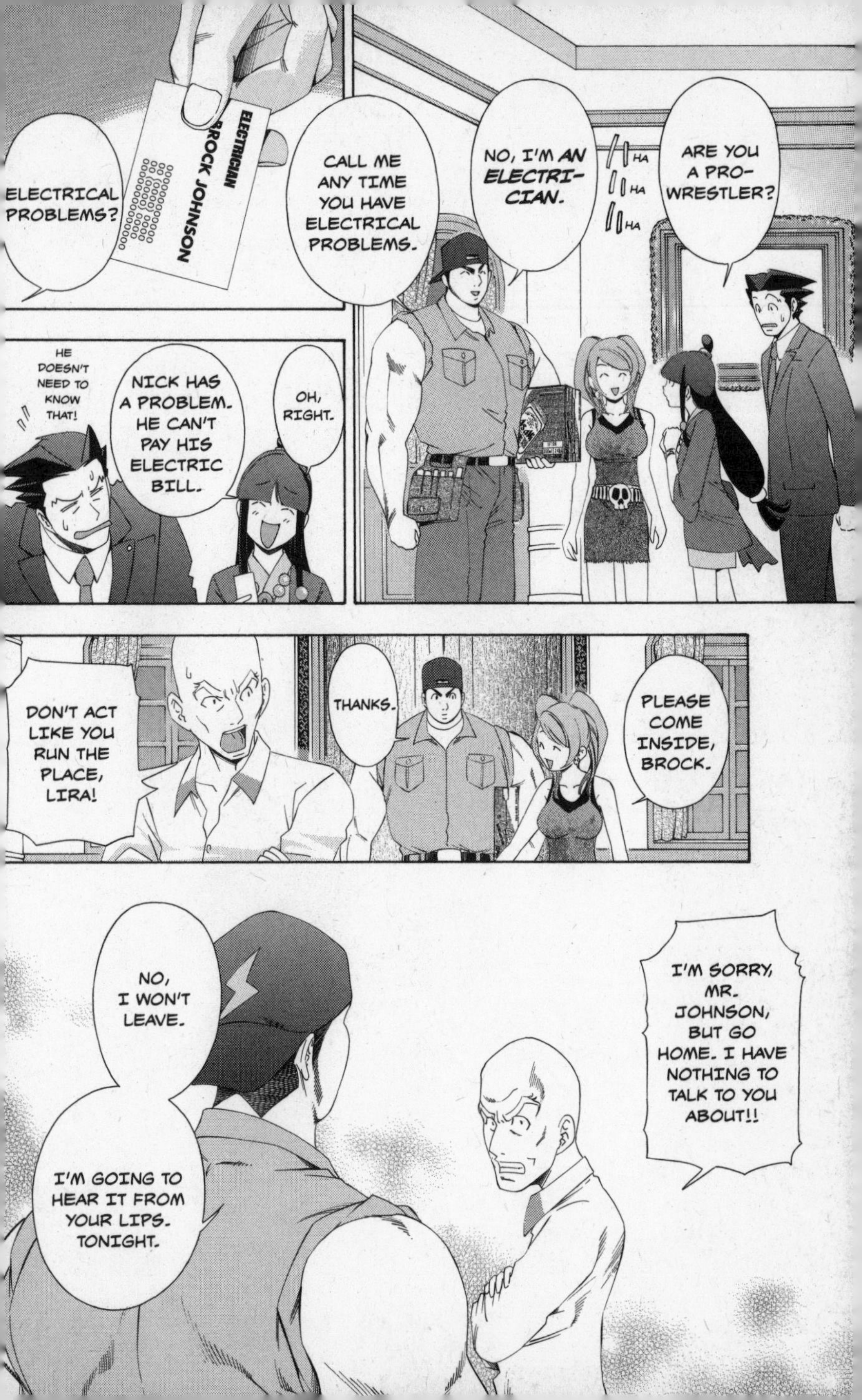
ARE YOU A PRO-WRESTLER?
HA HA HA
NO, I'M AN ELECTRICIAN.
CALL ME ANY TIME YOU HAVE ELECTRICAL PROBLEMS.
ELECTRICIAN BROCK JOHNSON
ELECTRICAL PROBLEMS?
OH, RIGHT.
NICK HAS A PROBLEM. HE CAN'T PAY HIS ELECTRIC BILL.
HE DOESN'T NEED TO KNOW THAT!
PLEASE COME INSIDE, BROCK.
THANKS.
DON'T ACT LIKE YOU RUN THE PLACE, LIRA!
I'M SORRY, MR. JOHNSON, BUT GO HOME. I HAVE NOTHING TO TALK TO YOU ABOUT!!
NO, I WON'T LEAVE.
I'M GOING TO HEAR IT FROM YOUR LIPS. TONIGHT.

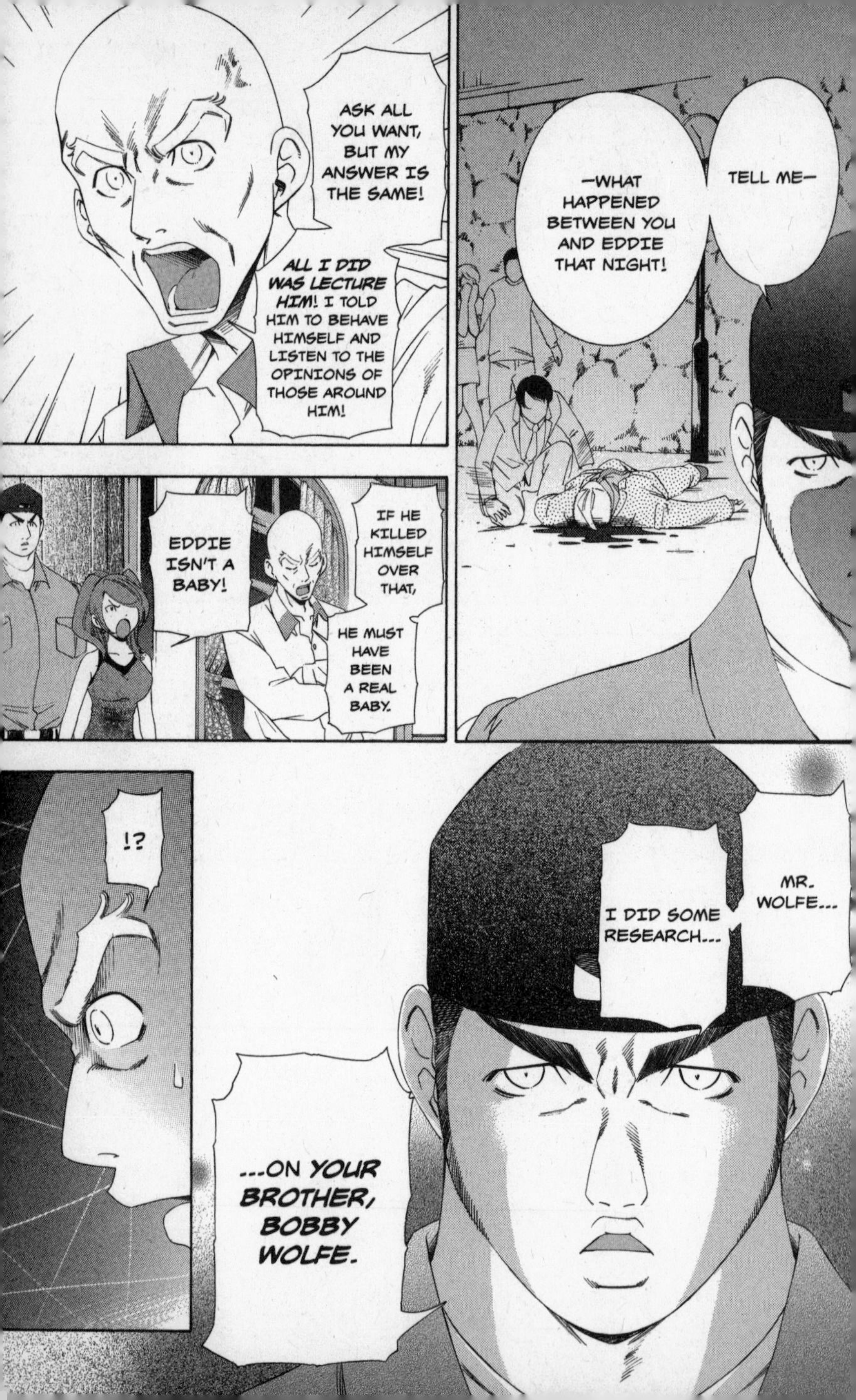
TELL ME—
—WHAT HAPPENED BETWEEN YOU AND EDDIE THAT NIGHT!
ASK ALL YOU WANT, BUT MY ANSWER IS THE SAME!
ALL I DID WAS LECTURE HIM! I TOLD HIM TO BEHAVE HIMSELF AND LISTEN TO THE OPINIONS OF THOSE AROUND HIM!
IF HE KILLED HIMSELF OVER THAT,
HE MUST HAVE BEEN A REAL BABY.
EDDIE ISN'T A BABY!
MR. WOLFE...
I DID SOME RESEARCH...
...ON YOUR BROTHER, BOBBY WOLFE.
!?

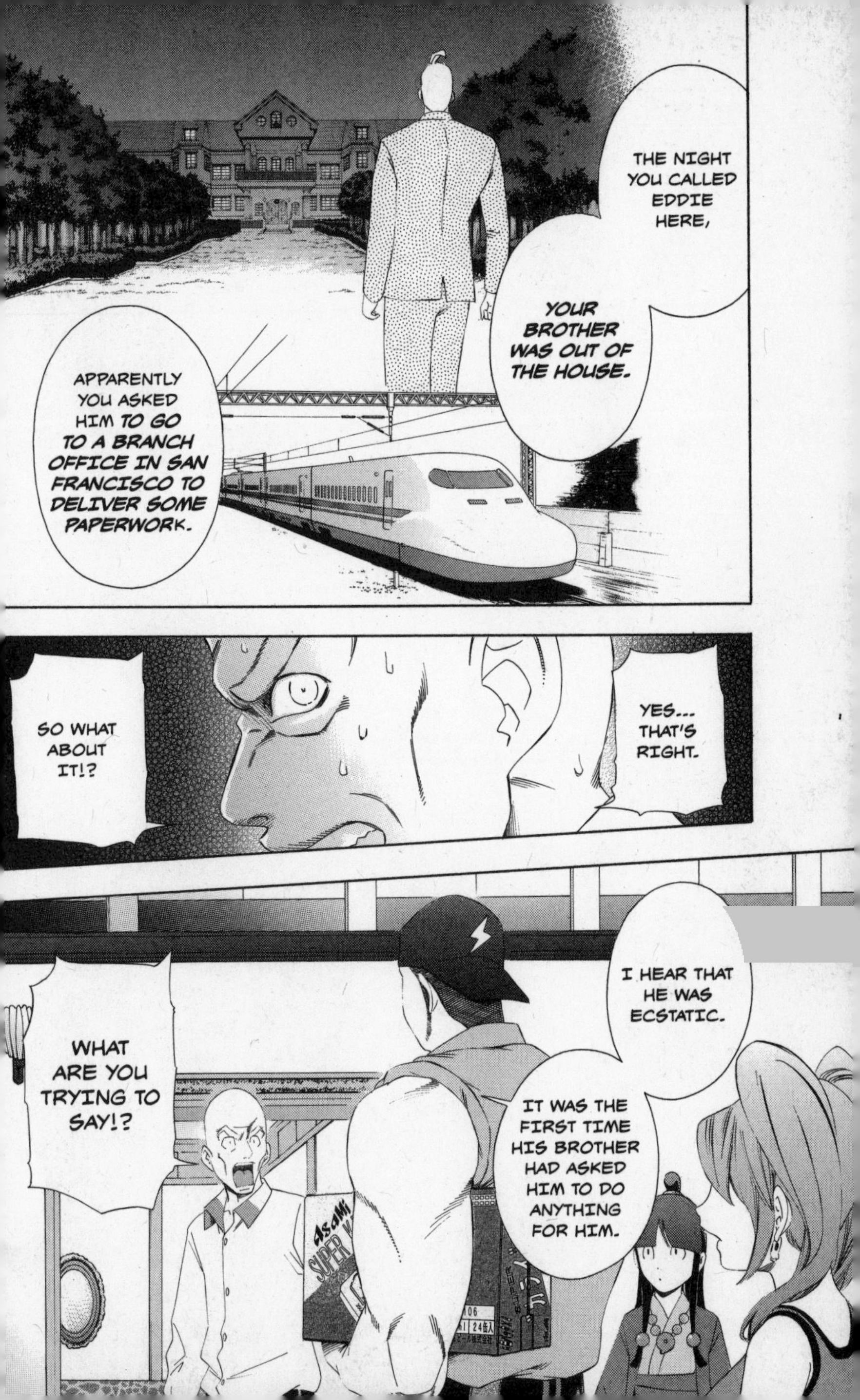
THE NIGHT YOU CALLED EDDIE HERE,
YOUR BROTHER WAS OUT OF THE HOUSE.
APPARENTLY YOU ASKED HIM TO GO TO A BRANCH OFFICE IN SAN FRANCISCO TO DELIVER SOME PAPERWORK.
YES... THAT'S RIGHT.
SO WHAT ABOUT IT!?
I HEAR THAT HE WAS ECSTATIC.
IT WAS THE FIRST TIME HIS BROTHER HAD ASKED HIM TO DO ANYTHING FOR HIM.
WHAT ARE YOU TRYING TO SAY!?

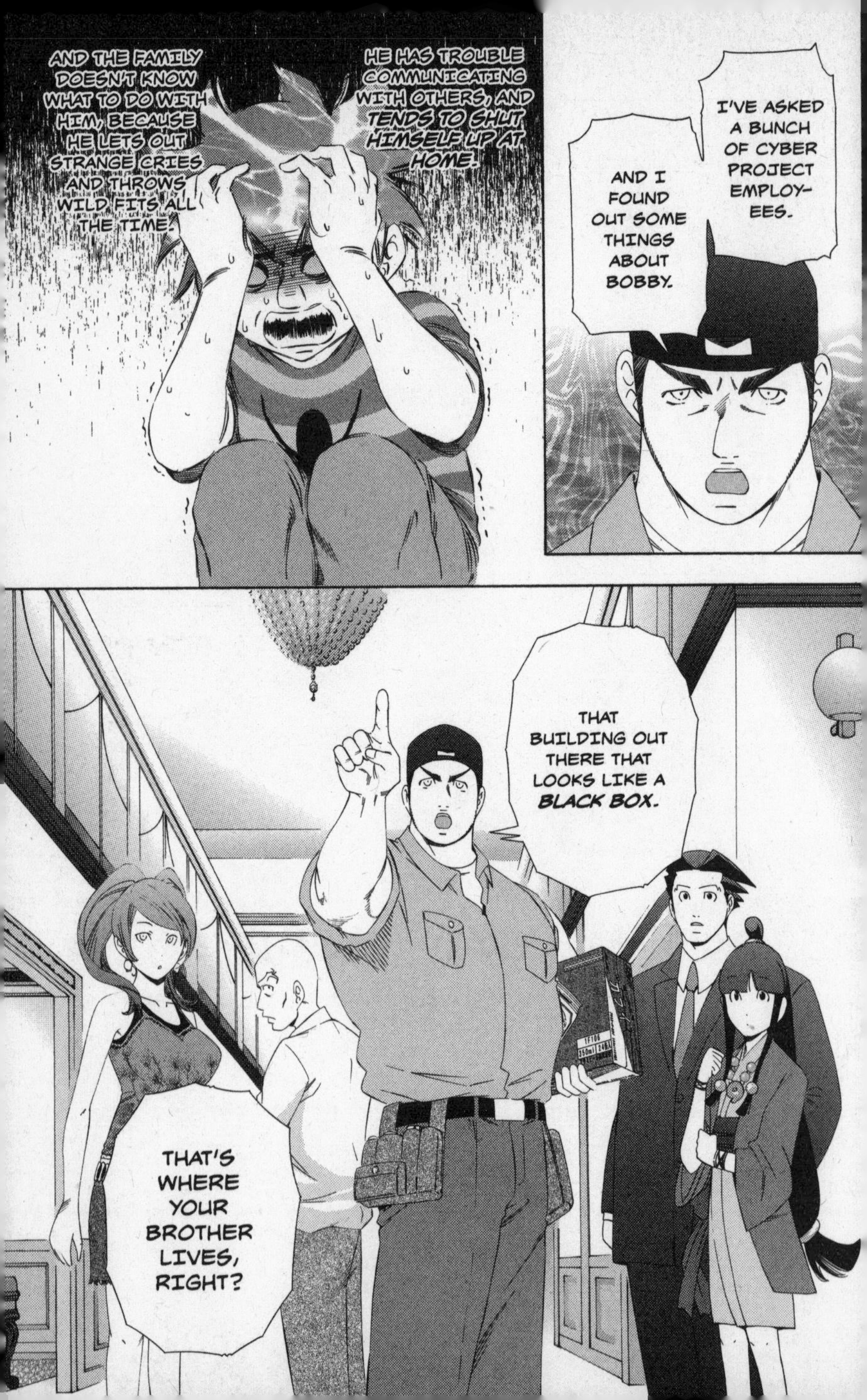
I'VE ASKED A BUNCH OF CYBER PROJECT EMPLOY-EES.
AND I FOUND OUT SOME THINGS ABOUT BOBBY.
HE HAS TROUBLE COMMUNICATING WITH OTHERS, AND *TENDS TO SHUT HIMSELF UP AT HOME.*
AND THE FAMILY DOESN'T KNOW WHAT TO DO WITH HIM, BECAUSE HE LETS OUT STRANGE CRIES AND THROWS WILD FITS ALL THE TIME.
THAT BUILDING OUT THERE THAT LOOKS LIKE A *BLACK BOX.*
THAT'S WHERE YOUR BROTHER LIVES, RIGHT?

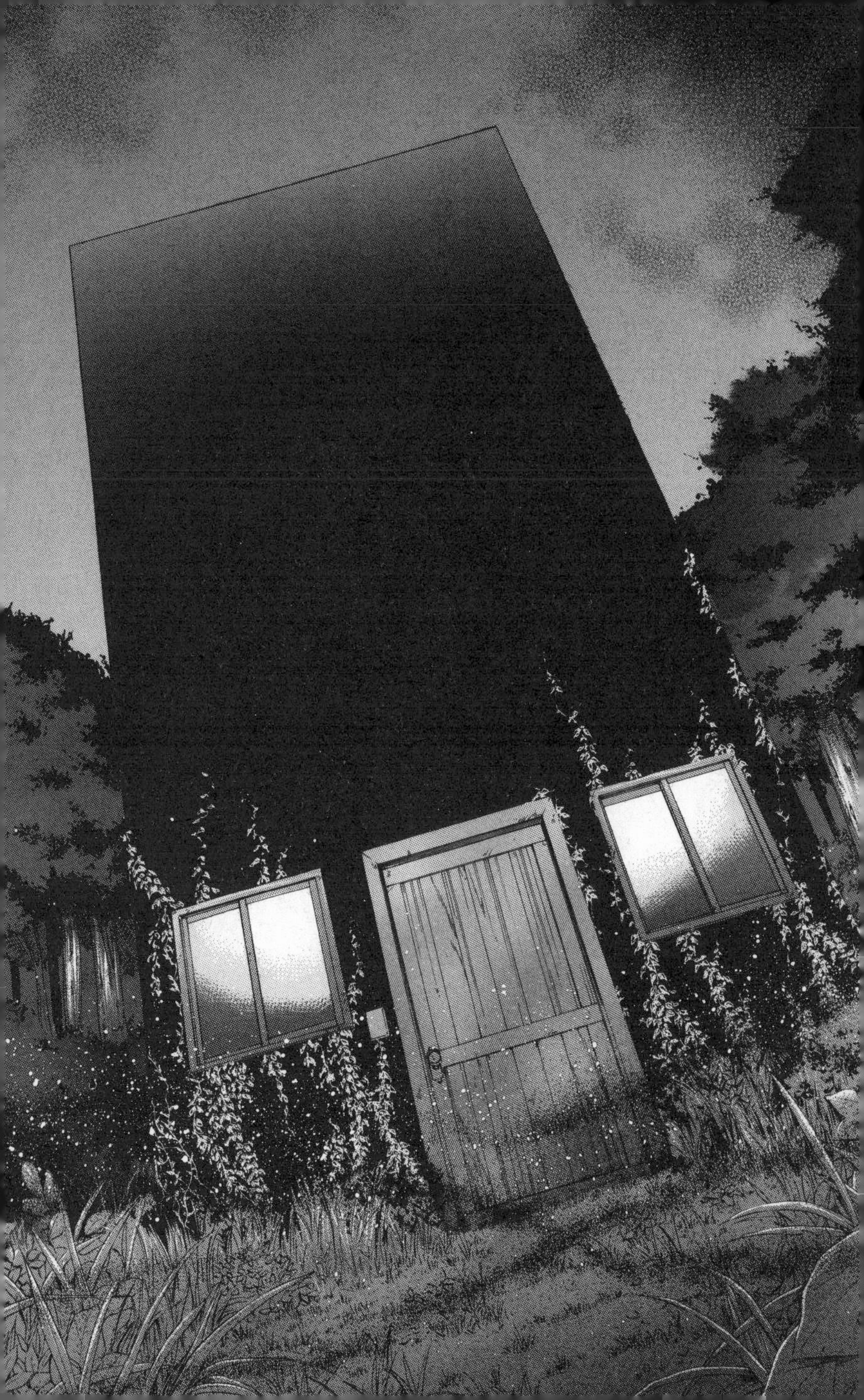

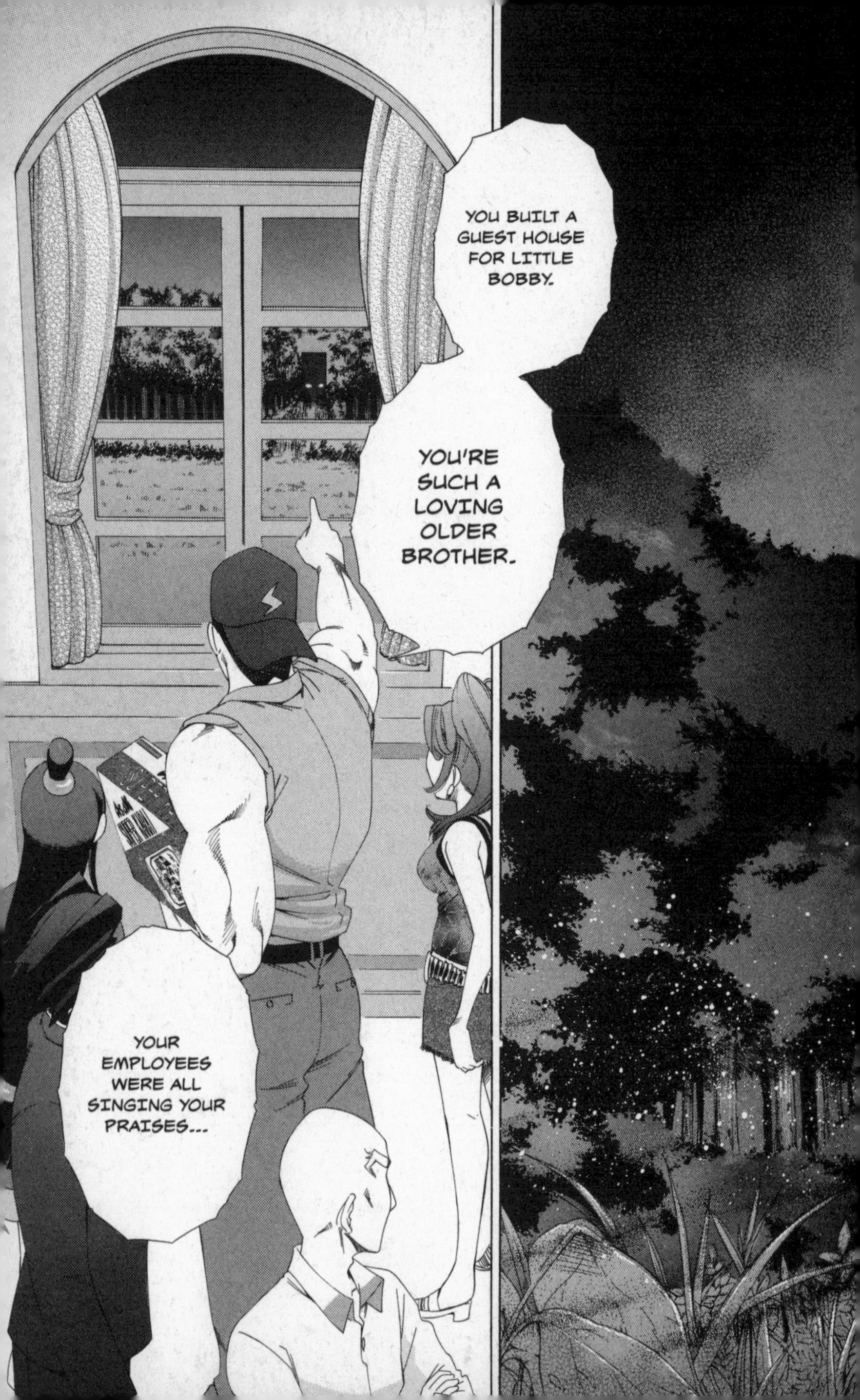
YOU BUILT A GUEST HOUSE FOR LITTLE BOBBY.
YOU'RE SUCH A LOVING OLDER BROTHER.
YOUR EMPLOYEES WERE ALL SINGING YOUR PRAISES...

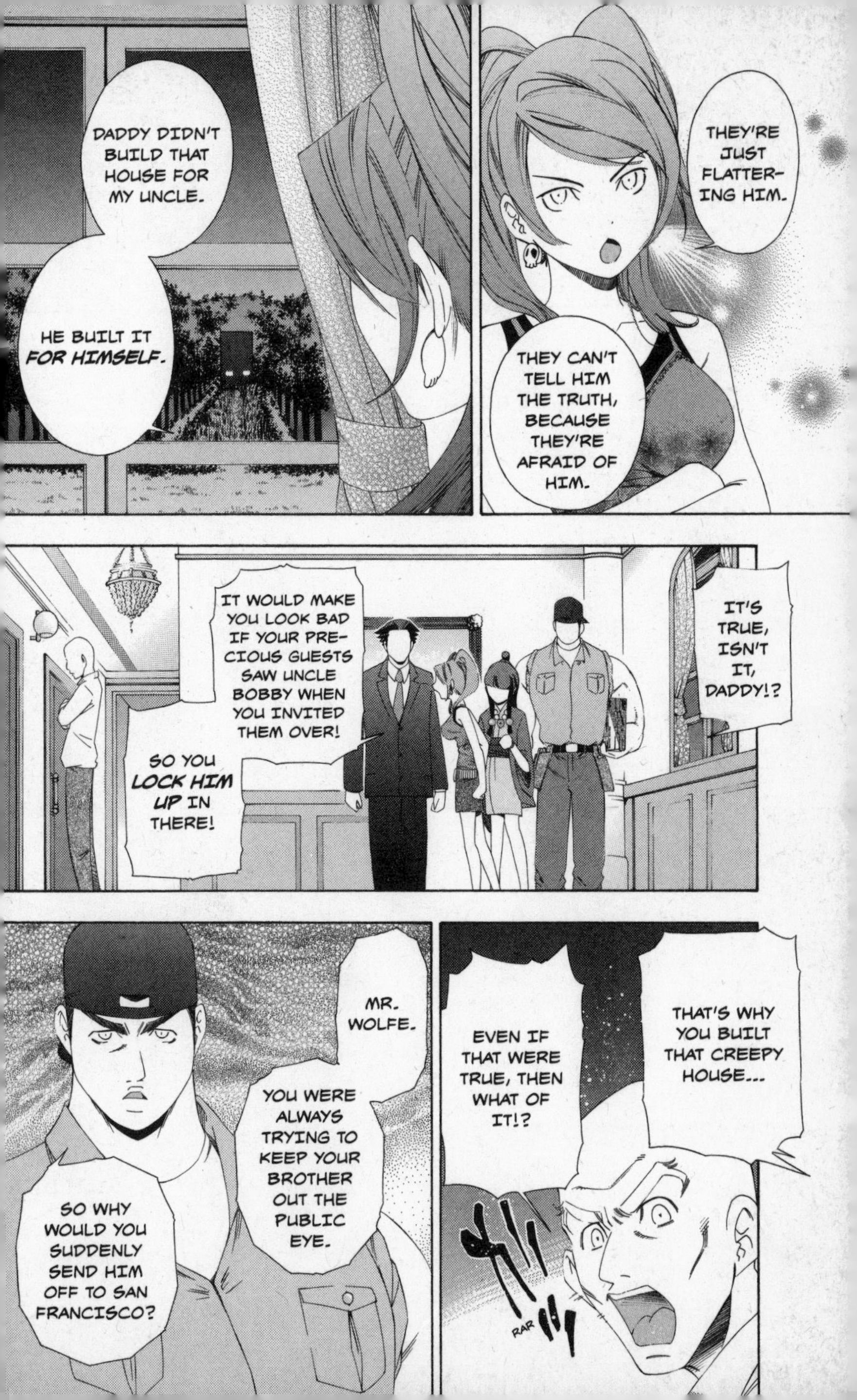
THEY'RE JUST FLATTERING HIM.
THEY CAN'T TELL HIM THE TRUTH, BECAUSE THEY'RE AFRAID OF HIM.
DADDY DIDN'T BUILD THAT HOUSE FOR MY UNCLE.
HE BUILT IT FOR HIMSELF.
IT'S TRUE, ISN'T IT, DADDY!?
IT WOULD MAKE YOU LOOK BAD IF YOUR PRECIOUS GUESTS SAW UNCLE BOBBY WHEN YOU INVITED THEM OVER!
SO YOU LOCK HIM UP IN THERE!
THAT'S WHY YOU BUILT THAT CREEPY HOUSE...
EVEN IF THAT WERE TRUE, THEN WHAT OF IT!?
RAR
MR. WOLFE.
YOU WERE ALWAYS TRYING TO KEEP YOUR BROTHER OUT THE PUBLIC EYE.
SO WHY WOULD YOU SUDDENLY SEND HIM OFF TO SAN FRANCISCO?

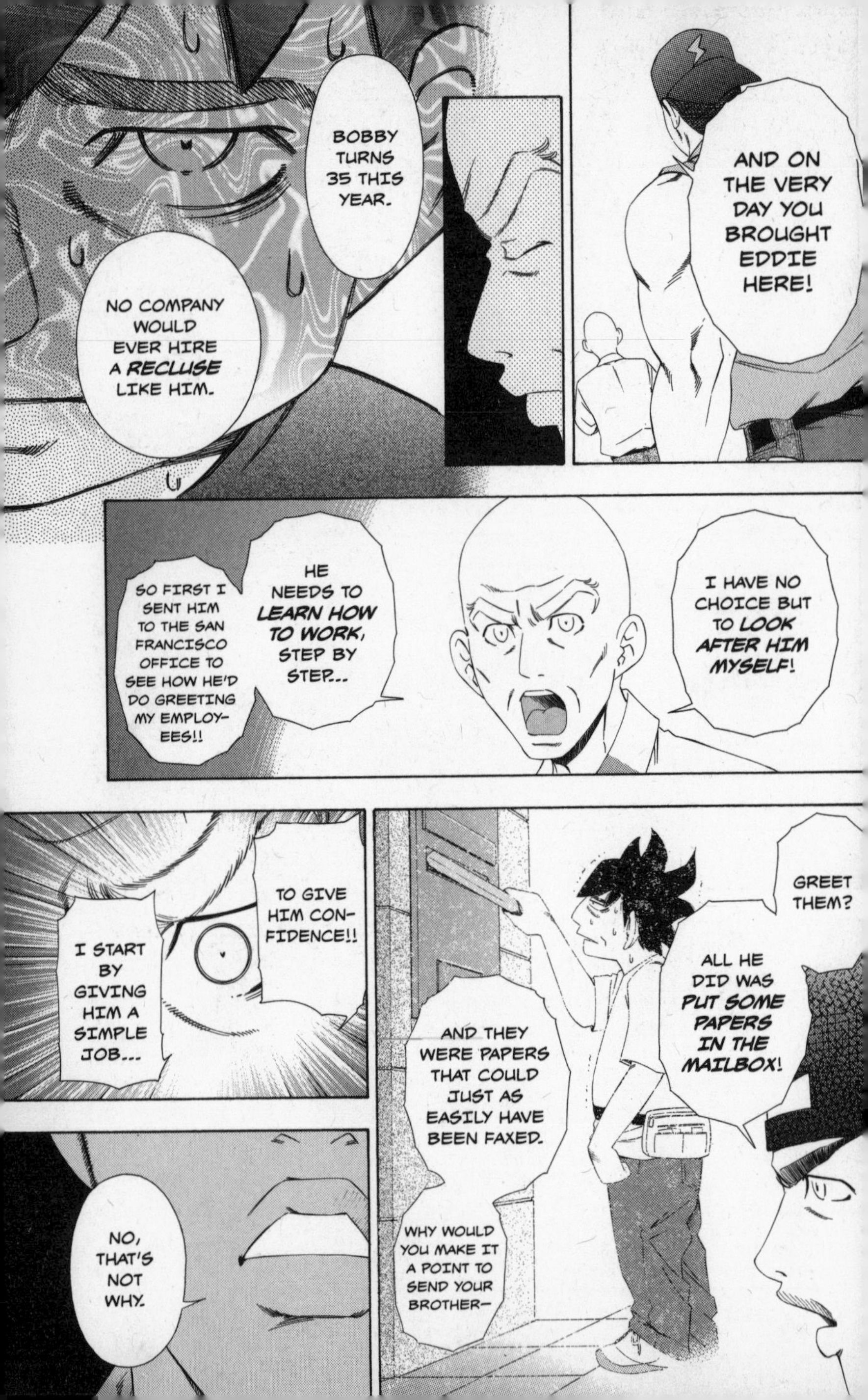
AND ON THE VERY DAY YOU BROUGHT EDDIE HERE!
BOBBY TURNS 35 THIS YEAR.
NO COMPANY WOULD EVER HIRE A *RECLUSE* LIKE HIM.
I HAVE NO CHOICE BUT TO *LOOK AFTER HIM MYSELF*!
HE NEEDS TO *LEARN HOW TO WORK*, STEP BY STEP...
SO FIRST I SENT HIM TO THE SAN FRANCISCO OFFICE TO SEE HOW HE'D DO GREETING MY EMPLOY-EES!!
GREET THEM?
ALL HE DID WAS *PUT SOME PAPERS IN THE MAILBOX*!
AND THEY WERE PAPERS THAT COULD JUST AS EASILY HAVE BEEN FAXED.
WHY WOULD YOU MAKE IT A POINT TO SEND YOUR BROTHER—
TO GIVE HIM CON-FIDENCE!!
I START BY GIVING HIM A SIMPLE JOB...
NO, THAT'S NOT WHY.

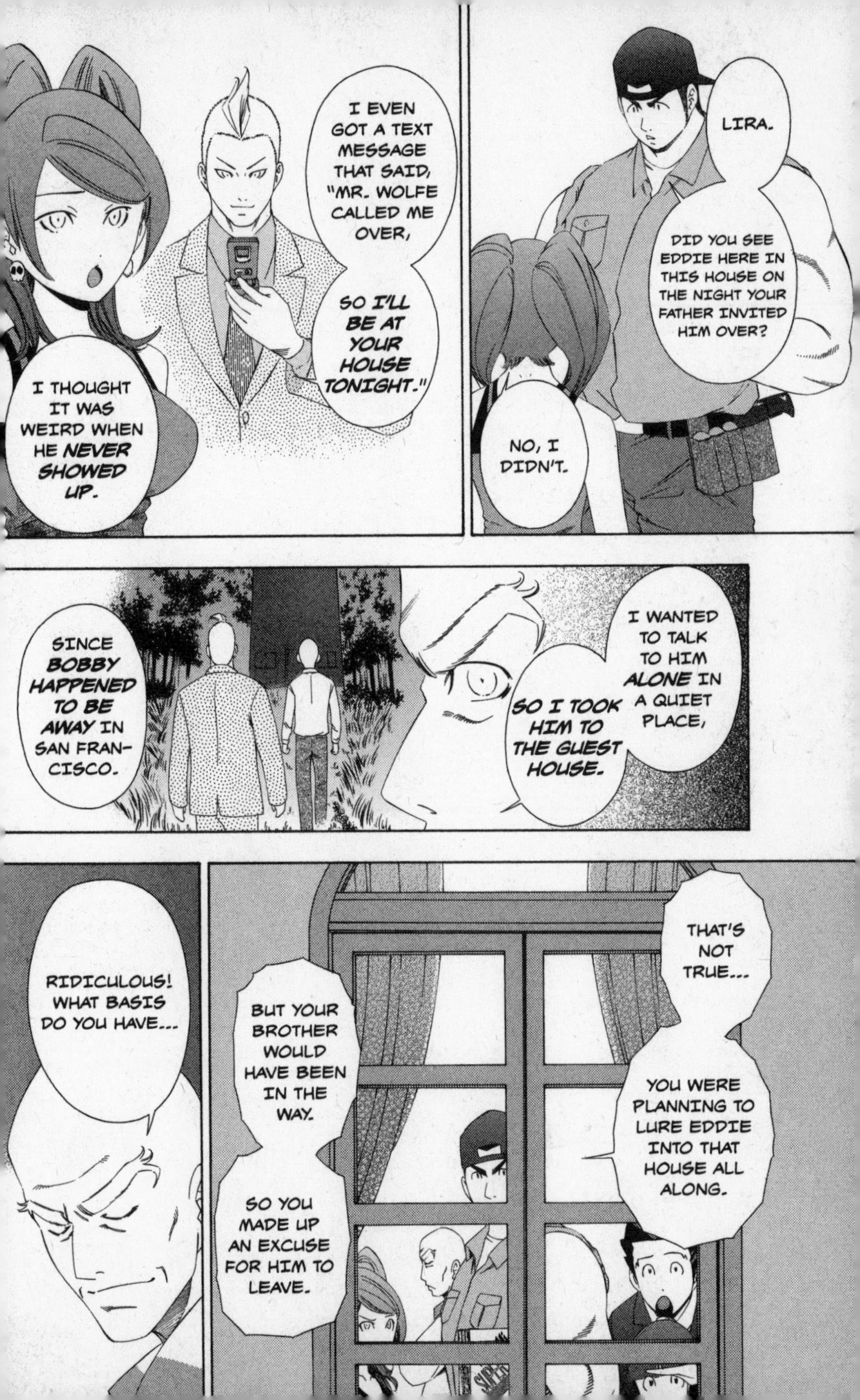
LIRA.
DID YOU SEE EDDIE HERE IN THIS HOUSE ON THE NIGHT YOUR FATHER INVITED HIM OVER?
NO, I DIDN'T.
I EVEN GOT A TEXT MESSAGE THAT SAID, "MR. WOLFE CALLED ME OVER,
SO I'LL BE AT YOUR HOUSE TONIGHT."
I THOUGHT IT WAS WEIRD WHEN HE NEVER SHOWED UP.
I WANTED TO TALK TO HIM ALONE IN A QUIET PLACE,
SO I TOOK HIM TO THE GUEST HOUSE.
SINCE BOBBY HAPPENED TO BE AWAY IN SAN FRAN-CISCO.
THAT'S NOT TRUE...
YOU WERE PLANNING TO LURE EDDIE INTO THAT HOUSE ALL ALONG.
BUT YOUR BROTHER WOULD HAVE BEEN IN THE WAY.
SO YOU MADE UP AN EXCUSE FOR HIM TO LEAVE.
RIDICULOUS! WHAT BASIS DO YOU HAVE...

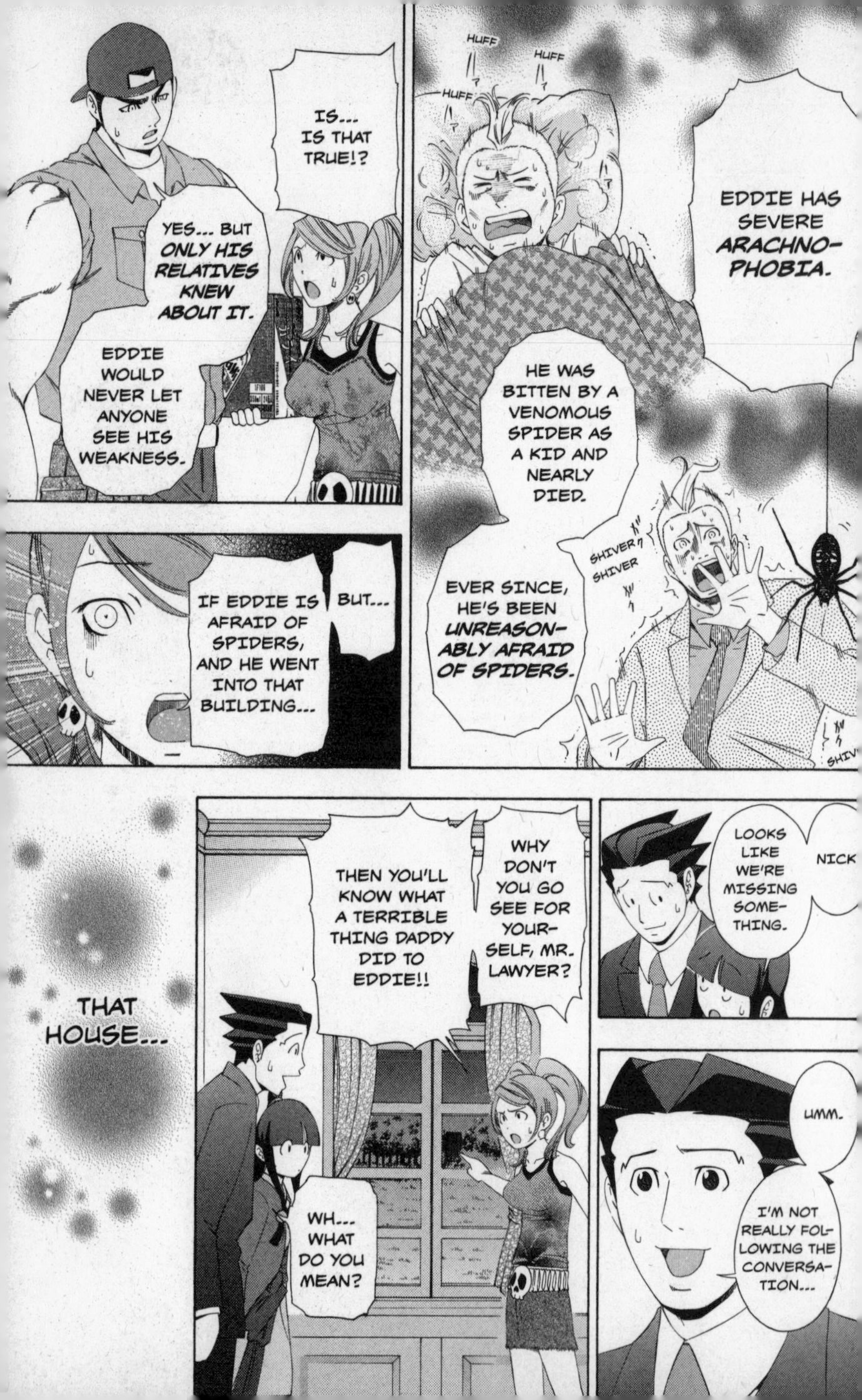
HUFF
HUFF
HUFF
EDDIE HAS SEVERE ARACHNOPHOBIA.
HE WAS BITTEN BY A VENOMOUS SPIDER AS A KID AND NEARLY DIED.
EVER SINCE, HE'S BEEN UNREASONABLY AFRAID OF SPIDERS.
SHIVER
SHIVER
SHIV
IS... IS THAT TRUE!?
YES... BUT ONLY HIS RELATIVES KNEW ABOUT IT.
EDDIE WOULD NEVER LET ANYONE SEE HIS WEAKNESS.
BUT...
IF EDDIE IS AFRAID OF SPIDERS, AND HE WENT INTO THAT BUILDING...
NICK
LOOKS LIKE WE'RE MISSING SOMETHING.
UMM.
I'M NOT REALLY FOLLOWING THE CONVERSATION...
WHY DON'T YOU GO SEE FOR YOURSELF, MR. LAWYER?
THEN YOU'LL KNOW WHAT A TERRIBLE THING DADDY DID TO EDDIE!!
WH... WHAT DO YOU MEAN?
THAT HOUSE...

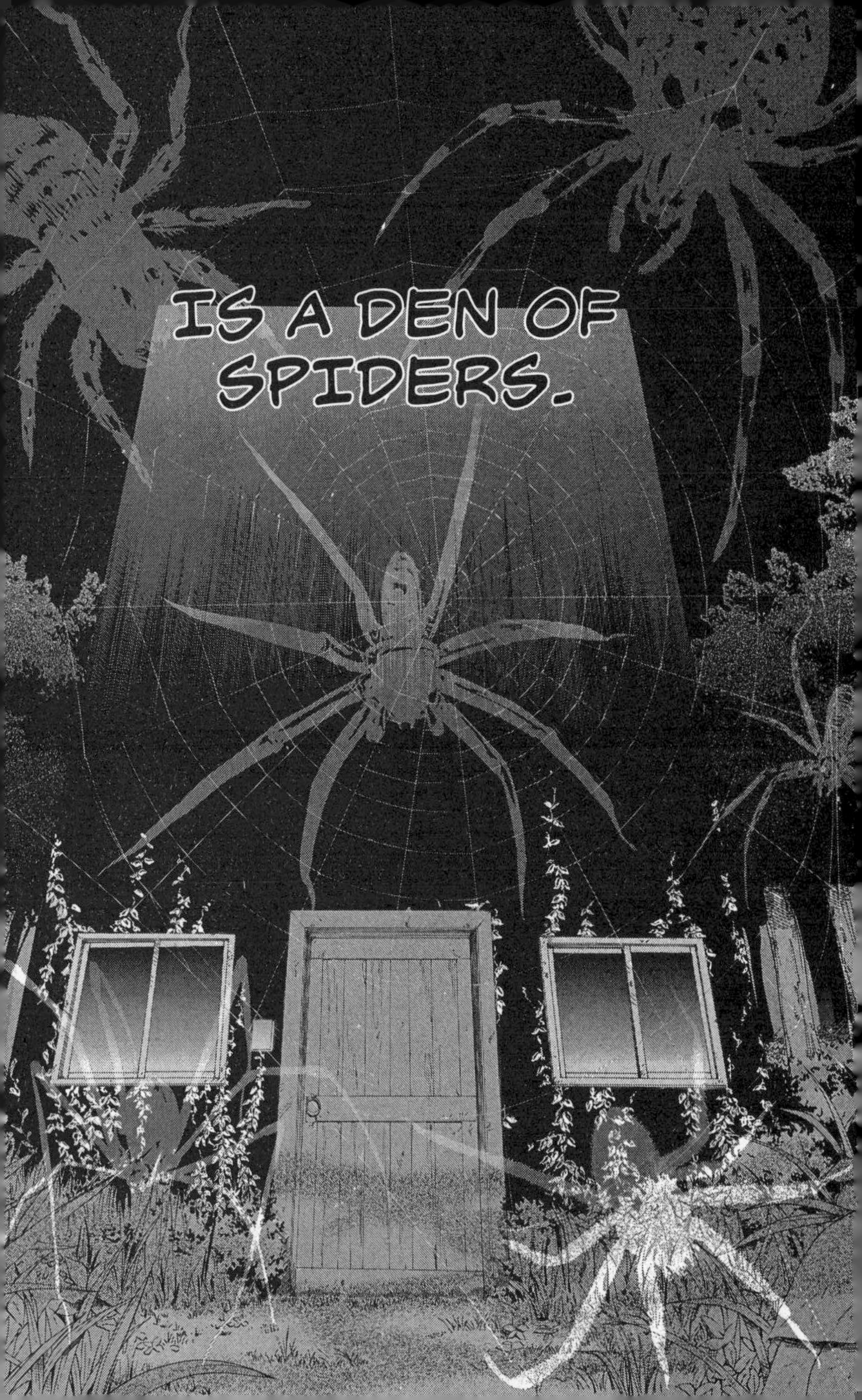
IS A DEN OF SPIDERS.

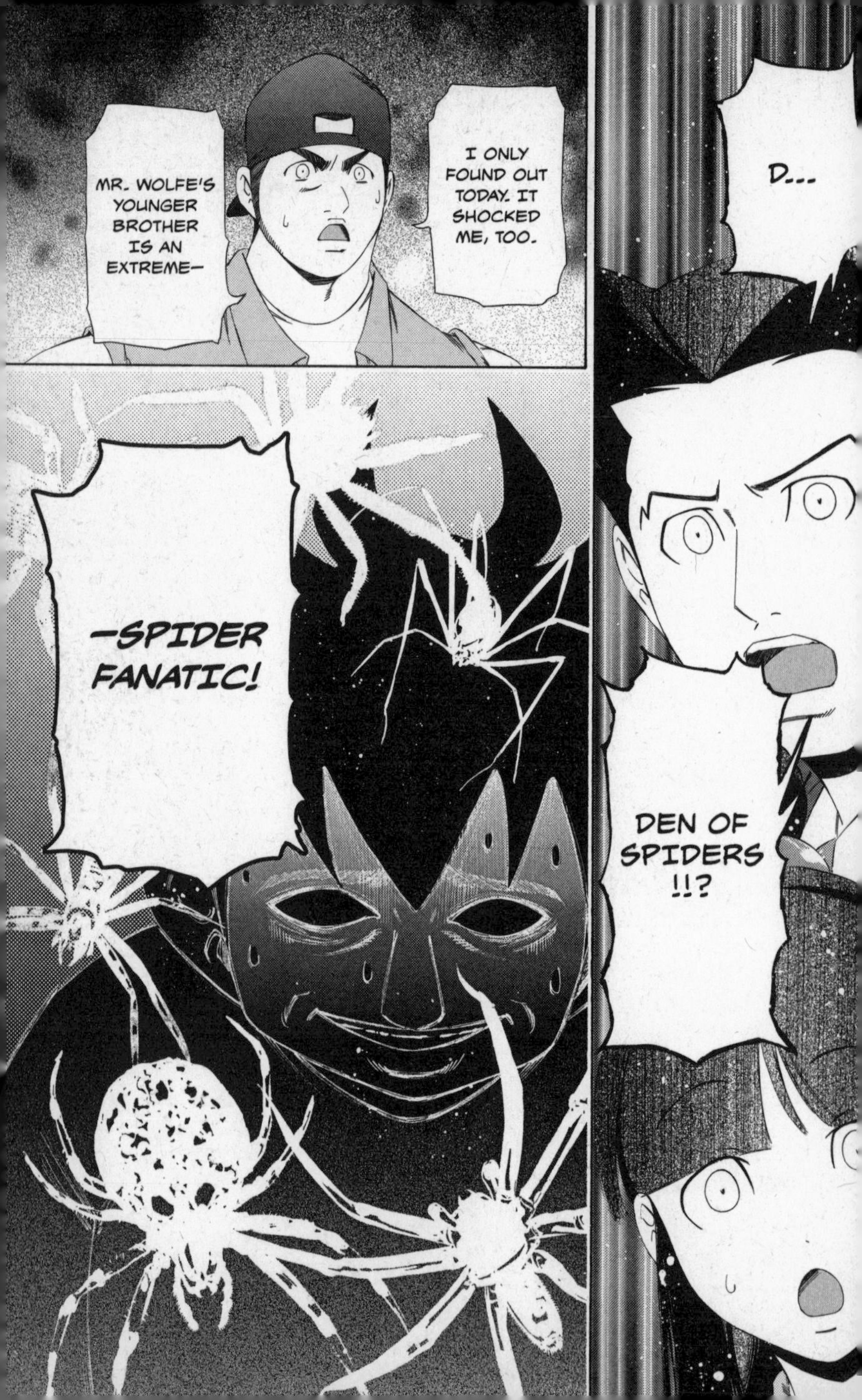
D...
DEN OF SPIDERS !!?
I ONLY FOUND OUT TODAY. IT SHOCKED ME, TOO.
MR. WOLFE'S YOUNGER BROTHER IS AN EXTREME—
—SPIDER FANATIC!

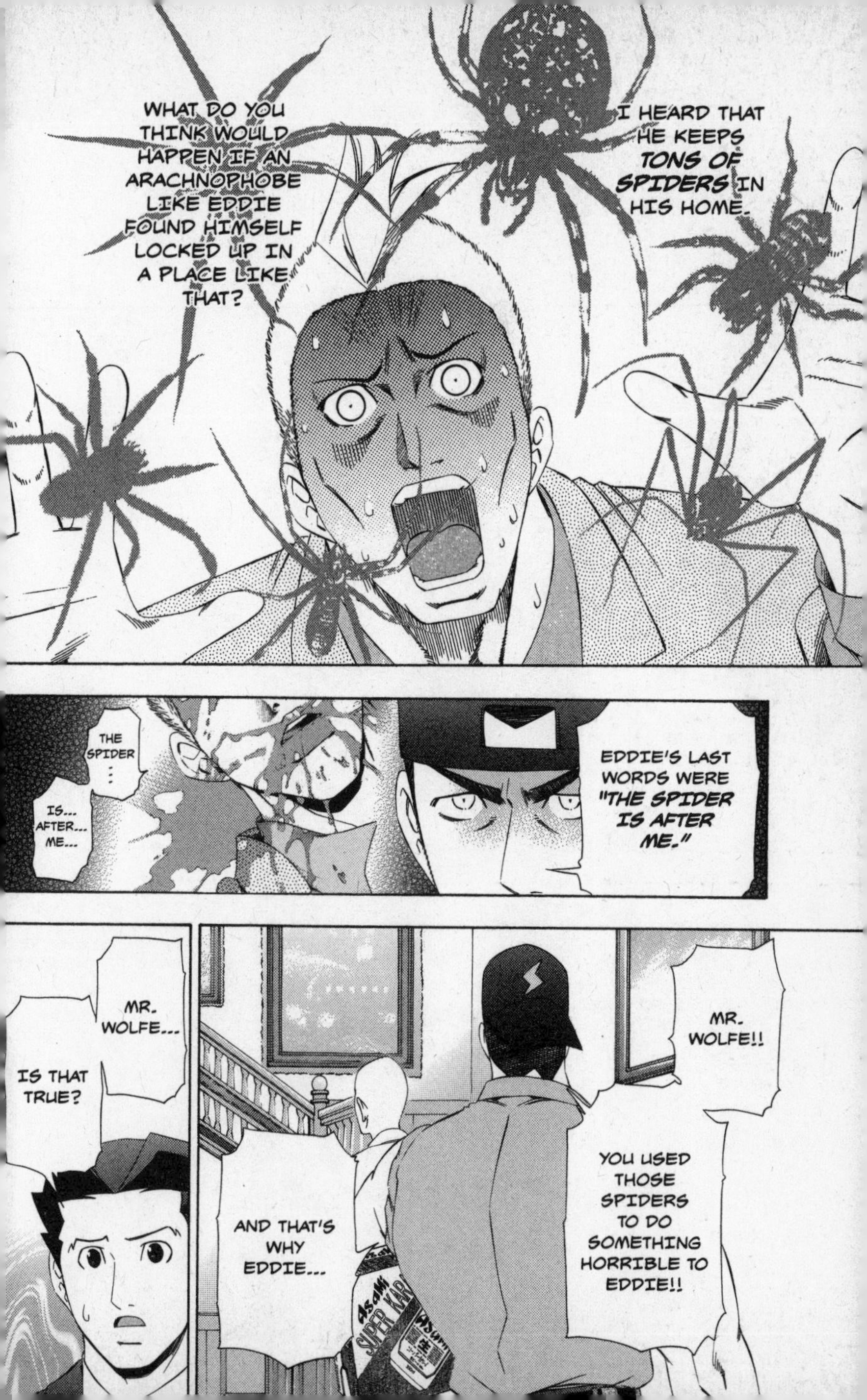
I HEARD THAT HE KEEPS TONS OF SPIDERS IN HIS HOME.
WHAT DO YOU THINK WOULD HAPPEN IF AN ARACHNOPHOBE LIKE EDDIE FOUND HIMSELF LOCKED UP IN A PLACE LIKE THAT?
EDDIE'S LAST WORDS WERE "THE SPIDER IS AFTER ME."
THE SPIDER ...
IS... AFTER... ME...
MR. WOLFE!!
YOU USED THOSE SPIDERS TO DO SOMETHING HORRIBLE TO EDDIE!!
AND THAT'S WHY EDDIE...
MR. WOLFE...
IS THAT TRUE?

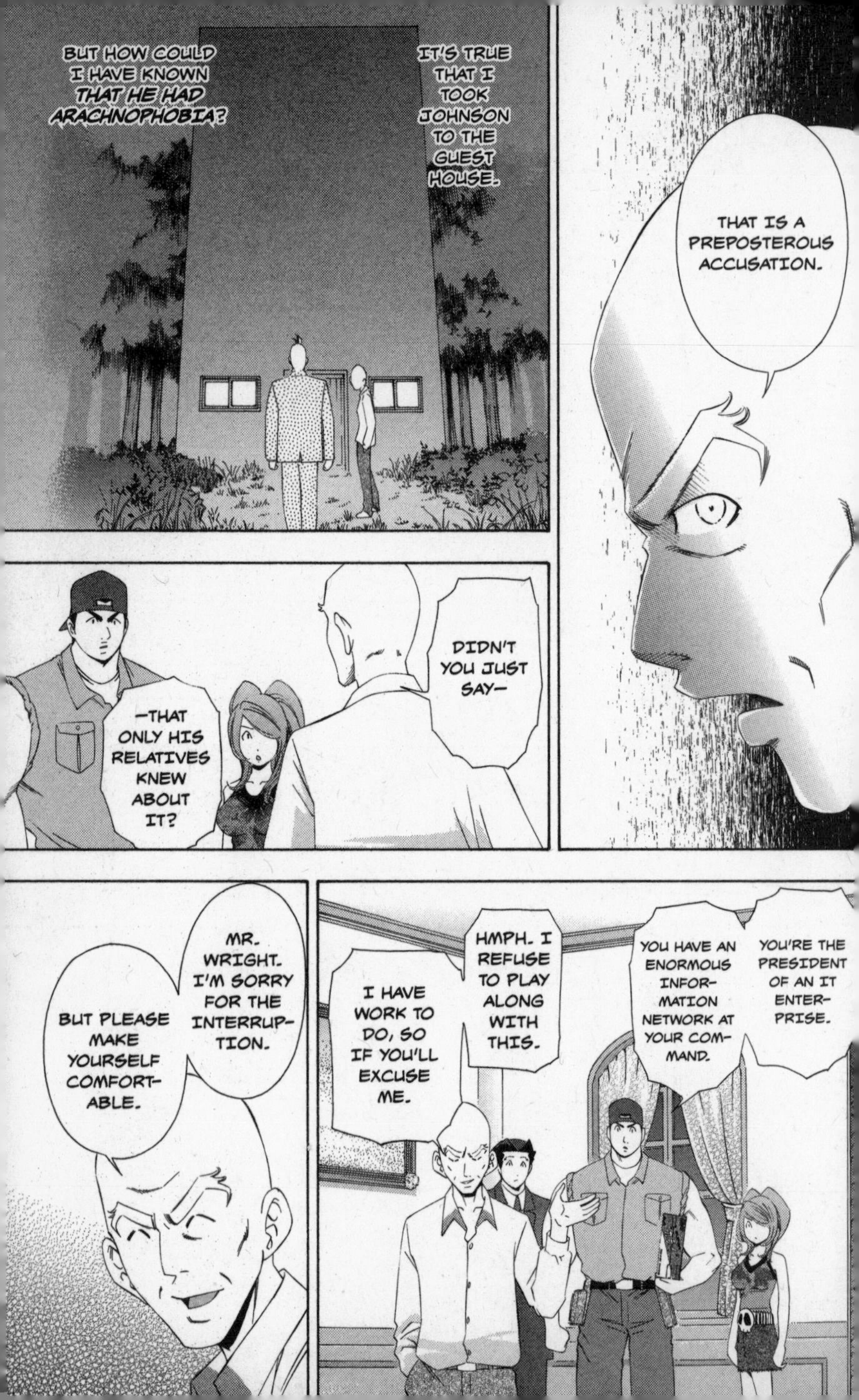
THAT IS A PREPOSTEROUS ACCUSATION.
IT'S TRUE THAT I TOOK JOHNSON TO THE GUEST HOUSE.
BUT HOW COULD I HAVE KNOWN *THAT HE HAD ARACHNOPHOBIA?*
DIDN'T YOU JUST SAY—
—THAT ONLY HIS RELATIVES KNEW ABOUT IT?
YOU'RE THE PRESIDENT OF AN IT ENTERPRISE.
YOU HAVE AN ENORMOUS INFORMATION NETWORK AT YOUR COMMAND.
HMPH. I REFUSE TO PLAY ALONG WITH THIS.
I HAVE WORK TO DO, SO IF YOU'LL EXCUSE ME.
MR. WRIGHT. I'M SORRY FOR THE INTERRUPTION.
BUT PLEASE MAKE YOURSELF COMFORTABLE.

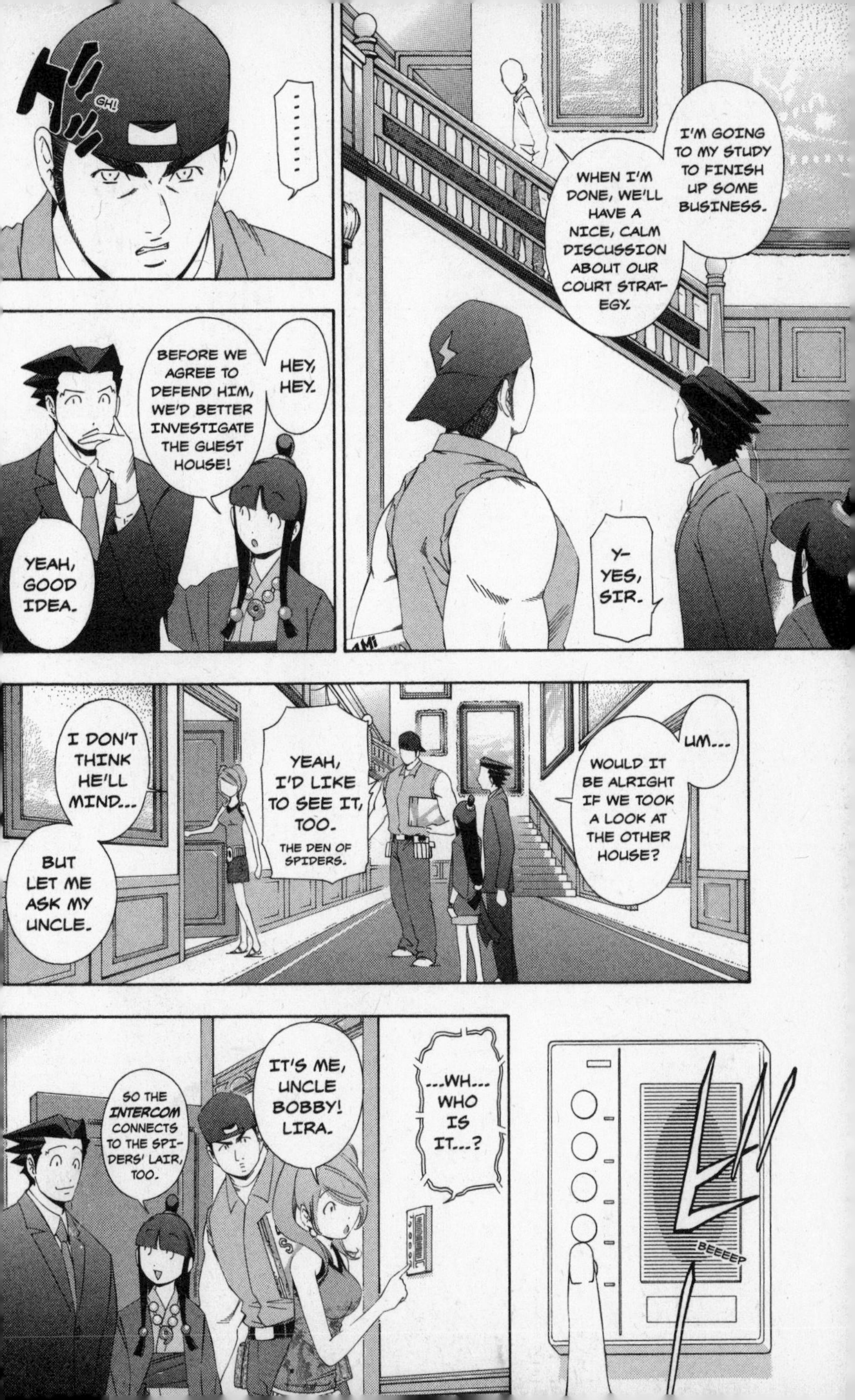
I'M GOING TO MY STUDY TO FINISH UP SOME BUSINESS.
WHEN I'M DONE, WE'LL HAVE A NICE, CALM DISCUSSION ABOUT OUR COURT STRATEGY.
Y-YES, SIR.
GH!
......
HEY, HEY.
BEFORE WE AGREE TO DEFEND HIM, WE'D BETTER INVESTIGATE THE GUEST HOUSE!
YEAH, GOOD IDEA.
UM...
WOULD IT BE ALRIGHT IF WE TOOK A LOOK AT THE OTHER HOUSE?
YEAH, I'D LIKE TO SEE IT, TOO.
THE DEN OF SPIDERS.
I DON'T THINK HE'LL MIND...
BUT LET ME ASK MY UNCLE.
BEEEEP
...WH... WHO IS IT...?
IT'S ME, UNCLE BOBBY! LIRA.
SO THE *INTERCOM* CONNECTS TO THE SPIDERS' LAIR, TOO.

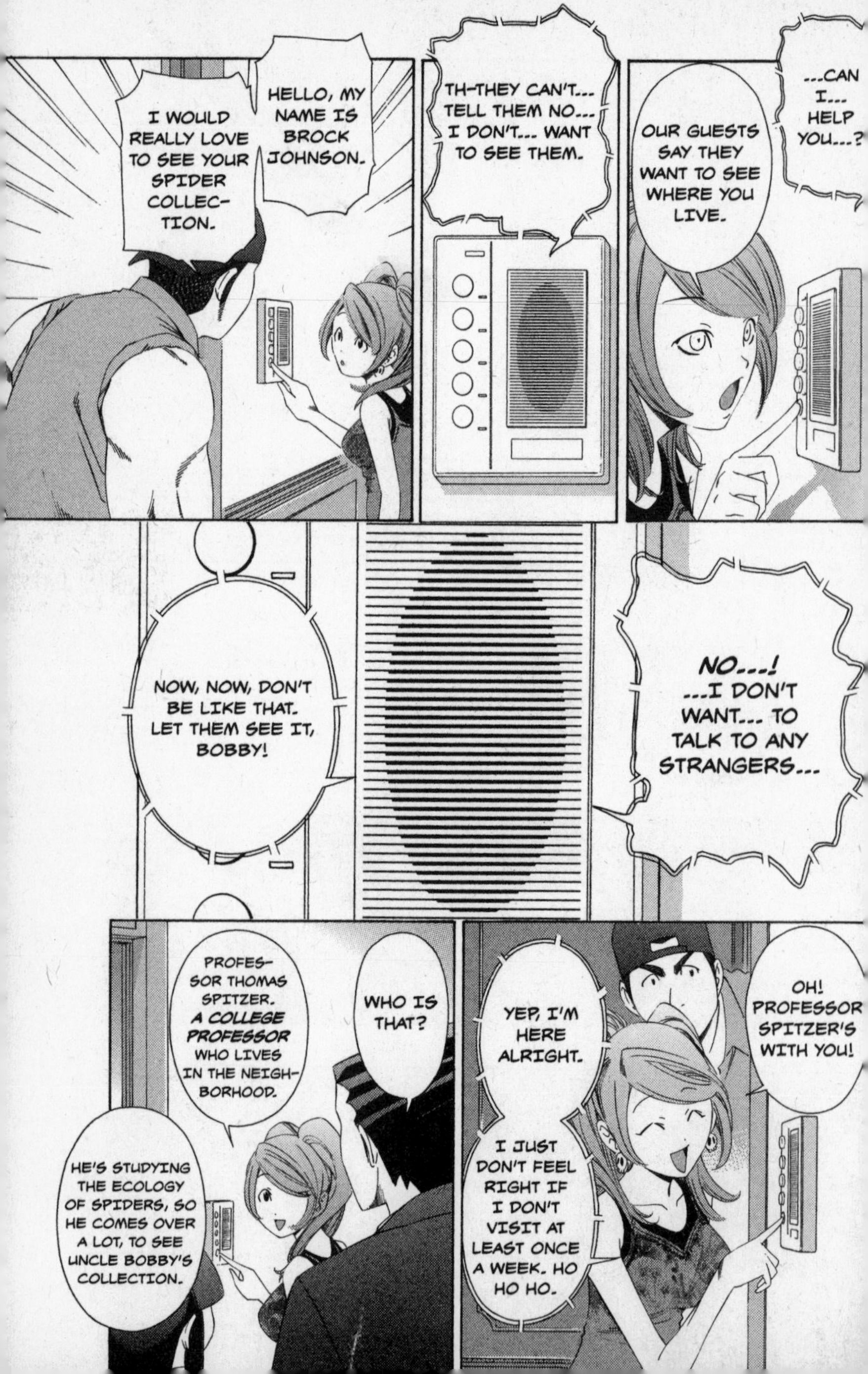
...CAN I... HELP YOU...?
OUR GUESTS SAY THEY WANT TO SEE WHERE YOU LIVE.
TH-THEY CAN'T... TELL THEM NO... I DON'T... WANT TO SEE THEM.
HELLO, MY NAME IS BROCK JOHNSON.
I WOULD REALLY LOVE TO SEE YOUR SPIDER COLLECTION.
*NO...!* ...I DON'T WANT... TO TALK TO ANY STRANGERS...
NOW, NOW, DON'T BE LIKE THAT. LET THEM SEE IT, BOBBY!
OH! PROFESSOR SPITZER'S WITH YOU!
YEP, I'M HERE ALRIGHT.
I JUST DON'T FEEL RIGHT IF I DON'T VISIT AT LEAST ONCE A WEEK. HO HO HO.
WHO IS THAT?
PROFESSOR THOMAS SPITZER. *A COLLEGE PROFESSOR* WHO LIVES IN THE NEIGHBORHOOD.
HE'S STUDYING THE ECOLOGY OF SPIDERS, SO HE COMES OVER A LOT, TO SEE UNCLE BOBBY'S COLLECTION.

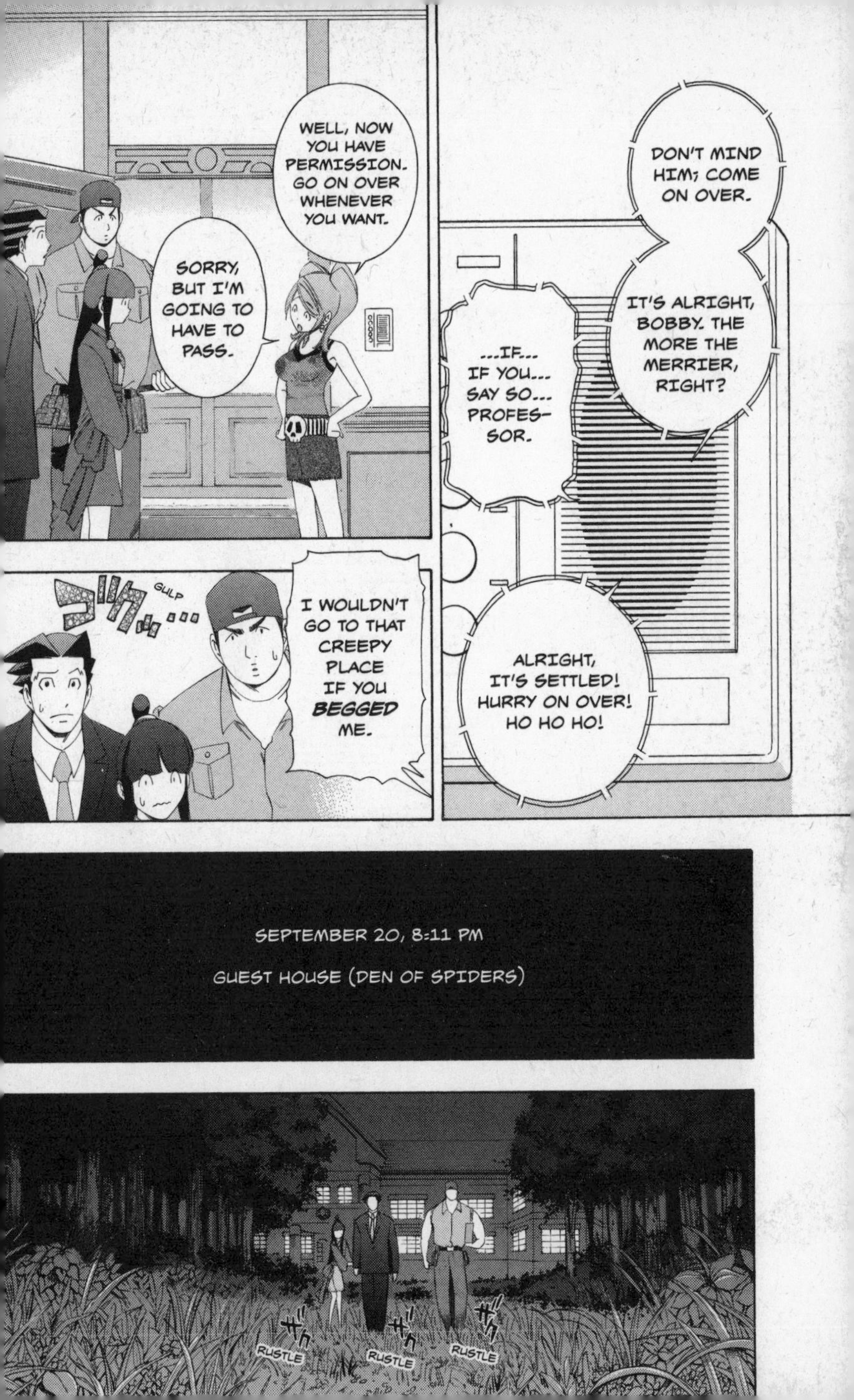
DON'T MIND HIM; COME ON OVER.
IT'S ALRIGHT, BOBBY. THE MORE THE MERRIER, RIGHT?
...IF... IF YOU... SAY SO... PROFES-SOR.
ALRIGHT, IT'S SETTLED! HURRY ON OVER! HO HO HO!
WELL, NOW YOU HAVE PERMISSION. GO ON OVER WHENEVER YOU WANT.
SORRY, BUT I'M GOING TO HAVE TO PASS.
I WOULDN'T GO TO THAT CREEPY PLACE IF YOU *BEGGED* ME.
GULP
SEPTEMBER 20, 8:11 PM
GUEST HOUSE (DEN OF SPIDERS)
RUSTLE
RUSTLE
RUSTLE

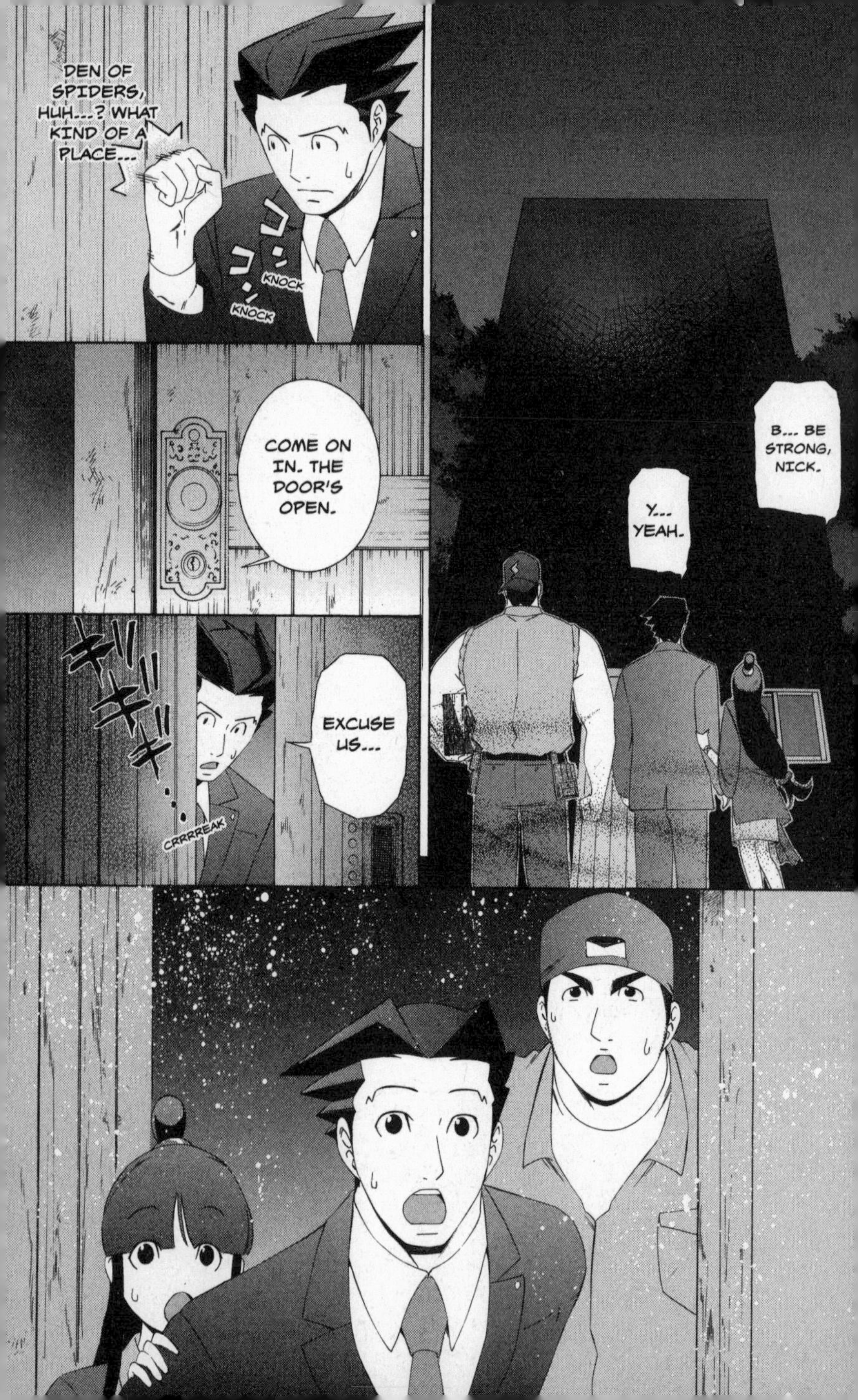
B... BE STRONG, NICK.
Y... YEAH.
DEN OF SPIDERS, HUH...? WHAT KIND OF A PLACE...
KNOCK
KNOCK
COME ON IN. THE DOOR'S OPEN.
EXCUSE US...
CRRRREAK

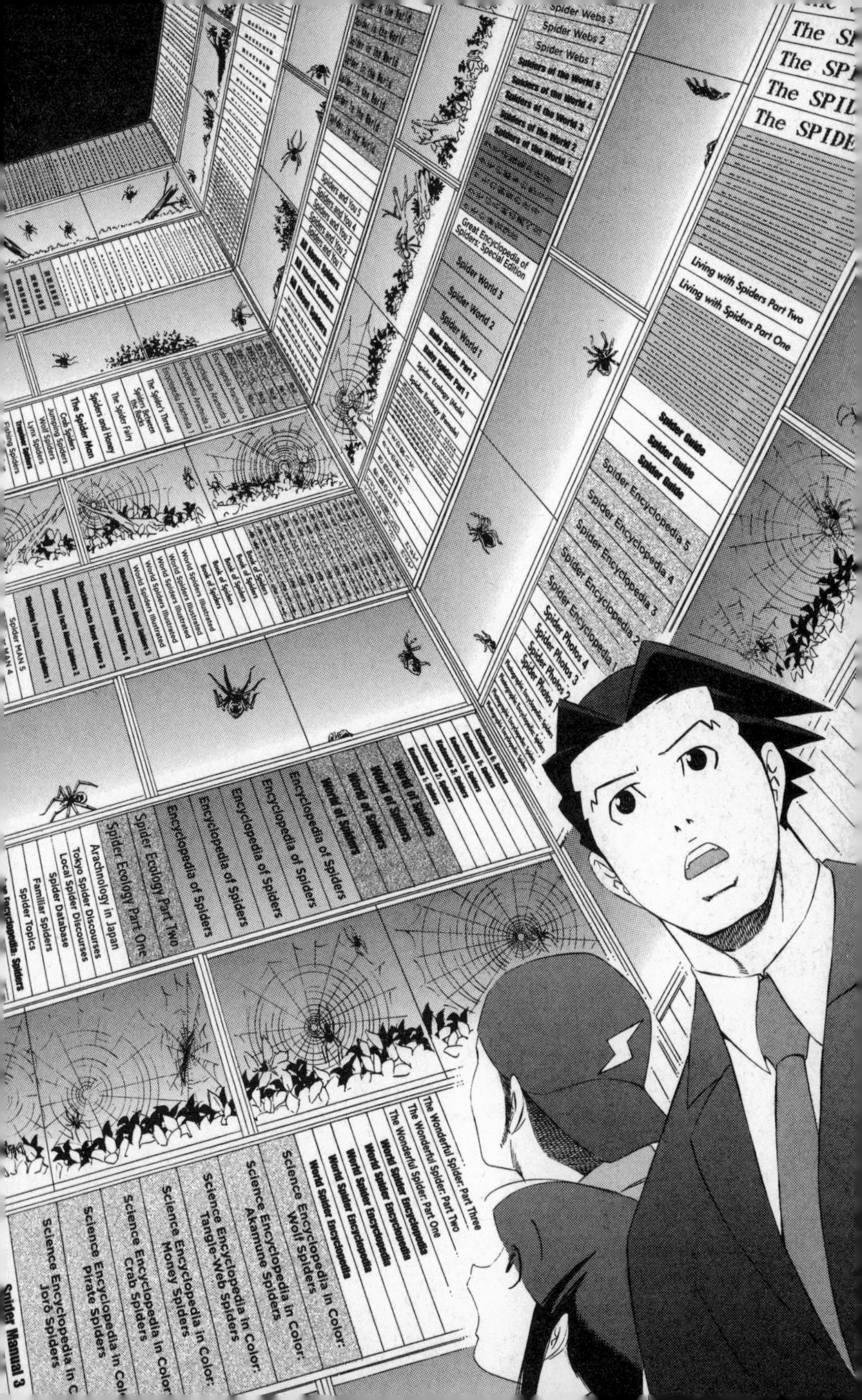
Spider Webs 3
Spider Webs 2
Spider Webs 1
Spiders of the World 5
Spiders of the World 4
Spiders of the World 3
Spiders of the World 2
Spiders of the World 1
Living with Spiders Part Two
Living with Spiders Part One
Great Encyclopedia of Spiders: Special Edition
Spider World 3
Spider World 2
Spider World 1
Baby Spider Part 2
Baby Spider Part 1
Spider Ecology (Male)
Spider Ecology (Female)
Spiders and You 5
Spiders and You 4
Spiders and You 3
Spiders and You 2
Spiders and You 1
All About Spiders
All About Spiders
All About Spiders
All About Spiders
Spider Guide
Spider Guide
Spider Guide
Spider Encyclopedia 5
Spider Encyclopedia 4
Spider Encyclopedia 3
Spider Encyclopedia 2
Spider Encyclopedia 1
Spider Photos 4
Spider Photos 3
Spider Photos 2
Spider Photos 1
The Spider's Thread
Spiders Between the Rocks
The Spider Fairy
Spiders and Honey
The Spider Man
Crab Spiders
Wolf Spiders
Jumping Spiders
Lynx Spiders
Trapdoor Spiders
Fishing Spiders
Book of Spiders
Book of Spiders
Book of Spiders
World Spiders Illustrated
World Spiders Illustrated
World Spiders Illustrated
Spider MAN 5
World of Spiders
World of Spiders
World of Spiders
Encyclopedia of Spiders
Encyclopedia of Spiders
Encyclopedia of Spiders
Encyclopedia of Spiders
Spider Ecology Part Two
Spider Ecology Part One
Arachnology in Japan
Tokyo Spider Discourses
Local Spider Database
Spider Database
Familiar Spiders
Spider Topics
The Wonderful Spider: Part Three
The Wonderful Spider: Part Two
The Wonderful Spider: Part One
World Spider Encyclopedia
World Spider Encyclopedia
World Spider Encyclopedia
World Spider Encyclopedia
World Spider Encyclopedia
Science Encyclopedia in Color: Wolf Spiders
Science Encyclopedia in Color: Akamune Spiders
Science Encyclopedia in Color: Tangle-Web Spiders
Science Encyclopedia in Color: Money Spiders
Science Encyclopedia in Color: Crab Spiders
Science Encyclopedia in Color: Pirate Spiders
Science Encyclopedia in Color: Jorō Spiders

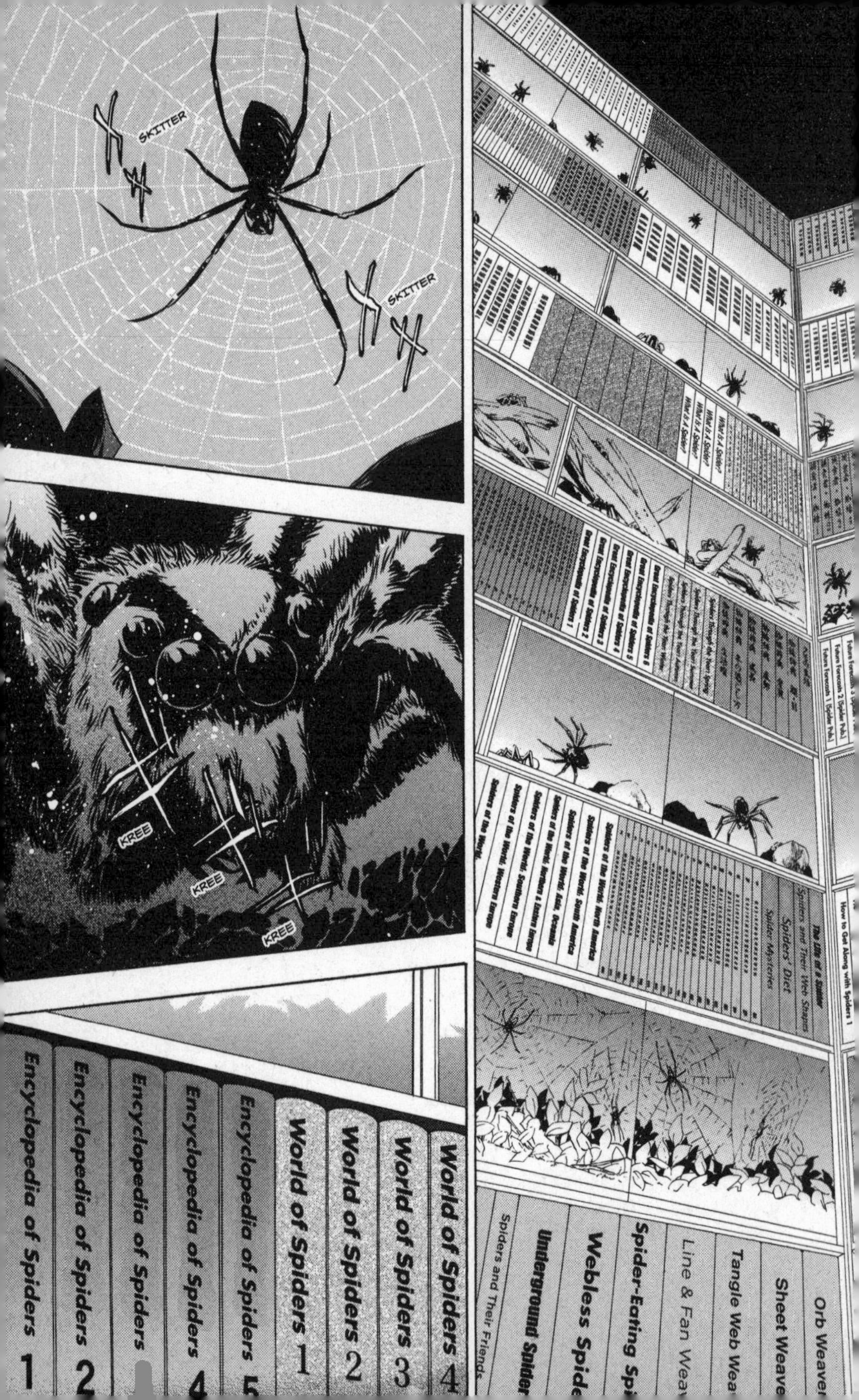
What Is A Spider?
What Is A Spider?
What Is A Spider?
Future Forecasts 2 (Spider Pub.)
Future Forecasts 1 (Spider Pub.)
Great Encyclopedia of Spiders 6
Great Encyclopedia of Spiders 5
Great Encyclopedia of Spiders 4
Great Encyclopedia of Spiders 3
Great Encyclopedia of Spiders 2
Great Encyclopedia of Spiders 1
Spiders Through the Year: Spring
Spiders Through the Year: Summer
Spiders Through the Year: Autumn
Spiders Through the Year: Winter
How to Get Along with Spiders 1
The Life of a Spider
Spiders and Their Web Shapes
Spiders' Diet
Spider Mysteries
Spiders of the World: North America
Spiders of the World: South America
Spiders of the World: Asia, Oceania
Spiders of the World: Northern & Eastern Europe
Spiders of the World: Southern Europe
Spiders of the World: Western Europe
Spiders of the World
Orb Weave
Sheet Weave
Tangle Web Wea
Line & Fan Wea
Spider-Eating Sp
Webless Spide
Underground Spider
Spiders and Their Friends
SKITTER
SKITTER
KREE
KREE
KREE
World of Spiders 4
World of Spiders 3
World of Spiders 2
World of Spiders 1
Encyclopedia of Spiders 5
Encyclopedia of Spiders 4
Encyclopedia of Spiders
Encyclopedia of Spiders 2
Encyclopedia of Spiders 1

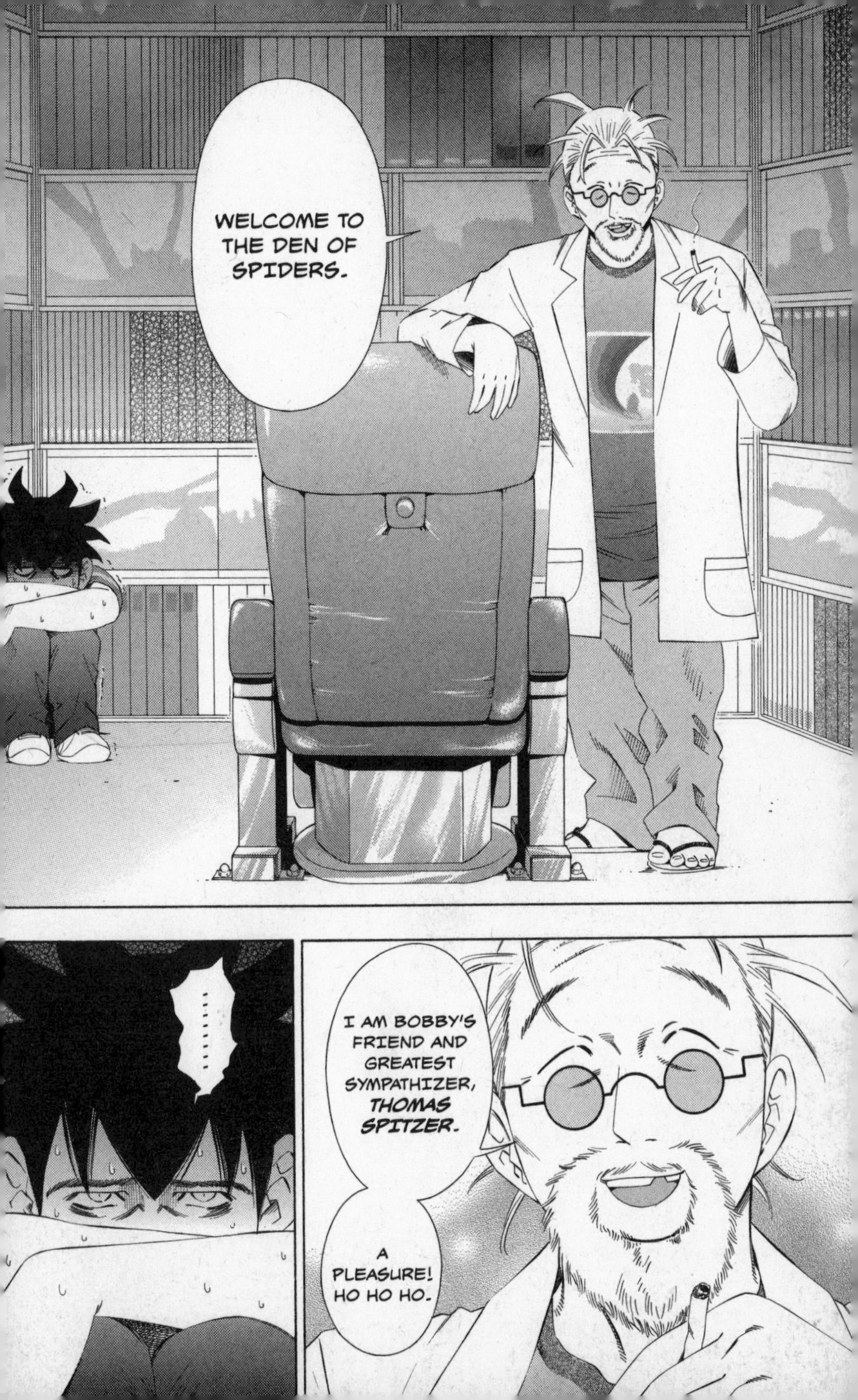
WELCOME TO THE DEN OF SPIDERS.
I AM BOBBY'S FRIEND AND GREATEST SYMPATHIZER, *THOMAS SPITZER*.
A PLEASURE! HO HO HO.
.......

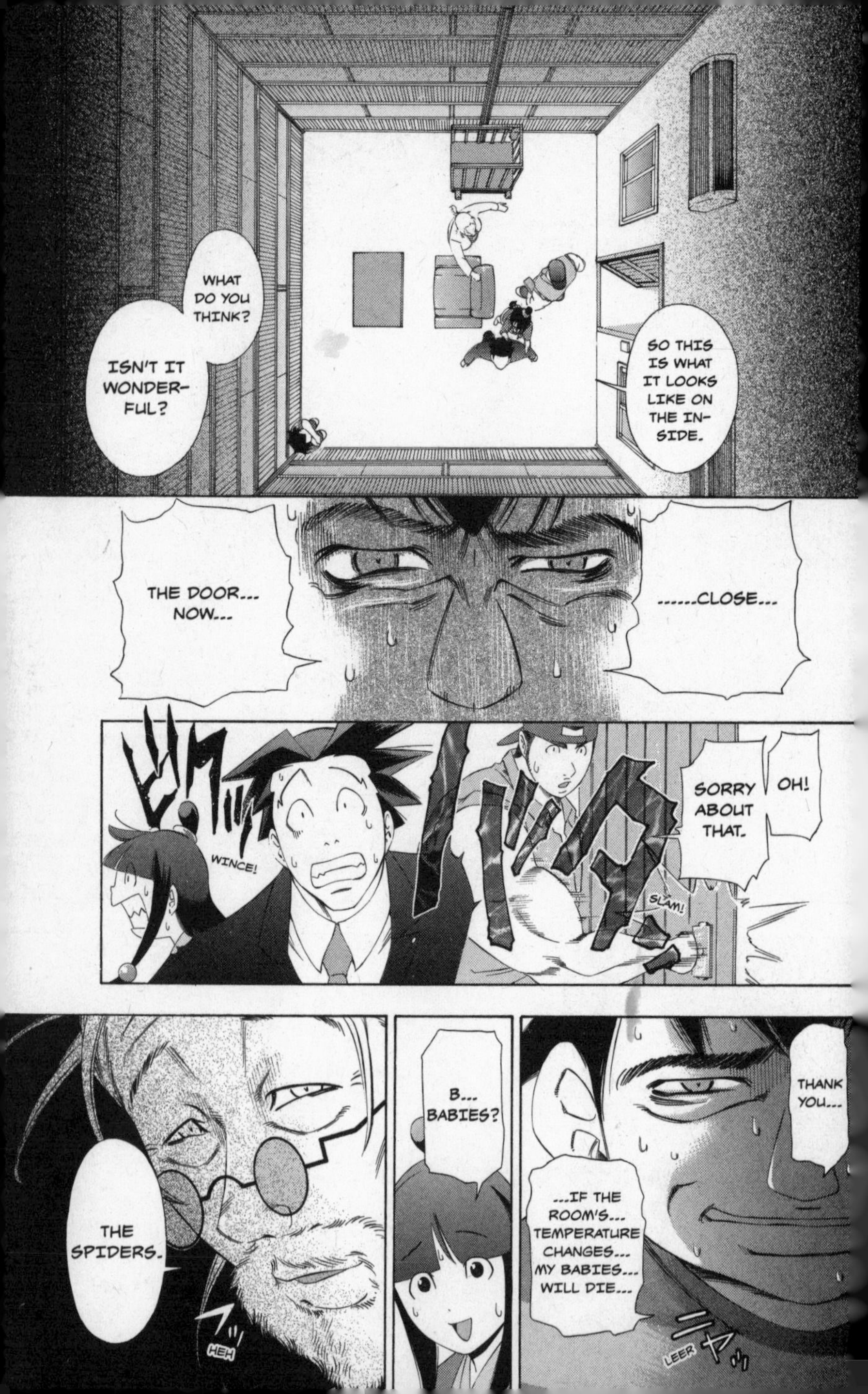
SO THIS IS WHAT IT LOOKS LIKE ON THE IN-SIDE.
WHAT DO YOU THINK?
ISN'T IT WONDER-FUL?
......CLOSE...
THE DOOR... NOW...
OH!
SORRY ABOUT THAT.
SLAM!
WINCE!
THANK YOU...
...IF THE ROOM'S... TEMPERATURE CHANGES... MY BABIES... WILL DIE...
LEER
B... BABIES?
THE SPIDERS.
HEH

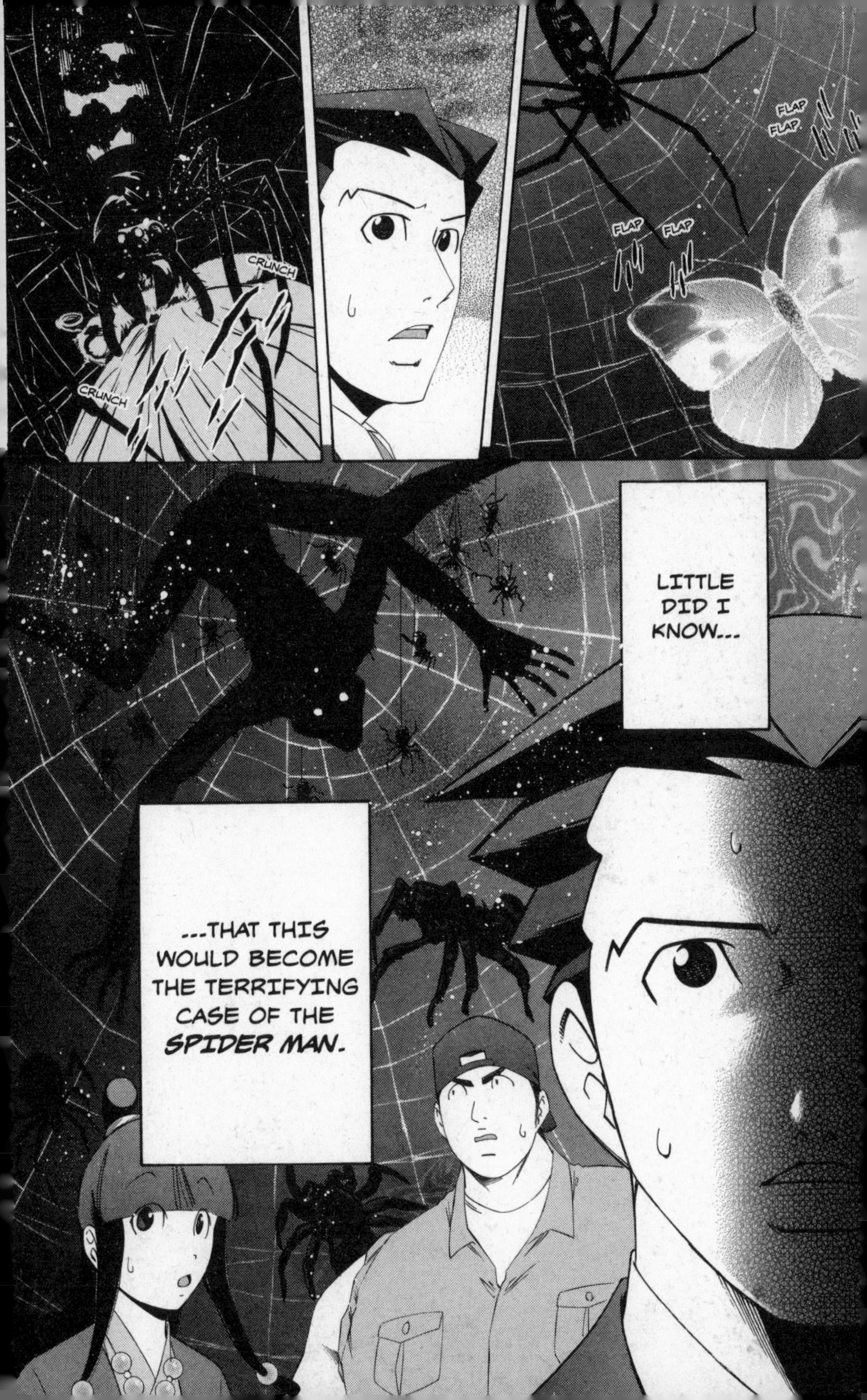
FLAP
FLAP
FLAP
FLAP
CRUNCH
CRUNCH
LITTLE DID I KNOW...
...THAT THIS WOULD BECOME THE TERRIFYING CASE OF THE *SPIDER MAN*.

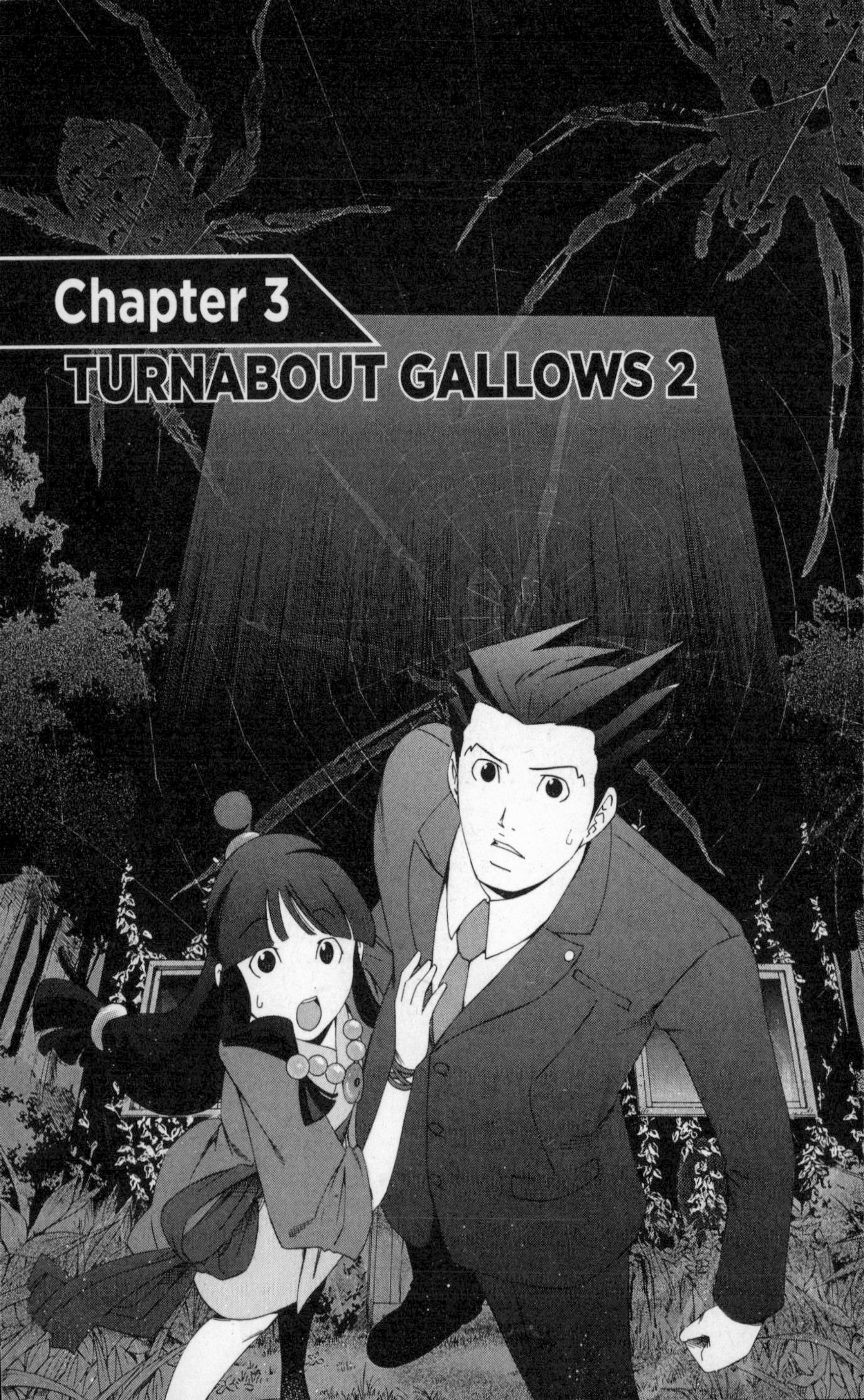
Chapter 3
TURNABOUT GALLOWS 2

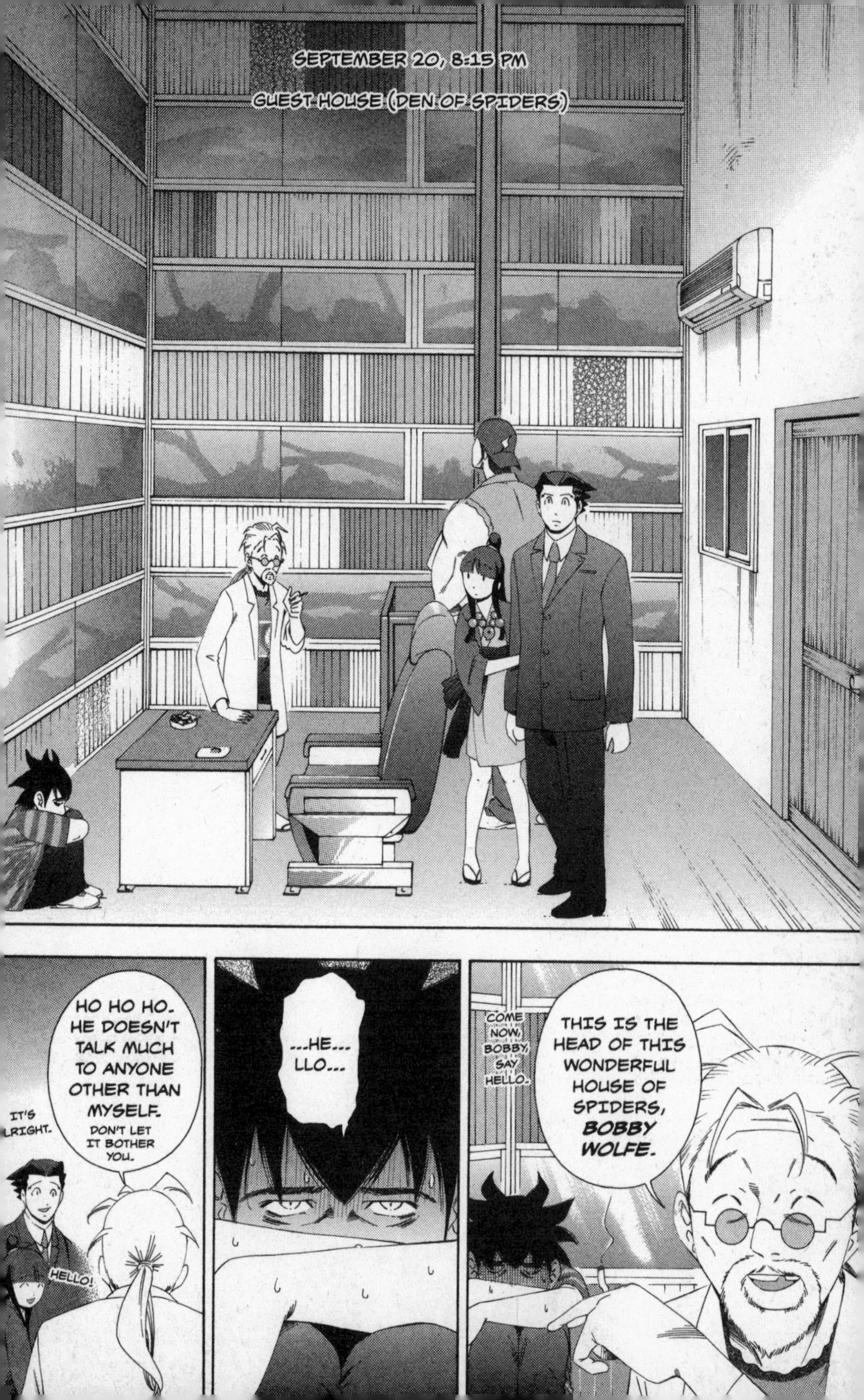
SEPTEMBER 20, 8:15 PM
GUEST HOUSE (DEN OF SPIDERS)
THIS IS THE HEAD OF THIS WONDERFUL HOUSE OF SPIDERS, ***BOBBY WOLFE.***
COME NOW, BOBBY, SAY HELLO.
...HE... LLO...
HO HO HO. HE DOESN'T TALK MUCH TO ANYONE OTHER THAN MYSELF.
DON'T LET IT BOTHER YOU.
IT'S LRIGHT.
HELLO!

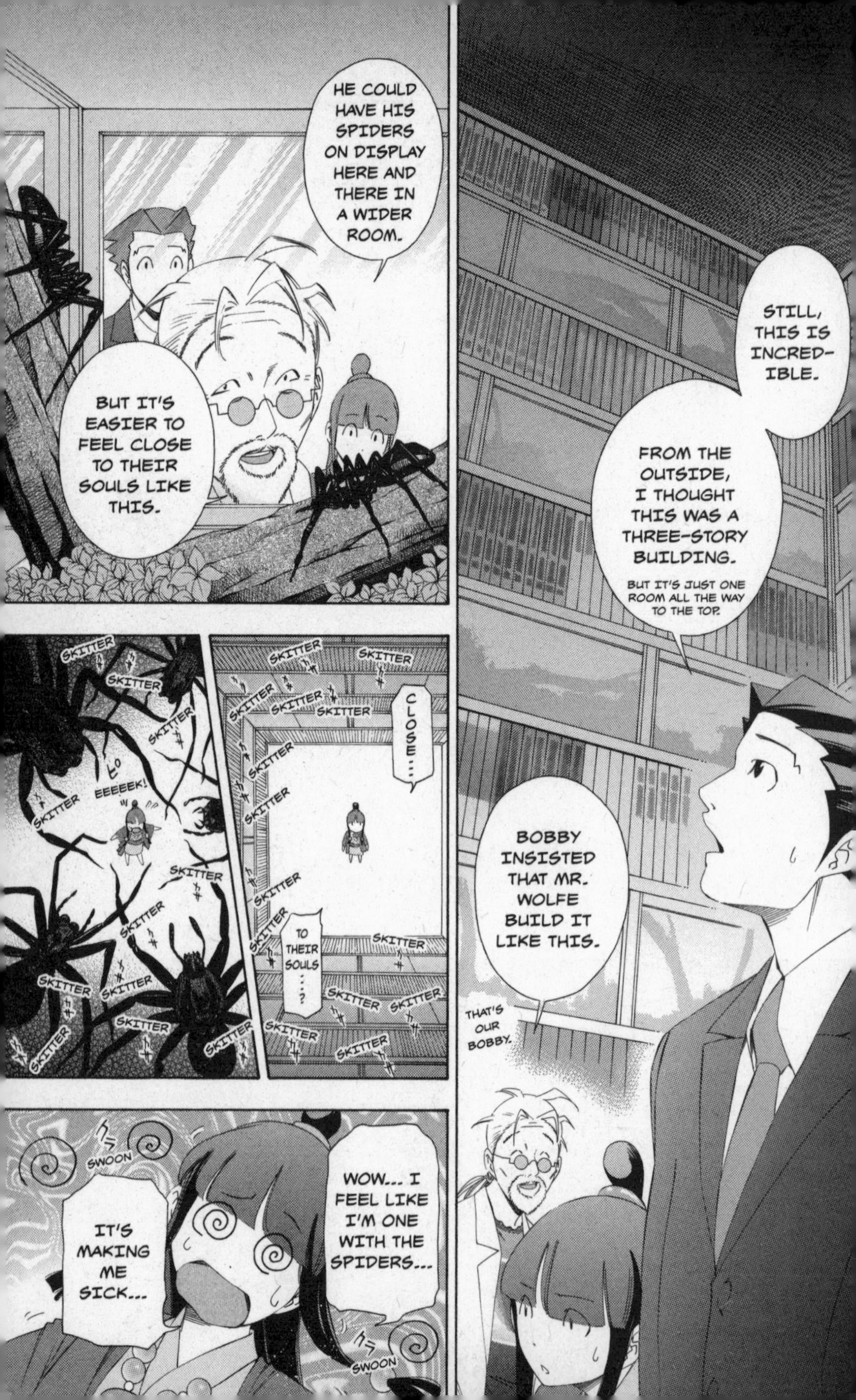
STILL, THIS IS INCREDIBLE.
FROM THE OUTSIDE, I THOUGHT THIS WAS A THREE-STORY BUILDING.
BUT IT'S JUST ONE ROOM ALL THE WAY TO THE TOP.
BOBBY INSISTED THAT MR. WOLFE BUILD IT LIKE THIS.
THAT'S OUR BOBBY.
HE COULD HAVE HIS SPIDERS ON DISPLAY HERE AND THERE IN A WIDER ROOM.
BUT IT'S EASIER TO FEEL CLOSE TO THEIR SOULS LIKE THIS.
CLOSE...
SKITTER SKITTER
SKITTER SKITTER SKITTER
TO THEIR SOULS...?
SKITTER SKITTER SKITTER
EEEEEK!
SKITTER SKITTER SKITTER
WOW... I FEEL LIKE I'M ONE WITH THE SPIDERS...
SWOON
IT'S MAKING ME SICK...
SWOON

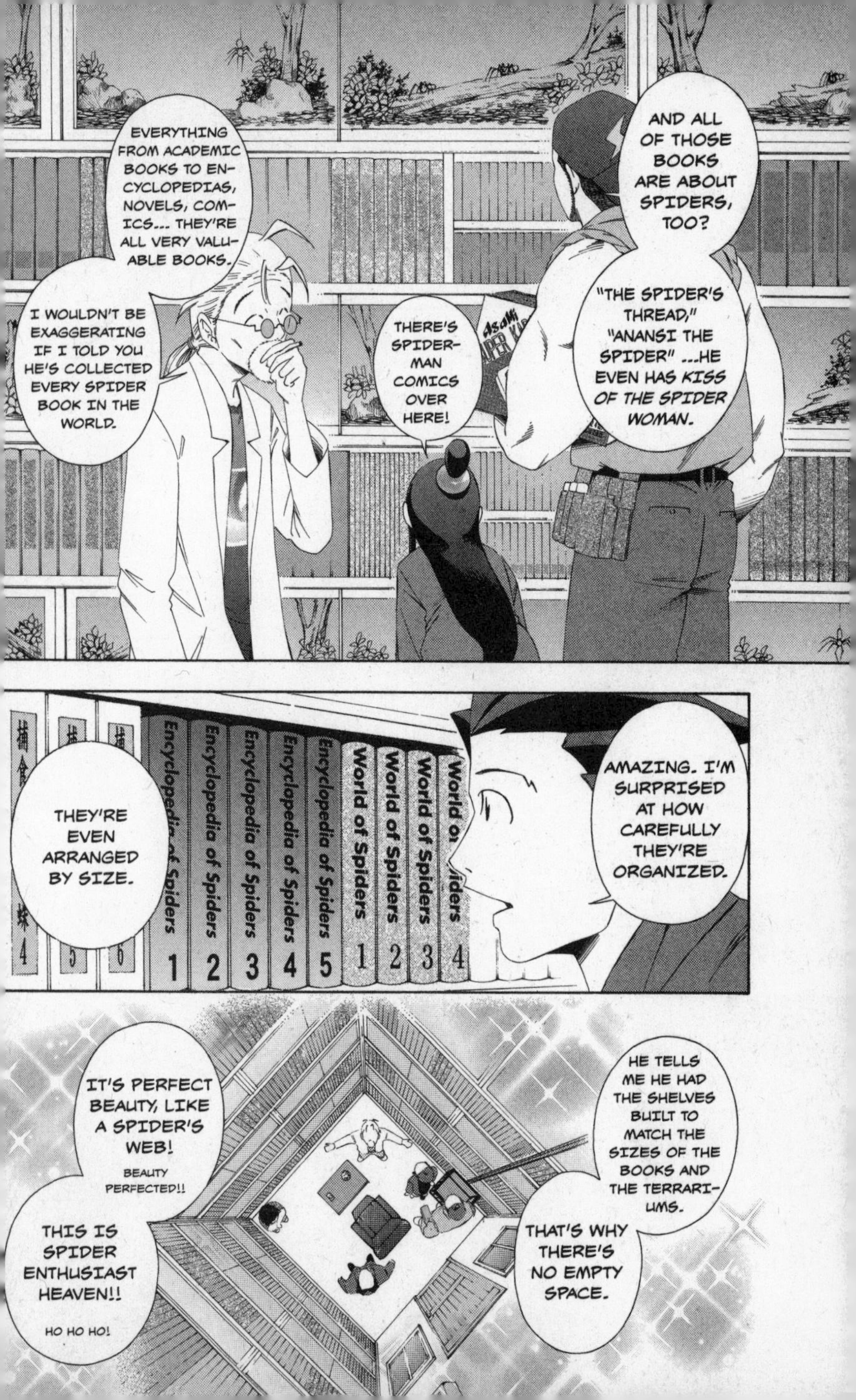
AND ALL OF THOSE BOOKS ARE ABOUT SPIDERS, TOO?
EVERYTHING FROM ACADEMIC BOOKS TO ENCYCLOPEDIAS, NOVELS, COMICS... THEY'RE ALL VERY VALUABLE BOOKS.
I WOULDN'T BE EXAGGERATING IF I TOLD YOU HE'S COLLECTED EVERY SPIDER BOOK IN THE WORLD.
THERE'S SPIDER-MAN COMICS OVER HERE!
"THE SPIDER'S THREAD," "ANANSI THE SPIDER" ...HE EVEN HAS *KISS OF THE SPIDER WOMAN*.
AMAZING. I'M SURPRISED AT HOW CAREFULLY THEY'RE ORGANIZED.
THEY'RE EVEN ARRANGED BY SIZE.
Encyclopedia of Spiders 1
Encyclopedia of Spiders 2
Encyclopedia of Spiders 3
Encyclopedia of Spiders 4
Encyclopedia of Spiders 5
World of Spiders 1
World of Spiders 2
World of Spiders 3
HE TELLS ME HE HAD THE SHELVES BUILT TO MATCH THE SIZES OF THE BOOKS AND THE TERRARIUMS.
THAT'S WHY THERE'S NO EMPTY SPACE.
IT'S PERFECT BEAUTY, LIKE A SPIDER'S WEB!
BEAUTY PERFECTED!!
THIS IS SPIDER ENTHUSIAST HEAVEN!!
HO HO HO!

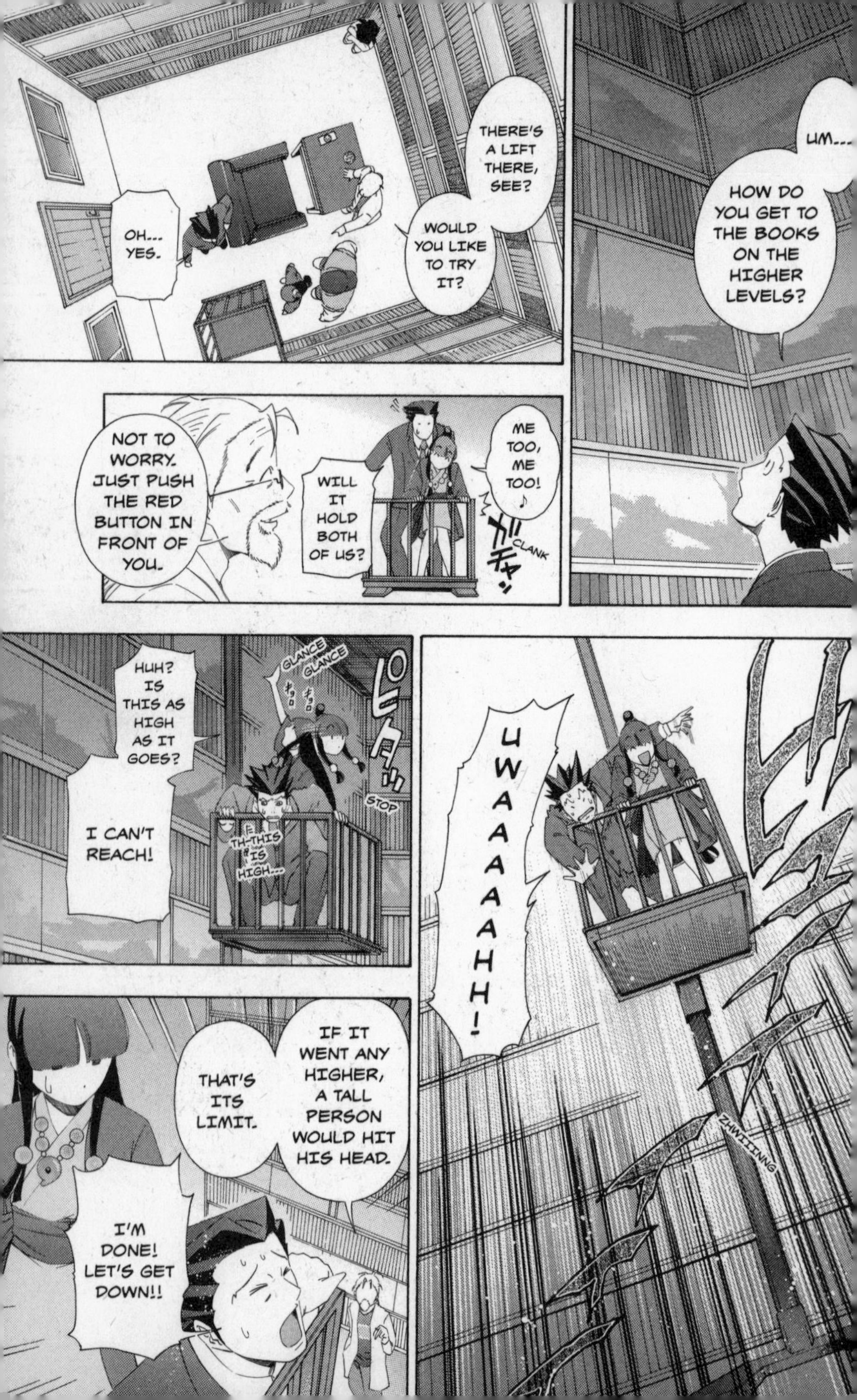
UM...
HOW DO YOU GET TO THE BOOKS ON THE HIGHER LEVELS?
THERE'S A LIFT THERE, SEE?
WOULD YOU LIKE TO TRY IT?
OH... YES.
ME TOO, ME TOO! ♪
CLANK
WILL IT HOLD BOTH OF US?
NOT TO WORRY. JUST PUSH THE RED BUTTON IN FRONT OF YOU.
UWAAAAAAHH!
ZHWIIIINNG
GLANCE
GLANCE
HUH? IS THIS AS HIGH AS IT GOES?
STOP
TH-THIS IS HIGH...
I CAN'T REACH!
IF IT WENT ANY HIGHER, A TALL PERSON WOULD HIT HIS HEAD.
THAT'S ITS LIMIT.
I'M DONE! LET'S GET DOWN!!

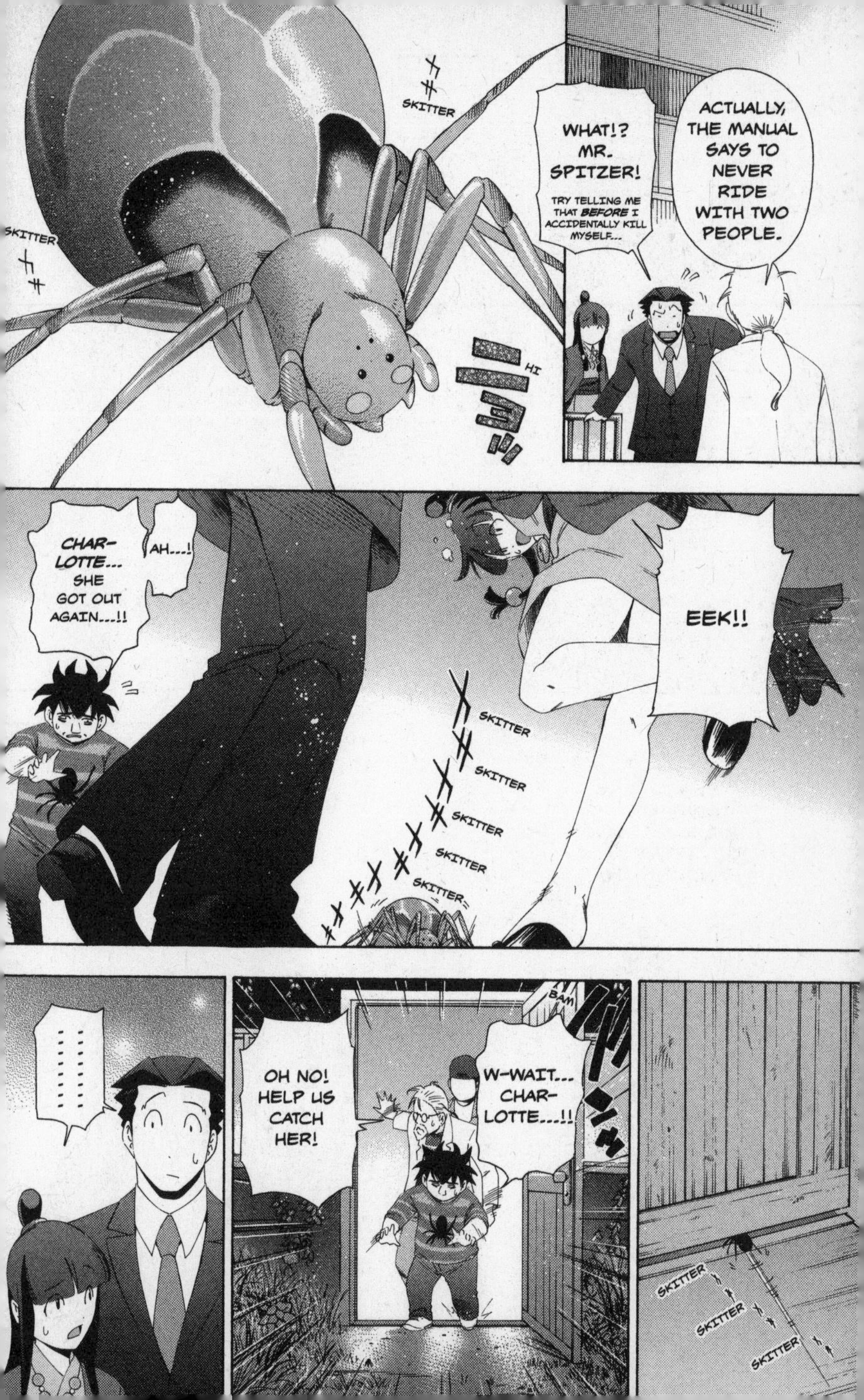
ACTUALLY, THE MANUAL SAYS TO NEVER RIDE WITH TWO PEOPLE.
WHAT!? MR. SPITZER!
TRY TELLING ME THAT *BEFORE* I ACCIDENTALLY KILL MYSELF...
SKITTER
HI
SKITTER
EEK!!
SKITTER
SKITTER
SKITTER
SKITTER
SKITTER
AH...!
CHAR-LOTTE... SHE GOT OUT AGAIN...!!
SKITTER
SKITTER
SKITTER
BAM
W-WAIT... CHAR-LOTTE...!!
OH NO! HELP US CATCH HER!
......

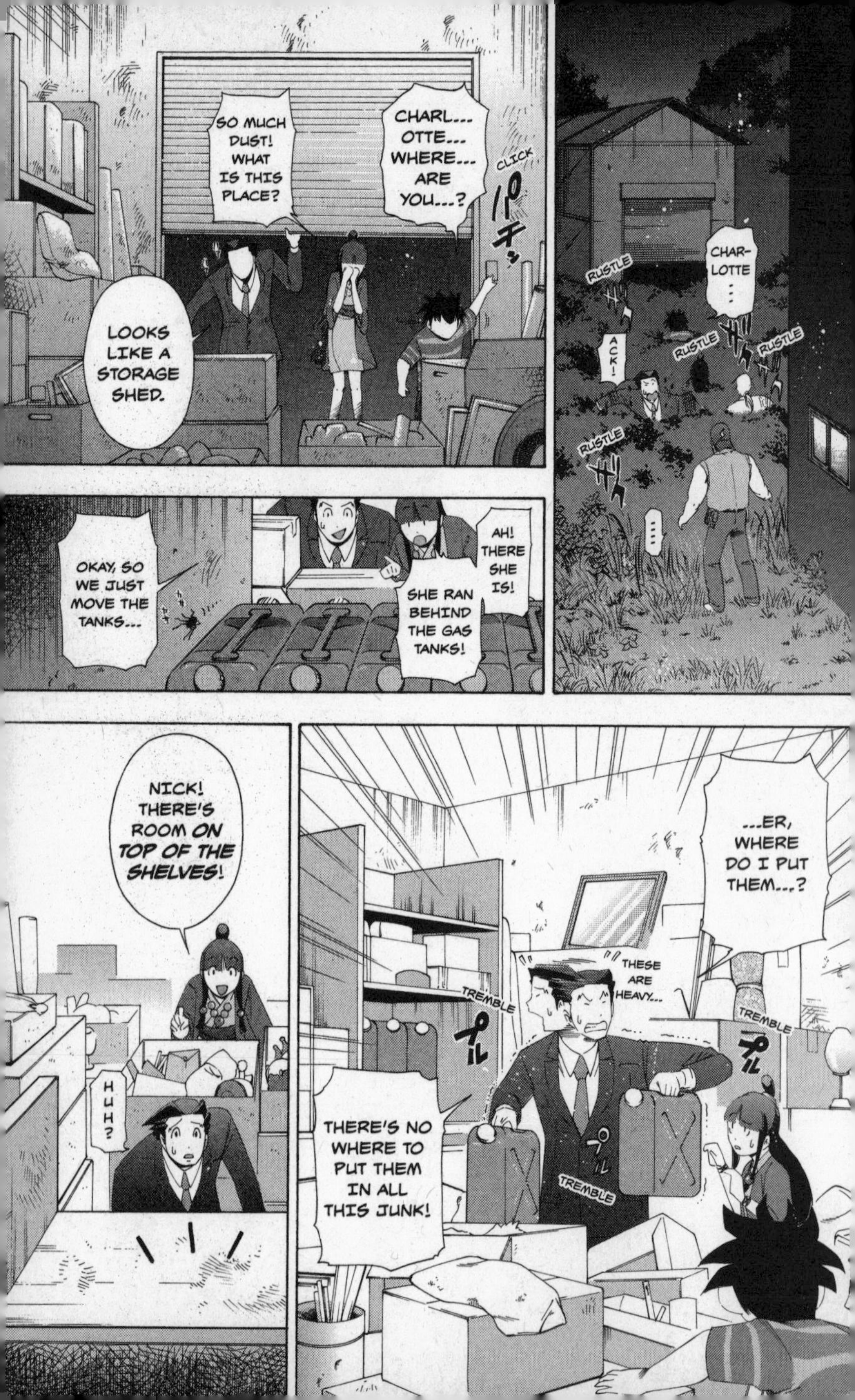
CHAR-LOTTE...
RUSTLE
ACK!
RUSTLE
RUSTLE
RUSTLE
...
CLICK
CHARL... OTTE... WHERE... ARE YOU...?
SO MUCH DUST! WHAT IS THIS PLACE?
LOOKS LIKE A STORAGE SHED.
AH! THERE SHE IS!
SHE RAN BEHIND THE GAS TANKS!
OKAY, SO WE JUST MOVE THE TANKS...
...ER, WHERE DO I PUT THEM...?
TREMBLE
THESE ARE HEAVY...
TREMBLE
TREMBLE
THERE'S NO WHERE TO PUT THEM IN ALL THIS JUNK!
NICK! THERE'S ROOM ON TOP OF THE SHELVES!
HUH?

CLINK
CLINK

THERE SHE IS! WE FOUND HER!!

U... UPSY-DAISY...

CHAR... LOTTE...

EEEEEK! EEEEEK! I CAUGHT HER! WHAT WAS I THINKING!!?

WHAT DO I DO!? IT'S SKIT-TERING AROUND! EEEK! EEEK!

WHAM

WHAM

WHAM

H-HOLD ON... I'LL FIND A CASE FOR HER...!!

FLUSTER

FLUSTER

GOTCHA!

HA!!

CLAP!

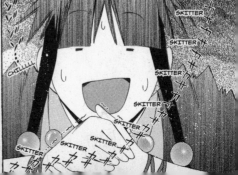

SKITTER

SKITTER

SKITTER

SKITTER

CHILLLL

SKITTER

SKITTER

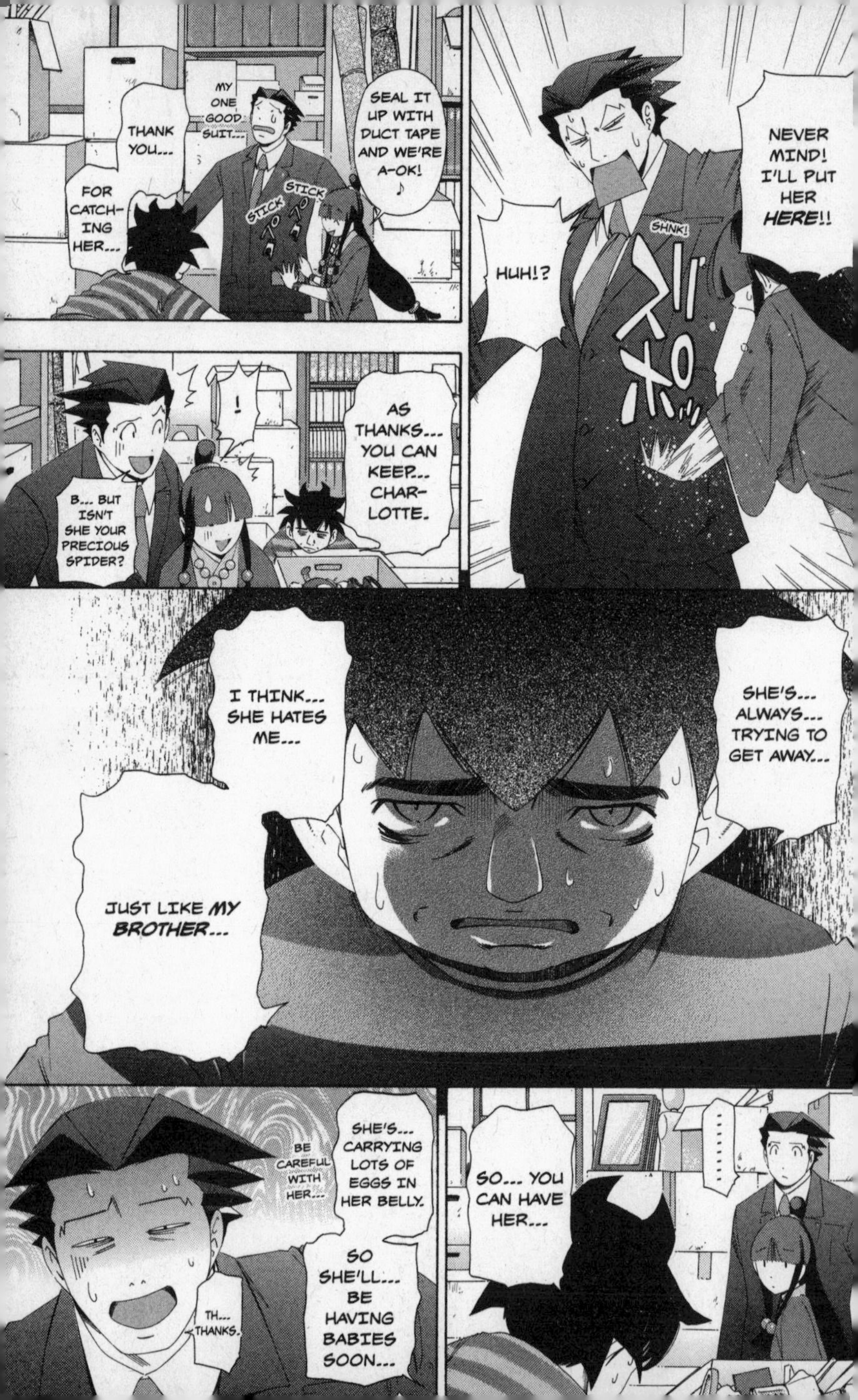

NEVER MIND! I'LL PUT HER *HERE*!!
SHNK!
HUH!?
SEAL IT UP WITH DUCT TAPE AND WE'RE A-OK! ♪
STICK
STICK
MY ONE GOOD SUIT...
THANK YOU...
FOR CATCHING HER...
AS THANKS... YOU CAN KEEP... CHARLOTTE.
!
B... BUT ISN'T SHE YOUR PRECIOUS SPIDER?
SHE'S... ALWAYS... TRYING TO GET AWAY...
I THINK... SHE HATES ME...
JUST LIKE *MY BROTHER*...
.......
SO... YOU CAN HAVE HER...
SHE'S... CARRYING LOTS OF EGGS IN HER BELLY.
BE CAREFUL WITH HER...
SO SHE'LL... BE HAVING BABIES SOON...
TH... THANKS.

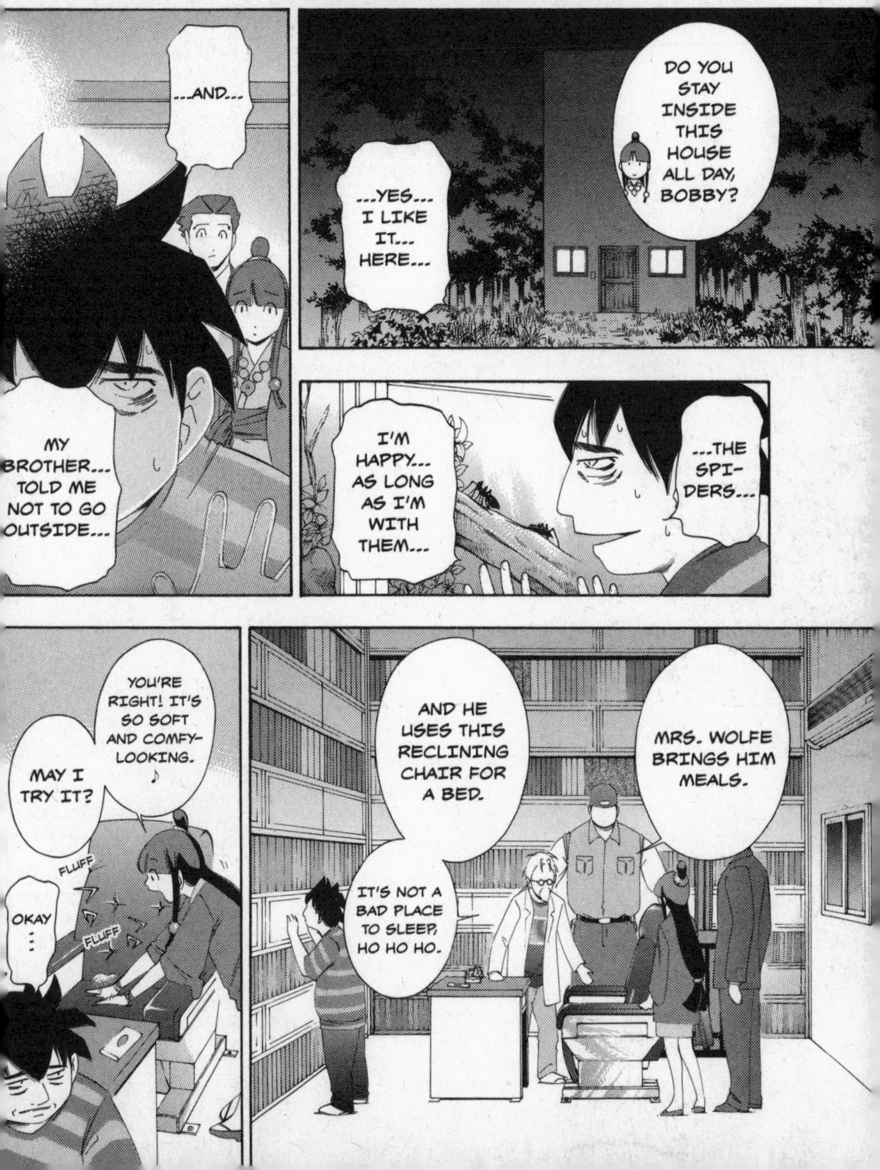
DO YOU STAY INSIDE THIS HOUSE ALL DAY, BOBBY?
...YES... I LIKE IT... HERE...
...THE SPIDERS...
I'M HAPPY... AS LONG AS I'M WITH THEM...
...AND...
MY BROTHER... TOLD ME NOT TO GO OUTSIDE...
MRS. WOLFE BRINGS HIM MEALS.
AND HE USES THIS RECLINING CHAIR FOR A BED.
IT'S NOT A BAD PLACE TO SLEEP, HO HO HO.
YOU'RE RIGHT! IT'S SO SOFT AND COMFY-LOOKING. ♪
MAY I TRY IT?
FLUFF
FLUFF
OKAY...

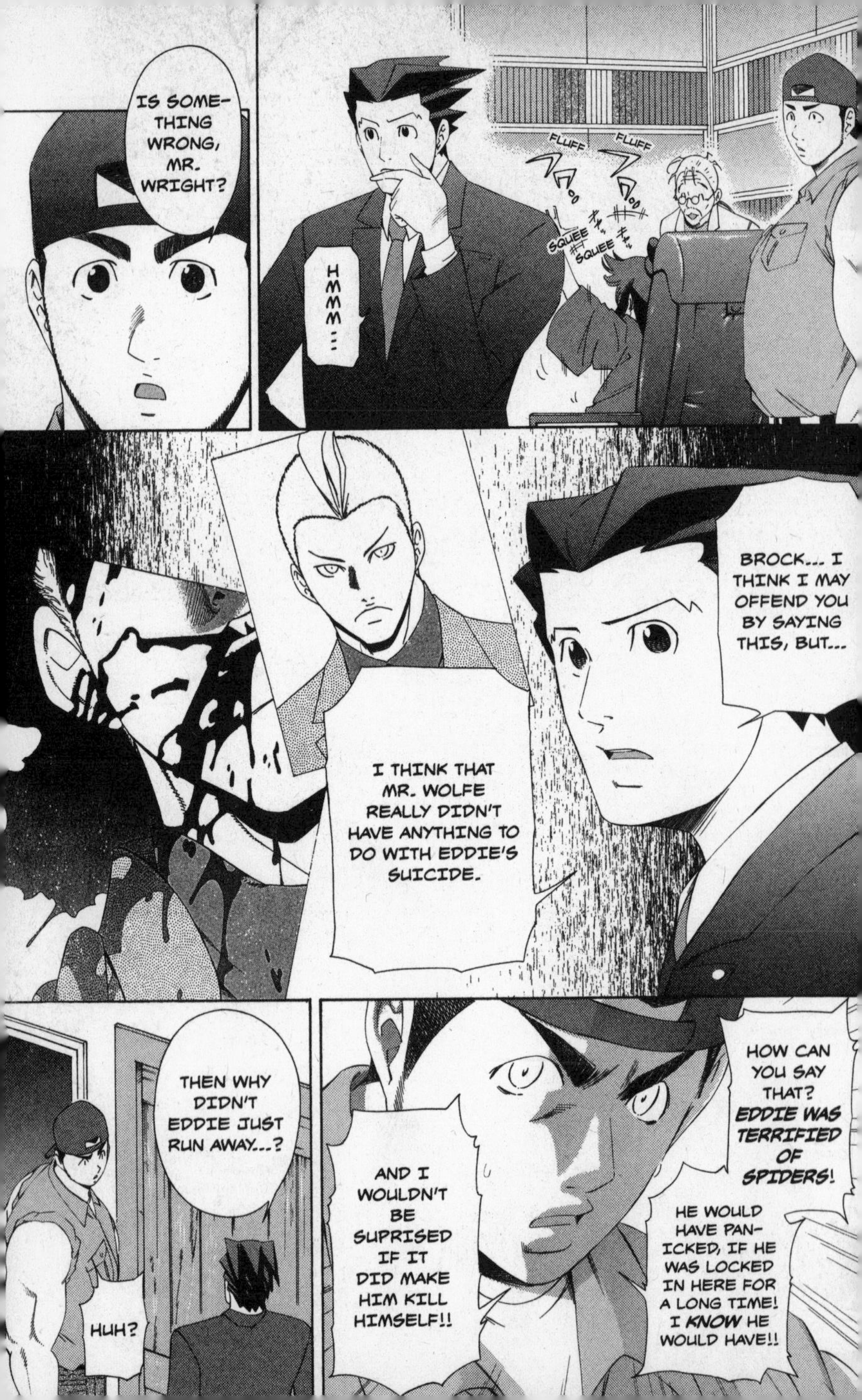
FLUFF
FLUFF
SQUEE
SQUEE
HMMM...
IS SOMETHING WRONG, MR. WRIGHT?
BROCK... I THINK I MAY OFFEND YOU BY SAYING THIS, BUT...
I THINK THAT MR. WOLFE REALLY DIDN'T HAVE ANYTHING TO DO WITH EDDIE'S SUICIDE.
HOW CAN YOU SAY THAT? *EDDIE WAS TERRIFIED OF SPIDERS!*
HE WOULD HAVE PANICKED, IF HE WAS LOCKED IN HERE FOR A LONG TIME! I *KNOW* HE WOULD HAVE!!
AND I WOULDN'T BE SUPRISED IF IT DID MAKE HIM KILL HIMSELF!!
THEN WHY DIDN'T EDDIE JUST RUN AWAY...?
HUH?

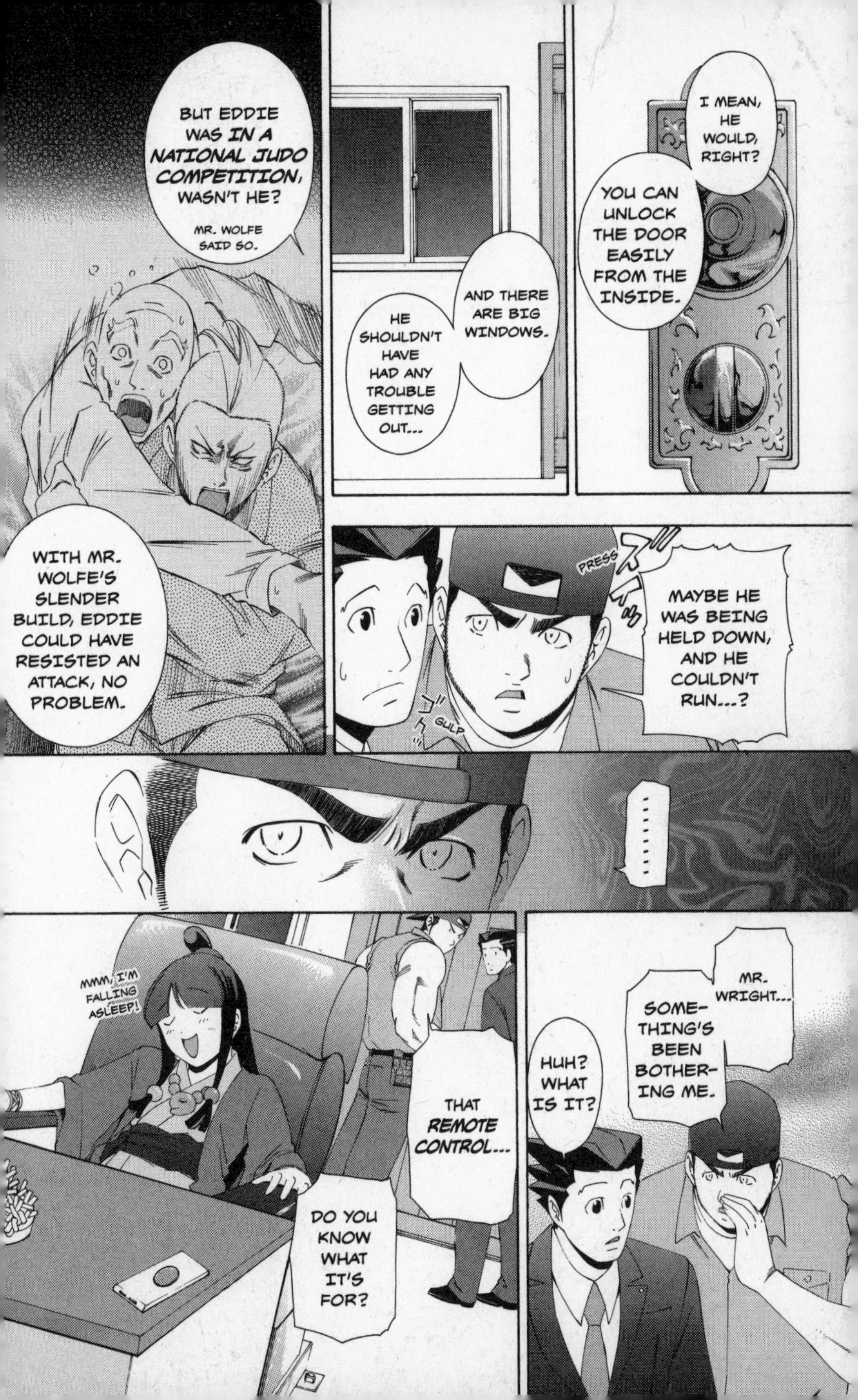
I MEAN, HE WOULD, RIGHT?
YOU CAN UNLOCK THE DOOR EASILY FROM THE INSIDE.
AND THERE ARE BIG WINDOWS.
HE SHOULDN'T HAVE HAD ANY TROUBLE GETTING OUT...
PRESS
MAYBE HE WAS BEING HELD DOWN, AND HE COULDN'T RUN...?
GULP
BUT EDDIE WAS IN A NATIONAL JUDO COMPETITION, WASN'T HE?
MR. WOLFE SAID SO.
WITH MR. WOLFE'S SLENDER BUILD, EDDIE COULD HAVE RESISTED AN ATTACK, NO PROBLEM.
........
MR. WRIGHT...
SOME-THING'S BEEN BOTHER-ING ME.
HUH? WHAT IS IT?
MMM, I'M FALLING ASLEEP!
THAT REMOTE CONTROL...
DO YOU KNOW WHAT IT'S FOR?

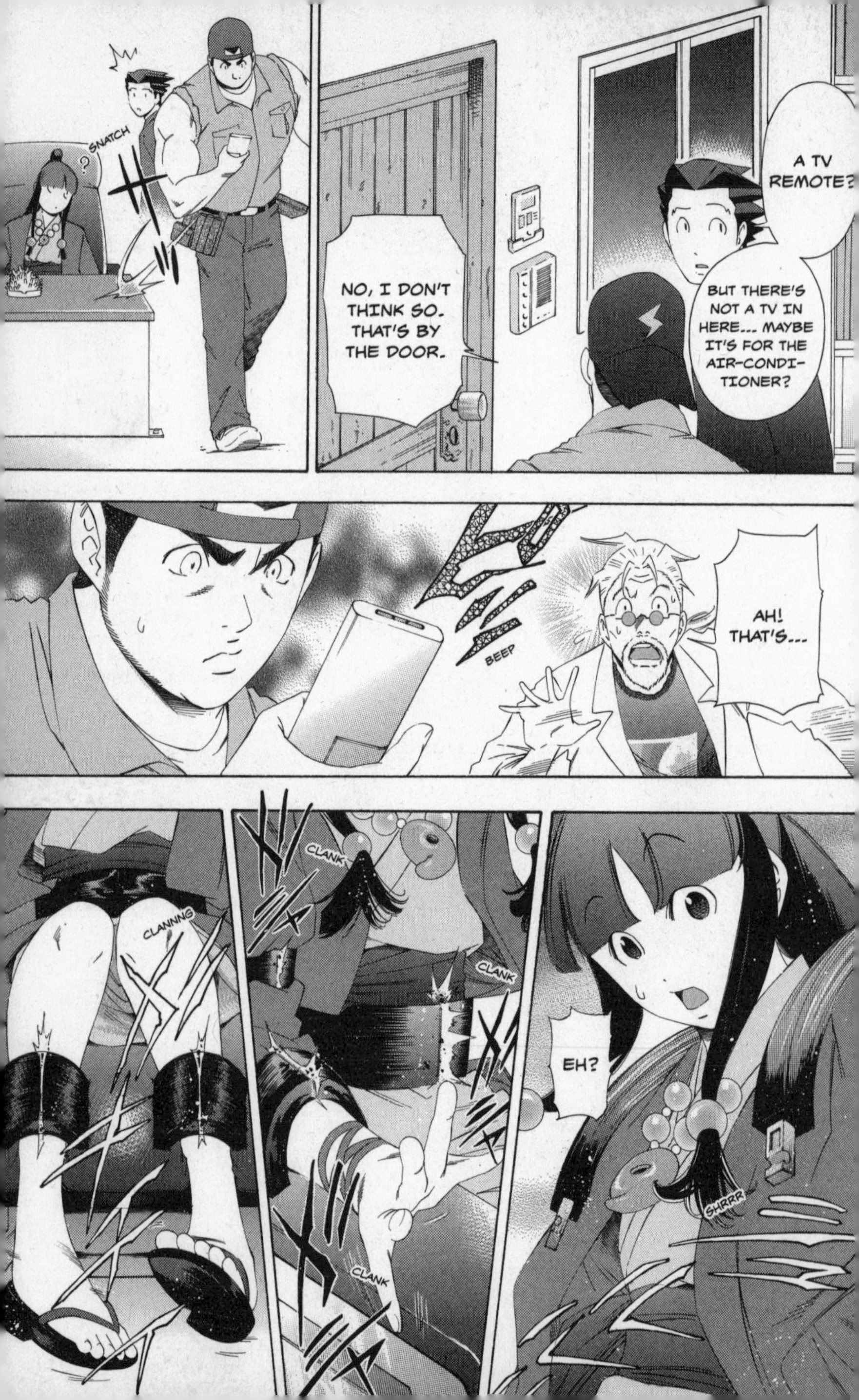
A TV REMOTE?
BUT THERE'S NOT A TV IN HERE... MAYBE IT'S FOR THE AIR-CONDITIONER?
NO, I DON'T THINK SO. THAT'S BY THE DOOR.
SNATCH
?
AH! THAT'S...
BEEP
EH?
SHRRR
CLANK
CLANK
CLANK
CLANNNG

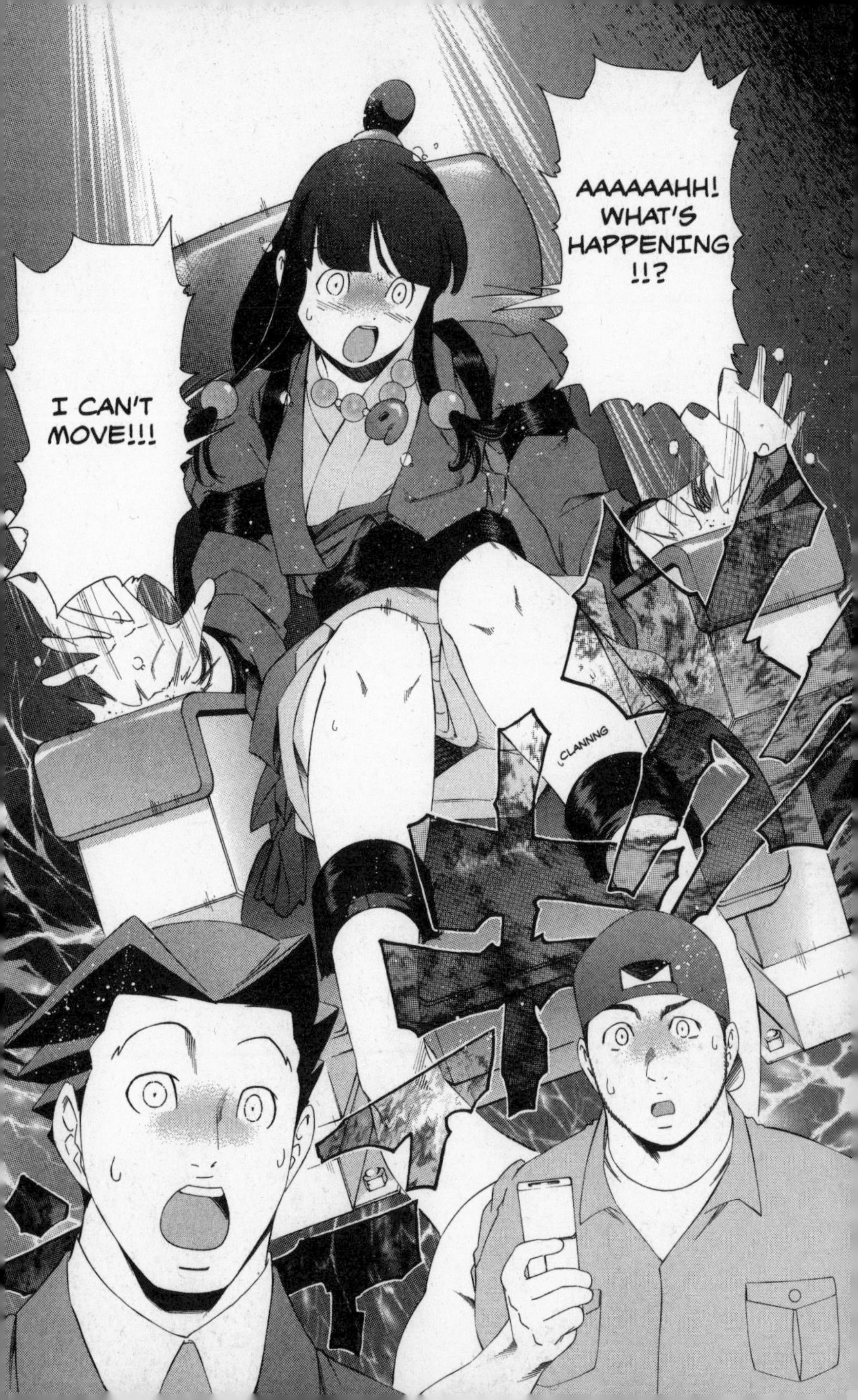
AAAAAAHH! WHAT'S HAPPENING !!?
I CAN'T MOVE!!!
CLANNNG

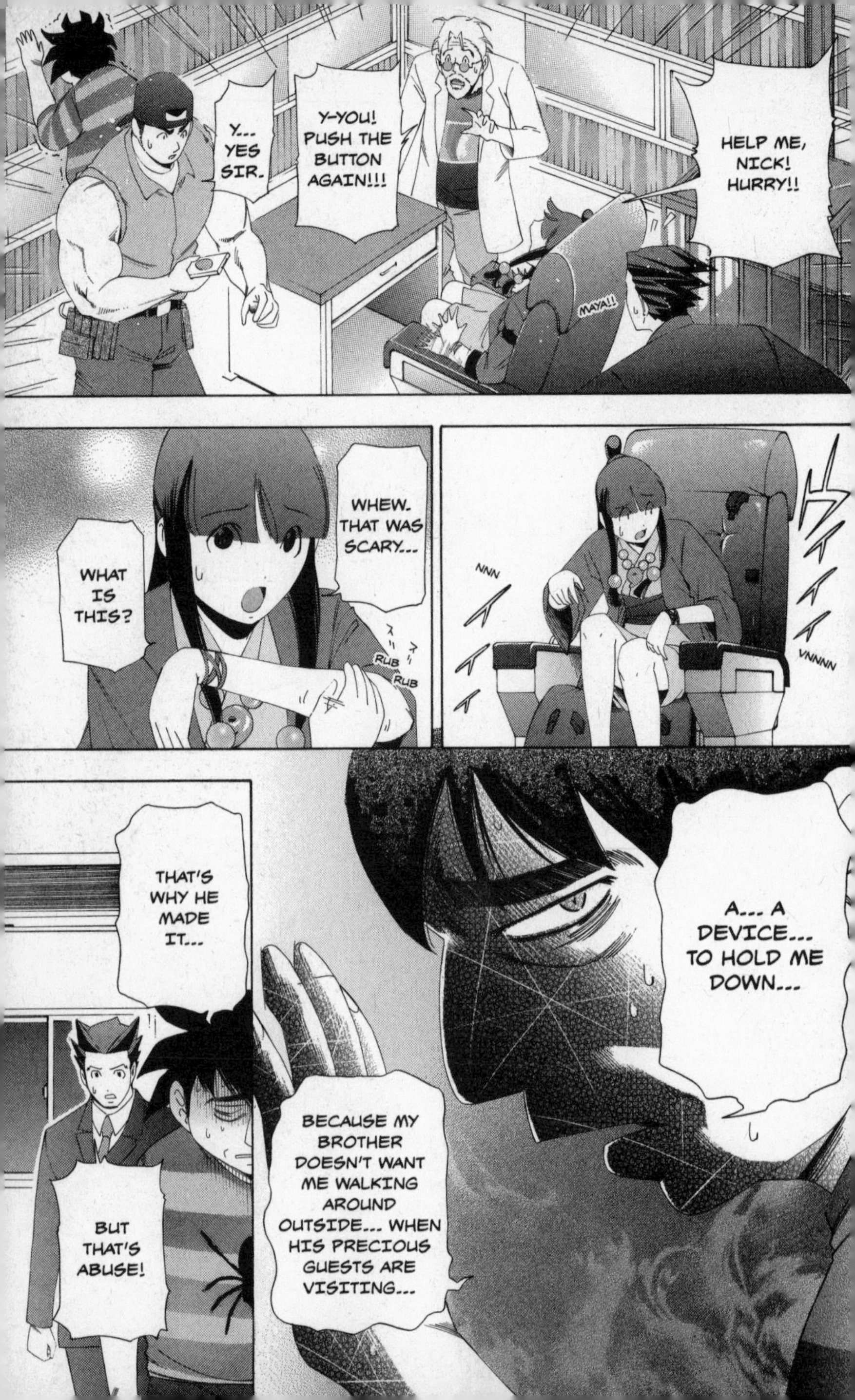
HELP ME, NICK! HURRY!!
MAYA!!
Y-YOU! PUSH THE BUTTON AGAIN!!!
Y... YES SIR.
NNN
VNNNN
WHEW. THAT WAS SCARY...
WHAT IS THIS?
RUB RUB
A... A DEVICE... TO HOLD ME DOWN...
BECAUSE MY BROTHER DOESN'T WANT ME WALKING AROUND OUTSIDE... WHEN HIS PRECIOUS GUESTS ARE VISITING...
THAT'S WHY HE MADE IT...
BUT THAT'S ABUSE!

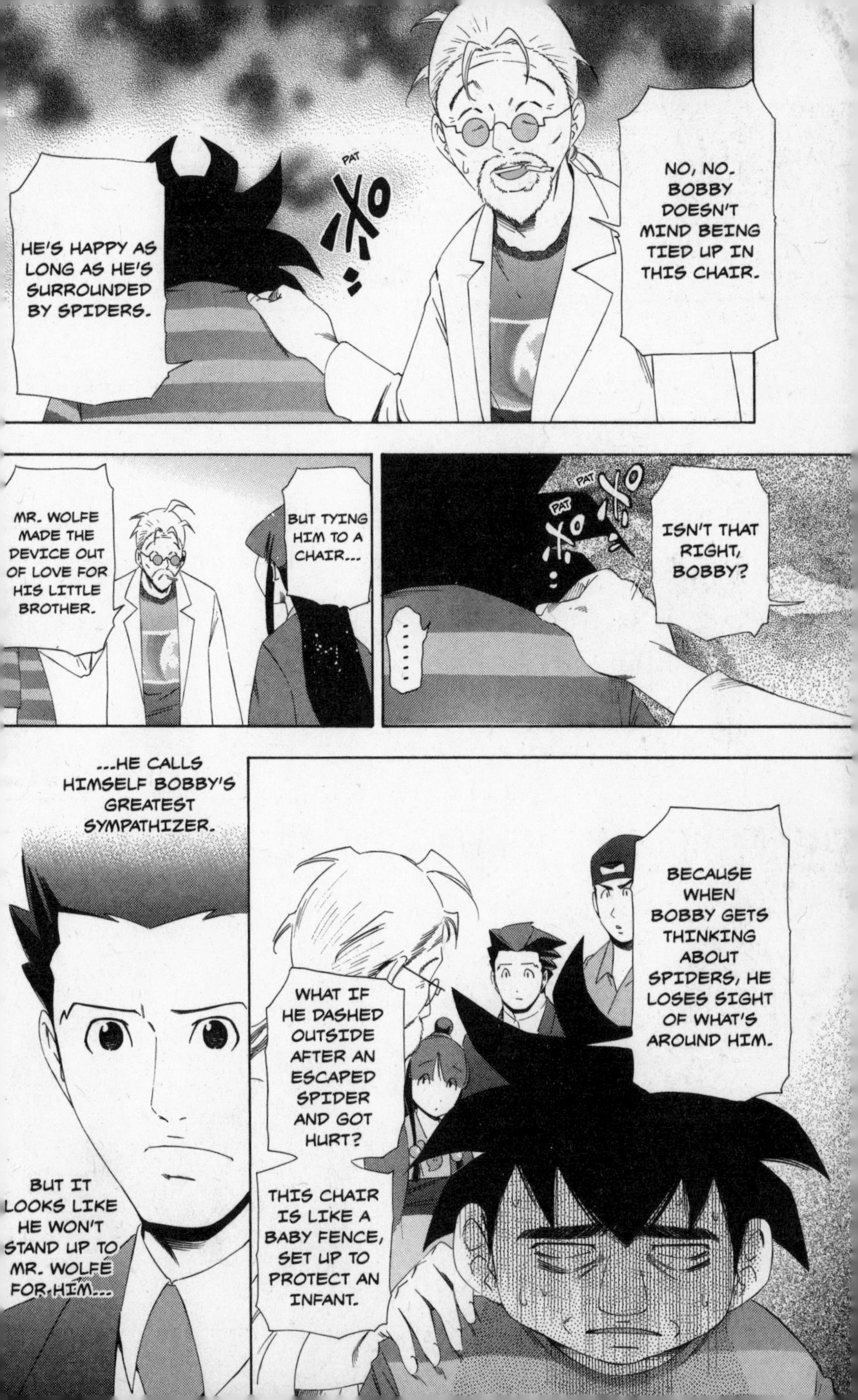

NO, NO. BOBBY DOESN'T MIND BEING TIED UP IN THIS CHAIR.
PAT
HE'S HAPPY AS LONG AS HE'S SURROUNDED BY SPIDERS.
ISN'T THAT RIGHT, BOBBY?
PAT
PAT
......
BUT TYING HIM TO A CHAIR...
MR. WOLFE MADE THE DEVICE OUT OF LOVE FOR HIS LITTLE BROTHER.
BECAUSE WHEN BOBBY GETS THINKING ABOUT SPIDERS, HE LOSES SIGHT OF WHAT'S AROUND HIM.
WHAT IF HE DASHED OUTSIDE AFTER AN ESCAPED SPIDER AND GOT HURT?
THIS CHAIR IS LIKE A BABY FENCE, SET UP TO PROTECT AN INFANT.
...HE CALLS HIMSELF BOBBY'S GREATEST SYMPATHIZER.
BUT IT LOOKS LIKE HE WON'T STAND UP TO MR. WOLFE FOR HIM...

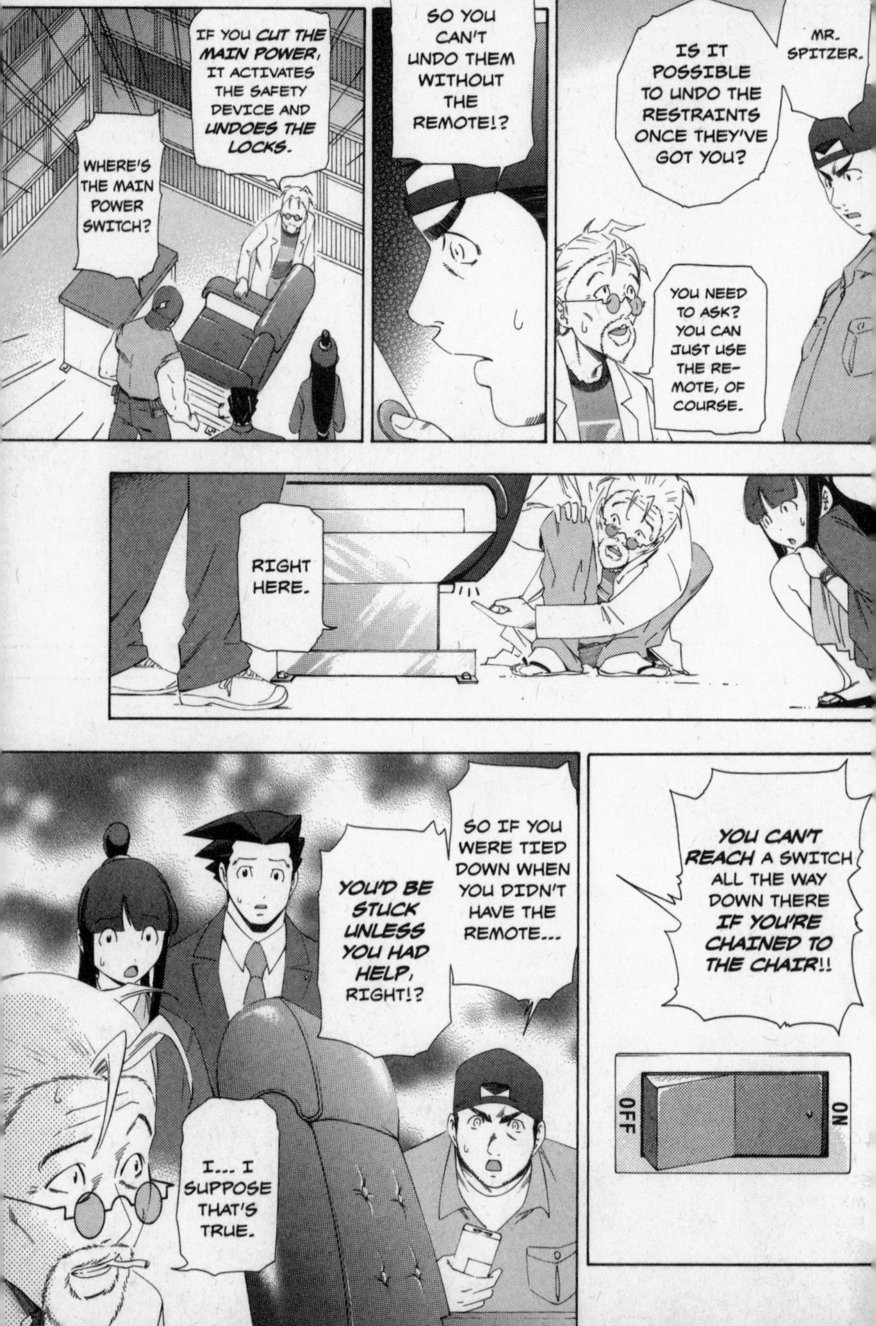
MR. SPITZER.
IS IT POSSIBLE TO UNDO THE RESTRAINTS ONCE THEY'VE GOT YOU?
YOU NEED TO ASK? YOU CAN JUST USE THE RE-MOTE, OF COURSE.
SO YOU CAN'T UNDO THEM WITHOUT THE REMOTE!?
IF YOU *CUT THE MAIN POWER*, IT ACTIVATES THE SAFETY DEVICE AND *UNDOES THE LOCKS*.
WHERE'S THE MAIN POWER SWITCH?
RIGHT HERE.
*YOU CAN'T REACH* A SWITCH ALL THE WAY DOWN THERE *IF YOU'RE CHAINED TO THE CHAIR*!!
OFF
ON
SO IF YOU WERE TIED DOWN WHEN YOU DIDN'T HAVE THE REMOTE...
*YOU'D BE STUCK UNLESS YOU HAD HELP*, RIGHT!?
I... I SUPPOSE THAT'S TRUE.

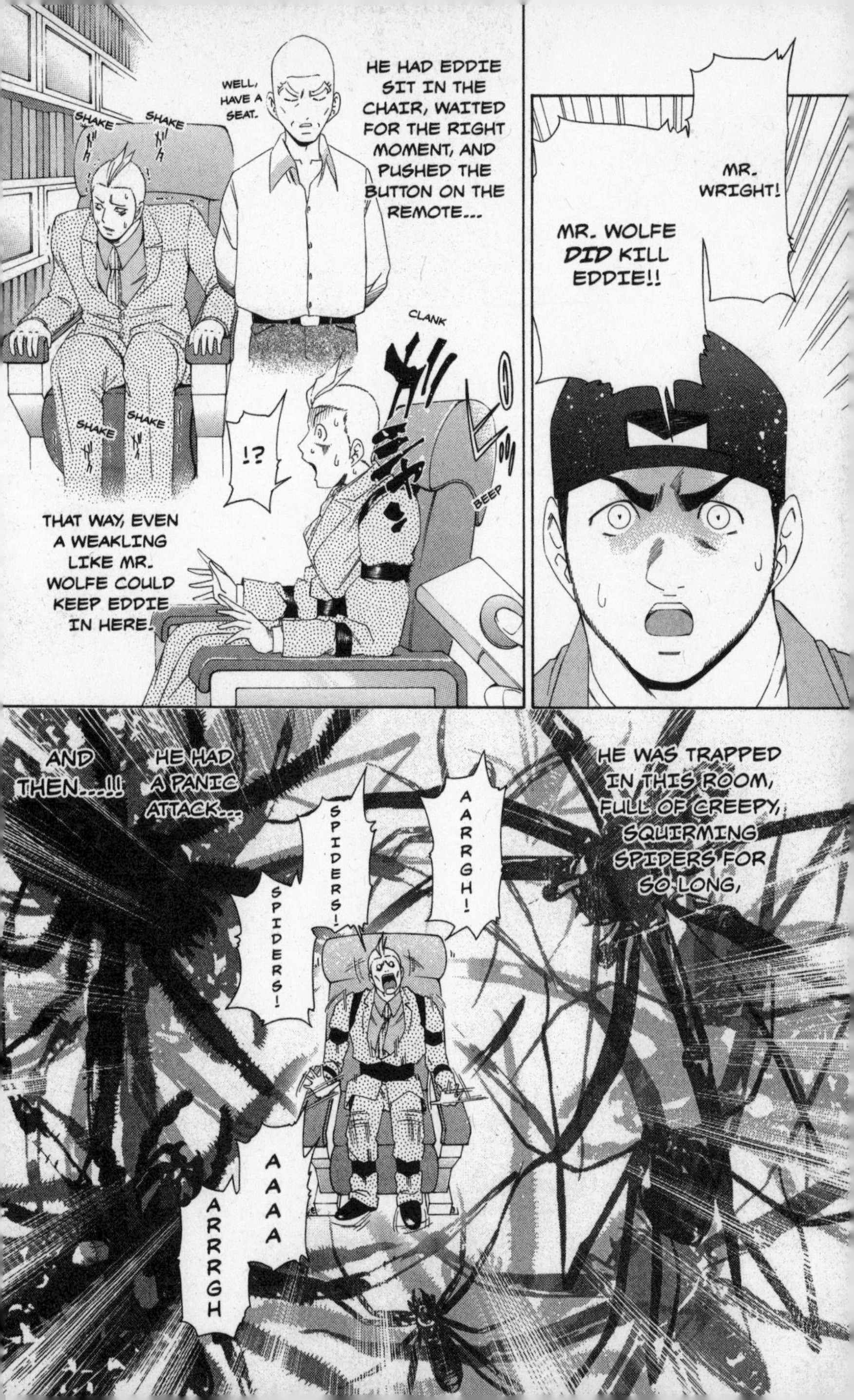
MR. WRIGHT!
MR. WOLFE *DID* KILL EDDIE!!
HE HAD EDDIE SIT IN THE CHAIR, WAITED FOR THE RIGHT MOMENT, AND PUSHED THE BUTTON ON THE REMOTE...
WELL, HAVE A SEAT.
SHAKE
SHAKE
SHAKE
SHAKE
CLANK
BEEP
!?
THAT WAY, EVEN A WEAKLING LIKE MR. WOLFE COULD KEEP EDDIE IN HERE.
HE WAS TRAPPED IN THIS ROOM, FULL OF CREEPY, SQUIRMING SPIDERS FOR SO LONG,
AARRGH!
SPIDERS! SPIDERS!
HE HAD A PANIC ATTACK...
AND THEN...!!
AAAA
ARRRGH

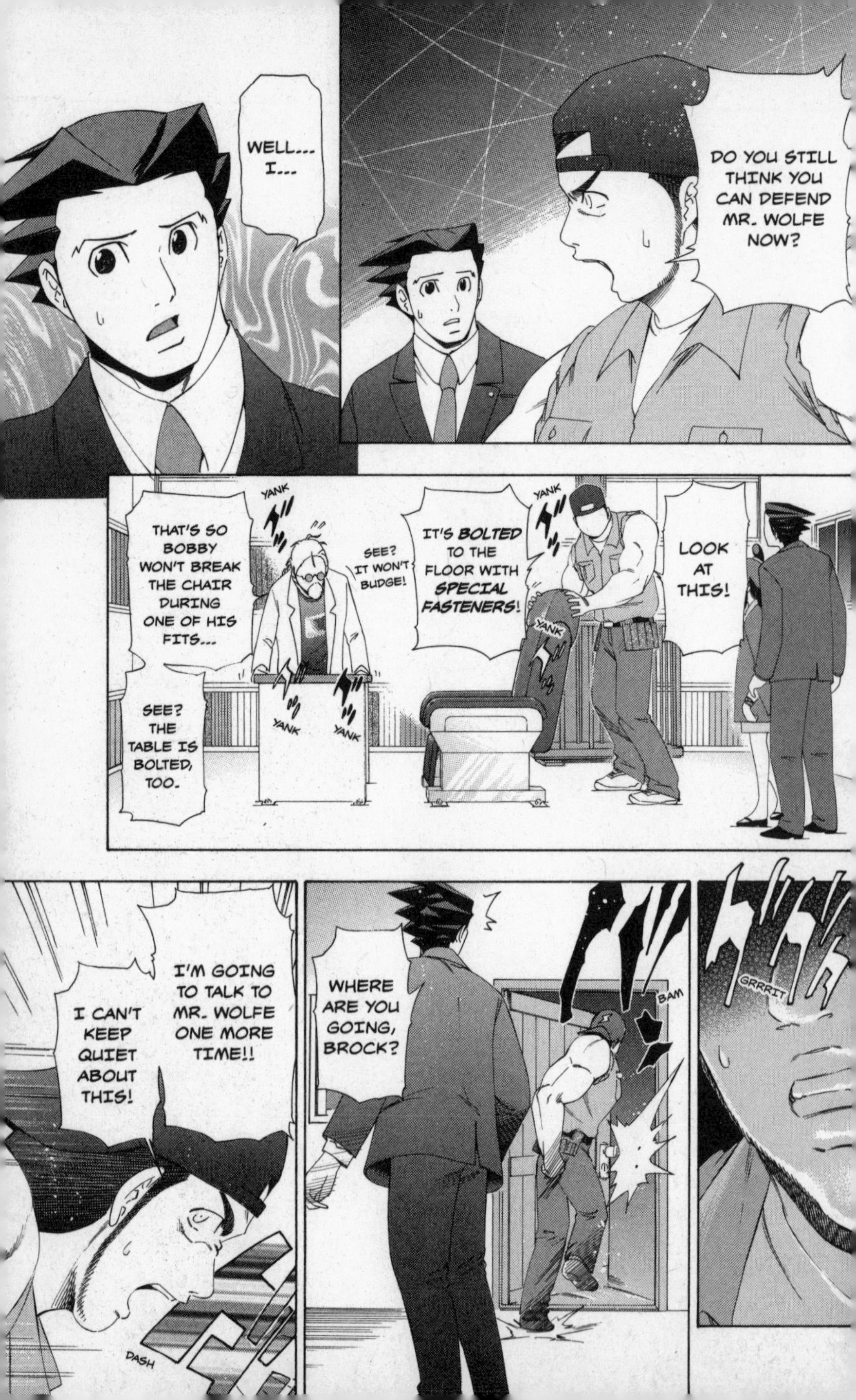
DO YOU STILL THINK YOU CAN DEFEND MR. WOLFE NOW?
WELL... I...
LOOK AT THIS!
YANK
IT'S BOLTED TO THE FLOOR WITH SPECIAL FASTENERS!
YANK
SEE? IT WON'T BUDGE!
YANK
THAT'S SO BOBBY WON'T BREAK THE CHAIR DURING ONE OF HIS FITS...
SEE? THE TABLE IS BOLTED, TOO.
YANK
YANK
GRRRIT
BAM
WHERE ARE YOU GOING, BROCK?
I'M GOING TO TALK TO MR. WOLFE ONE MORE TIME!!
I CAN'T KEEP QUIET ABOUT THIS!
DASH

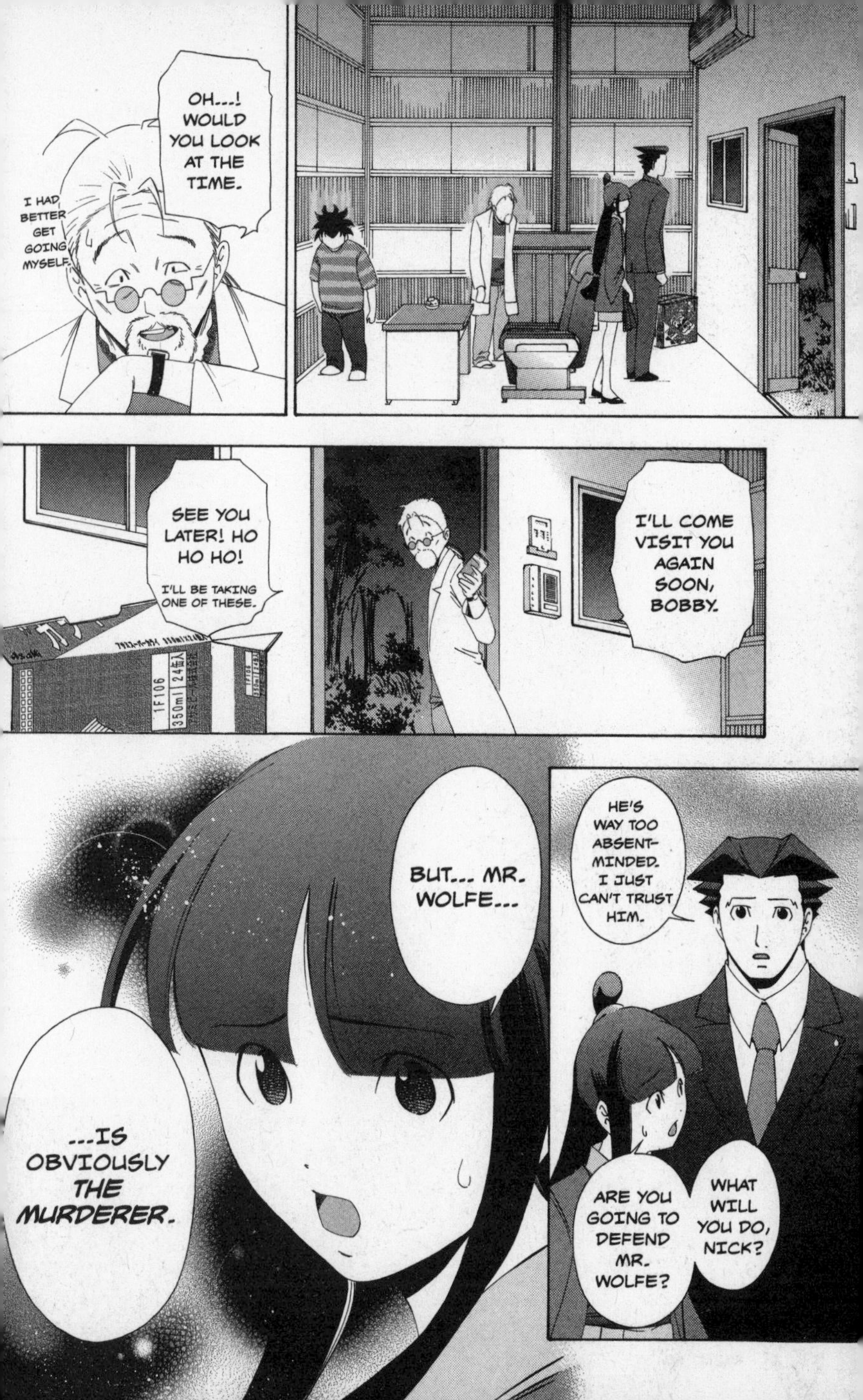
OH...! WOULD YOU LOOK AT THE TIME.
I HAD BETTER GET GOING MYSELF.
I'LL COME VISIT YOU AGAIN SOON, BOBBY.
SEE YOU LATER! HO HO HO!
I'LL BE TAKING ONE OF THESE.
HE'S WAY TOO ABSENT-MINDED. I JUST CAN'T TRUST HIM.
WHAT WILL YOU DO, NICK?
ARE YOU GOING TO DEFEND MR. WOLFE?
BUT... MR. WOLFE...
...IS OBVIOUSLY *THE MURDERER*.

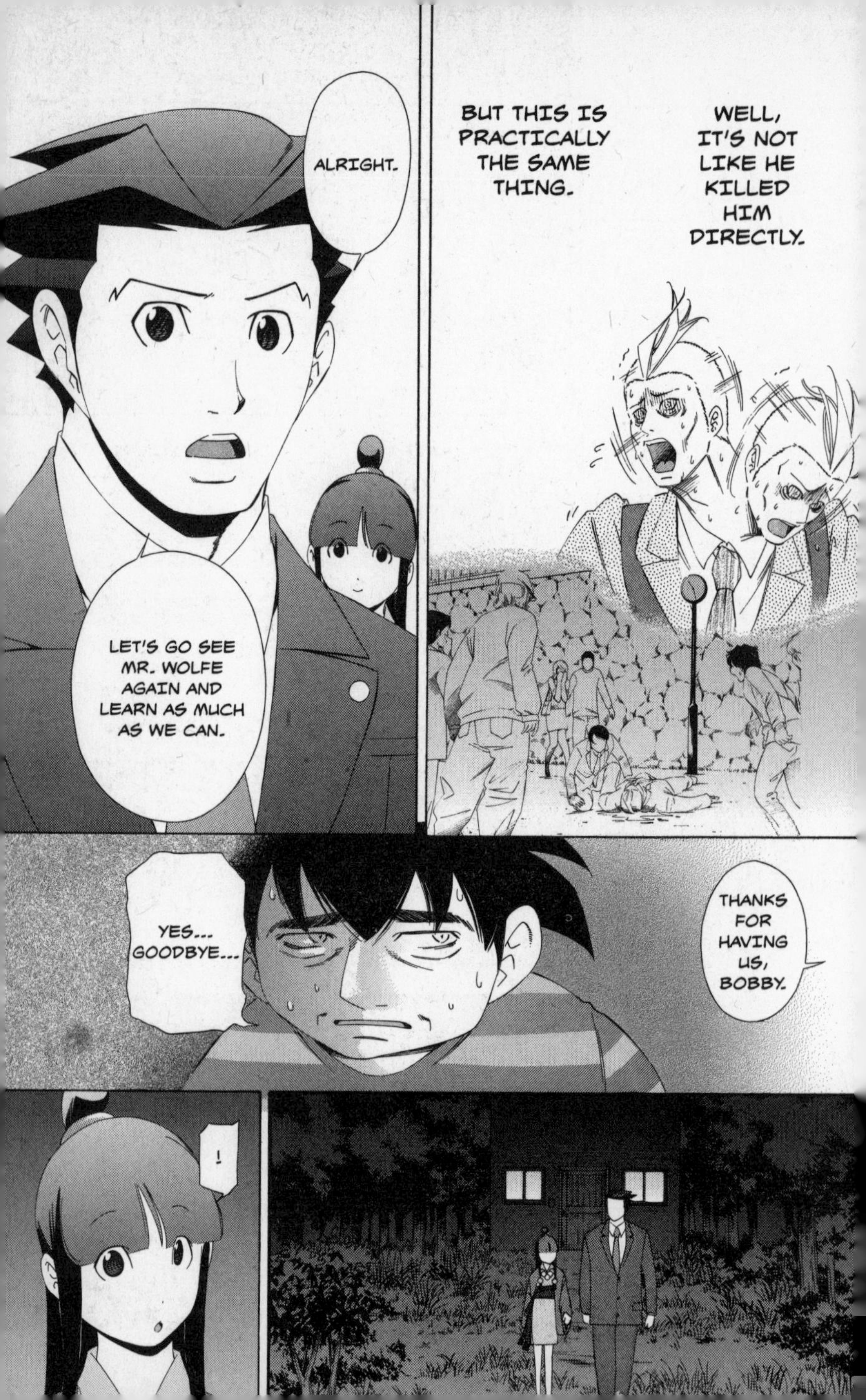
WELL, IT'S NOT LIKE HE KILLED HIM DIRECTLY.
BUT THIS IS PRACTICALLY THE SAME THING.
ALRIGHT.
LET'S GO SEE MR. WOLFE AGAIN AND LEARN AS MUCH AS WE CAN.
THANKS FOR HAVING US, BOBBY.
YES... GOODBYE...
!

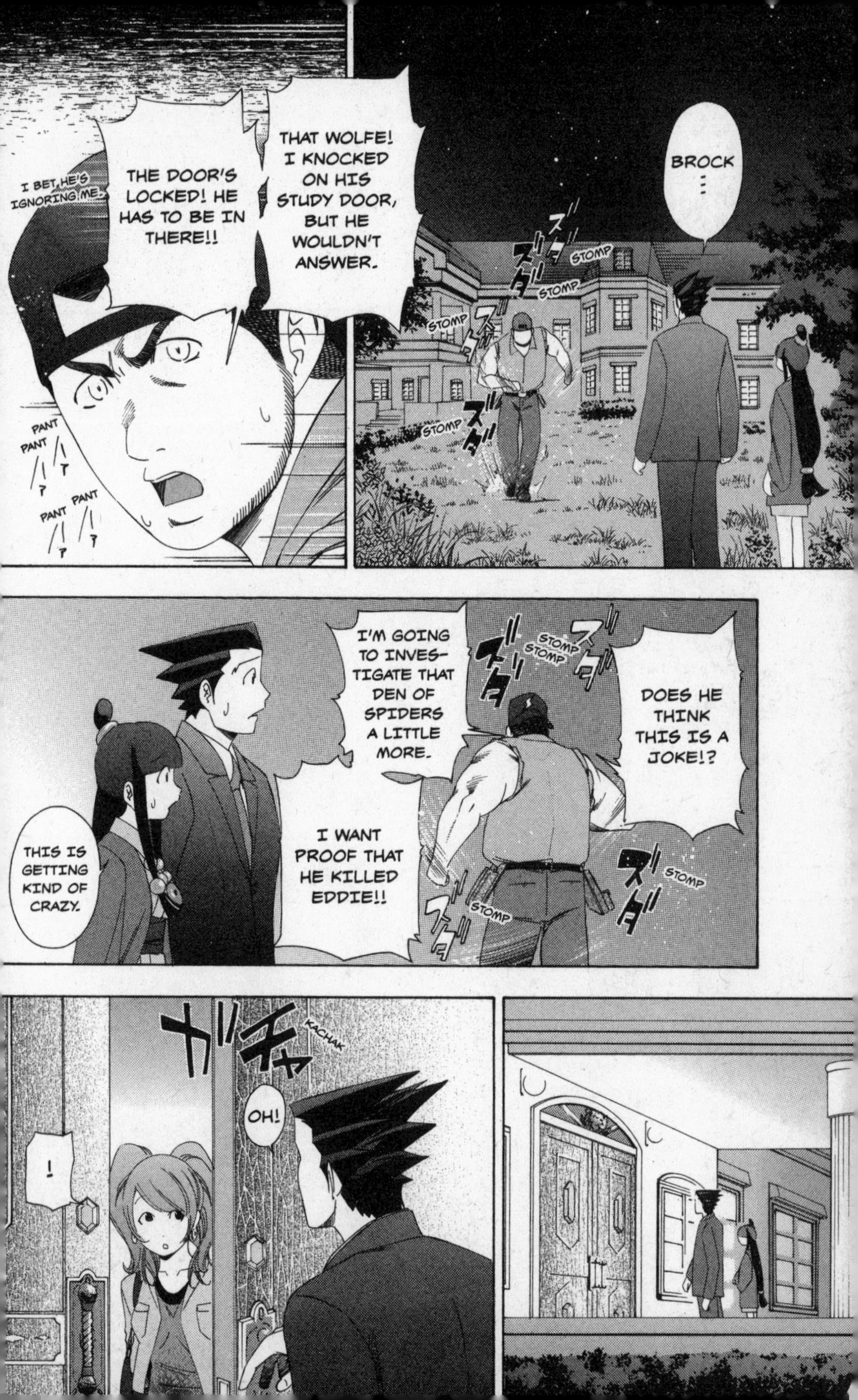
BROCK ...
STOMP
STOMP
STOMP
STOMP
THAT WOLFE! I KNOCKED ON HIS STUDY DOOR, BUT HE WOULDN'T ANSWER.
THE DOOR'S LOCKED! HE HAS TO BE IN THERE!!
I BET HE'S IGNORING ME.
PANT PANT
PANT PANT
DOES HE THINK THIS IS A JOKE!?
STOMP STOMP
I'M GOING TO INVES-TIGATE THAT DEN OF SPIDERS A LITTLE MORE.
I WANT PROOF THAT HE KILLED EDDIE!!
STOMP
STOMP
THIS IS GETTING KIND OF CRAZY.
KACHAK
OH!
!

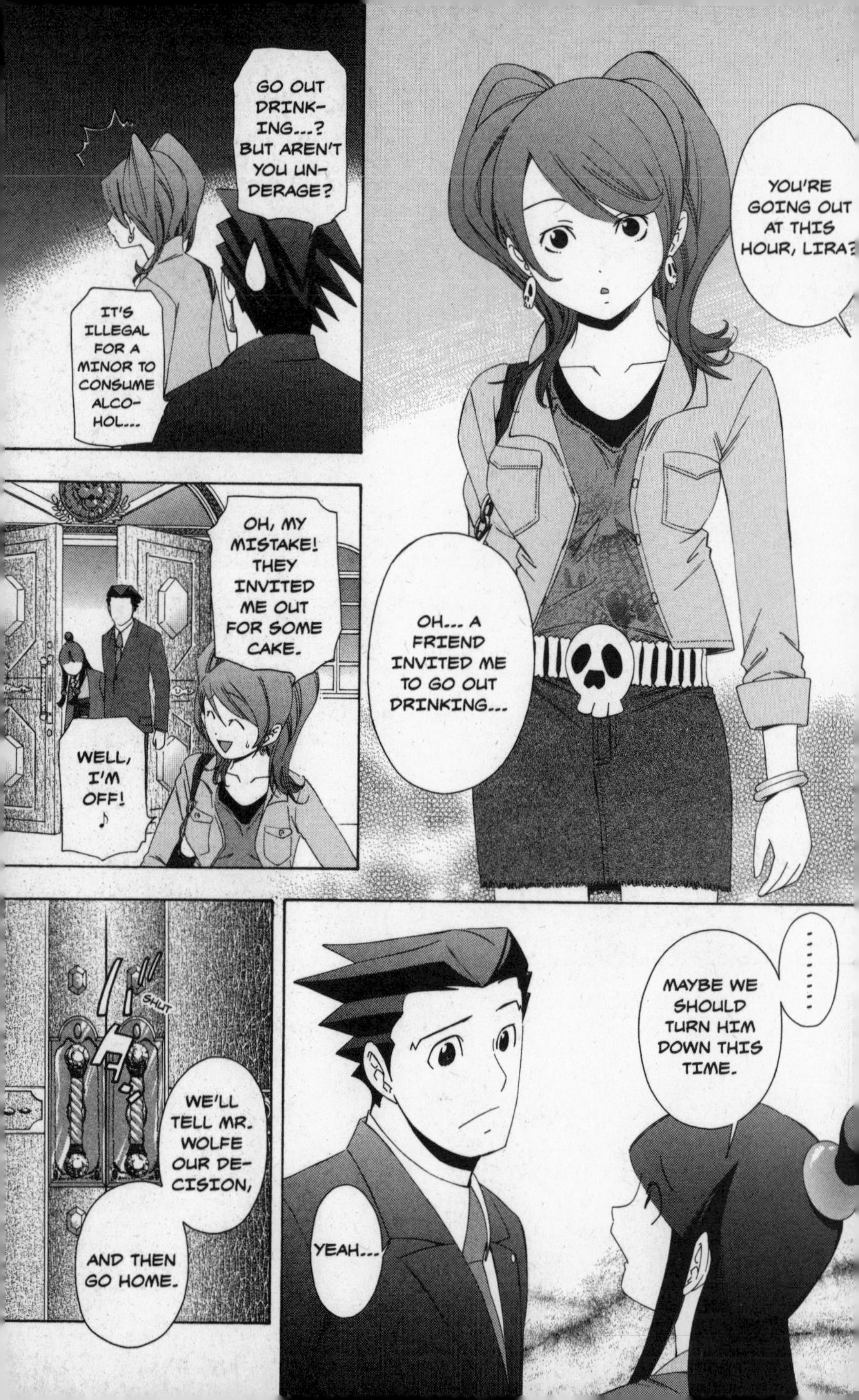
YOU'RE GOING OUT AT THIS HOUR, LIRA?
OH... A FRIEND INVITED ME TO GO OUT DRINKING...
GO OUT DRINKING...? BUT AREN'T YOU UNDERAGE?
IT'S ILLEGAL FOR A MINOR TO CONSUME ALCOHOL...
OH, MY MISTAKE! THEY INVITED ME OUT FOR SOME CAKE.
WELL, I'M OFF! ♪
......
MAYBE WE SHOULD TURN HIM DOWN THIS TIME.
YEAH...
SHUT
WE'LL TELL MR. WOLFE OUR DECISION,
AND THEN GO HOME.

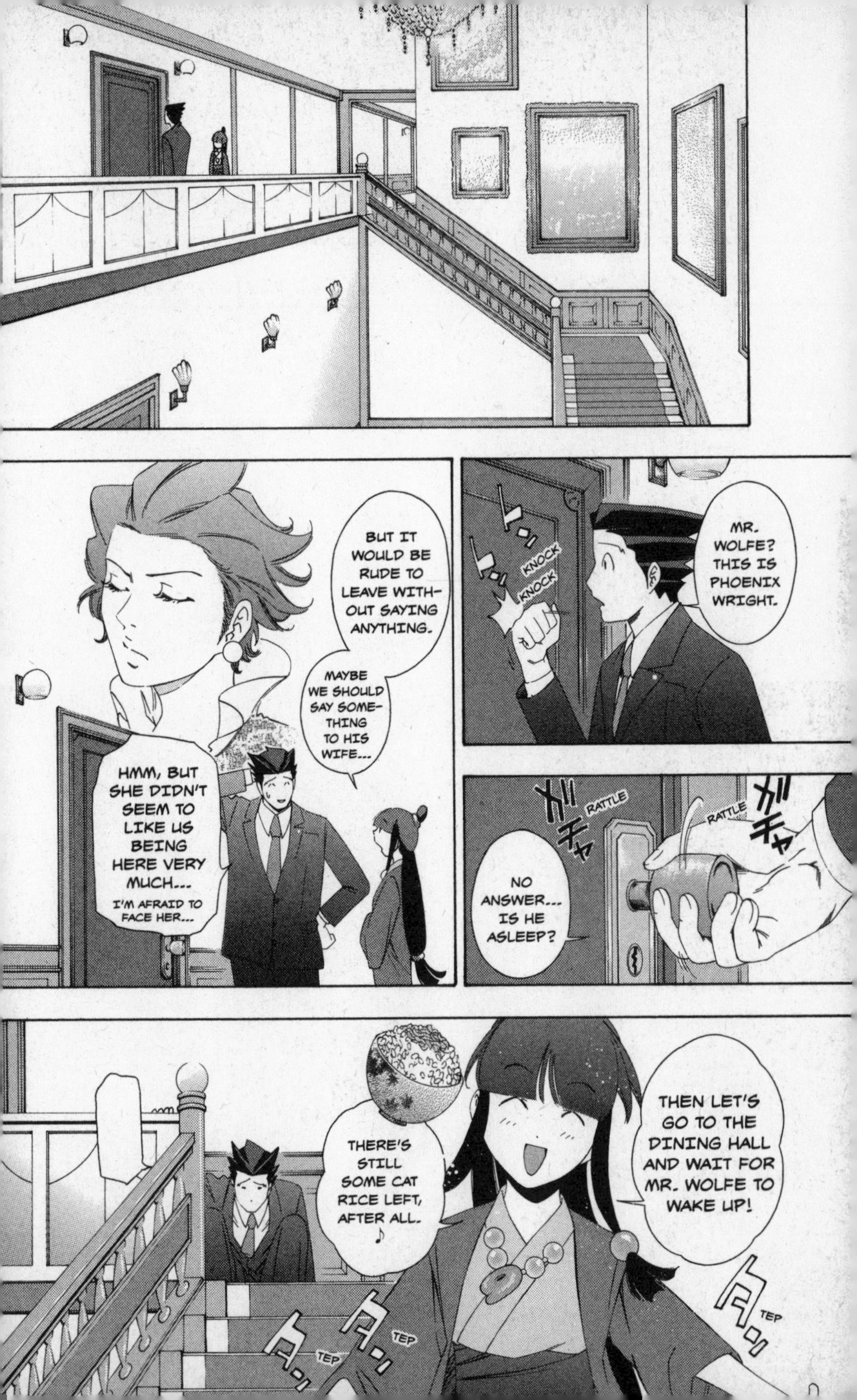
KNOCK
KNOCK
MR. WOLFE? THIS IS PHOENIX WRIGHT.
RATTLE
RATTLE
NO ANSWER... IS HE ASLEEP?
BUT IT WOULD BE RUDE TO LEAVE WITHOUT SAYING ANYTHING.
MAYBE WE SHOULD SAY SOMETHING TO HIS WIFE...
HMM, BUT SHE DIDN'T SEEM TO LIKE US BEING HERE VERY MUCH...
I'M AFRAID TO FACE HER...
THEN LET'S GO TO THE DINING HALL AND WAIT FOR MR. WOLFE TO WAKE UP!
THERE'S STILL SOME CAT RICE LEFT, AFTER ALL. ♪
TEP
TEP
TEP

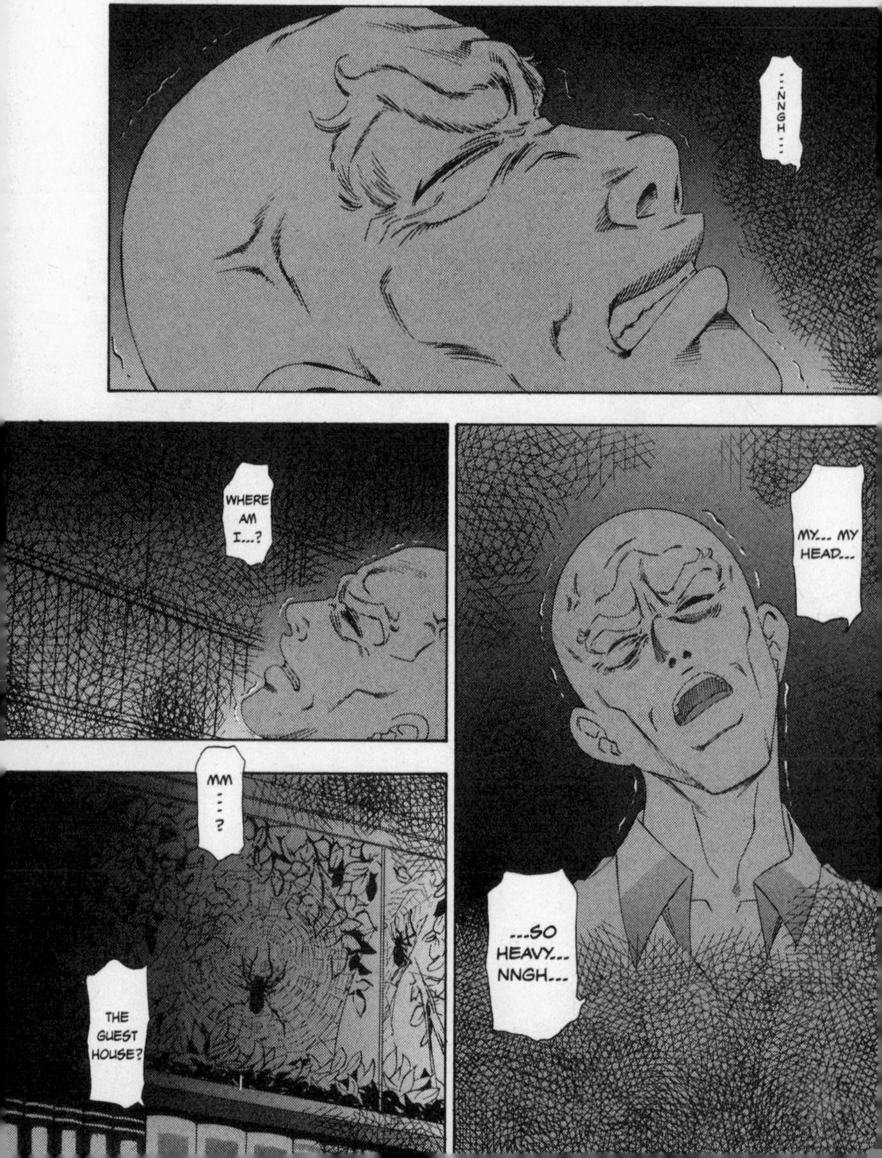
...NNGH...
MY... MY HEAD...
...SO HEAVY... NNGH...
WHERE AM I...?
MM...?
THE GUEST HOUSE?

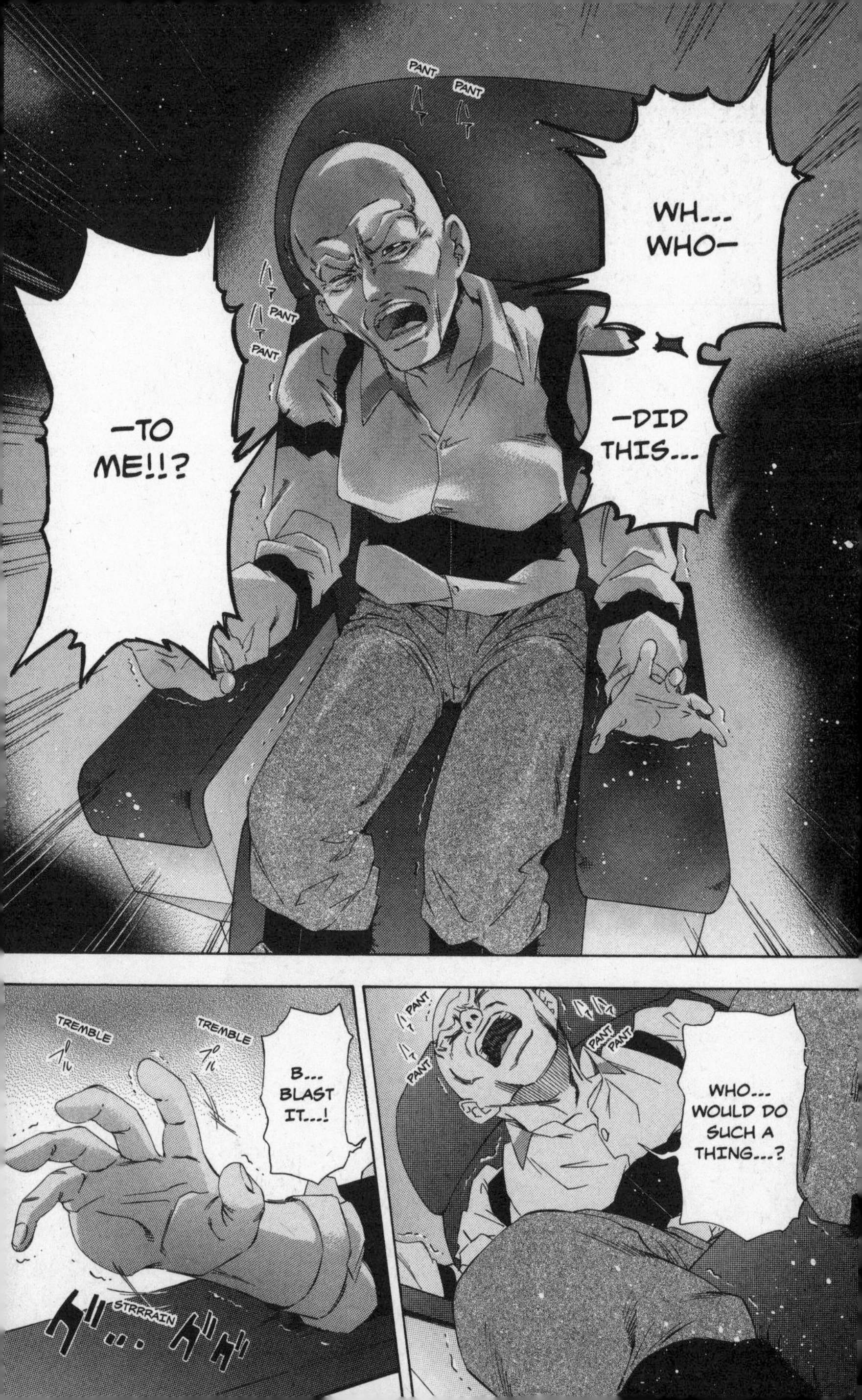
PANT
PANT
WH... WHO—
—DID THIS...
PANT
PANT
—TO ME!!?
PANT
PANT
PANT
PANT
WHO... WOULD DO SUCH A THING...?
TREMBLE
TREMBLE
B... BLAST IT...!
STRRRAIN

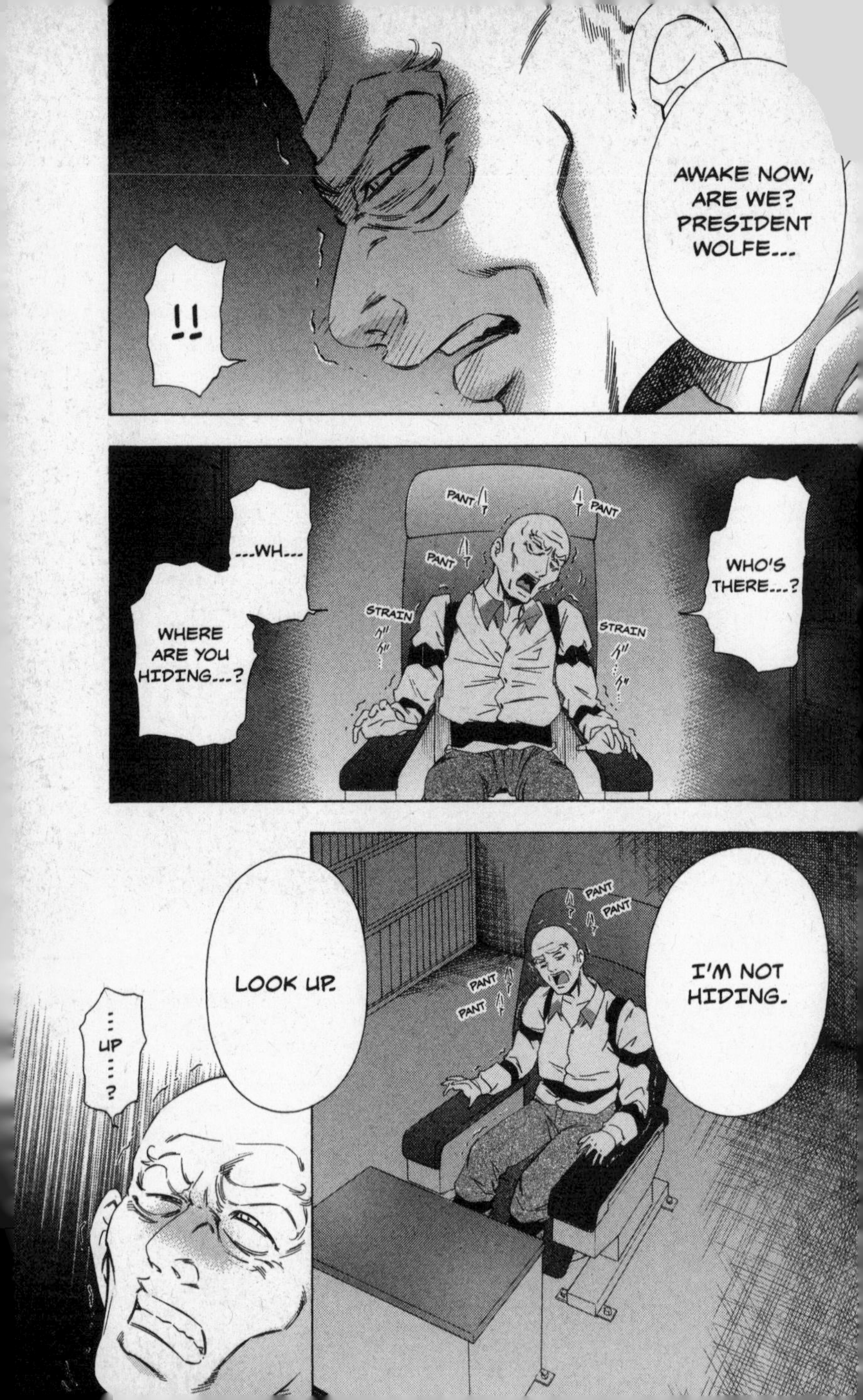
AWAKE NOW, ARE WE? PRESIDENT WOLFE...
!!
PANT
PANT
PANT
WHO'S THERE...?
...WH...
WHERE ARE YOU HIDING...?
STRAIN
STRAIN
PANT
PANT
I'M NOT HIDING.
PANT
PANT
LOOK UP.
...UP...?

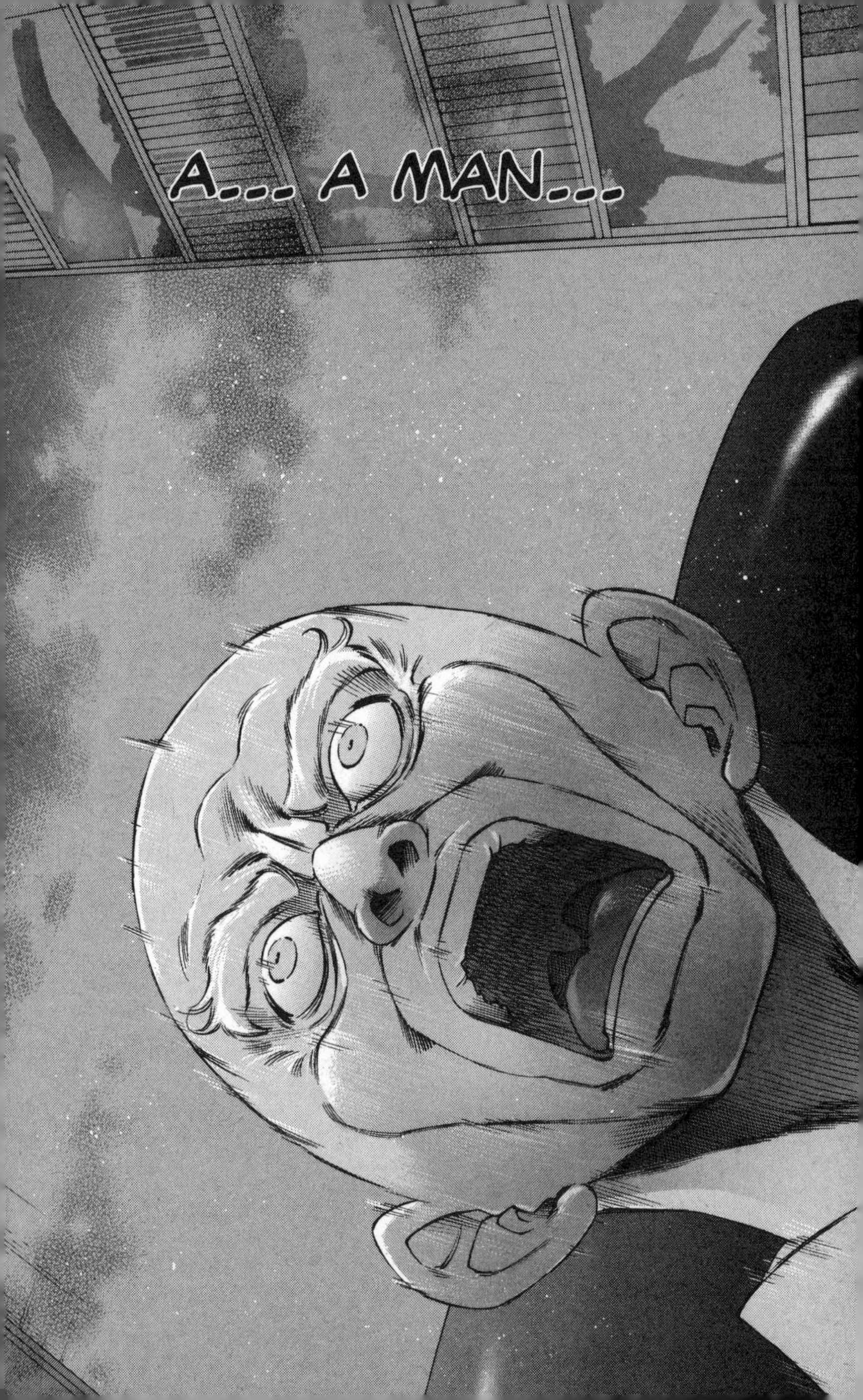
A... A MAN...

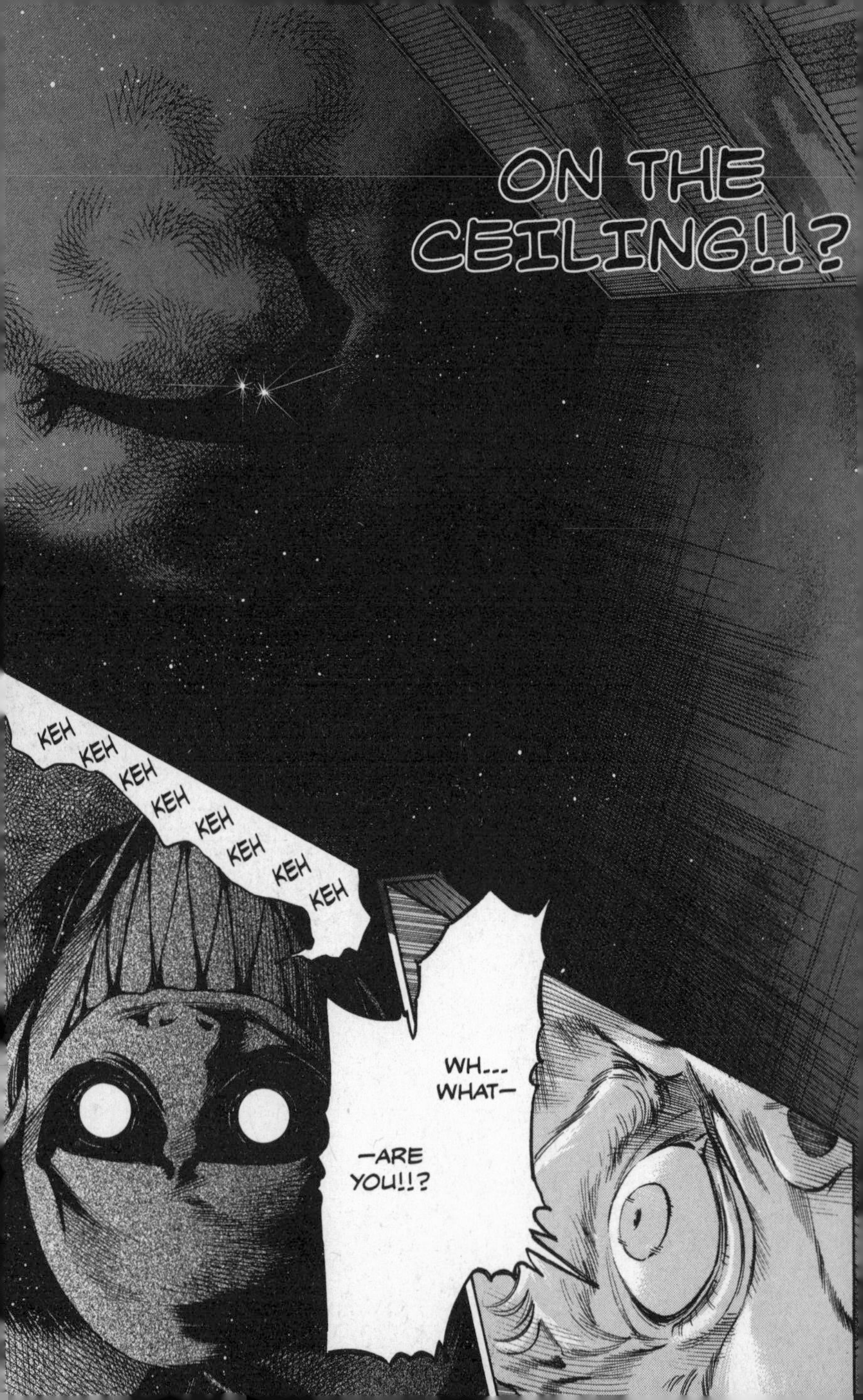
ON THE CEILING!!?
KEH KEH KEH KEH KEH KEH KEH KEH
WH... WHAT—
—ARE YOU!!?

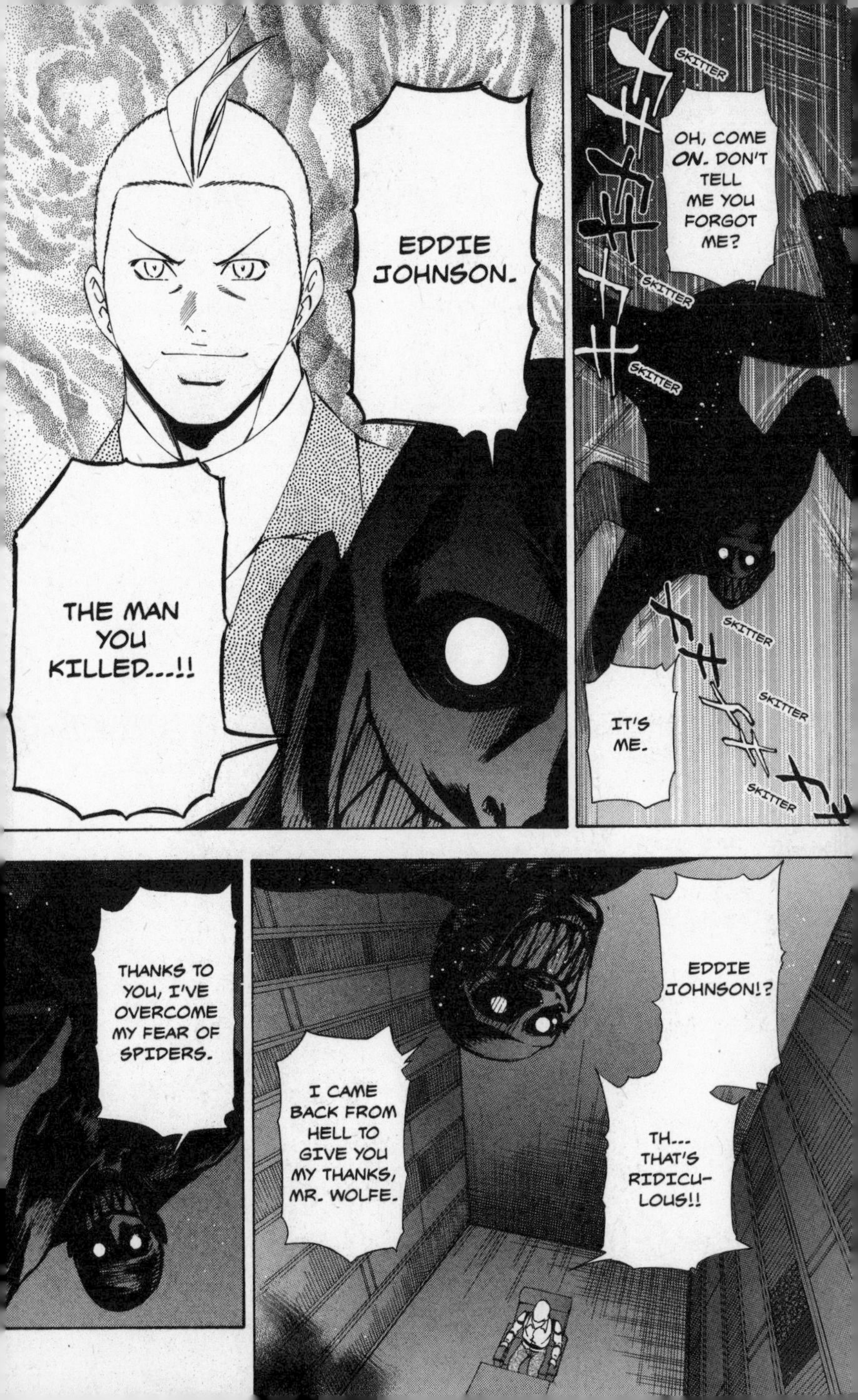
SKITTER
OH, COME ON. DON'T TELL ME YOU FORGOT ME?
SKITTER
SKITTER
SKITTER
SKITTER
IT'S ME.
SKITTER
EDDIE JOHNSON.
THE MAN YOU KILLED...!!
EDDIE JOHNSON!?
TH... THAT'S RIDICULOUS!!
I CAME BACK FROM HELL TO GIVE YOU MY THANKS, MR. WOLFE.
THANKS TO YOU, I'VE OVERCOME MY FEAR OF SPIDERS.

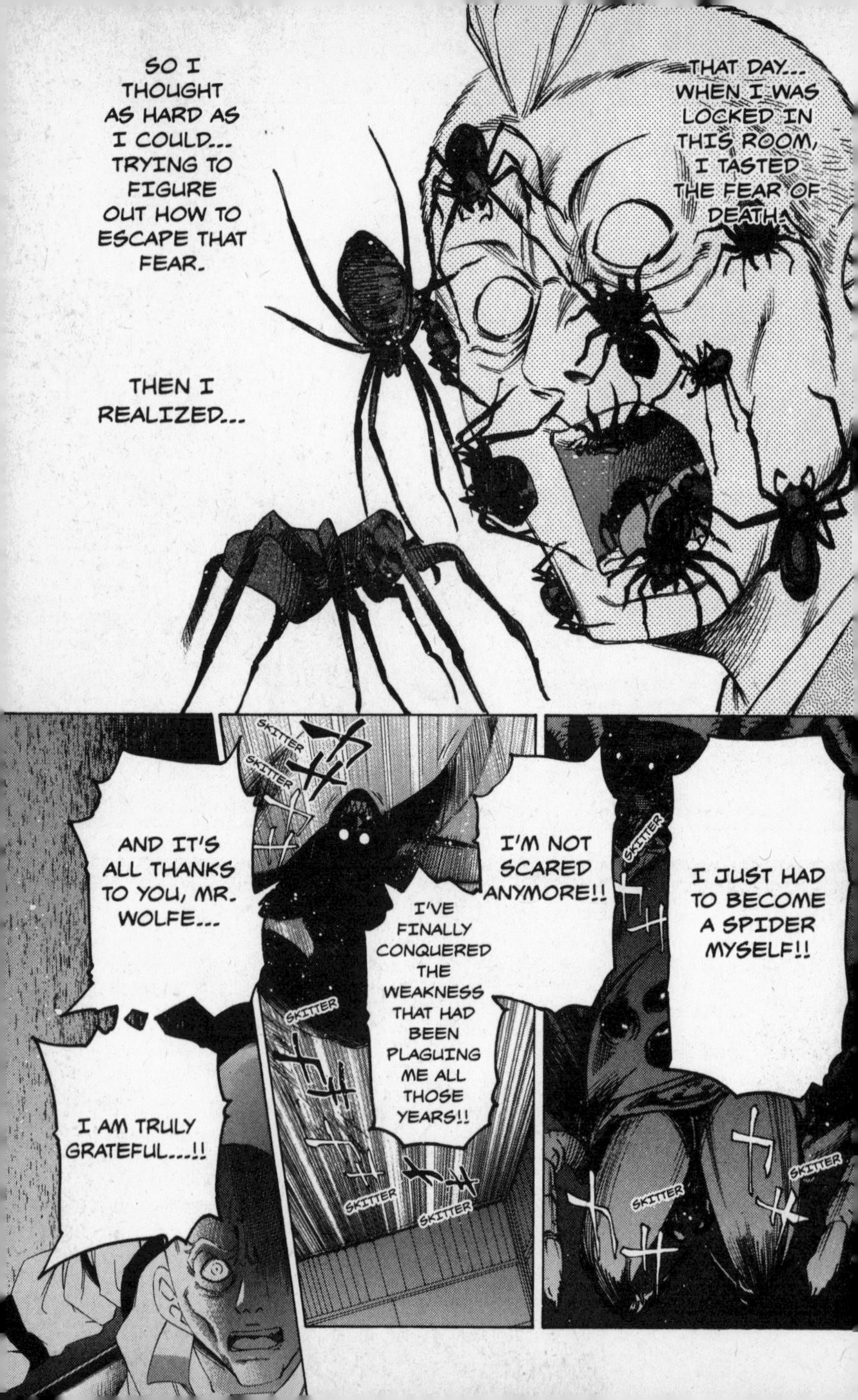
THAT DAY... WHEN I WAS LOCKED IN THIS ROOM, I TASTED THE FEAR OF DEATH.
SO I THOUGHT AS HARD AS I COULD... TRYING TO FIGURE OUT HOW TO ESCAPE THAT FEAR.
THEN I REALIZED...
SKITTER
I JUST HAD TO BECOME A SPIDER MYSELF!!
SKITTER
SKITTER
SKITTER
SKITTER
I'M NOT SCARED ANYMORE!!
I'VE FINALLY CONQUERED THE WEAKNESS THAT HAD BEEN PLAGUING ME ALL THOSE YEARS!!
SKITTER
SKITTER
SKITTER
SKITTER
AND IT'S ALL THANKS TO YOU, MR. WOLFE...
I AM TRULY GRATEFUL...!!

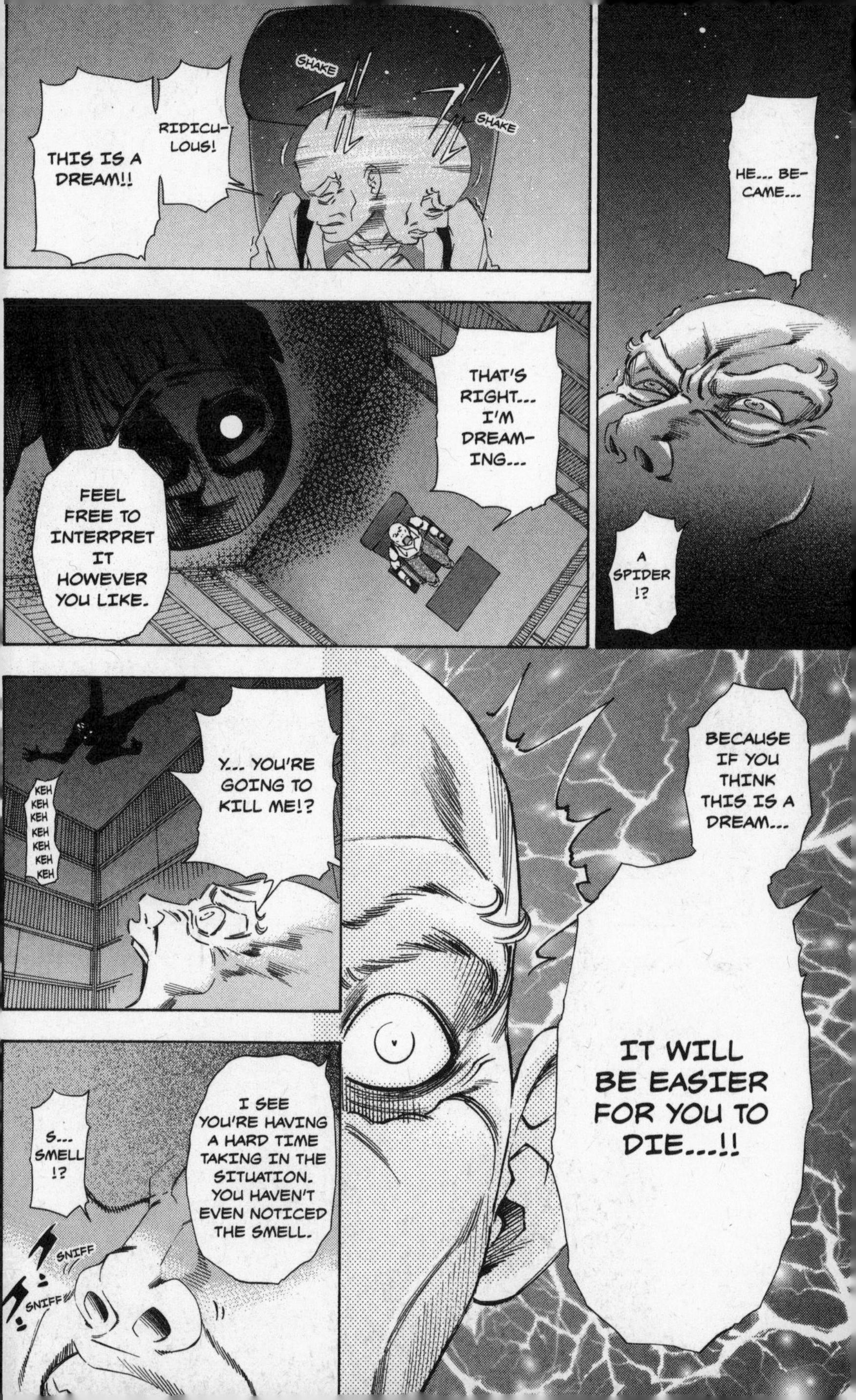
HE... BE-CAME...
A SPIDER!?
SHAKE
SHAKE
RIDICULOUS!
THIS IS A DREAM!!
THAT'S RIGHT... I'M DREAMING...
FEEL FREE TO INTERPRET IT HOWEVER YOU LIKE.
BECAUSE IF YOU THINK THIS IS A DREAM...
IT WILL BE EASIER FOR YOU TO DIE...!!
Y... YOU'RE GOING TO KILL ME!?
KEH KEH KEH KEH KEH KEH KEH
I SEE YOU'RE HAVING A HARD TIME TAKING IN THE SITUATION. YOU HAVEN'T EVEN NOTICED THE SMELL.
S... SMELL!?
SNIFF
SNIFF

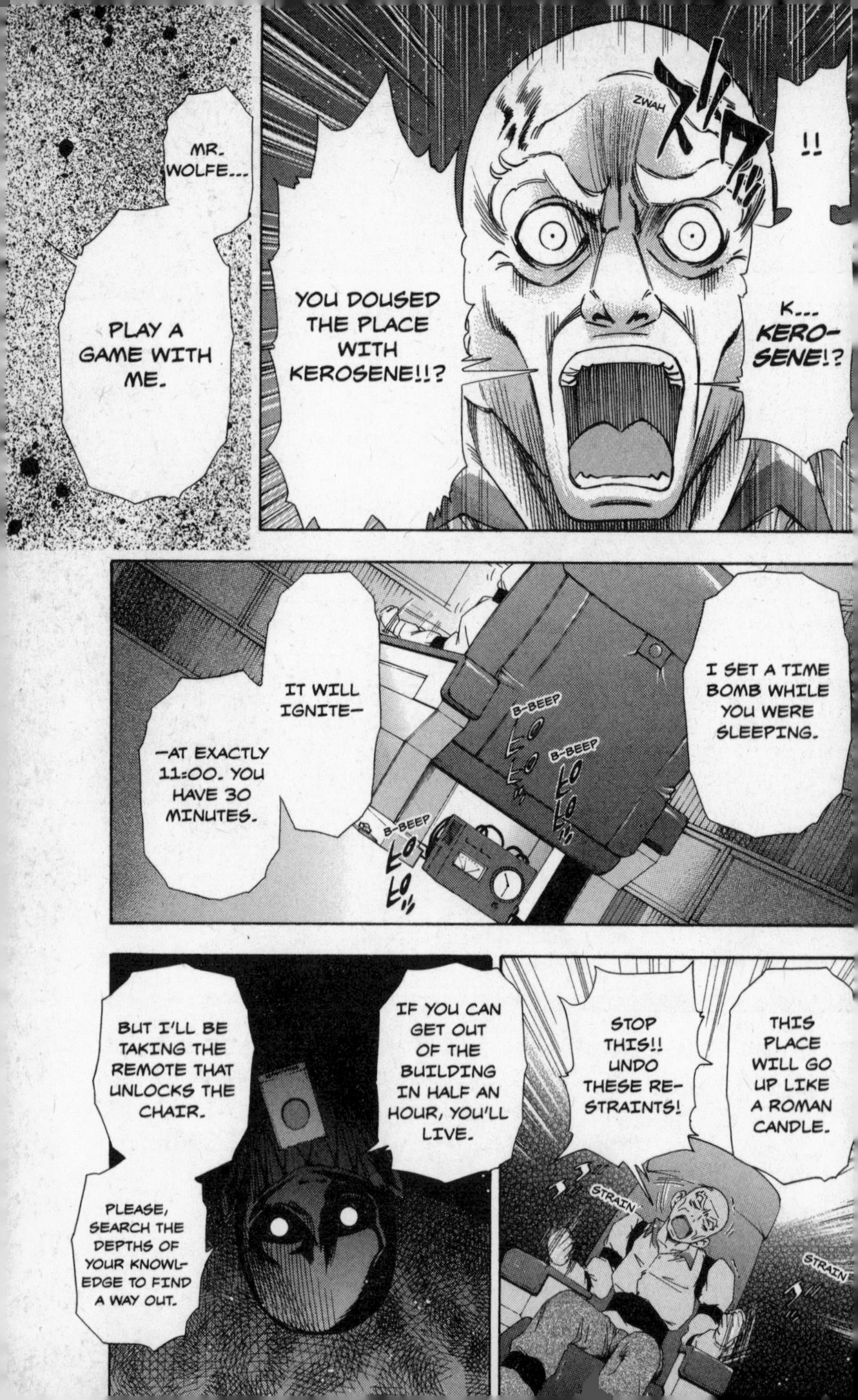
ZWAH
!!
K... KERO-SENE!?
YOU DOUSED THE PLACE WITH KEROSENE!!?
MR. WOLFE...
PLAY A GAME WITH ME.
I SET A TIME BOMB WHILE YOU WERE SLEEPING.
B-BEEP
B-BEEP
B-BEEP
IT WILL IGNITE—
—AT EXACTLY 11:00. YOU HAVE 30 MINUTES.
THIS PLACE WILL GO UP LIKE A ROMAN CANDLE.
STOP THIS!! UNDO THESE RE-STRAINTS!
STRAIN
STRAIN
IF YOU CAN GET OUT OF THE BUILDING IN HALF AN HOUR, YOU'LL LIVE.
BUT I'LL BE TAKING THE REMOTE THAT UNLOCKS THE CHAIR.
PLEASE, SEARCH THE DEPTHS OF YOUR KNOWL-EDGE TO FIND A WAY OUT.

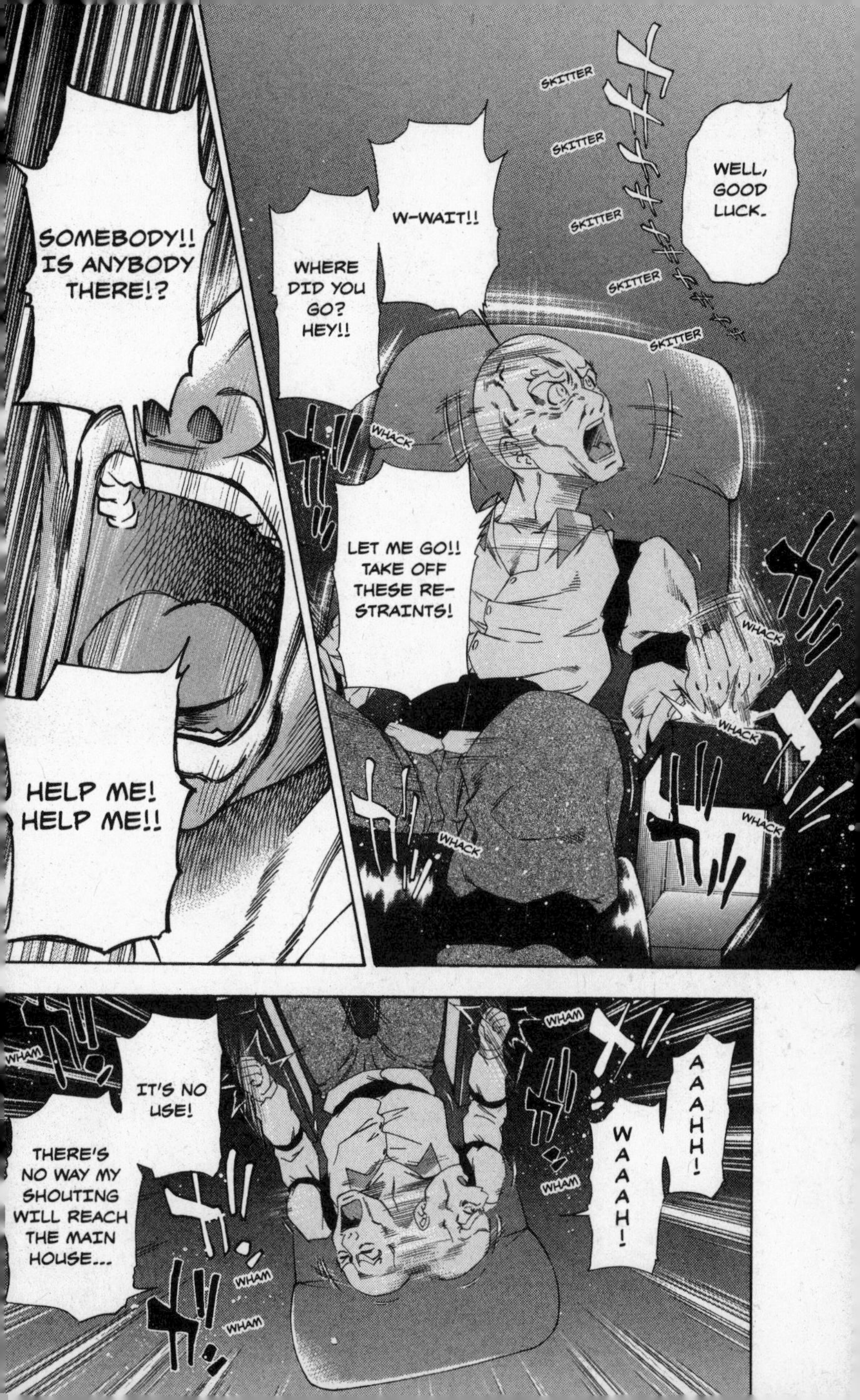
WELL, GOOD LUCK.
SKITTER
SKITTER
SKITTER
SKITTER
SKITTER
W-WAIT!!
WHERE DID YOU GO? HEY!!
WHACK
LET ME GO!! TAKE OFF THESE RE-STRAINTS!
WHACK
WHACK
WHACK
WHACK
SOMEBODY!! IS ANYBODY THERE!?
HELP ME! HELP ME!!
AAAAHH!
WAAAAH!
WHAM
WHAM
IT'S NO USE!
THERE'S NO WAY MY SHOUTING WILL REACH THE MAIN HOUSE...
WHAM
WHAM
WHAM

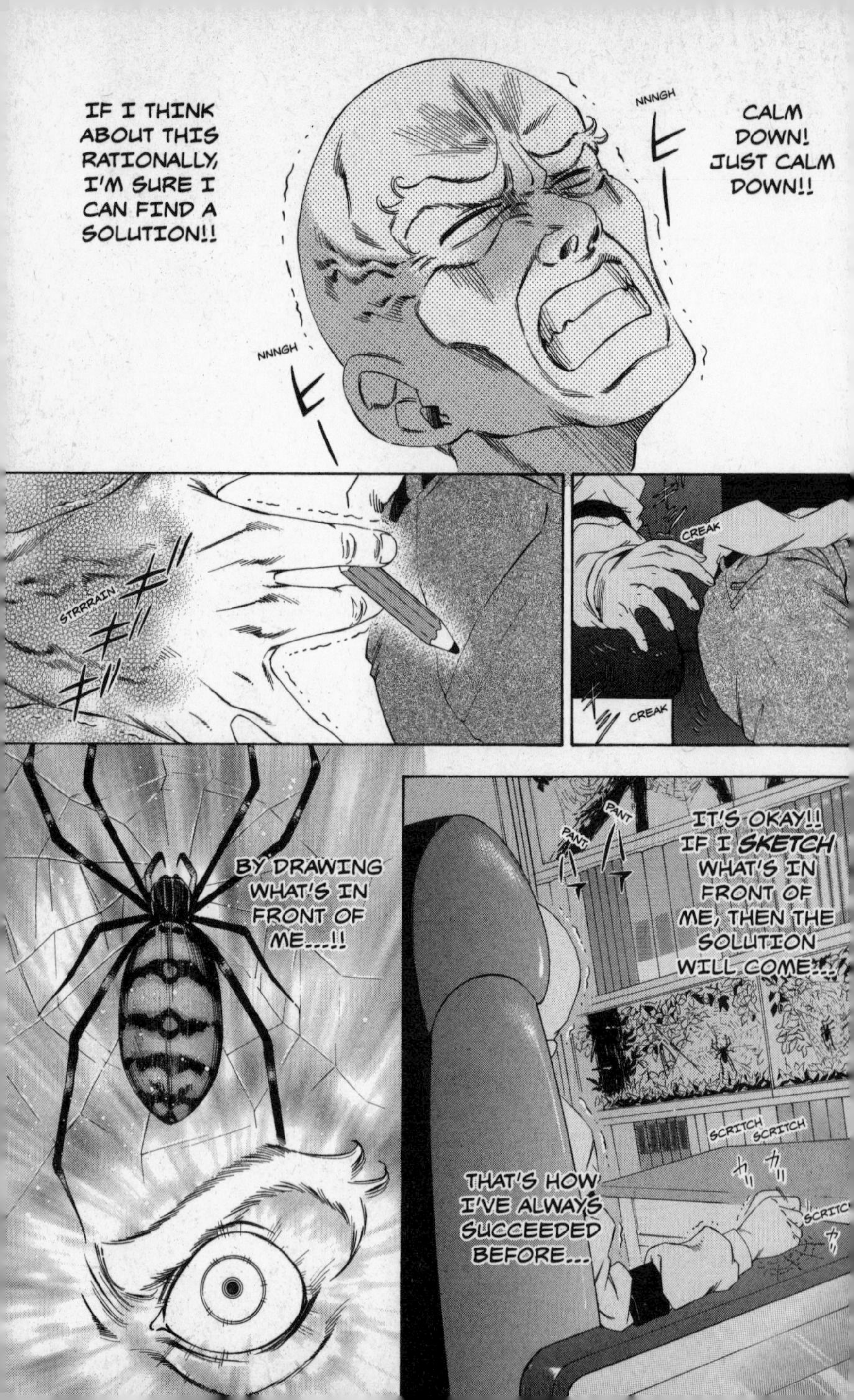
NNNGH
CALM DOWN! JUST CALM DOWN!!
IF I THINK ABOUT THIS RATIONALLY, I'M SURE I CAN FIND A SOLUTION!!
NNNGH
CREAK
CREAK
STRRRAIN
PANT
PANT
IT'S OKAY!! IF I *SKETCH* WHAT'S IN FRONT OF ME, THEN THE SOLUTION WILL COME...
SCRITCH
SCRITCH
THAT'S HOW I'VE ALWAYS SUCCEEDED BEFORE...
BY DRAWING WHAT'S IN FRONT OF ME...!!

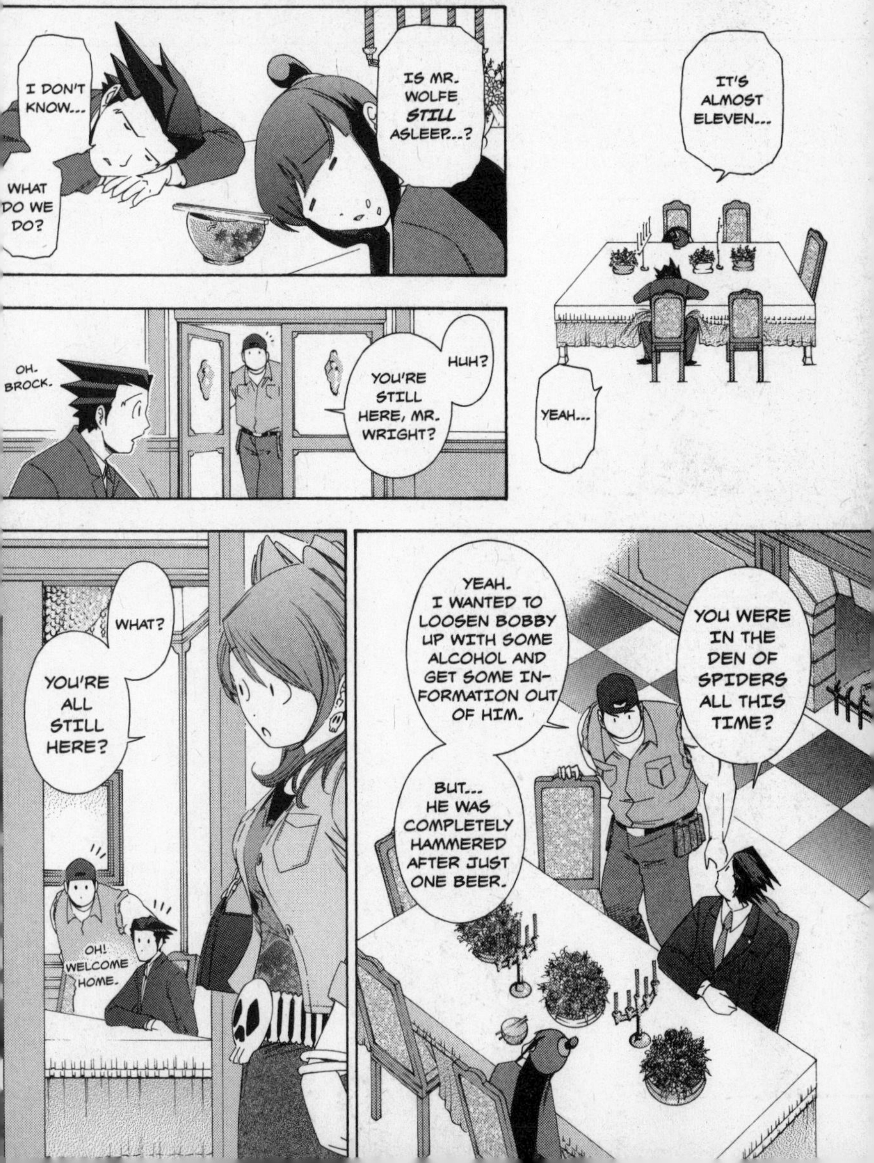
IT'S ALMOST ELEVEN...
YEAH...
IS MR. WOLFE STILL ASLEEP...?
I DON'T KNOW...
WHAT DO WE DO?
HUH?
YOU'RE STILL HERE, MR. WRIGHT?
OH. BROCK.
YOU WERE IN THE DEN OF SPIDERS ALL THIS TIME?
YEAH. I WANTED TO LOOSEN BOBBY UP WITH SOME ALCOHOL AND GET SOME IN-FORMATION OUT OF HIM.
BUT... HE WAS COMPLETELY HAMMERED AFTER JUST ONE BEER.
WHAT?
YOU'RE ALL STILL HERE?
OH! WELCOME HOME.

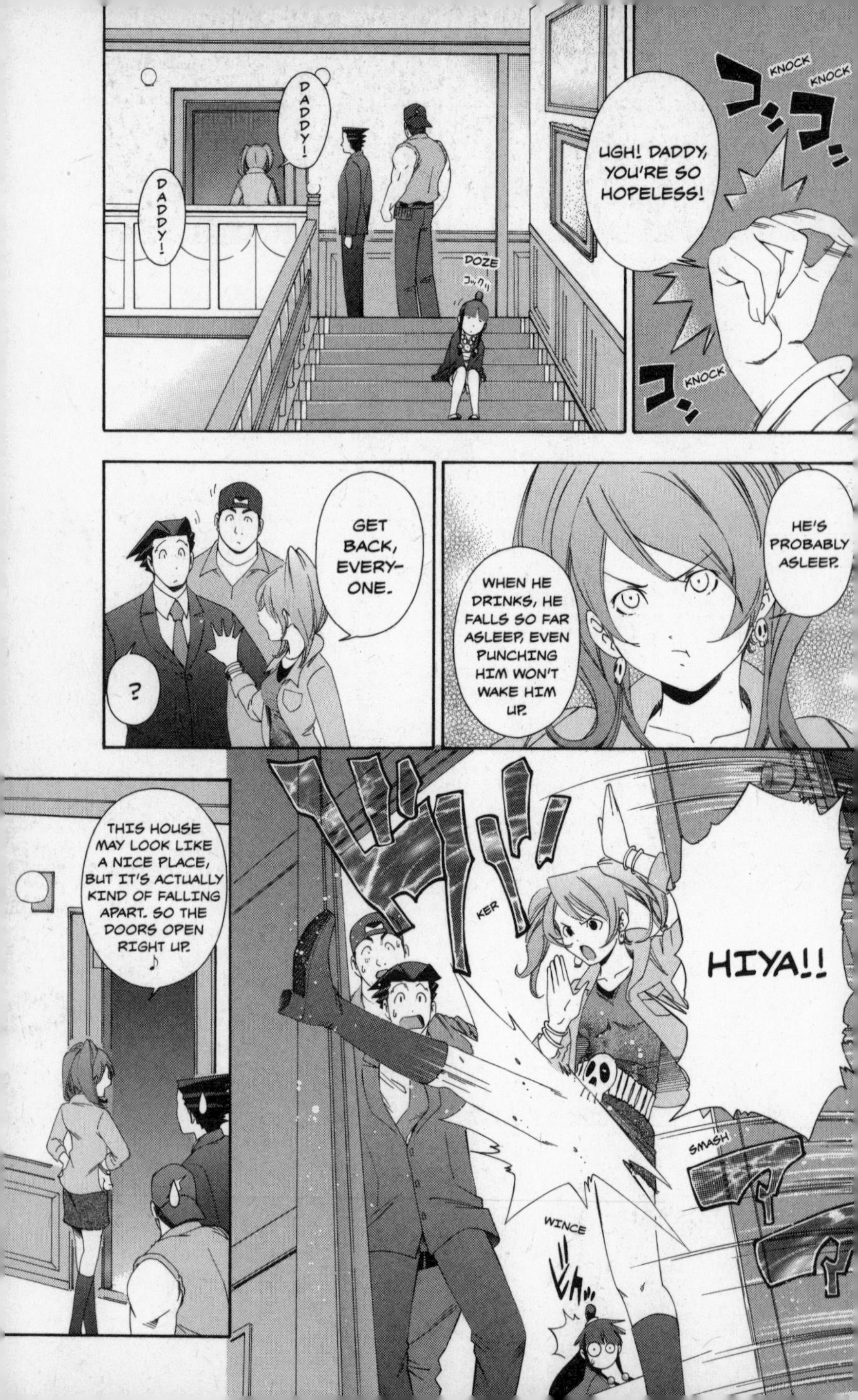
KNOCK
KNOCK
UGH! DADDY, YOU'RE SO HOPELESS!
KNOCK
DADDY!
DADDY!
DOZE
HE'S PROBABLY ASLEEP.
WHEN HE DRINKS, HE FALLS SO FAR ASLEEP, EVEN PUNCHING HIM WON'T WAKE HIM UP.
GET BACK, EVERY-ONE.
?
HIYA!!
KER
SMASH
WINCE
THIS HOUSE MAY LOOK LIKE A NICE PLACE, BUT IT'S ACTUALLY KIND OF FALLING APART. SO THE DOORS OPEN RIGHT UP. ♪

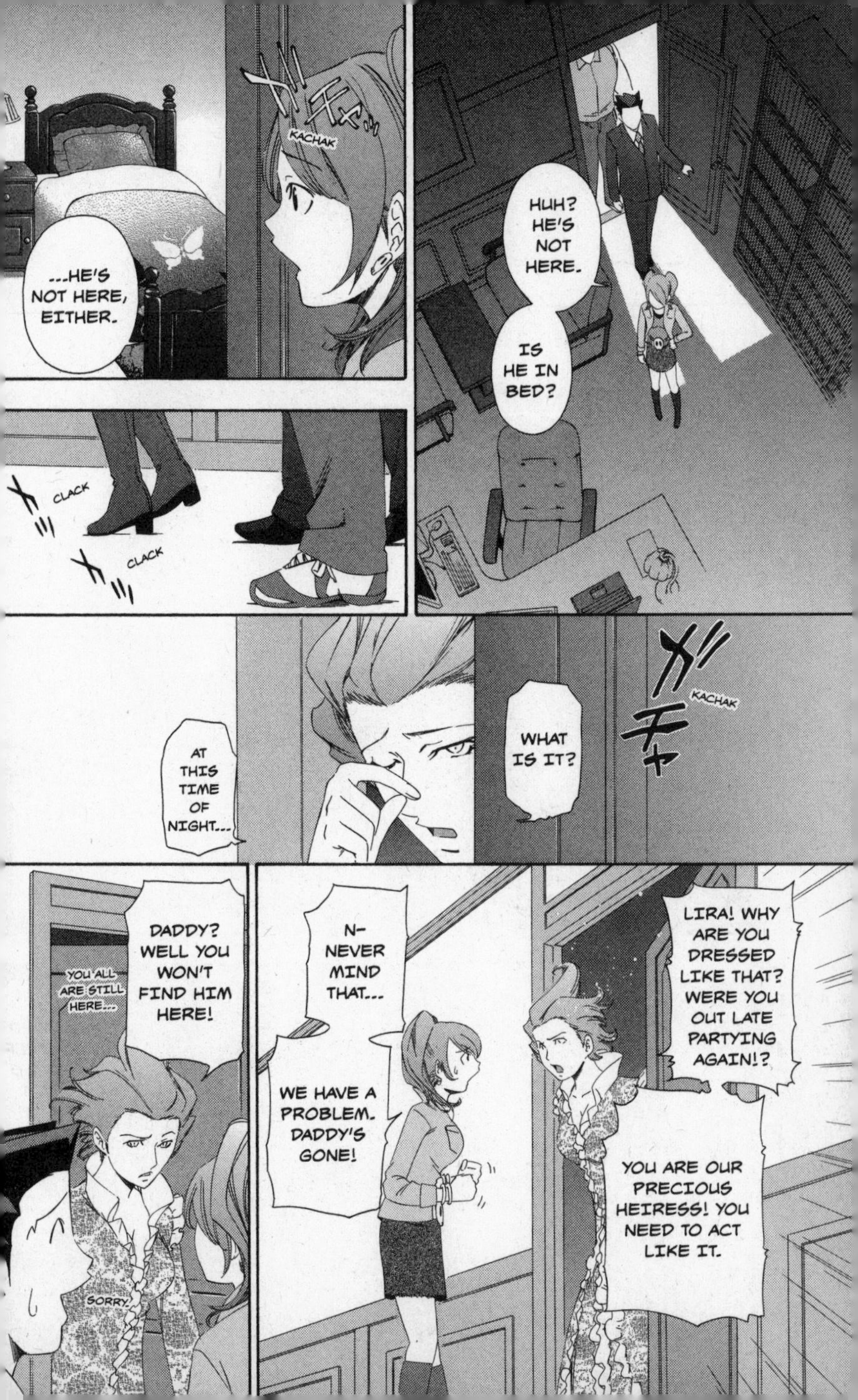
HUH? HE'S NOT HERE.
IS HE IN BED?
KACHAK
...HE'S NOT HERE, EITHER.
CLACK
CLACK
KACHAK
WHAT IS IT?
AT THIS TIME OF NIGHT...
LIRA! WHY ARE YOU DRESSED LIKE THAT? WERE YOU OUT LATE PARTYING AGAIN!?
YOU ARE OUR PRECIOUS HEIRESS! YOU NEED TO ACT LIKE IT.
N- NEVER MIND THAT...
WE HAVE A PROBLEM. DADDY'S GONE!
DADDY? WELL YOU WON'T FIND HIM HERE!
YOU ALL ARE STILL HERE...
SORRY.

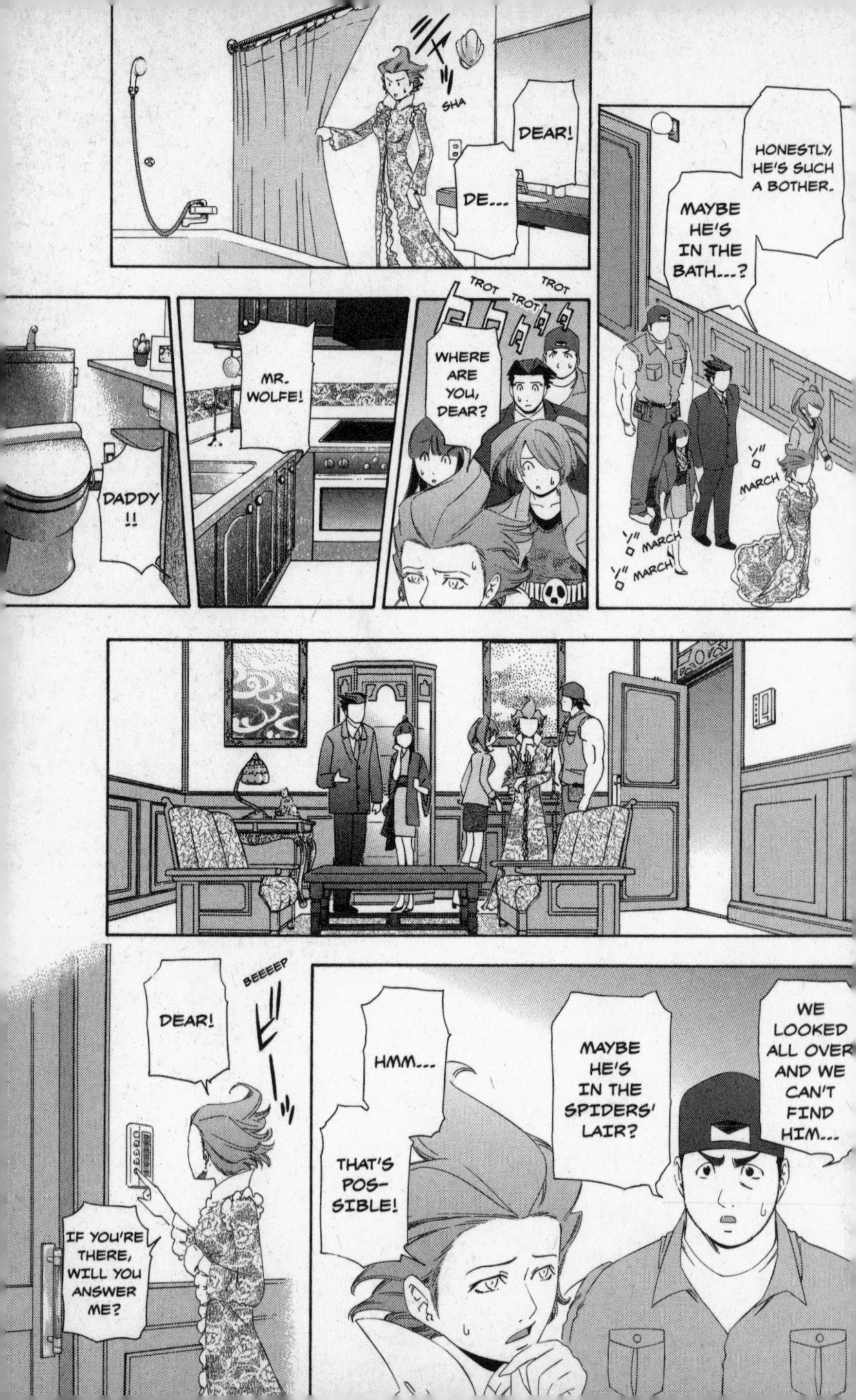
HONESTLY, HE'S SUCH A BOTHER.
MAYBE HE'S IN THE BATH...?
MARCH
MARCH
MARCH
DEAR!
DE...
SHA
TROT
TROT
TROT
WHERE ARE YOU, DEAR?
MR. WOLFE!
DADDY!!
WE LOOKED ALL OVER AND WE CAN'T FIND HIM...
MAYBE HE'S IN THE SPIDERS' LAIR?
HMM...
THAT'S POS-SIBLE!
BEEEEP
DEAR!
IF YOU'RE THERE, WILL YOU ANSWER ME?

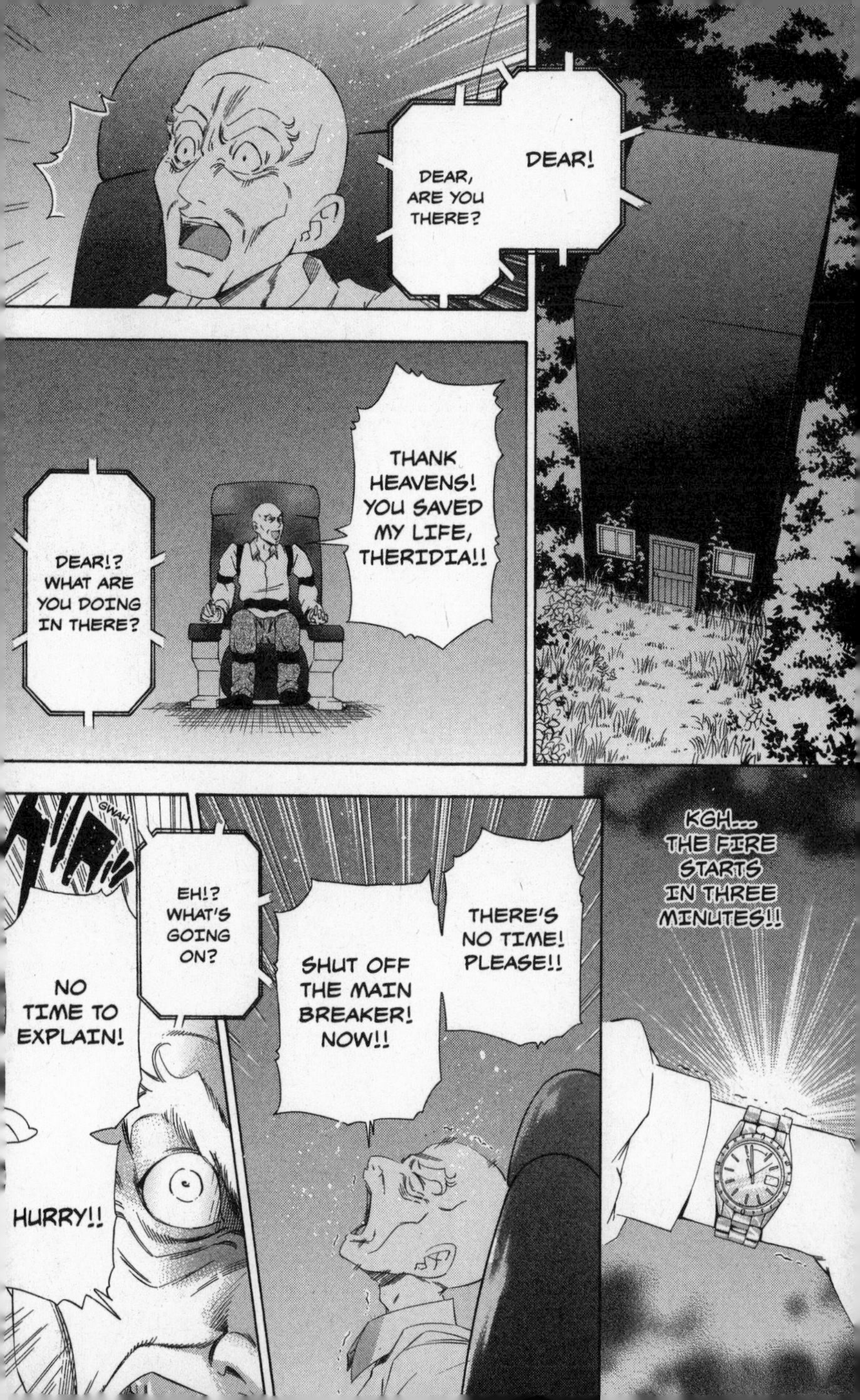
DEAR!
DEAR, ARE YOU THERE?
THANK HEAVENS! YOU SAVED MY LIFE, THERIDIA!!
DEAR!? WHAT ARE YOU DOING IN THERE?
KGH... THE FIRE STARTS IN THREE MINUTES!!
THERE'S NO TIME! PLEASE!!
SHUT OFF THE MAIN BREAKER! NOW!!
EH!? WHAT'S GOING ON?
GWAH
NO TIME TO EXPLAIN!
HURRY!!

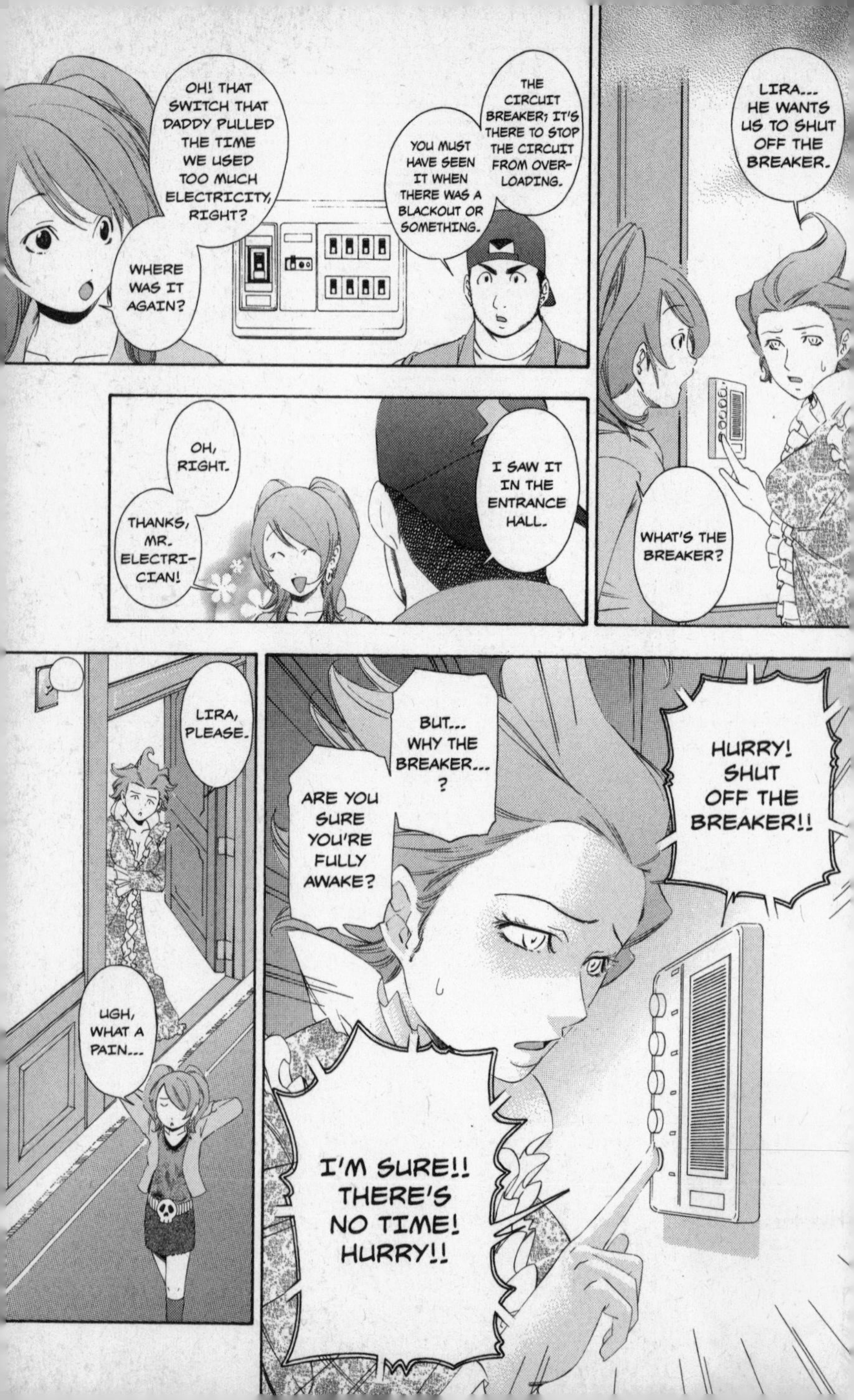
LIRA... HE WANTS US TO SHUT OFF THE BREAKER.
WHAT'S THE BREAKER?
THE CIRCUIT BREAKER; IT'S THERE TO STOP THE CIRCUIT FROM OVER-LOADING.
YOU MUST HAVE SEEN IT WHEN THERE WAS A BLACKOUT OR SOMETHING.
OH! THAT SWITCH THAT DADDY PULLED THE TIME WE USED TOO MUCH ELECTRICITY, RIGHT?
WHERE WAS IT AGAIN?
I SAW IT IN THE ENTRANCE HALL.
OH, RIGHT.
THANKS, MR. ELECTRI-CIAN!
HURRY! SHUT OFF THE BREAKER!!
BUT... WHY THE BREAKER...?
ARE YOU SURE YOU'RE FULLY AWAKE?
I'M SURE!! THERE'S NO TIME! HURRY!!
LIRA, PLEASE.
UGH, WHAT A PAIN...

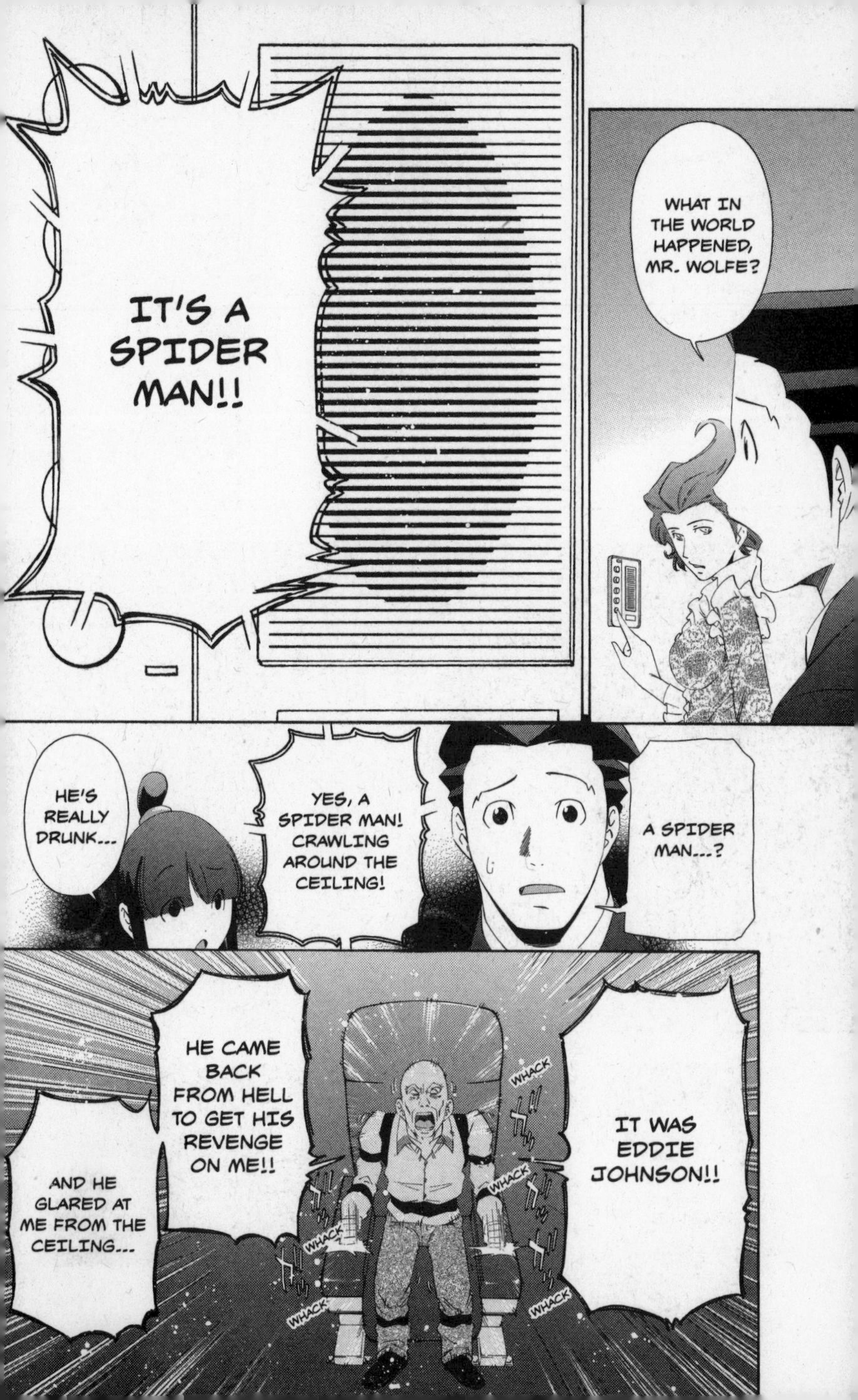
WHAT IN THE WORLD HAPPENED, MR. WOLFE?
IT'S A SPIDER MAN!!
A SPIDER MAN...?
YES, A SPIDER MAN! CRAWLING AROUND THE CEILING!
HE'S REALLY DRUNK...
IT WAS EDDIE JOHNSON!!
WHACK
WHACK
WHACK
WHACK
WHACK
HE CAME BACK FROM HELL TO GET HIS REVENGE ON ME!!
AND HE GLARED AT ME FROM THE CEILING...

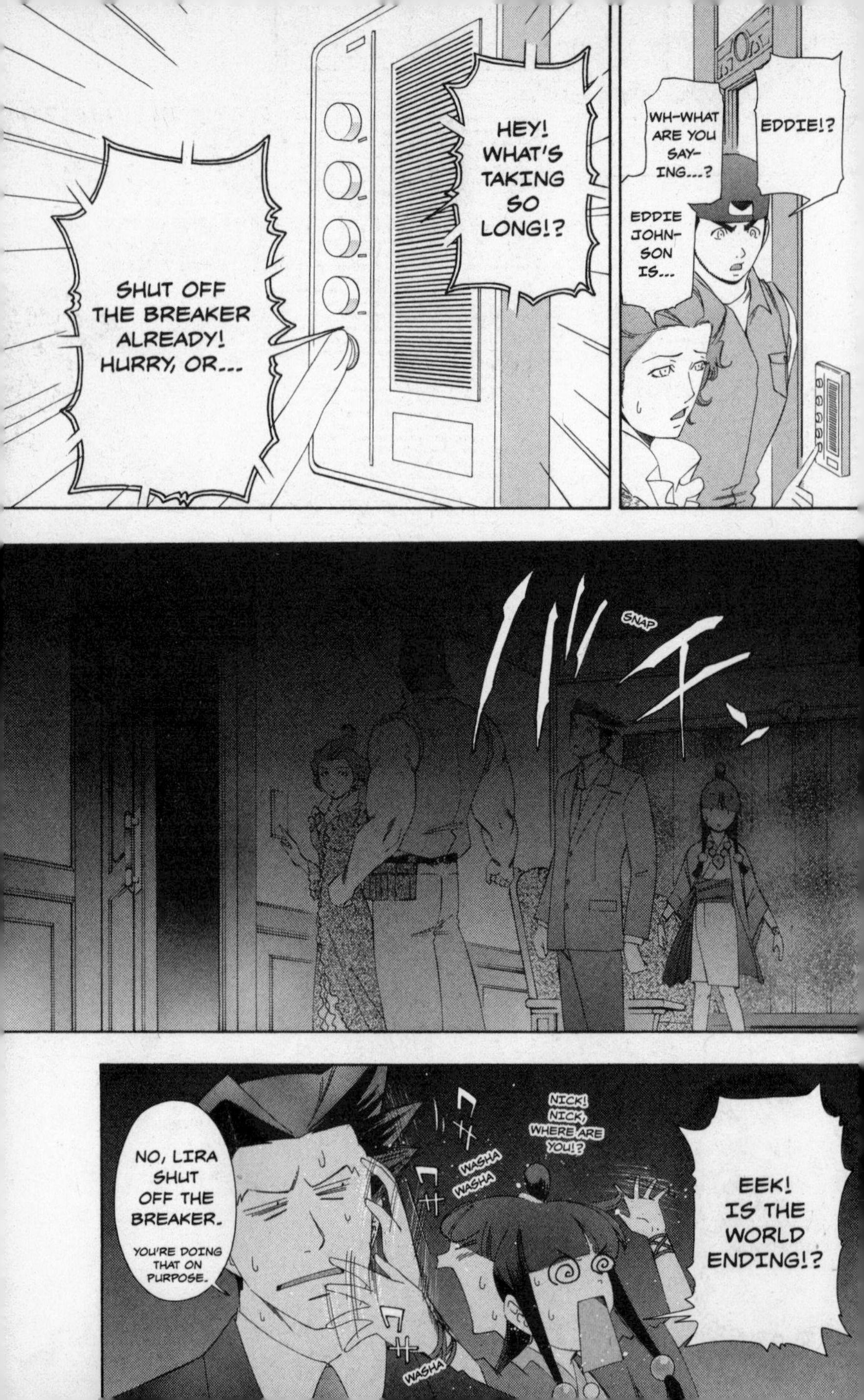
EDDIE!?
WH-WHAT ARE YOU SAY-ING...?
EDDIE JOHN-SON IS...
HEY! WHAT'S TAKING SO LONG!?
SHUT OFF THE BREAKER ALREADY! HURRY, OR...
SNAP
EEK! IS THE WORLD ENDING!?
NICK! NICK, WHERE ARE YOU!?
WASHA WASHA
NO, LIRA SHUT OFF THE BREAKER.
YOU'RE DOING THAT ON PURPOSE.
WASHA

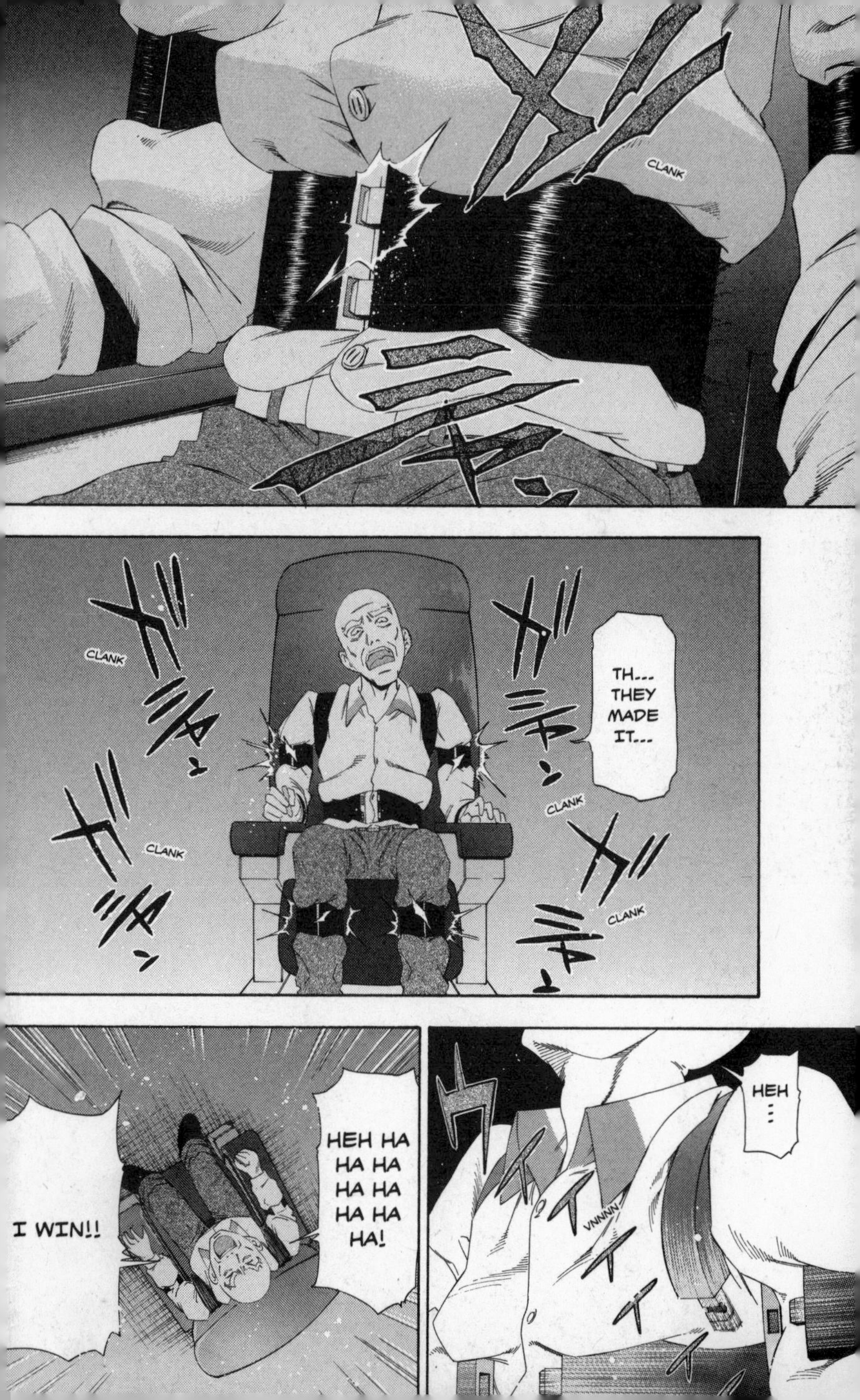
CLANK
TH... THEY MADE IT...
CLANK
CLANK
CLANK
CLANK
HEH ...
VNNNN
HEH HA HA HA HA HA HA HA HA!
I WIN!!

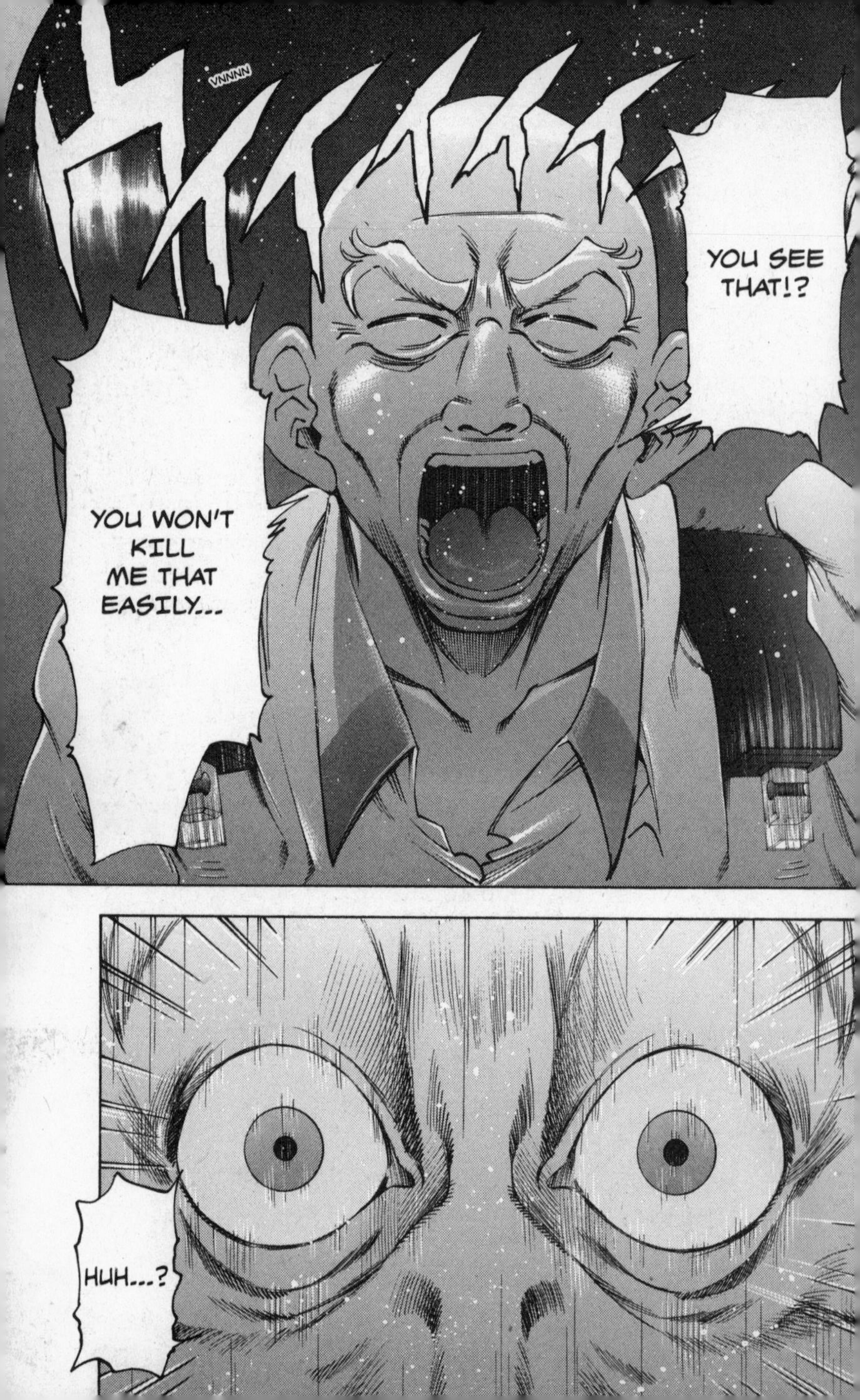
VNNNN
YOU SEE THAT!?
YOU WON'T KILL ME THAT EASILY...
HUH...?

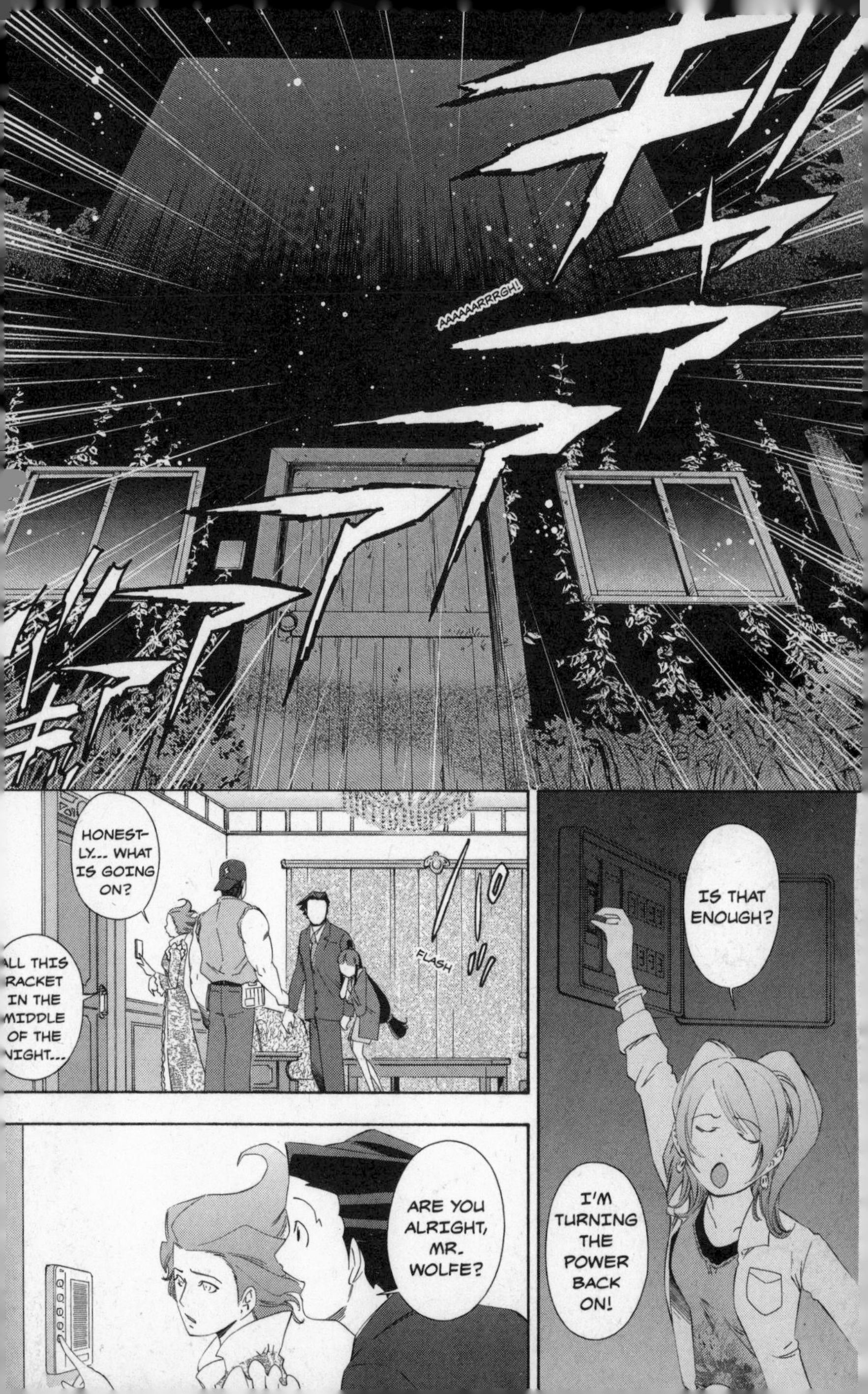
AAAAAARRRGH!
IS THAT ENOUGH?
I'M TURNING THE POWER BACK ON!
FLASH
HONESTLY... WHAT IS GOING ON?
ALL THIS RACKET IN THE MIDDLE OF THE NIGHT...
ARE YOU ALRIGHT, MR. WOLFE?

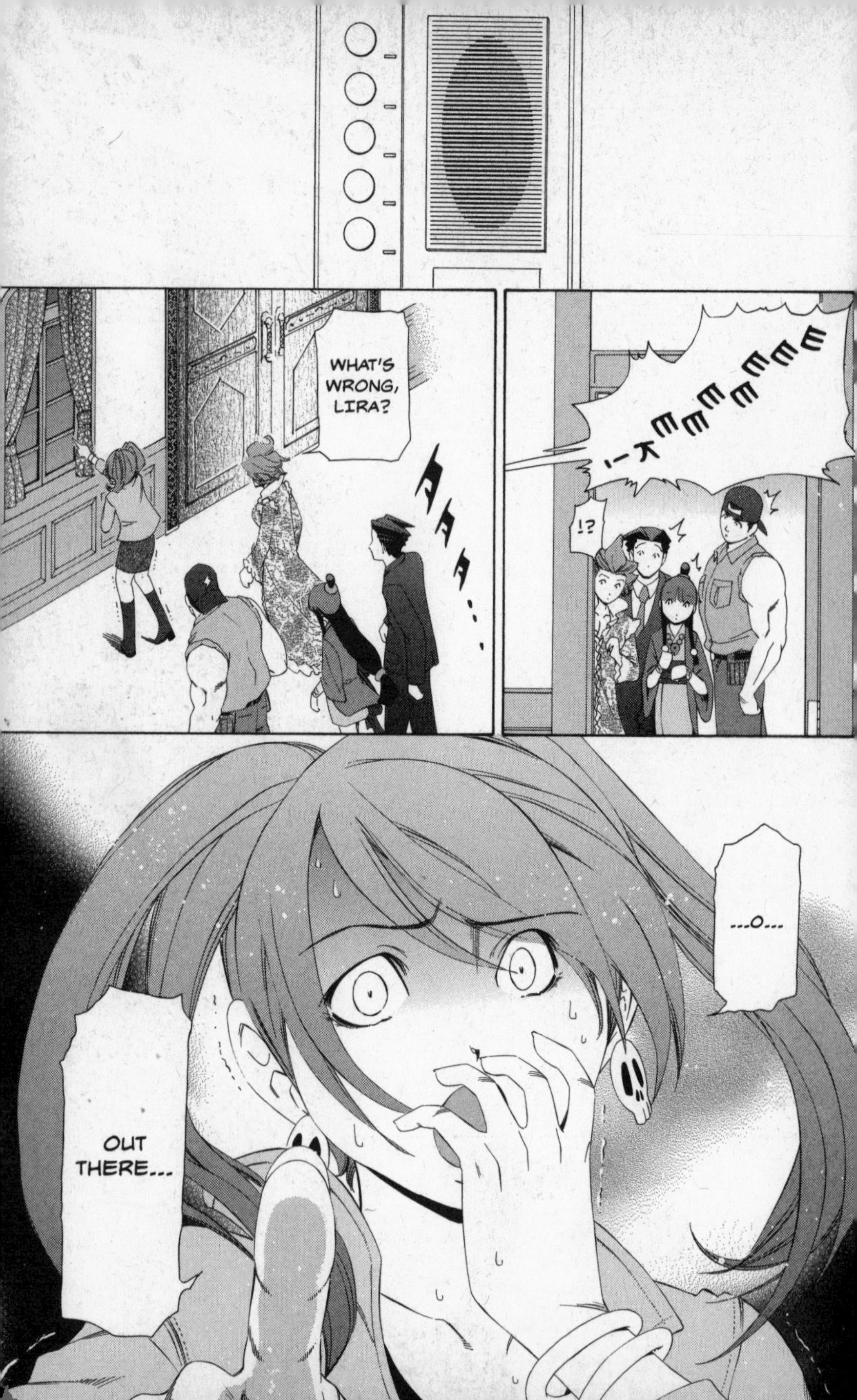
WEEEEEEEK-!
!?
WHAT'S WRONG, LIRA?
タタタ...
...O...
OUT THERE...

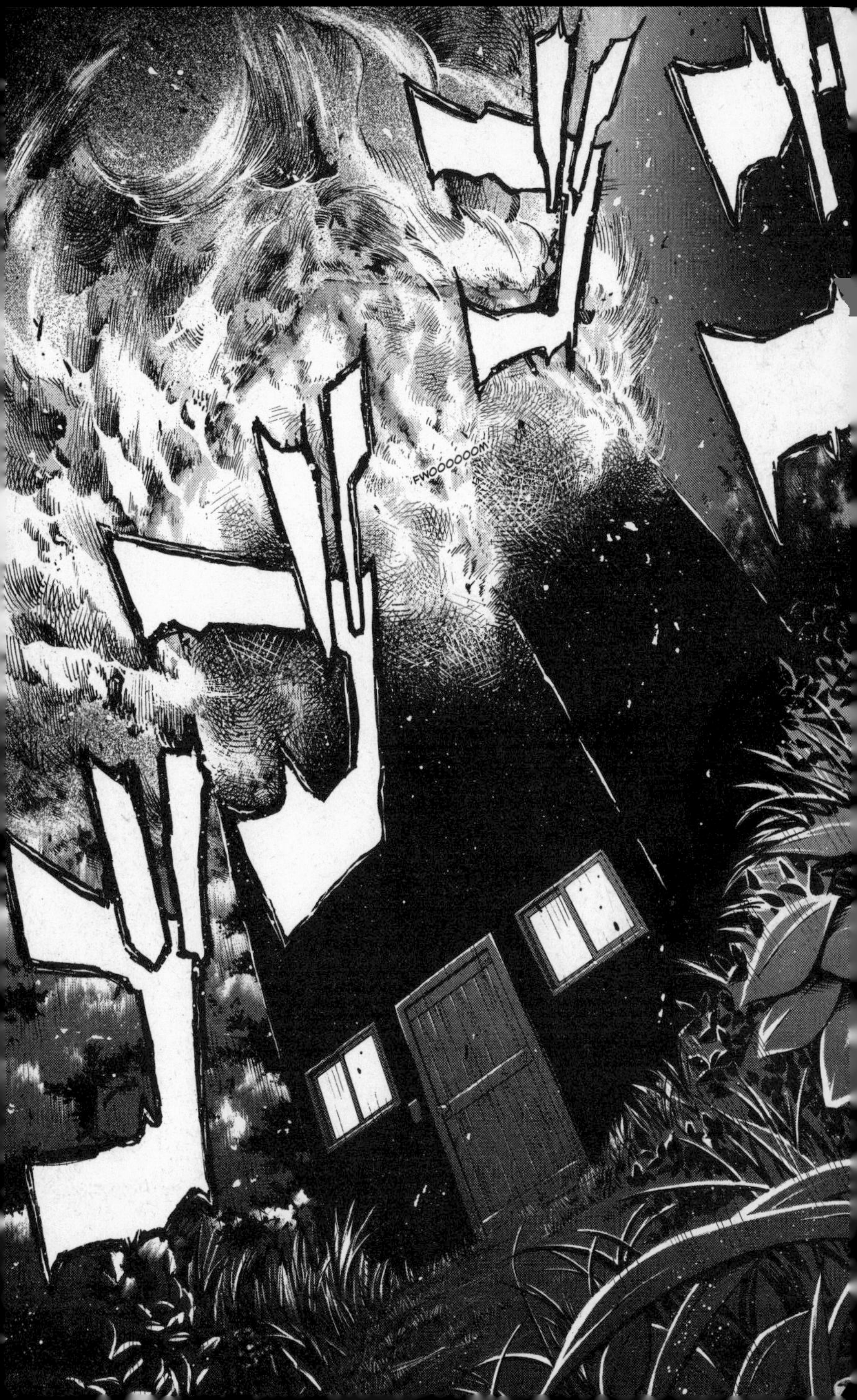
FWOOOOOOM

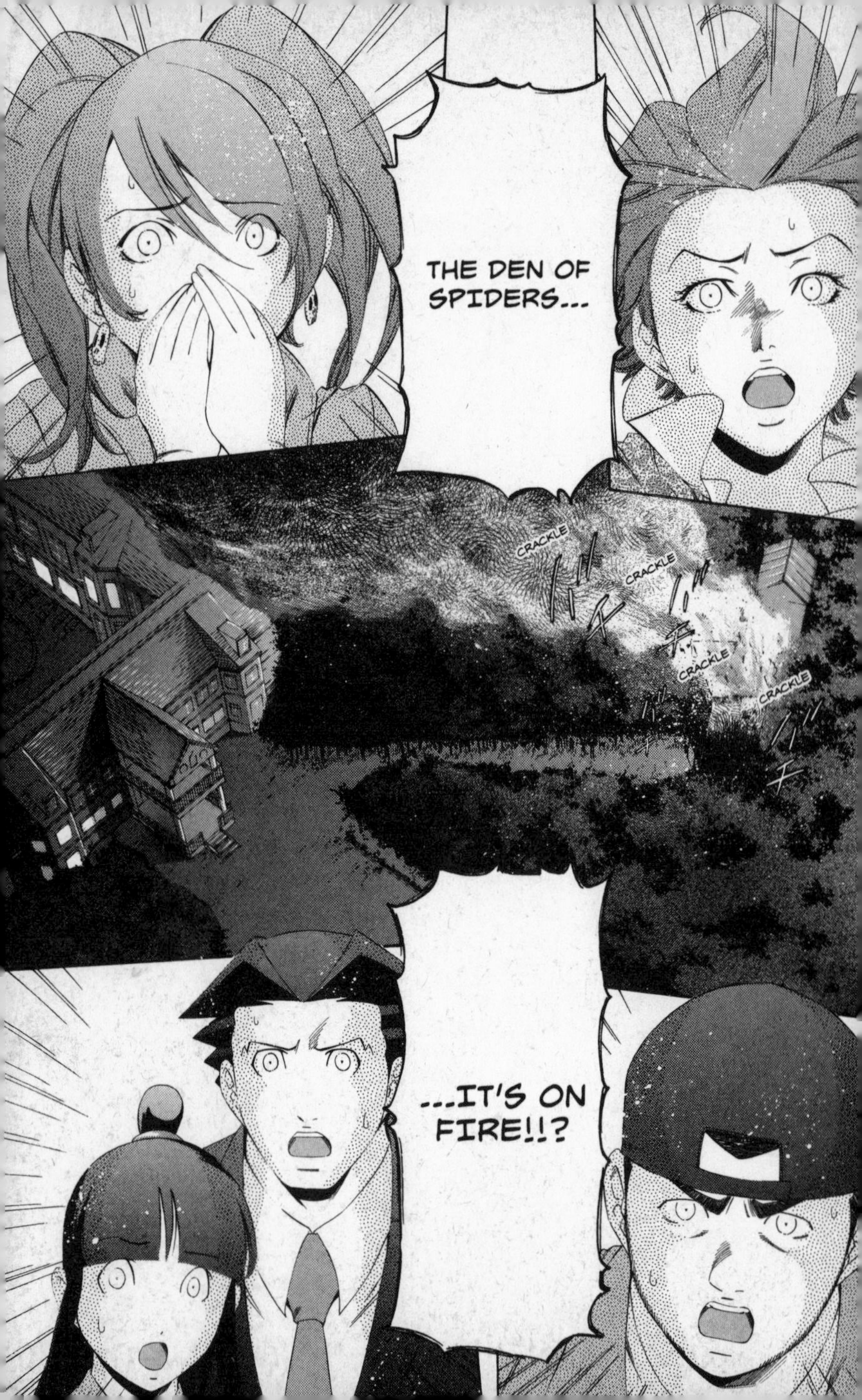
THE DEN OF SPIDERS...
CRACKLE
CRACKLE
CRACKLE
CRACKLE
...IT'S ON FIRE!!?

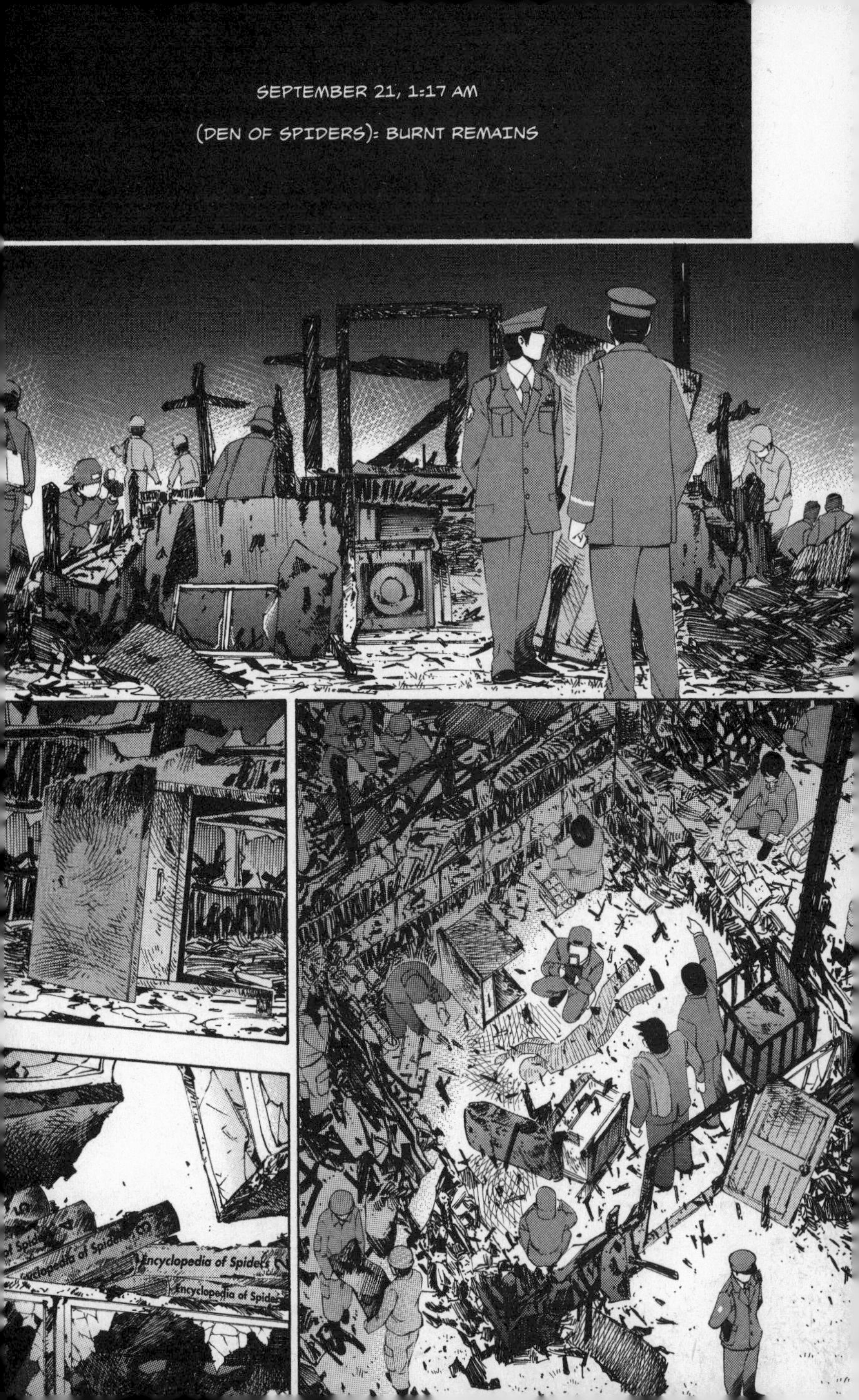
SEPTEMBER 21, 1:17 AM
(DEN OF SPIDERS): BURNT REMAINS
Encyclopedia of Spiders
Encyclopedia of Spider

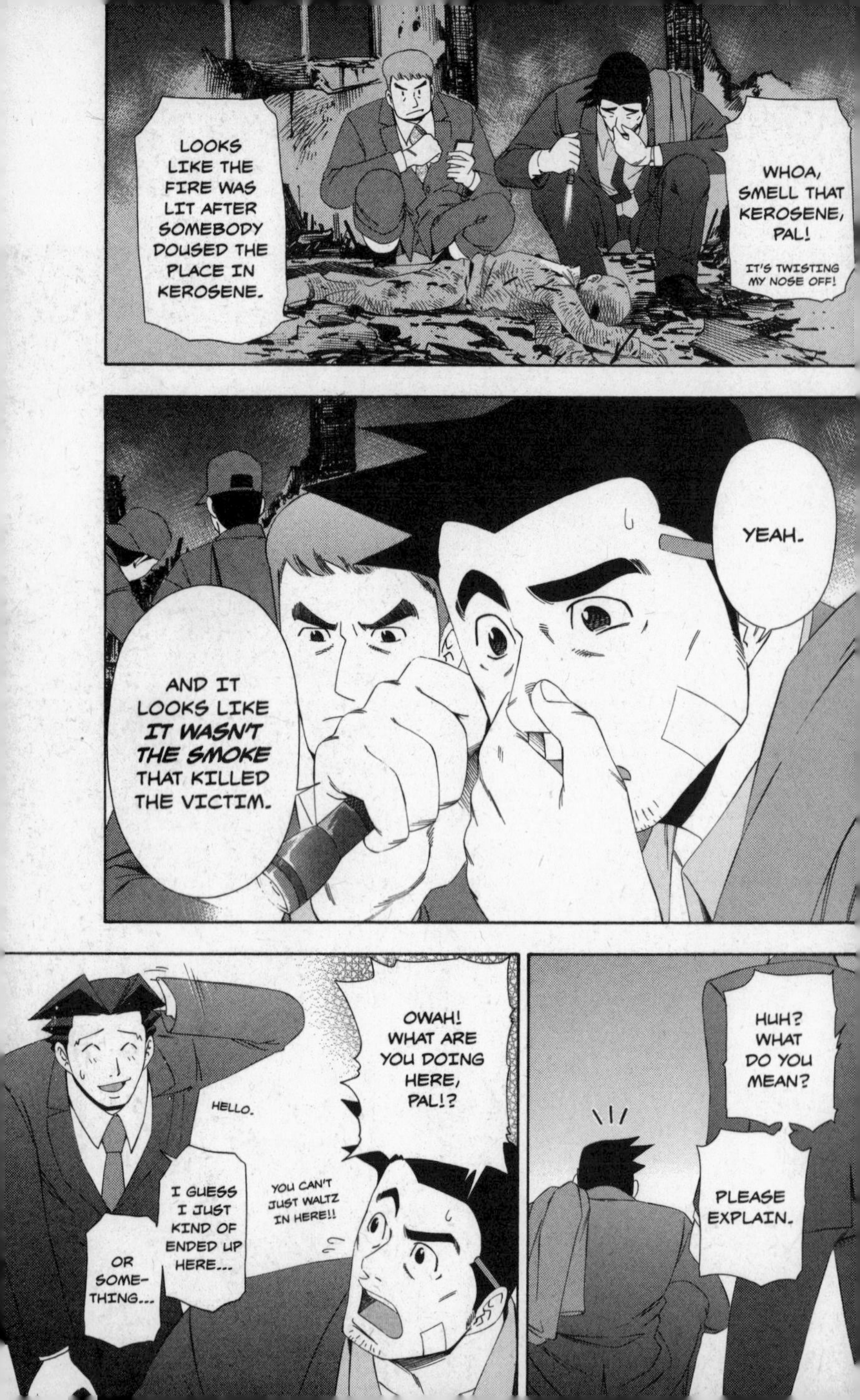
WHOA, SMELL THAT KEROSENE, PAL!
IT'S TWISTING MY NOSE OFF!
LOOKS LIKE THE FIRE WAS LIT AFTER SOMEBODY DOUSED THE PLACE IN KEROSENE.
YEAH.
AND IT LOOKS LIKE *IT WASN'T THE SMOKE* THAT KILLED THE VICTIM.
HUH? WHAT DO YOU MEAN?
PLEASE EXPLAIN.
OWAH! WHAT ARE YOU DOING HERE, PAL!?
YOU CAN'T JUST WALTZ IN HERE!!
HELLO.
I GUESS I JUST KIND OF ENDED UP HERE...
OR SOME-THING...

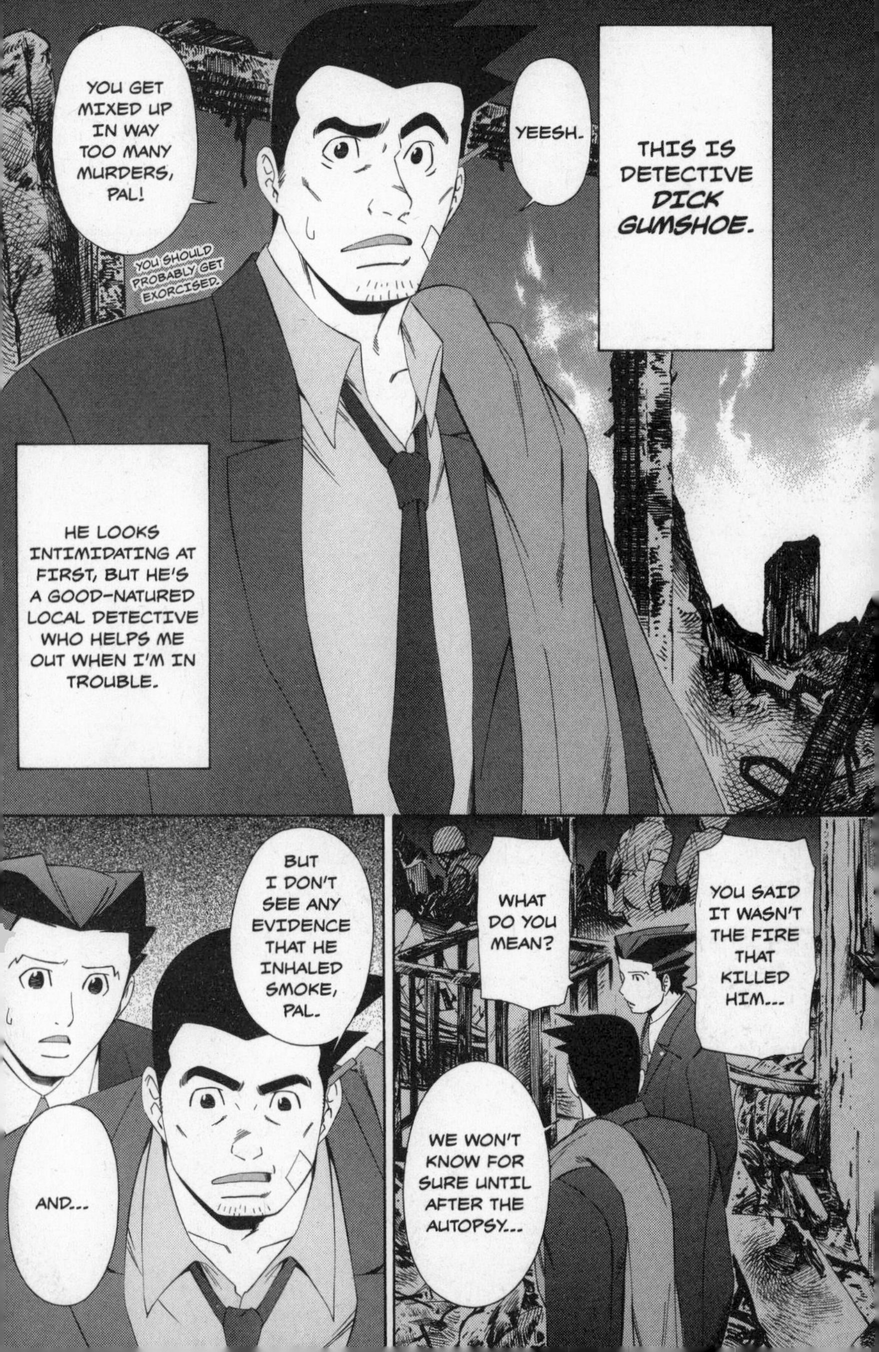
THIS IS DETECTIVE DICK GUMSHOE.
YEESH.
YOU GET MIXED UP IN WAY TOO MANY MURDERS, PAL!
YOU SHOULD PROBABLY GET EXORCISED.
HE LOOKS INTIMIDATING AT FIRST, BUT HE'S A GOOD-NATURED LOCAL DETECTIVE WHO HELPS ME OUT WHEN I'M IN TROUBLE.
YOU SAID IT WASN'T THE FIRE THAT KILLED HIM...
WHAT DO YOU MEAN?
WE WON'T KNOW FOR SURE UNTIL AFTER THE AUTOPSY...
BUT I DON'T SEE ANY EVIDENCE THAT HE INHALED SMOKE, PAL.
AND...

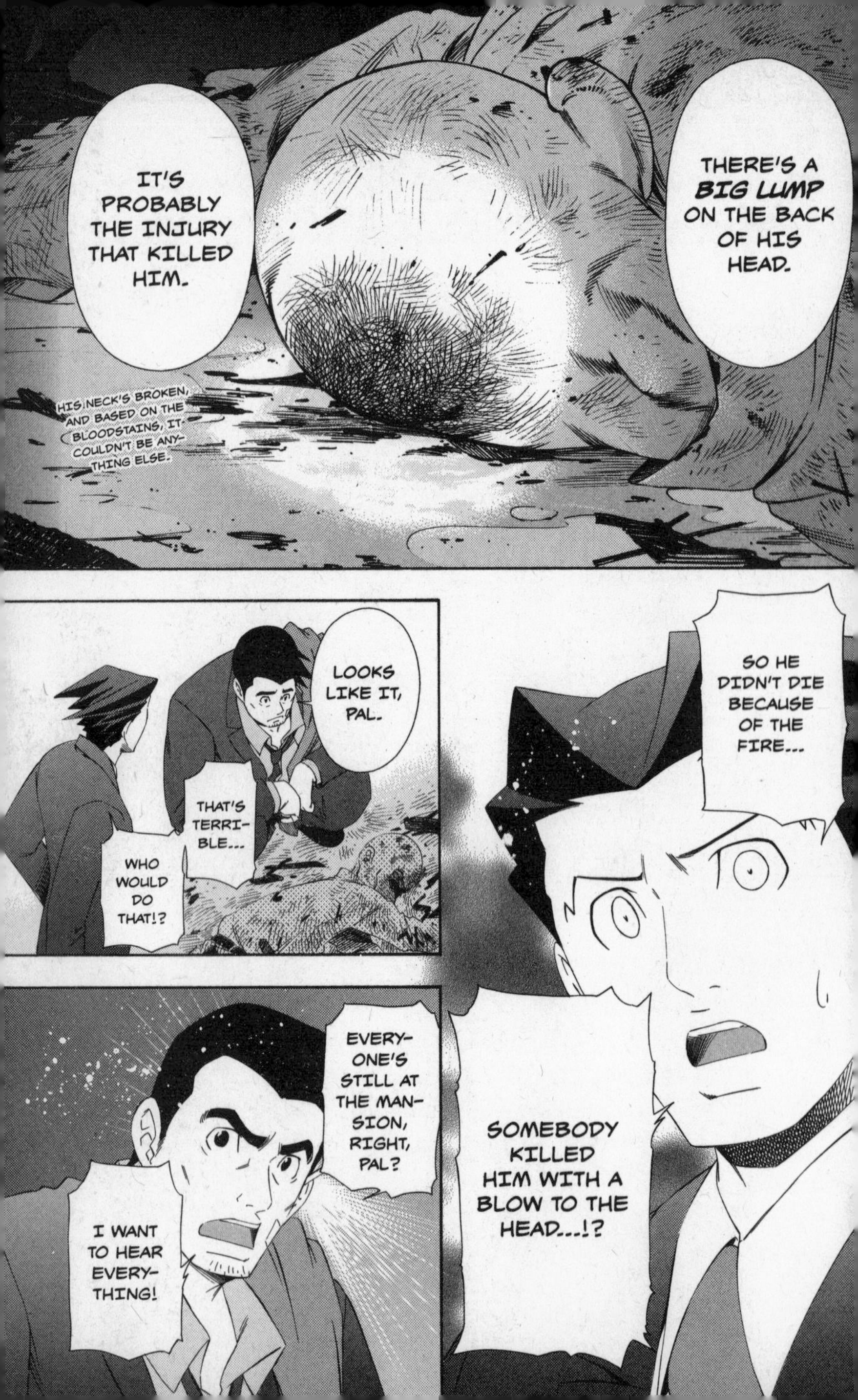
THERE'S A *BIG LUMP* ON THE BACK OF HIS HEAD.
IT'S PROBABLY THE INJURY THAT KILLED HIM.
HIS NECK'S BROKEN, AND BASED ON THE BLOODSTAINS, IT COULDN'T BE ANY-THING ELSE.
SO HE DIDN'T DIE BECAUSE OF THE FIRE...
SOMEBODY KILLED HIM WITH A BLOW TO THE HEAD...!?
LOOKS LIKE IT, PAL.
THAT'S TERRI-BLE...
WHO WOULD DO THAT!?
EVERY-ONE'S STILL AT THE MAN-SION, RIGHT, PAL?
I WANT TO HEAR EVERY-THING!

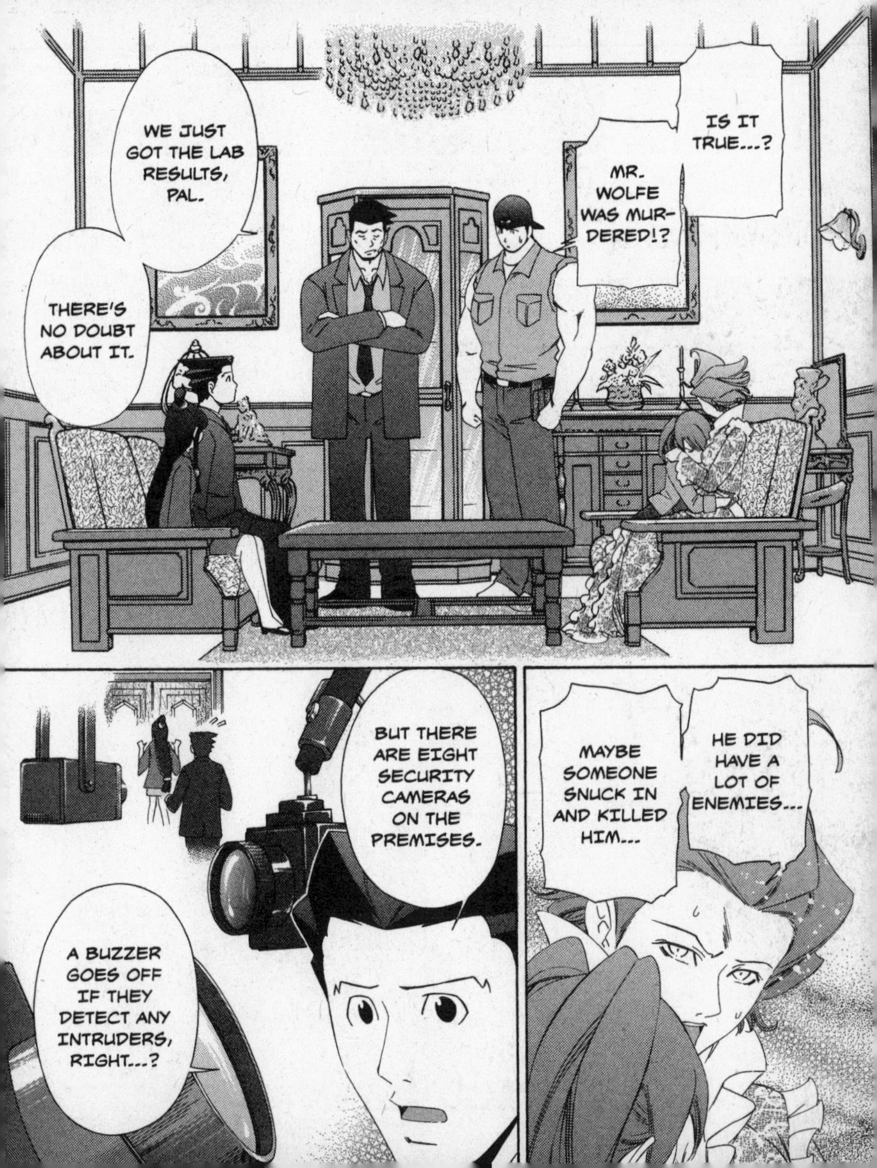
IS IT TRUE...?
MR. WOLFE WAS MUR- DERED!?
WE JUST GOT THE LAB RESULTS, PAL.
THERE'S NO DOUBT ABOUT IT.
HE DID HAVE A LOT OF ENEMIES...
MAYBE SOMEONE SNUCK IN AND KILLED HIM...
BUT THERE ARE EIGHT SECURITY CAMERAS ON THE PREMISES.
A BUZZER GOES OFF IF THEY DETECT ANY INTRUDERS, RIGHT...?

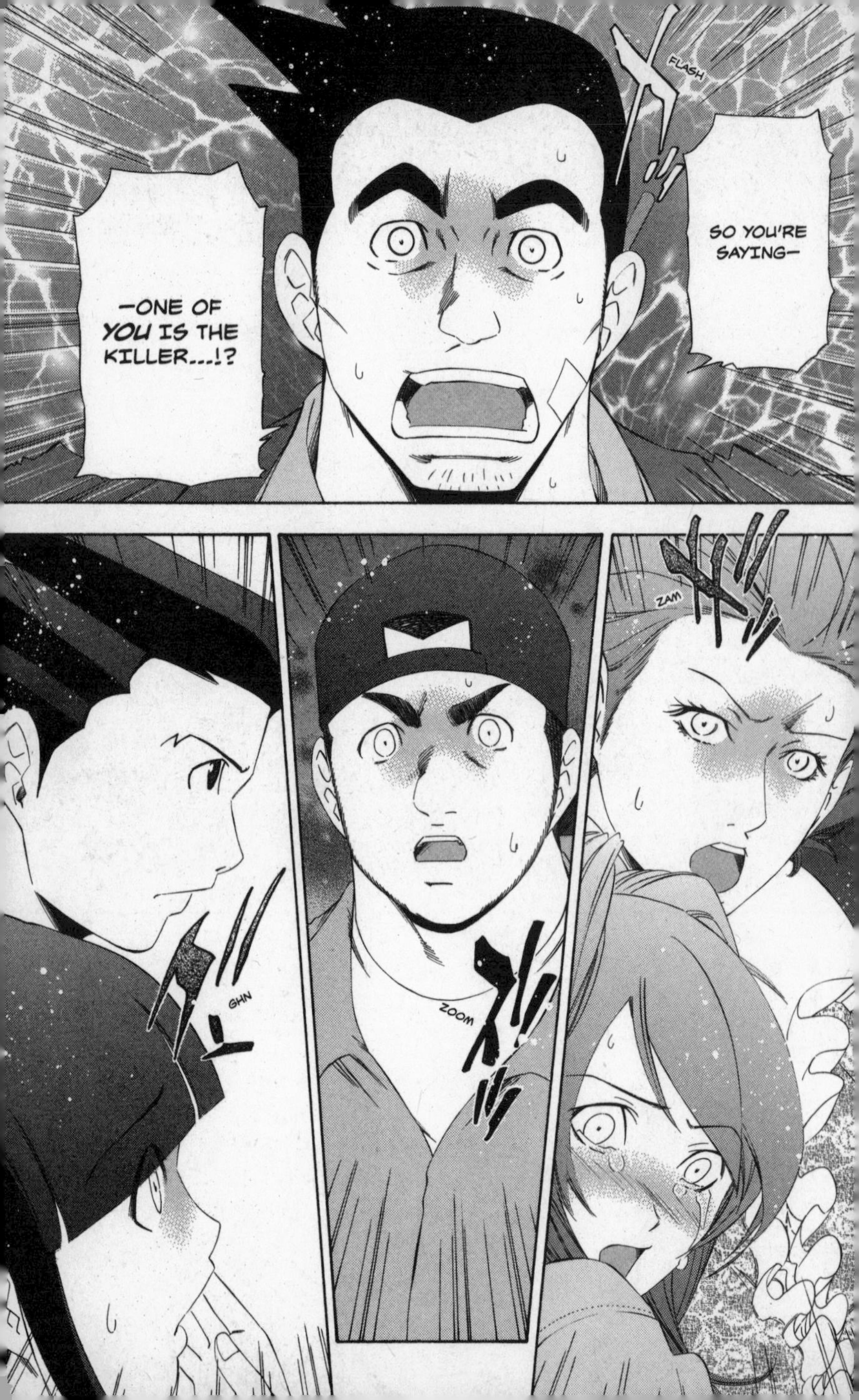
FLASH
SO YOU'RE SAYING—
—ONE OF *YOU* IS THE KILLER...!?
ZAM
ZOOM
GHN

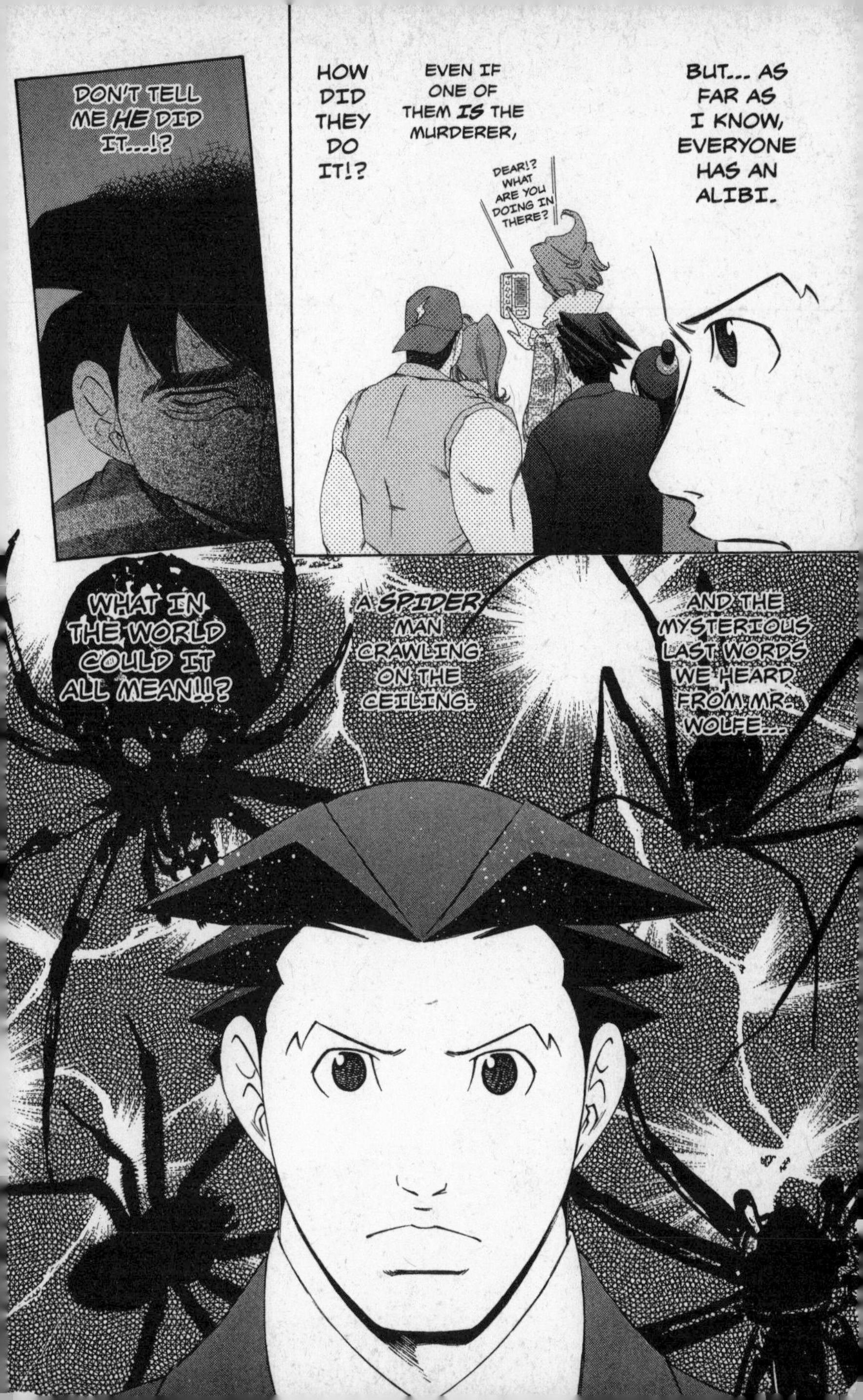
BUT... AS FAR AS I KNOW, EVERYONE HAS AN ALIBI.
EVEN IF ONE OF THEM IS THE MURDERER,
DEAR!? WHAT ARE YOU DOING IN THERE?
HOW DID THEY DO IT!?
DON'T TELL ME HE DID IT...!?
AND THE MYSTERIOUS LAST WORDS WE HEARD FROM MR. WOLFE...
A SPIDER MAN CRAWLING ON THE CEILING.
WHAT IN THE WORLD COULD IT ALL MEAN!!?

Phoenix Wright
Ace Attorney™

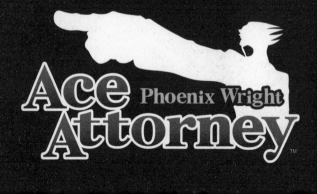

# TRANSLATION NOTES

Japanese is a tricky language for most Westerners, and trans-ation is often more art than science. For your edification and eading pleasure, here are notes on some of the places where we could have gone in a different direction with our translation of he work, or where a Japanese cultural reference is used.

**You're so spoony, Larry, page 15**

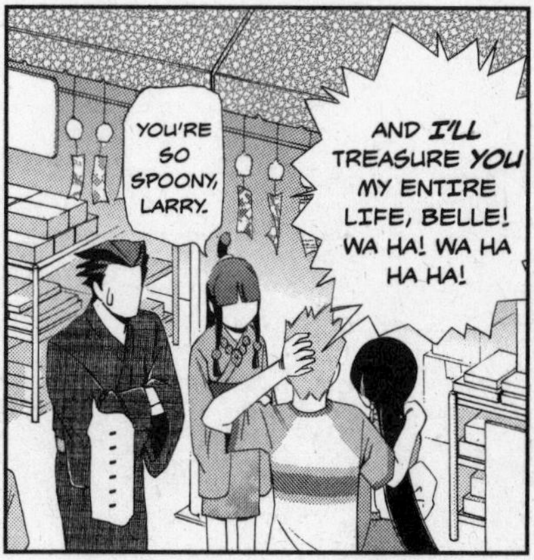
AND I'LL TREASURE YOU MY ENTIRE LIFE, BELLE! WA HA! WA HA HA HA!
YOU'RE SO SPOONY, LARRY.

Maya is commenting simultane-ously on Larry's amorousness as vell as the praises he sings for his new love. (In some circles, it's common knowledge that bards are spoony.) In the Japanese, she ays that the underpart of Larry's nose is growing. This is partially a reference to one's nose grow-ing due to boasts of questionable veracity, but mostly a reference to the Japanese idiom wherein the underside of a nose being long indicates that a man likes the ladies.

**This is the kind of card you see on wind chimes!, page 50**

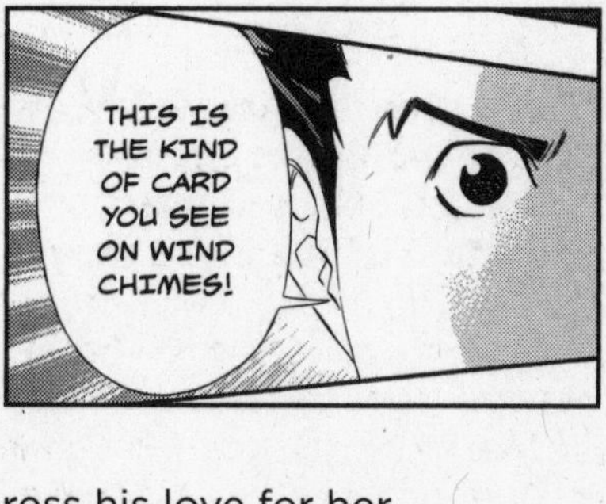
THIS IS THE KIND OF CARD YOU SEE ON WIND CHIMES!

Japanese wind chimes, like the ones featured at the Gourd Lake estival, have a card hanging from he clapper in the bell. The card catches the wind, causing the bell o chime. These cards can have poems or wishes written on them. n the case of Larry's gift to Belle, he card is covered in hearts, to express his love for her.

**Cat rice, page 99**

Rice with fish flakes is known as cat rice, or *nekomanma* in Japan. Mr. Wolfe makes the dish sound fancier by calling it that, but it's actually a very cheap dish, which is why Phoenix and Maya have already had quite enough of it.

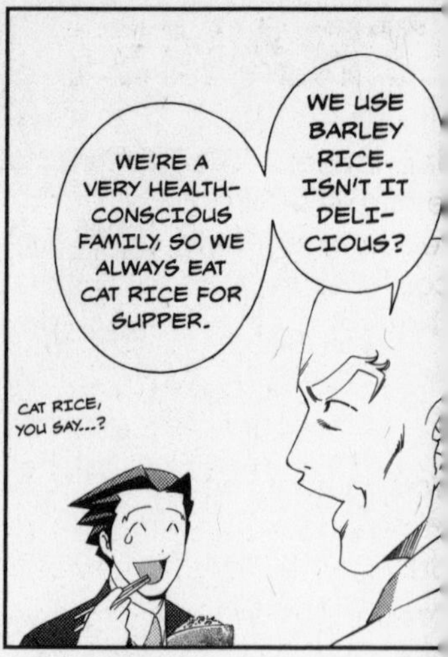
WE USE BARLEY RICE. ISN'T IT DELI-CIOUS?
WE'RE A VERY HEALTH-CONSCIOUS FAMILY, SO WE ALWAYS EAT CAT RICE FOR SUPPER.
CAT RICE, YOU SAY...?

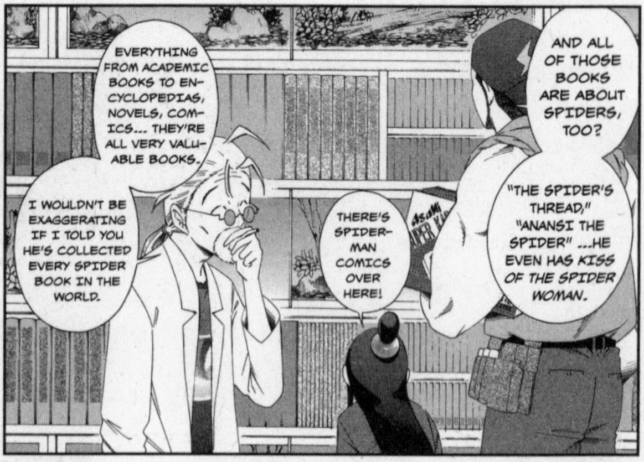
AND ALL OF THOSE BOOKS ARE ABOUT SPIDERS, TOO?
EVERYTHING FROM ACADEMIC BOOKS TO EN-CYCLOPEDIAS, NOVELS, COM-ICS... THEY'RE ALL VERY VALU-ABLE BOOKS.
"THE SPIDER'S THREAD," "ANANSI THE SPIDER" ...HE EVEN HAS *KISS OF THE SPIDER WOMAN.*
THERE'S SPIDER-MAN COMICS OVER HERE!
I WOULDN'T BE EXAGGERATING IF I TOLD YOU HE'S COLLECTED EVERY SPIDER BOOK IN THE WORLD.

**"The Spider's Thread," "Anansi the Spider," and *Kiss of the Spider Woman*, page 134**

These are only a few samples to illustrate how vast Bobby's collection of spider books is. "The Spider's Thread" is a Japanese short story about a sinner whose one good deed in life is that he saved a spider, and that spider's thread gives him a chance to escape from hell. "Anansi the Spider" is an Ashanti folk hero. *Kiss of the Spider Woman* is an Argentinian novel about two prisoners in Buenos Aires who form an intimate relationship, and actually has very little to do with spiders.

# PREVIEW OF PHOENIX WRIGHT: ACE ATTORNEY 2

We're pleased to present you a preview from *Phoenix Wright: Ace Attorney 2*. Please check our website (www.kodanshacomics.com) to see when this volume will be available in English. For now you'll have to make do with Japanese!

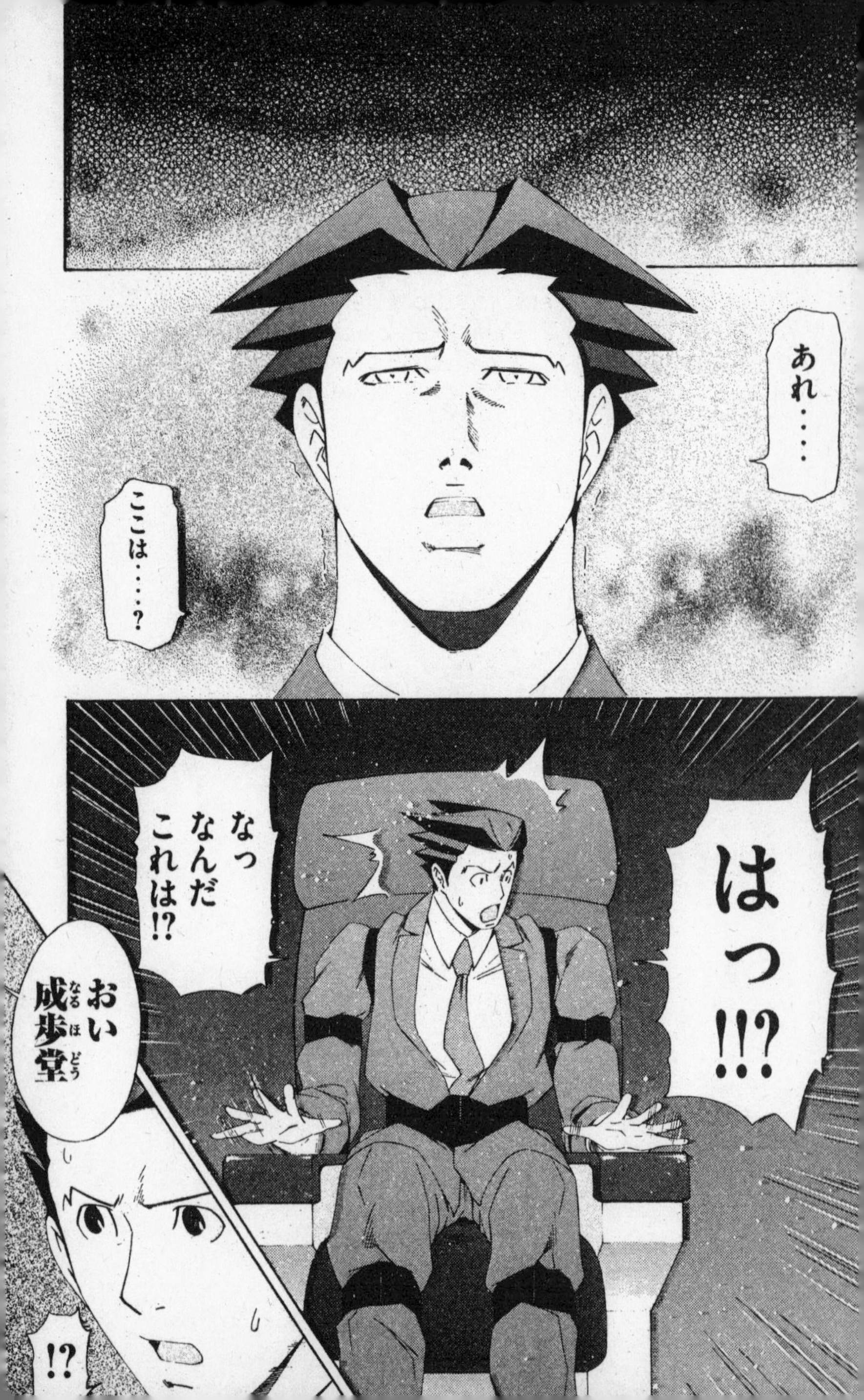
あれ・・・・
ここは・・・・？
はっ!!?
なっ なんだ これは!?
おい 成歩堂
!?

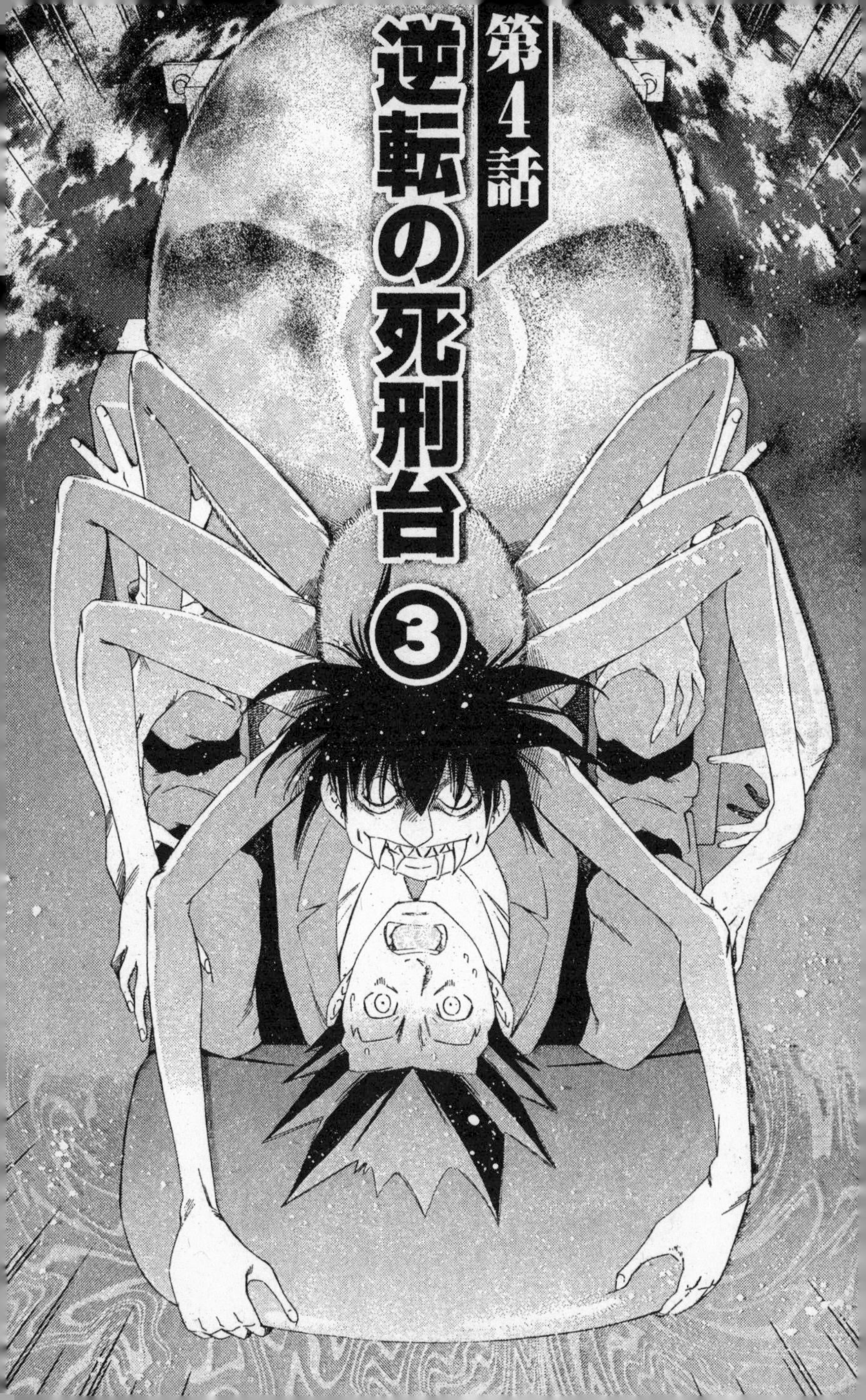
第4話
逆転の死刑台③

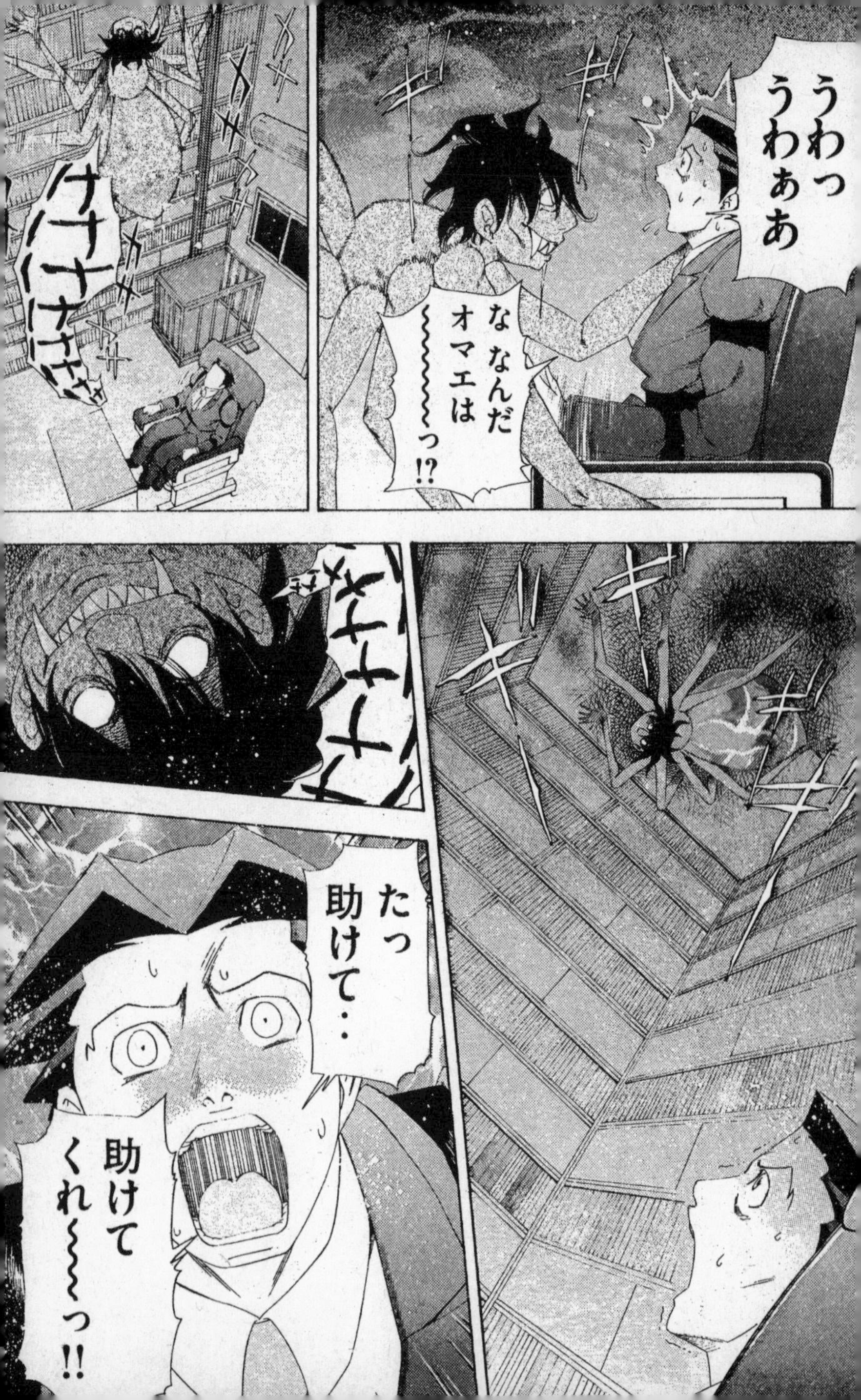
うわっ
うわぁあ
ななんだ
オマエは
〜〜〜〜っ!?
たっ
助けて・・
助けて
くれ〜〜っ!!

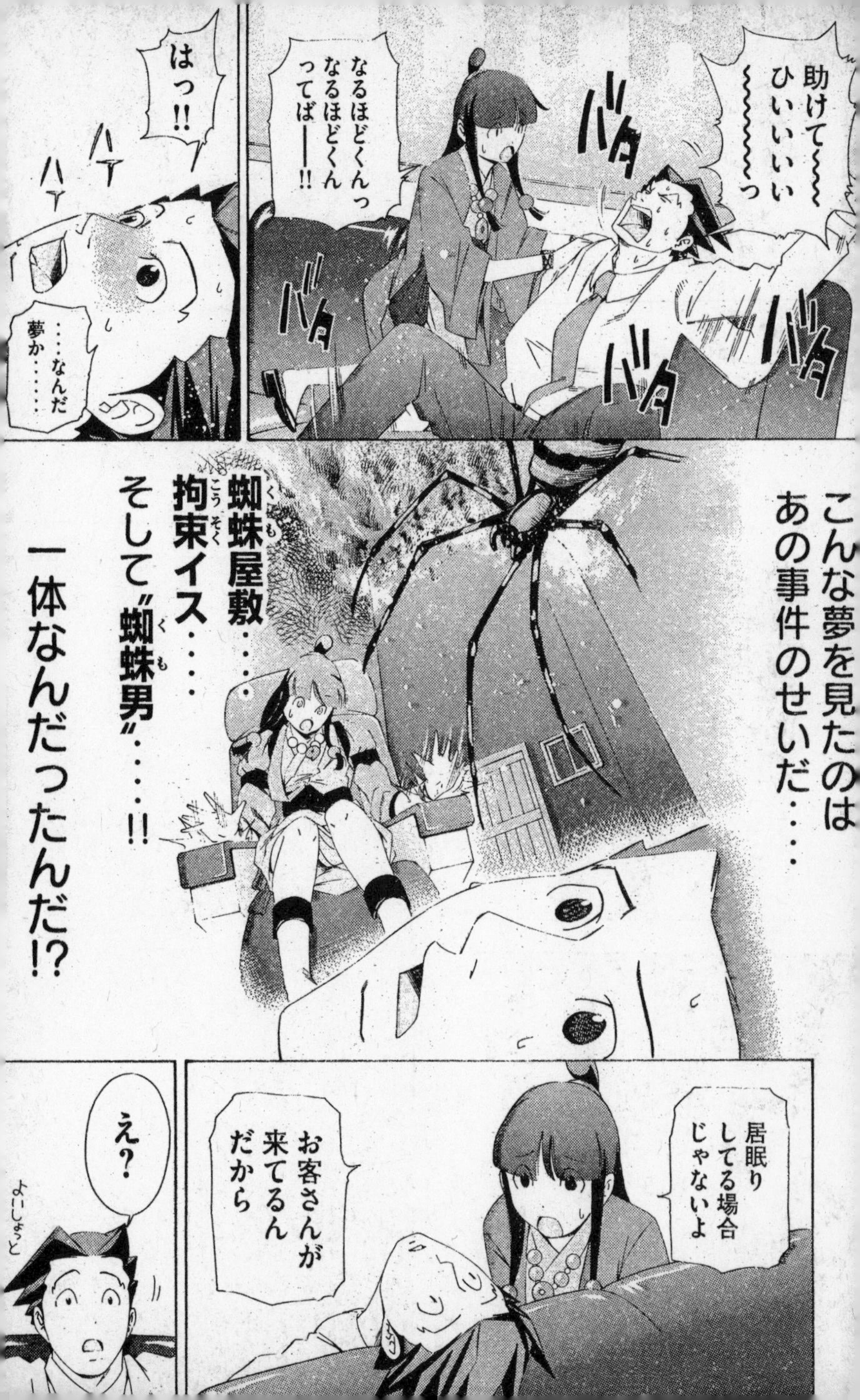
助けて〜〜〜
ひぃいいいい〜〜〜っ
バタ
バタ
バタ
バタ
なるほどくんっ なるほどくんってば——!!
はっ!!
ハァ
ハァ
……なんだ 夢か……
こんな夢を見たのは
あの事件のせいだ……
蜘蛛屋敷……
拘束イス……
そして〝蜘蛛男〟……!!
一体なんだったんだ!?
居眠りしてる場合じゃないよ
お客さんが来てるんだから
え?
よいしょっと

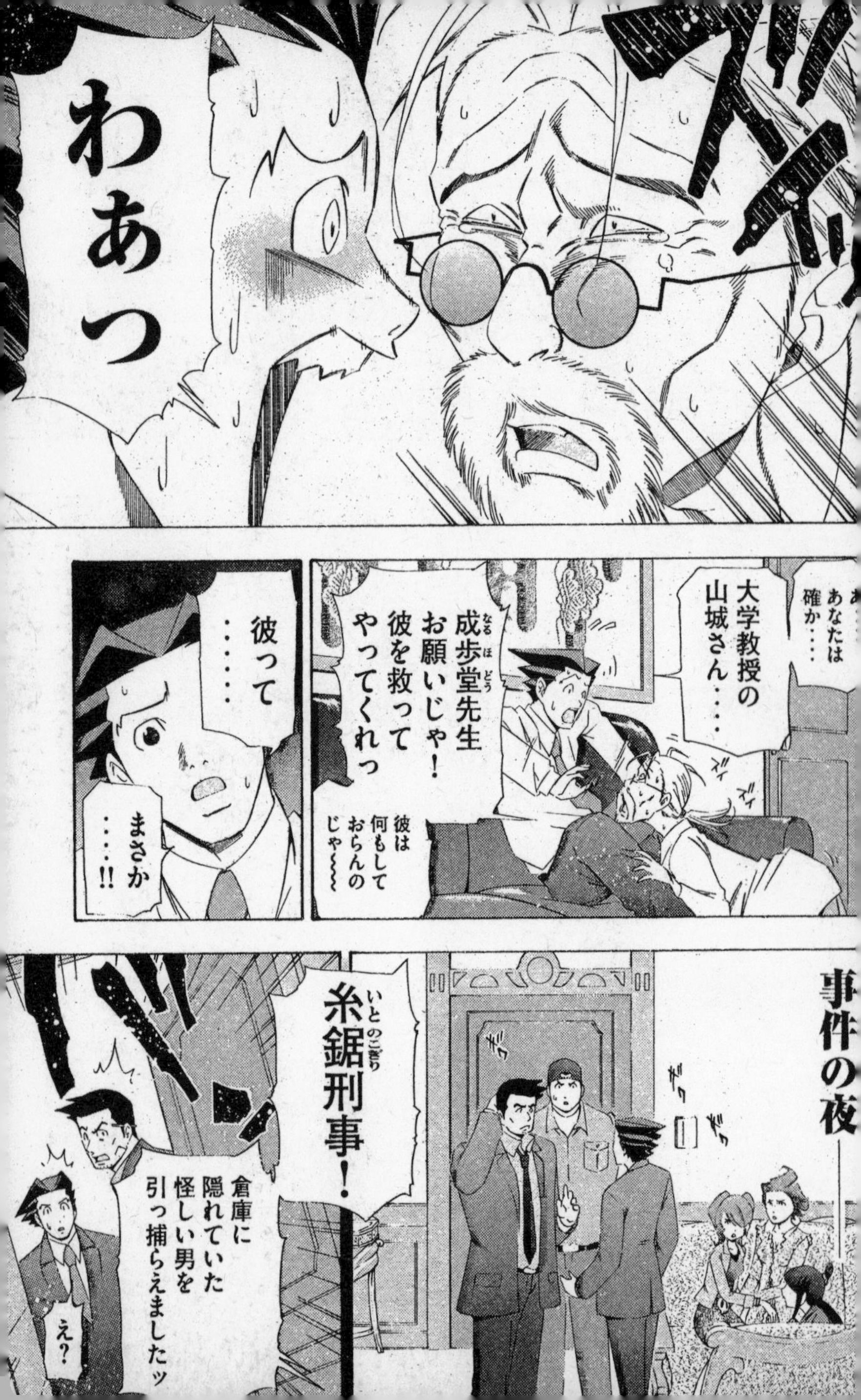
わあっ
あ
あなたは確か……
大学教授の山城さん……
成歩堂先生お願いじゃ！彼を救ってやってくれっ
彼は何もしておらんのじゃ〜〜
彼って……
まさか……!!
事件の夜——
糸鋸刑事！
倉庫に隠れていた怪しい男を引っ捕らえましたッ
え？

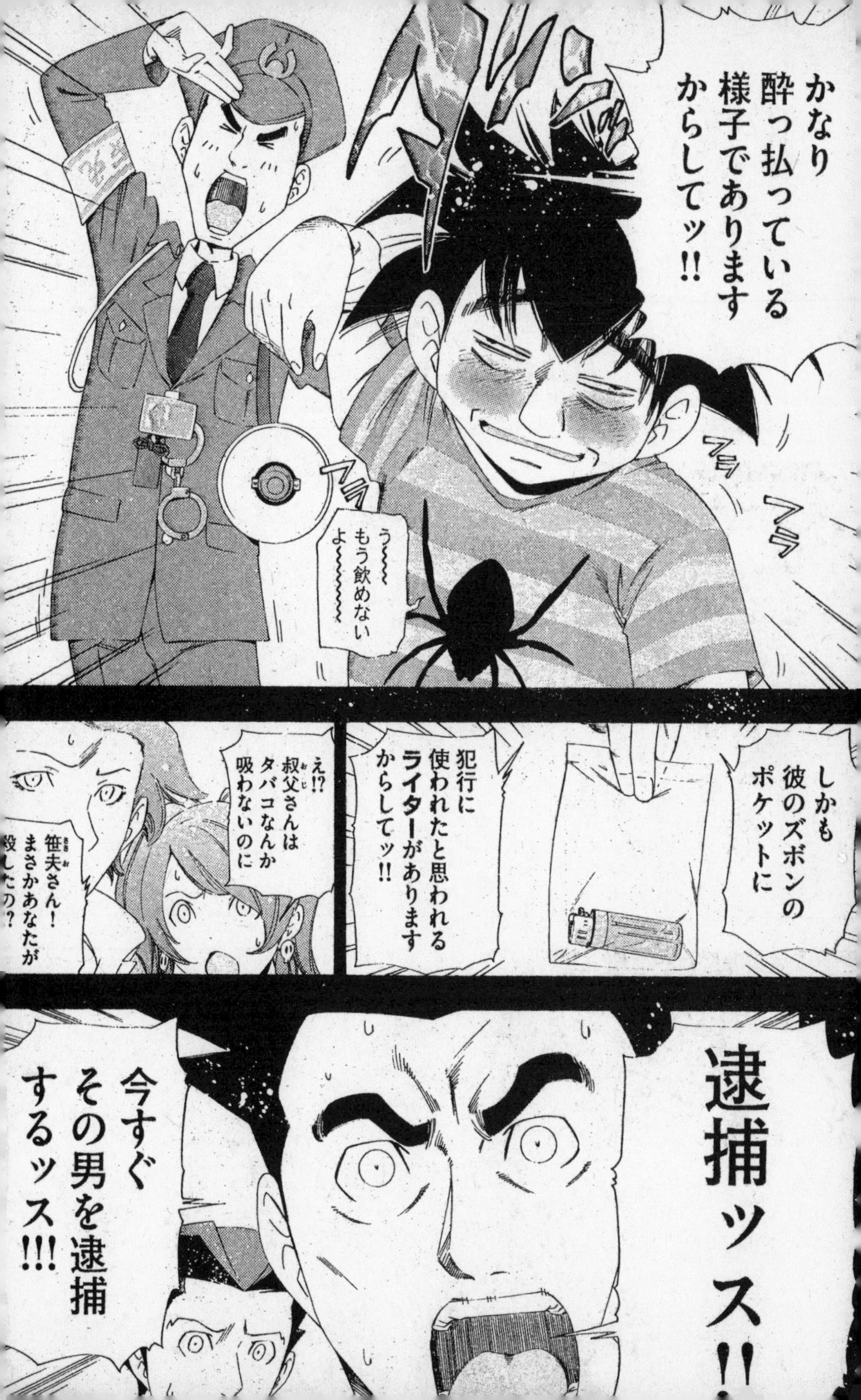
かなり酔っ払っている様子でありますからしてッ!!
う〜〜もう飲めないよ〜〜〜〜
しかも彼のズボンのポケットに
犯行に使われたと思われるライターがありますからしてッ!!
え!? 叔父さんはタバコなんか吸わないのに
笹夫さん! まさかあなたが殺したの?
逮捕ッス!!
今すぐその男を逮捕するッス!!!

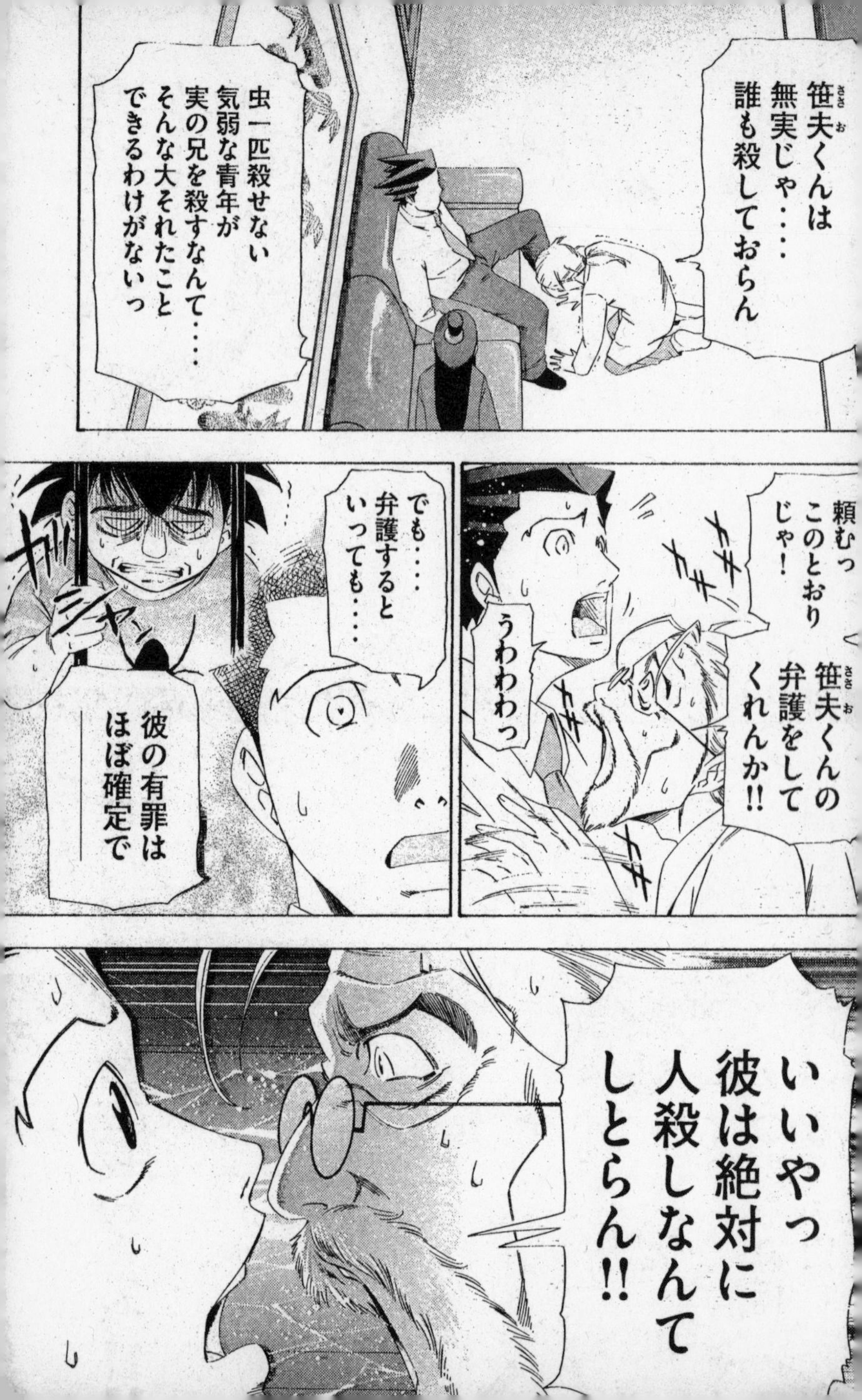
笹夫くんは無実じゃ・・・・誰も殺しておらん
虫一匹殺せない気弱な青年が実の兄を殺すなんて・・・・そんな大それたことできるわけがないいっ
頼むっこのとおりじゃ！
笹夫くんの弁護をしてくれんか!!
うわわわわっ
でも・・・・弁護するといっても・・・・
ガシャン
——彼の有罪はほぼ確定で——
いいやっ彼は絶対に人殺しなんてしとらん!!

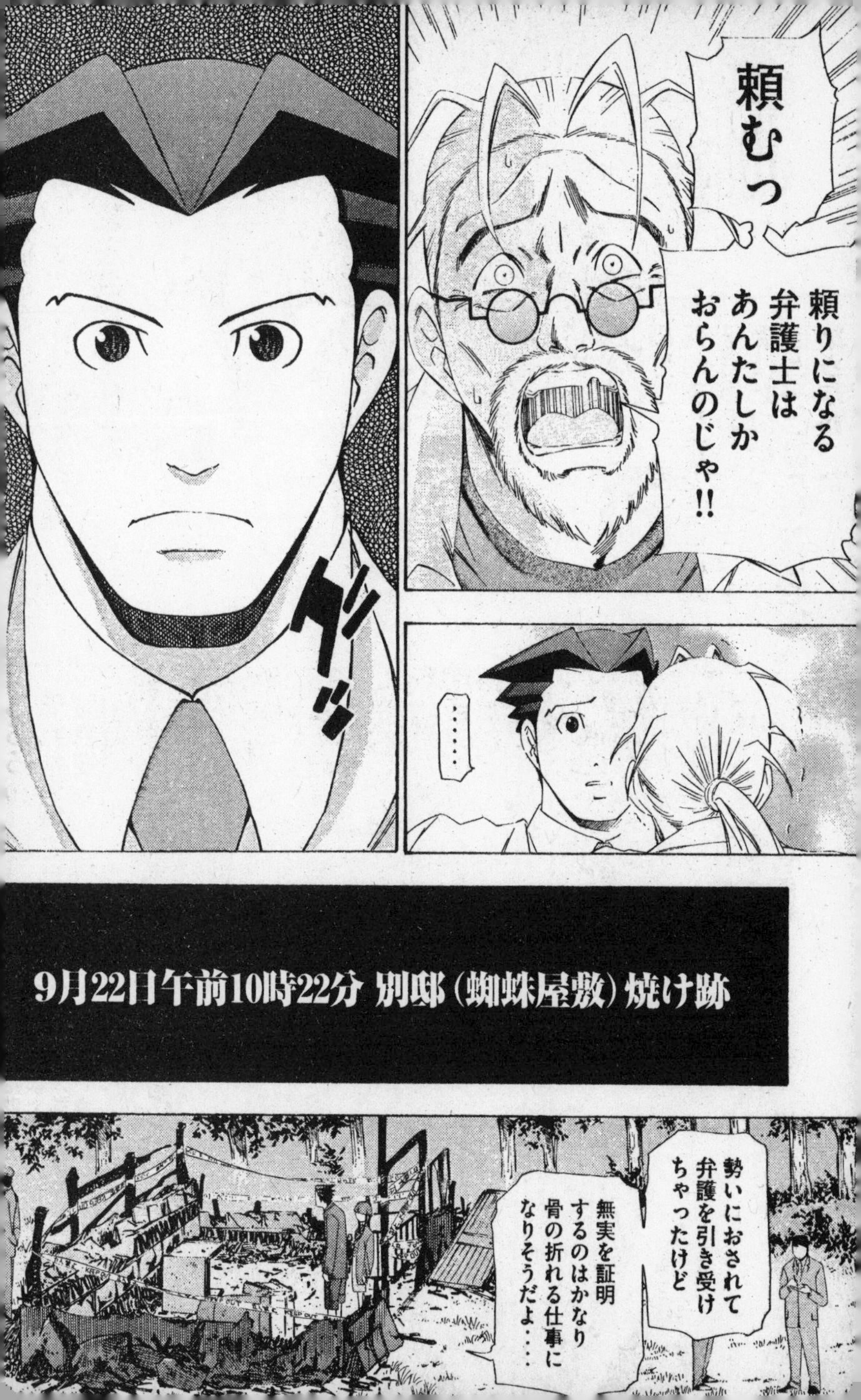
頼むっ
頼りになる弁護士はあんたしかおらんのじゃ!!
……
ダンッ
9月22日午前10時22分 別邸（蜘蛛屋敷）焼け跡
勢いにおされて弁護を引き受けちゃったけど
無実を証明するのはかなり骨の折れる仕事になりそうだよ・・・・

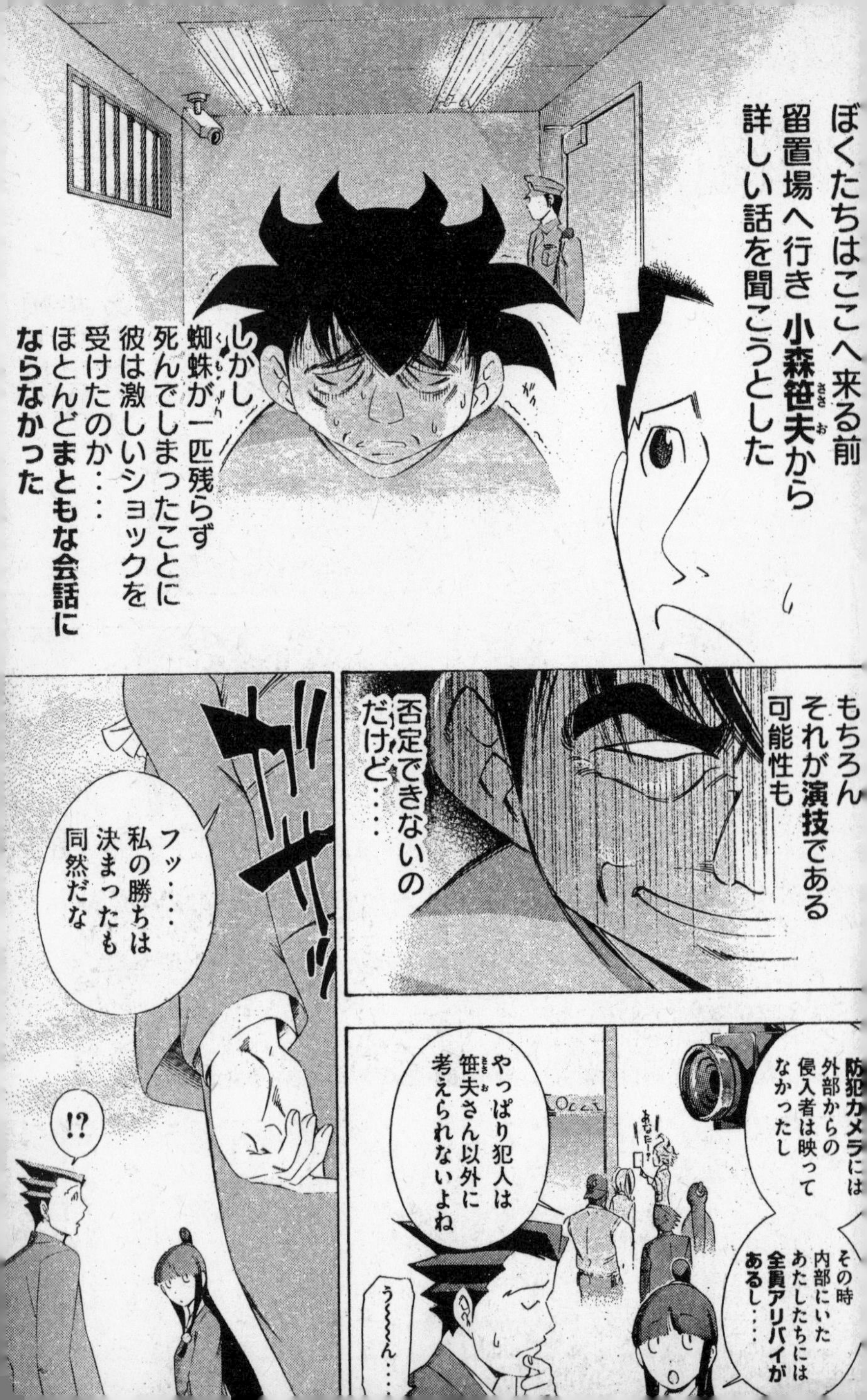
ぼくたちはここへ来る前 留置場へ行き 小森笹夫から 詳しい話を聞こうとした
しかし 蜘蛛が一匹残らず 死んでしまったことに 彼は激しいショックを 受けたのか・・・・ ほとんどまともな会話に ならなかった
もちろん それが演技である 可能性も
否定できないの だけど・・・・
防犯カメラには 外部からの 侵入者は映って なかったし
その時 内部にいた あたしたちには 全員アリバイが あるし・・・・
やっぱり犯人は 笹夫さん以外に 考えられないよね
う〜〜〜ん・・・・
ガサッ
フッ・・・・ 私の勝ちは 決まったも 同然だな
!?

# FROM HIRO MASHIMA, CREATOR OF **RAVE MASTER**

# FAIRY TAIL

FAIRY TAIL 1
Hiro Mashima Creator of Rave Master

FAIRY TAIL 2
Hiro Mashima Creator of Rave Master

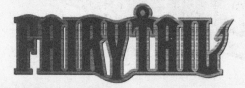

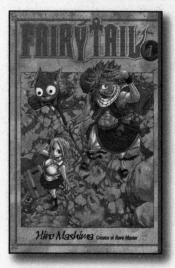

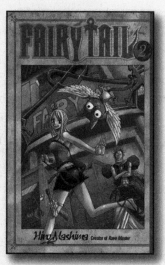

**Lucy has always dreamed of joining the Fairy Tail, a club for the most powerful sorcerers in the land. But once she becomes a member, the fun really starts!**

***Special extras in each volume! Read them all!***

RATING T AGES 13+

**VISIT WWW.KODANSHACOMICS.COM TO:**

- View release date calendars for upcoming volumes
- Find out the latest about new Kodansha Comics series

KC KODANSHA COMICS

# NEGIMA!™
## MAGISTER NEGI MAGI

### BY KEN AKAMATSU

**N**egi Springfield is a ten-year-old wizard teaching English at an all-girls Japanese school. He dreams of becoming a master wizard like his legendary father, the Thousand Master. At first his biggest concern was concealing his magic powers, because if he's ever caught using them publicly, he thinks he'll be turned into an ermine! But in a world that gets stranger every day, it turns out that the strangest people of all are Negi's students! From a librarian with a magic book to a centuries-old vampire, from a robot to a ninja, Negi will risk his own life to protect the girls in his care!

Ages: 16+

*Special extras in each volume! Read them all!*

**KC KODANSHA COMICS**

**VISIT WWW.KODANSHACOMICS.COM TO:**
• View release date calendars for upcoming volumes
• Find out the latest about new Kodansha Comics series

# TOMARE!
## [STOP!]

**You are going the wrong way!**

**Manga is a completely different type of reading experience.**

**To start at the *beginning*, go to the *end*!**

That's right! Authentic manga is read the traditional Japanese way—from right to left, exactly the *opposite* of how American books are read. It's easy to follow: Just go to the other end of the book, and read each page—and each panel—from right side to left side, starting at the top right. Now you're experiencing manga as it was meant to be.